The Dalton Boys

David Allin

"Crimes, like virtues, are their own rewards."

--George Farquhar

For my father, who taught me the power of words.

Contents

FOREWORD

In 1860 my great-great-grandfather, William H. Allin, came to the southeastern Kansas town of Coffeyville, a mile from the border of what was then Indian Territory, and Allins have lived in that city ever since. When I was a child growing up in Oklahoma, my father would often take me to Coffeyville to visit my grandparents, and it was there that I was introduced to the Daltons. In a traditional family joke, my father once took me to the Elmwood cemetery where Bob and Grat Dalton are buried, and he told me that if I leaned over their graves and loudly asked, "What are you doing down there, boys?", they would answer me by saying "Nothing at all." He was right, of course. He also took me to see the Dalton Defenders Museum, and back at my grandfather's house he showed me the cracked and stiff leather gunbelt and bridle that once belonged to Bob Dalton. At the time these things sparked only a mild interest in me, but in the intervening years my curiosity about these famous outlaws grew until finally I was driven to find out more. I wanted to understand how and why these young men, with an almost identical background to my father's, had become famous criminals. This search turned out to be harder than I expected.

When I began looking for books about the Daltons, I discovered that there were only a few, and they were mostly outdated and of suspect validity. Until recently, most of what has been written about the Dalton gang was at best inaccurate, and at worst totally fabricated. Numerous books, usually dime novels and such "flash literature," were published immediately following the gang's demise, and these slim volumes were examples of yellow journalism at its worst. Unfortunately, later authors based more serious works about the Daltons on these dubious references without verifying their accuracy, thus perpetuating many myths and misconceptions. I quickly realized that if I wanted a true account of the Daltons, I would have to write it myself.

In order to find the truth, I bypassed virtually all the books and articles that had previously been published and went to primary sources—original documents and accounts uncorrupted by revisionist historians. I found that there are voluminous records of court testimony and other legal documents relating to the Daltons on file in the National Archives, and contemporary newspapers are preserved on microfilm at various state historical societies. These sources, combined with certain eye-witness reports that appeared to be reasonably reliable, provided the information need to recreate the Dalton story. Utilizing skills I had developed in twenty years as a military intelligence analyst, I collected all this data, collated it, organized it with timelines and maps, and used deductive reasoning and inference to fill in the few remaining gaps in the record. Once I had established the facts, the story almost told itself. At the end of each chapater I have provided author's notes which list the sources for that chapter, how they were interpreted, and related information.

Emmett Dalton, the only survivor of the gang, wrote two books about their exploits after he was released from prison. The first, and more accurate of the two books, was called *Beyond the Law*, and it became indispensable in researching this book, since Emmett was, understandably, the only one who could tell what the Daltons had been doing when not in the public view. While his memoirs were essential, they had to be taken with a large grain of salt. Emmett was hardly an unbiased observer, and he wrote this first book in 1908, over fifteen years after the events he described. In addition to containing factual errors and a muddled sequence of events that can charitably be attributed to a faulty memory, Emmett's account is also tainted by a personal agenda that is readily apparent.

Despite his claim that the sole purpose of the book was to warn young people about the evils of a life of crime, Emmett devotes much of this brief work to explaining that he was not really personally involved in most of the crimes, and that he even tried to talk the others out of committing them. The weight of evidence from court records and other accounts, on the other hand, shows that he willingly took part in almost all their crimes. Motivated by this desire to exculpate himself, Emmett sometimes simply failed to mention his criminal acts, and other times claimed they were done by someone else, someone who was now conveniently dead or perhaps never existed at all.

When he was not proclaiming his own innocence, Emmett was often trying to enhance the image of his brother Bob. Emmett obviously admired Bob to the point of hero-worship, and he continually attributed noble motives and deeds to Bob that were at the least exaggerated, if not totally fictitious. This attempt at mitigation also caused Emmett to totally ignore certain events, and exaggerate or minimize others.

Finally, and more commendably, Emmet avoided positively identifying many of the people who had assisted them during their criminal career, thus protecting them from prosecution or harassment by reporters. In some cases he avoided any mention of them, and in others he changed their names and gave them false background stories. In those cases where I was unable to determine the true identify of such individuals, I used the name Emmet had given them.

When he was not protecting his friends, glorifying Bob, or distancing himself from his crimes, it appears that Emmett tried to tell the truth about his past. While he frequently omitted inconvenient facts, and often used ambiguous wording to obscure unpleasant realities, there is no evidence that he made anything up out of whole cloth. Although some of the events he described could not be independently verified, neither could they be disproved. Those events that did not obviously serve Emmett's personal agenda, and otherwise rang true, were included in this book.

The Daltons were to some extent a product of their environment, and it is important to understand the political and cultural atmosphere of that turbulent era and how it influenced them. In the early nineteenth century the federal government had forcibly relocated several eastern Indian tribes, including the so-called Five Civilized Tribes, to western lands that were at the time considered undesirable by whites. In this newly-created Indian Territory, which eventually became Oklahoma, these tribes were allowed to establish their own "nations," complete with limited sovereignty and self-government. Many Indians had brought black slaves with them to their new lands, but after the Civil War these blacks were freed and made full members of their respective tribes. White men, on the other hand, were forbidden to own land in this territory, although they could go there to trade with the Indians, and could lease land from them for farming and ranching.

This system worked reasonably well at first, but towards the end of the century, as the rest of the country became civilized, more and more whites began moving into the nation's last untamed frontier. They were taking advantage of the fact that the Indian authorities had no jurisdiction over whites, and the only laws that applied to non-Indians were federal laws enforced by an undermanned and overworked cadre of deputy marshals operating out of Judge Isaac Parker's court in Fort Smith, Arkansas. These lawmen were additionally frustrated and hampered by the inane official emphasis on enforcing the laws against "introducing" whiskey into the territory.

Beginning in 1889, Indian Territory was whittled away by the piecemeal opening of selected sections to white settlement. Sometimes by land rush, and sometimes by allotment, these areas in the western half of the territory were rapidly overrun and occupied by white men, who named the expanding region Oklahoma Territory. Towns sprang up overnight, railroads were extended in all directions, and deputy marshals struggled to maintain order in this chaotic territory until local governments could be formed and police forces organized. Meanwhile, in the steadily diminishing Indian Territory, the civilized tribes fought a losing political battle to remain independent. The ensuing turmoil provided ample opportunities for political corruption, commercial exploitation, and crime. Like many others, the Daltons found these opportunities hard to resist.

Virtually all of the events portrayed in this book occurred as described, and are documented in the author's notes, but the book was written in the style of a novel. This makes the book more accessible and enjoyable to read, and allows a better insight into the personalities of the individuals involved. As author E. L. Doctorow once remarked, "The historian will tell you what happened. The novelist will tell you what it felt like." Whenever possible actual statements and dialogue are included, and they are supplemented by imagined conversations interpolated from events, established speech patterns, and a personal familiarity with local idioms. Think of this as a docu-novel, the written equivalent of docudramas on TV and movies based on real events.

CHAPTER 1

Sunday, November 27, 1887

It was a cold morning in the Cherokee Nation, and so far there was little heat coming from the weak sunlight that streaked through the trees along the Arkansas River southwest of Fort Smith. Deputy Marshal Jim Cole grunted as he threw the saddle over his horse. A few feet away Frank Dalton, another deputy marshal, squatted down and placed some small logs on the campfire, then held his open hands over the flames. Dalton's horse was already saddled and waiting. With hands numb from the frigid air, Cole stooped down and buckled the cinch across his animal's chest. It was a quiet winter morning, and the only sound besides the crackling of the campfire was the snoring coming from Dalton's tent.

Cole tugged on the saddle's pommel to make sure it was tight, then picked up his Winchester from where he had left it leaning against a tree and slipped it into the leather scabbard tied to the right side of the saddle. He had arrived at Dalton's camp the day before, just at sundown, to deliver a writ. Cole gave Frank one for Dave Smith on the charge of larceny, and he had another writ on Smith, this one for "introducing" and selling whiskey in the Indian Territory. Although it was only a couple miles back to Fort Smith, Dalton had invited Cole to spend the night at his camp, and Cole readily accepted. He had counted on the invitation, in fact, since he had no money to pay for lodging or food.

Frank Dalton and his two-man posse had arrived at Fort Smith on Friday with a load of prisoners, and after turning the felons over to the jailer had gone back across the river to camp in the bottoms. When Cole had arrived with the writs, he and Frank had decided to go after Smith together, since Cole knew where Smith was camped. What Cole didn't tell Dalton was that he had already had a run-in with Dave Smith, and Cole had heard that Smith was threatening to kill Cole the next time he saw him.

“You ought to get a pistol,” Dalton remarked as Cole joined him at the fire to warm his hands and get one more cup of coffee.

Cole nodded. “As soon as I get enough money ahead.” The deputies were poorly paid, and money came slowly, but Cole’s problem was that he could never hold on to it when he got it. Somehow it was quickly spent on women and liquor, and there was never enough left for things like guns and clothes. In fact, the black wool overcoat he was wearing at that moment was borrowed from Frank’s little brother Bob, one of the two young men asleep in the tent. Bob, who was only eighteen, and Bud Heady, a couple years older, comprised Frank’s posse and acted as guards over the prisoners he collected on his patrol through the Nations. They would not be needed to arrest a petty criminal like Smith, so Frank had decided to let them sleep in.

“You ready?” Dalton asked. Cole nodded, then stood up and stretched. He tossed the dregs that remained in his coffee cup, scoured the tin cup with a handful of sand, and stuffed it into his saddle bag. Dalton straightened his lank frame as well, and was adjusting his pistol belt. Seemingly oblivious to the cold, Dalton had his overcoat open over his dark grey suit. The tobacco-colored overcoat was similar to the one Cole had borrowed, not surprising since both had been made by the Daltons’ mother up in Coffeyville. Jim felt a twinge of envy as he watched Dalton stride over to mount his horse. Frank Dalton was a favorite of Judge Parker, and was generally regarded as one of the best lawmen in the territory. Utterly dedicated to enforcing the law, he was even respected by most of the criminals, both because of his competence and because of his reputation for fair treatment.

It didn’t hurt any that Frank looked the part, just like the heroes on the covers of dime novels. Tall, lean, and handsome, with the steely-eyed gaze of a man who had seen it all, Frank wasn’t afraid of anything. His suit was always clean and neat, and his tall boots were always polished. On his head he wore a neat gray hat with a short rounded crown and a flat narrow brim that might have looked silly on most men, but Frank wore it with authority. Jim Cole had been a deputy for almost as long as Dalton, but he had had occasional problems. Although nothing had been said officially, Cole knew that

Marshal Carroll and some of the others considered him too quick to use force. To Cole's way of thinking, however, if you didn't strike first, you were taking a chance on getting killed. And as far as he was concerned, everyone was a criminal until proven otherwise.

Cole's horse snorted steam as he mounted. The two men guided their horses out onto the muddy and rutted wagon road that paralleled the river and turned toward the southwest. "You know Payne's Clearing, near Cook's Place?" Cole asked.

"Heard of it, never been there," Dalton answered.

"It's a wood-cutters camp. There's maybe three houses and a couple tents. Smith's supposed to be staying in one of the tents."

"Is he armed?"

"I think he's got a Winchester."

"Think he'll resist?"

Cole took a moment to consider this. "Naw," he finally said dismissively. "He's a coward. He'll probably piss his pants when we show up."

Dalton gave Cole a strange look, which Cole pretended not to notice. They rode on in silence. Switching hands holding the reins, Cole would alternately stick his free hand in his coat for warmth, then use the warmed hand to cover his ears that ached from the freezing wind.

As they rode, the low winter sun behind cast long, distorted shadows of them across the ground. The yellow and brown stalks of dried grass were crushed in countless random trails that wove among the scattered rocks, bushes, and clumps of leafless trees. This area, just across the river from Fort Smith, was heavily trafficked by the traders, settlers, and government agents who had business, legal and otherwise, in the Indian Nations. They passed numerous camps, and places where camps had been, as they followed the winding road into a more heavily forested area.

Riding through the woods, Cole could see the increasing evidence of a logging operation, with stumps and sawed branches littering the forest floor. They had gone only a couple miles from

Dalton's camp when Cole reined in his horse and pointed off to the left.

"That's Payne's Clearing," he said. A wagon track wound through the trees into a large cleared area just visible between the barren branches. Situated on rising ground, the clearing was about five hundred yards across. Cole and Dalton turned their horses up the wagon trail and passed through the screen of trees into the clearing itself.

There was a scattering of log cabins and tens, mostly around the periphery of the clearing. The muddy ground in between had hundreds of tree stumps jutting out like broken teeth, and among them were random piles of logs and assorted wood-cutting equipment. Near the center of the clearing was a tent cabin, its front facing west, away from the marshals. The walls were three logs high, and canvas had been stretched over a frame to make a roof. Smoke from a campfire rose in the still air in front of the tent. As they came out of the trees, Cole saw a flash of movement as a woman walked from the fire and ducked into the tent.

"Think she saw us?" Cole asked worriedly.

"Maybe," Dalton answered indifferently. Cole felt a flash of unreasoning anger over his partner's lack of concern. About thirty feet from the back of the tent they stopped their horses and dismounted, drawing their rifles from their saddle holsters. Leaving their horses loose, they cautiously moved toward the tent. Dalton went around the south side of the tent, while Cole circled around the north. Cole peered around the northwest corner cautiously, but saw only the campfire and Dalton, who had casually walked around with his Winchester hanging loosely at his side. Not wanting to be outdone in the bravery department, Cole rushed forward and stuck the barrel of his rifle through the flaps of the tent door. Then all hell broke loose.

Someone inside grabbed the end of his gun, and Cole stepped backward in surprise. Still clutching the rifle barrel, a woman with stringy black hair followed him out, screaming unintelligibly at him, her eyes wild with fury. Dave Smith burst out of the tent right behind her, a Winchester held ready in his hands. Seeing that Cole was struggling with the woman, Smith turned to face Dalton.

"Hold up! Hold up!" Dalton commanded, trying to defuse the situation. "We don't want any trouble here." Events were spinning out of control.

At point blank range, Smith pulled the trigger and shot Dalton in the chest. Almost simultaneously there was a pistol shot from inside the tent, and Cole jerked his rifle out of the woman's hands, unintentionally firing a round into the air. Lunging after him, the wild woman grabbed for his rifle again, and Cole tripped over a tent rope as he backed away. He dropped into a sitting position with a jarring thump, while Smith shot at him over the woman's shoulder. Cole felt a streak of fire as the bulled creased his right breast.

Scrambling to his feet while he worked the lever on his rifle, Cole saw four more people run out of the tent, two men and two women. Apparently believing he had killed Cole, Smith had turned away from him was looking around the south side of the tent, in the direction that Dalton had staggered after being shot. Smith fired again, aiming down as if Dalton were on the ground, and Cole raised his own rifle his shoulder and squeezed the trigger. The blast recoiled against his shoulder, and through the smoke Cole saw Smith jerk and fall on his face. One of the other two men ducked back in the tent, while the third man, holding a bundle in his arms, ran off toward a nearby cabin with one of the women.

There was another pistol shot from inside the ten. Cole couldn't tell where it had been aimed, and didn't want to wait and find out. He sprinted down the gentle slope to the northwest, firing a shot wildly back at the tent as he ran. He heard a woman screech "Lord a mercy, I'm killed!" There was no time to think about it.

When he came to the trees at the edge of the clearing, he took cover behind one with a fat trunk. His heart racing, he looked back at the tent, his panting breath making clouds of fog. From this angle he could not see the front of the tent, but he could still see the first woman, the one who had grabbed his rifle, standing by the fire and screaming in frightened rage. Dalton was out of sight on the far side of the tent, and Cole had no idea if he were alive or dead. At the moment his only concern was his own life.

Cole saw movement at the front of the tent, and a man's head and shoulders appeared above the low corner of the cabin, bending over to pick something up. Thinking the man was getting Smith's Winchester, Cole took aim and fired, and was satisfied as the man stumbled and dropped. He had just re-cocked his rifle when there was another pistol shot from inside the ten, and a round passed overhead, showering Cole with bits of twigs. From the smoke Cole could tell that someone inside the tent was firing through a chink at the northwest corner. He fired back, and as he worked the cocking handle again there was another shot from the tent. This time the bullet struck the tree in front of Cole, making a nasty thunk when it slammed into the soft wood.

Deciding that this tree was not big enough, Cole darted back to larger one and slid to the ground behind it. A pistol shot followed him, and he heard the air crack as the bullet slapped past him. From his new position he pulled off another round at the tent, then jerked the handle down to eject the spent cartridge. When he pulled the lever back up, he felt the minute difference in resistance and heard the hollow sound of the action. He opened the breech part way and inspected the chamber. It was just as he feared—he was out of ammunition. He ducked as the unseen shooter in the tent sent another round crashing through the trees.

Although he knew it was useless, he patted his pockets, hoping to find some more cartridges. He had left all his spare ammunition with his horse, which had run away when all the shooting started. Rapidly he went over his options, which were few. The man in the tent would soon notice he was not returning fire and correctly guess the reason. Frank might still be alive, but he was out of reach. Cole had no idea how serious his own wound was, either. There seemed no other choice; he would have to go back to Fort Smith for help. Crouching low, he ran through the trees and bushes back to the wagon road. Once he was out of sight of the tent, he straightened up and began walking briskly back up the road, rehearsing what he would tell the Marshal.

Charles Woodall had watched the shootout, which he would later refer to as "the difficulty," from inside his cabin about fifty yards southeast of Smith's tent. When the shooting stopped, he went to the front door, but hesitated about approaching the scene of the dispute. He wanted to wait and make sure there would be no more gun play. As he stood in the doorway, he took in the grisly scene.

Woodall could not see the area immediately in front of the tent, though he could see Dave Smith's motionless legs lying in the mud. Mrs. Smith was still standing near the fire, screaming and pulling at her hair, while a few hundred feet away the Pearson couple was standing in mute terror, having barely escaped the carnage. Mr. Pearson gently handed the baby he was carrying over to his wife. Mrs. Smith finally noticed the gunshots had ceased, and her screams subsided to a sob. Weakly she approached the tent and went inside.

No sooner had the distraught woman gone in than a young man came out of the tent with a pistol in his hand. Woodall recognized him as Will Towerly, an unpleasant teen-aged scoundrel who had ridden in with Dave Smith the previous Tuesday. Although the pistol belonged to Smith, Woodall had never seen Towerly without it, just as Smith had always carried the Winchester with him. Towerly, unwashed and unshaven, gazed around the clearing with narrowed eyes, then shoved the pistol into its holster with an air of satisfaction. He looked down at the bodies strewn in front of the tent, then stepped over them to the southeast corner and picked up a Winchester. It was Dalton's. The deputy had dropped it when Smith first shot him, and it had come to rest leaning against the log wall of the tent.

Towerly observed the breech as he pushed the cocking lever part way down, the pulled it back up. He walked over to near where Dalton lay. Woodall had watched earlier from his window as the marshal had painfully crawled toward the back of the tent and taken cover behind a stump. His pistol lay on the ground beside him. When Towerly approached, Dalton pushed up on one elbow and raised his other hand to shoulder level in submission. The wind had died, and Dalton's quavering voice carried easily in the still air.

"For God's sake," he pleaded hoarsely, "don't shoot. I'm already a dead man."

Towerly stared at Dalton a moment, holding the rifle in both hands at his hip. Then, with no comment or expression, he fired. Dalton's head jerked and he collapsed in a heap. Towerly took a couple steps closer, stretched out the rifle until it was only a foot from Dalton's head, and fired again. Slowly the young man returned to the front of the tent, distractedly rubbing his left palm on his pants leg. He dropped the rifle against the wall of the tent and went inside.

A moment later he reappeared carrying a bridle and a blanket in his left hand. He bent down and picked up Dave Smith's Winchester in his right, then strolled down the slope to where Smith's horses were penned. He caught one, saddled it, and rode off to the southwest. Not until Towerly was out of sight did Woodall get up the nerve to go to the tent.

It was a horrible scene, with bodies tangled together in the mud, and blood making puddles in the footprints. People from the other houses and tents cautiously approached and offered their assistance, and soon the mess was being cleaned up.

Mrs. Dixon was already dead, and Woodall had some other men carry her to his house to be laid out. Leander Dixon, her husband, had a serious wound in his left shoulder, and he was carried into the tent and made comfortable, attended to by his sister Lizzie Smith, who was Dave Smith's wife and the one who had grabbed Cole's rifle. Dave Smith died before they could move him into the tent as well, so his body was wrapped in a sheet and left outside for burial. Mrs. Pearson took the Dixon's two children, an infant and a two-year-old, along with her own child, to James Raley's tent, while Jim Pearson saddled and went off to tell Mrs. Dixon's folks about the tragedy. Pearson had just returned when the posse from Fort Smith arrived.

Tuesday, November 29, 1887

Although it was late morning, the train station was dim and murky, its corners shrouded in shadows. The cloud cover that had moved in overnight kept Coffeyville gray and depressing, which was fitting under the circumstances. There was little of the winter daylight filtering in through the depot's dusty windows, and the station master had chosen not to turn up the gas lamps. Above the ticket window the big Regulator wall clock ticked like a metronome. Emmett Dalton watched the minute hand jerk to the next hash mark, then glanced out the window to the south again, looking for some sign that the train was coming. The twin rails that arrowed south across the Verdigris River into Indian Territory remained empty.

The railroads had made Coffeyville a major hub in southeast Kansas. Several lines intersected here, and its proximity to the border of Indian Territory made it a natural center for trade with the Nations. The town had grown and prospered, with brick buildings, paved sidewalks, and natural gas piped to most of the businesses and homes for heat and lighting. Originally from Missouri, the Dalton family had moved around a lot in Emmett's youth, finally settling in Coffeyville in 1882 following a short stay in the Cherokee Nation near Vinita. After five years, the longest he had ever lived in one place, Emmett now considered Coffeyville his home town.

There were only a few other people in the station, and they were quietly keeping to themselves. Perhaps they sensed the solemnity of Emmett's mission there; maybe they just had nothing to say. Emmett heaved a big sigh and tried to think about something else, but his brother's death was too overpowering. At only sixteen years of age, Emmett was the oldest male still living at home, the one who had to comfort his mother and sisters in their grief. His father and his brother Grat were out in California on business, and except for Frank and Bob, his other older brothers had moved to that western state several years before. Emmett had been compelled to provide strength and reassurance, when what he really wanted to do was lay down and cry. It was very hard to grow up all at once.

In the far distance he heard a train whistle, and to Emmett it seemed the most mournful cry he could imagine, but he was still glad to hear it. He stood up and walked to the window, through which he could make out the black shape of the engine spewing smoke as it slowed down from its run across the Cherokee Nation. He knew that when he first saw the engine, the last car of the train was still in Indian Territory, so close was Coffeyville to the border. The train's arrival was a mixed blessing for Emmett. It was bringing the body of his slain brother Frank, which would rekindle the grief he had been trying to suppress, but it also carried his brother Bob, who could take some of the load off Emmett's shoulders in dealing with the tragedy.

While the train was shuddering to a halt, Emmett stepped out onto the platform, hardly noticing the chill of the air as he left the heated depot. Expectantly he searched the windows for a familiar face, then switched his attention to the people who began climbing down from the passenger cars. Despite the occasion, he smiled as he saw Bob, and rushed over to greet him. Wearing a dark blue suit, a white shirt buttoned to the collar, boots with spurs, and a black slouch hat, Bob looked just like a deputy marshal should look. Bob's hands were full with suitcases and bags, but he tilted his head up with recognition when he saw Emmett, and the corners of his mouth turned up just a little. His alert blue eyes still showed a trace of red around the edges from recent tears, but he seemed outwardly calm and composed.

"How are you doing, Emmett?" Bob asked with sincere concern.

"Okay," Emmett responded. "I'm sure glad you're here now." The two brothers had always been close, and Emmett felt it even more now. Although Bob was only two years older, Emmett had always looked up to him, more so than to his other brothers, who had mostly already left home. Maybe it was because Bob was also taller. Over six feet, with a slim build, Bob had a handsome face and wavy dark hair, along with an easy-going confidence that drew all the young ladies. Emmett wanted nothing more than to be like Bob.

Bob shoved a lumpy feed sack at Emmett, who nearly dropped it when it weighed more than he expected. "What's this?" Emmett asked.

"Frank's stuff," Bob answered. "How's Mom doing?"

"It's been pretty hard on her. She insisted on doing a lot of the preparations herself. The funeral home, the minister. She wouldn't let me do it."

"Yeah, well, that's Mom," Bob commiserated.

Most of the people who had left the train began wandering away, leaving Emmett and Bob alone on the platform with another young man who waited nearby. Bob waved the young man over. "Emmett, this is Bud Heady. Bud, this is my little brother Emmett." They shook hands. Emmett knew from Frank's letters that Bud Heady had been one of Frank's guards along with Bob.

"There's the coffin," Bob said, pointing down the platform to where porters were unloading the baggage car. He began walking that direction, and Emmett had to hurry to catch up.

"The funeral home is supposed to have someone here to pick it up," Emmett said, the bag of Frank's possessions banging painfully against his leg. "The burial service is at three this afternoon, and they're supposed to bring the coffin out to the cemetery then." He saw a hearse backup up to the station. "Yeah, there they are."

Bob came to a stop beside the coffin, which was being loaded onto a luggage cart, and glared at the porters who were maneuvering it across the platform. "Careful!" he commanded them, although Emmett could detect no fault in their actions.

"Marshal Carroll sent me and Bud to escort Frank's body and make sure he got full honors," Bob explained to Emmett with a touch of pride. Bob supervised the loading of the coffin into the black-draped hearse, then watched as it drove away.

"The wagon's over here," Emmett said helpfully, motioning toward their old farm buckboard with its two-mule team. Emmett carefully laid the bag of Frank's personal effects into the bed of the wagon and pulled himself up onto the seat. Bob and Bud tossed their bags into the back of the wagon and climbed up on the seat with him. It was crowded with the three of them, but Emmett still managed to get the wagon turned and headed back to the family farm just outside of town.

It was a somber service at the graveside, with a cold wind biting through the Sunday clothes that the many mourners had worn. Frank had many friends, and Emmett was glad to see the service so well attended. Emmett had broken down and wept like a child, and he welcomed Bob's comforting arm around his shoulder. While his eyes glistened and his lips were grimly pressed together, Bob kept control of his emotions. He stood with military bearing, his head held high, and saluted when the coffin was lowered into the grave. Bob had wanted to fire his rifle in a salute as well, but their mother had refused to allow it.

After the funeral they had all gone back to the Dalton home, both family and friends. Other than Bud Heady, who had been invited to stay the night, the friends soon drifted away, leaving the family to its wake. Neighbors had brought over covered dishes of food, and Mrs. Dalton declined any help as she warmed them up and served the gathered clan. She was tightly wound, Emmett could see, and she put on a false front of cheerfulness as she bustled around serving and cleaning up. Every so often, though, someone would mention Frank's name, and Mrs. Dalton would collapse in tears, disappear into the bedroom with oldest sister Eva in her wake, and reappear a short time later. This left Emmett feeling helpless and confused.

Late that night, after everyone else had gone off to bed, Bob, Bud, and Emmett sat around the kitchen table in the flickering light of a single kerosene lantern and talked in low voices. Emmett felt honored to have been allowed to join them in what seemed a very adult, responsible conversation. At Emmett's request, Bob told the story of Frank's death again. Earlier, in deference to their mother, he had given a brief, sanitized version of the event, but now he told it in all its gory and lurid details, just as Jim Cole had told it to him. As he finished, Emmett found his own fists clenched in rage.

"Boy, I'd like to kill that Towerly guy!" Emmett hissed.

"The law will get him," Bud Heady promised.

"The marshal doubled the reward on him," Bob remarked "It's usually five hundred dollars in a case like this, but the marshal asked the Attorney General to make it a thousand."

"A thousand?" Emmett breathed. "It ought to be more. But I'd bring him in for free."

"Uh-huh" Bob said drily.

"Frank was a hell of a peace officer," Bud said, nodding seriously. "The marshal said he was one of the best he ever served with."

"He wants Grat to take his place," Bob announced.

"What?" Emmett gasped, caught completely by surprise. Grat had worked for Frank as a guard a few years earlier, but had not found it to his liking.

"The marshal said he would like to have me do it, but I'm still too young. Said he'd get into all kinds of trouble if he gave a commission to someone who couldn't vote. So he asked me to contact Grat and ask him to take Frank's place."

"What are you gonna do?" Emmett asked. Bob rubbed his beardless chin.

"I guess I'll work for Grat, if'n he takes the job. Where is Grat now? Does he know about Frank?"

"Mom wired everybody out in California—Bill, Litt, Ben, and Cole. Last we heard Dad and Grat were staying with Litt, so I guess they know by now, too." Their father, Lewis Dalton, had in recent years made a limited income by horse trading and running a string of race horses. He and Grat had taken some thoroughbreds out west to run in some races there, but so far had made little money at it. Mrs. Dalton depended mostly on the money Frank and Bob had sent her from their pay and whatever the farm outside Coffeyville could produce. Sometimes one of the four Dalton brothers who lived in California would send what they could, but it wasn't much.

"I'll wire Grat tomorrow," Bob said. "Don't tell Mom. She won't like the idea, and it's no use getting her more upset right now. Besides, Grat might not even want the job."

"I sure would," Emmett declared.

"Me, too," Bob admitted regretfully. "How about you, Bud?"

Heady shrugged. "I don't know. Maybe someday."

They were silent for a few minutes, staring at the dancing shadows of the flickering lantern. Finally Bob spoke again.

"That time the marshal asked Frank to be a hangman, that was something."

"Yep," Bud agreed.

"Tell it again," Emmett urged. He had heard the story several times, and it was no so real to him that he could imagine being there in the room. Bob leaned back in his chair, looked at the ceiling a moment, then started the tale.

"One day the marshal called for Frank to come to his office. When Frank got there, Colonel Carroll said, 'Well, Frank, knowing that you are cool-headed and will make no mistake, I have selected you from among all the deputies to spring the trap from under those poor boys who are to be hanged next Friday.' Old Frank, he drew himself up, took his commission out of his pocket and threw it on Carroll's desk. 'Well, Colonel,' he said, 'if that's all the use you have for me here is my commission. I'll shoot any man if it's in my line of duty, but I will never spring a trap, even from under a dog.'

"The marshal was real impressed, and he said, 'My boy, I don't blame you. I wouldn't either.' And he gave Frank back his commission. After that, none of the deputies were asked to be hangmen, and the other deputies were so glad Frank took a stand that they all chipped in and bought him a solid gold ring."

"He was buried with that ring," Emmett said solemnly, even though Bob and Bud were already well aware of the fact.

"Did you say Mom's already arranged for a headstone," Bob asked.

"Yesterday," Emmett answered. "She ordered a real nice one, about four feet tall."

"Good. Mr. Carroll paid me off and gave me what money was coming to Frank, even though the warrants ain't been sent to Washington yet. I'll give it to Mom to pay for the stone."

"That'd be good," Emmett said, nodding. "Burying Frank took most of the money she had saved back."

"Well, it's getting late," Bud said, stretching his arms out and yawning. "I think I'll hit the sack."

"Yeah, me, too," Bob said, pushing his chair back to get up. While Bob and Bud stretched out on bedrolls they put down in the parlor, Emmett went to his own bed in the room he shared with the youngest brother, Simon. As he undressed and slipped under the covers, he thought about all his brother Frank had accomplished, and he felt a swelling of pride. Now his brother Grat would become a deputy, maybe, and soon Bob would be one as well. The Daltons were gaining a reputation in Indian Territory, and Emmett was proud to have the name. Maybe soon he could join his brothers, and be one of the famous Dalton boys.

Saturday, December 4, 1887

A steady rain was streaming down from the leaden sky, and despite the fact that it was almost noon, the day remained dark and dreary. A strong north wind blew the chilling rain under the hats and down the collars of the two men as they rode, making them even more uncomfortable. With his wide-brimmed hat tilted toward the wind to block at least some of the spray, William A. Moody hunched his shoulders, having given up on making the flapping tails of his black slicker cover his legs. Moody was the posse for Deputy Marshal Ed Stockley, the man riding beside him on this miserable wet day. Disgustedly Moody watched the small but steady stream of water that was dripping from the brim of his hat right in front of his nose.

“How much farther you think it is?” Moody asked, vainly wiping the beads of water from his saddle’s pommel.

“Shouldn’t be more than a mile,” Stockley answered. Neither man had ever been in this area of the Choctaw Nation before, so finding Mrs. McKianey’s boarding house involved a lot of guesswork. Both men worked with Deputy Marshal Heck Thomas out of White Bead Hill, on the Washita River in the Chickasaw Nation about seventy miles to the west. They had been on their way to Fort Smith with a load of prisoners when Marshal Carroll sent word that they should go arrest Will Towerly, the man who had killed Frank Dalton.

So far it had been a long, boring trip. Before hearing about Frank Dalton, Thomas, Stockley, Moody, and some other guards had left White Bead with three wagons loaded with sixteen prisoners to make the long and arduous overland trip to Fort Smith. All along the way Heck Thomas had kept up a constant diatribe about the stupidity and waste of taking the prisoners by wagon, when the trains were right there. As he repeatedly pointed out, they could put the prisoners on a train at Pauls Valley, take them south to Gainesville, Texas, and then switch trains to one headed northeast that would eventually take them to Fort Smith. The trip would only take a couple days, and the savings from not paying all the travel pay and feeding costs to the deputies and guards would more than cover the cost of the train tickets.

Moody and Stockley had listened to Heck’s complaints with little comment. They were getting paid for transporting prisoners, and the longer it took to get them to the jail at Fort Smith, the more money the two men would make. They were naturally more interested in filling their own pockets than in saving the government money, so they would just nod and tell Heck that he had a point, without trying to encourage him. Moody suspected that Thomas was also influenced by his new bride, who had been visibly annoyed at Heck’s frequent trips away from home.

Moody had acknowledged that transporting prisoners at that time of year was an unpleasant experience, especially since there had been a lot of rain this year to turn the occasional excuse for a road into a morass of mud. The trip seemed to be taking forever, and all the men had been glad to arrive in McAlester the day before, where they were scheduled to take a rest. When they arrived, however, there had been a telegram waiting for Heck, a wire from Marshal Carroll. That evening Thomas called Stockley and Moody into the office of the local jail and gave them their orders: find and arrest Will Towerly.

One of the witnesses of Frank Dalton's murder had testified at the preliminary hearing for Leander Dixon that Towerly's father lived in the Stringtown area, just northwest of Atoka. Acting on that information, the marshal had somehow discovered that Towerly was hiding at Mrs. McKianey's boarding house, and had ordered Thomas to send someone after him. Heck had chosen Moody and Stockley as the best men for the job.

That morning the two lawmen had boarded a southbound train in McAlester and rode it to Atoka, the next town of any size along the railroad. Moody had gazed out the window at Stringtown as they passed it before they reached Atoka; it was only a few scattered cabins and tents, and had no depot. At Atoka they climbed down from the train and made their way up the muddy main street to a livery stable where they rented a couple horses and saddles. After asking directions, they rode out into the frigid rain and headed back in the direction they had come from. They forded the Muddy Boggy Creek that ran past the town and left the cleared land for the sodden forest.

"What are you gonna do with the reward money?" Moody asked casually. He gave his head a few rapid shakes, sending water flying from his hat like a wet dog.

"Reckon you'll get half of it," Stockley replied without looking at Moody.

"Well, that's mighty white of you," Moody said jokingly, but inwardly he was genuinely pleased and grateful. Being a posseman didn't pay worth a damn, and the extra five hundred dollars would come in really handy.

"But we ain't got it yet," Stockley reminded him. "The kid might be gone already, or never was there to begin with. Let's don't count our chickens afore they're hatched." Moody shrugged and nodded in agreement, but silently he catalogued the things he would buy with the money anyway, just in case.

The wagon tracks they were following meandered into a denser patch of woods, temporarily diminishing the force of the wind and allowing them to relax slightly. The barren tree branches were black against the scudding gray clouds, and the limbs creaked as they swayed in the breeze. Moody considered it a piss-poor day to be a law officer in Indian Territory.

The woods, which covered the crest of a low rounded hill, thinned out as the two men rode down the far side into the wide shallow valley beyond. Moody noticed that the rain had slackened to a drizzle, but as they rode out into the open valley, the wind seemed even more biting and miserable than before. In the middle of the valley was a large wooden house. It was a well-made frame house, two stories tall, with a covered porch that stretched across the front of the house. Above the porch roof was a small, inexpertly-painted sign that said, "Rooms." That had to be Mrs. McKianey's.

As they neared the unpainted structure, Moody noticed a thin trickle of smoke drifting from the metal stovepipe that jutted from the shingled roof. Lace curtains covered the windows. It seemed an unlikely place for a wanted man to hide. When they were within fifty feet of the front door, they reined in their horses. Stockley put his hand on the butt of his pistol, but left it in the holster. Moody had been carrying a Winchester across his lap, but now he lifted it and shook the water from it.

"Mrs. McKianey?" Stockley called out. "It's Marshal Stockley. We got word that Will Towerly's in there. Is that right?" They waited a minute, but there was no response, other than a flicker of movement as a curtain was briefly pulled aside. Motioning Moody to stay put, Stockley climbed down from his horse, drew his pistol, and started walking toward the house. He had gone only a few steps when the front door burst open and a young man with a rifle stepped out onto the porch. Thin, with uncombed dirty blonde hair and scraggly week-old beard, the boy wore no coat, just a faded plaid flannel shirt and baggy high-water black pants held up with suspenders. His wild eyes flicked back and forth between the two lawmen, and his rifle was held at the ready with both hands.

Stockley stopped in his tracks, but kept his pistol partially lowered at his side, in an attempt to appear less threatening.

"You Will Towerly?" Stockley asked.

"I god-damn reckon so!" Towerly spat out belligerently.

"U. S. Marshals. We got a writ for your arrest. Drop the rifle, son."

"I ain't your son, and I ain't droppin' no rifle." His voice was defiant, but there was a touch of fear discernible.

"You're in enough trouble as it is, kid. Why don't you just put down the gun and come along quietly. We don't want no shootin' here today."

"I killed one marshal, I can kill a couple more," Towerly croaked. Moody could see the kid's eyes starting to water, but whether he was crying or the tears were caused by the bitter wind, he couldn't say. Keeping his movements slow and gradual, Moody brought the barrel of his rifle up to bear directly on Towerly. He noted that Towerly was noticeably trembling.

"No need for that," Stockley cautioned the boy. "That'd just make things worse."

"Worse?" Towerly cackled like a maniac. "I'm gonna hang anyway, what's worse than that? Cain't hang me twice."

"You'll get a fair trial," Stockley assured him.

"Fair trial? From Judge Isaac Parker, the hangin' judge? I guess not!"

"You'll get a chance to tell your side of it." As Stockley talked, he had been easing closer to the porch. Moody watched silently, knowing the kid was right about hanging. Still, he hoped Ed could talk the boy down. The way Towerly was waving that rifle around made Moody very nervous.

"Fat lot of good it will do me," Towerly asserted, lowering his voice. "I know what'll happen. I ain't stupid, you know." He looked down disconsolately and allowed the barrel of his Winchester to sag.

"Come on, kid, let's go," Stockley said encouragingly, taking a step forward and stretching out his left hand. Towerly's head jerked up, and instantly he raised the rifle again and pulled the trigger, blasting Stockley at point-blank range. Moody watched, shocked, as Stockley stumbled backward and fired his pistol almost wildly as he fell to ground. Stockley's bullet struck Towerly in the right leg, and the boy twisted violently to one side and slammed his shoulder against the door frame. Immediately, before Towerly had a chance to recover, Moody fired his own rifle, then cocked and fired again and again, until Towerly slid down into a heap on the porch, his rifle trapped under his crumpled body.

Keeping his rifle trained on Towerly, who was motionless but moaning, Moody glanced over at Stockley. Though he had seen it happen, it only now registered that his friend was lying on his side in the wet brown grass, his hat askew and his legs twitching. Moody threw his leg over the saddle and slid to the ground, his Winchester still pointed at Towerly. Quickly edging over to Stockley, he knelt down beside him and rolled him onto his back. A ragged gasp escaped the deputy's open mouth, but his eyes remained tightly shut. There was a hole in the front of Stockley's slicker, and bright red blood was rhythmically surging out of it. Then, as Moody stared at the blood with horrified fascination, the pulsing stopped. A gentle hiss of air escaping from his lungs marked Stockley's last breath.

Moody stood up slowly, his legs stiff from the cold. He rubbed his eyes, then placed his rifle between his knees and took off his slicker. Picking up the rifle in one hand, he used the other to spread the coat over Stockley's head and torso. He stared down at the inert form for a moment, then turned and walked to the house.

A heavy-set middle-aged man in overalls and farmer shoes had come out of the house and knelt beside the fallen murderer, cradling the boy's head in his lap. As Moody stepped up onto the wooden porch, the man looked up at him with imploring eyes and said, "Did you have to shoot him?" Moody supposed the man was Towerly's father. He didn't answer, he just reached down and pulled Towerly's rifle from under him and leaned it against the wall out of reach. From the unnatural angles of his limbs, it was clear that

Towerly had a shattered arm and a broken leg, along with other wounds that were oozing blood all over his body.

Making soft clucking sounds with her tongue, an older woman in an apron came out with a patchwork quilt in her arms. Without a word to Moody or the father, she draped the brightly-colored quilt over Towerly until he was covered up to his neck. Tears were running down the sides of Towerly's face, and he croaked out a grateful "Thank you, ma'am." His father brushed away his son's tears and stroked his hair. Towerly looked up at Moody, who towered over him, with an expectant expression.

"Why'd you do it, fella?" Moody asked, genuinely puzzled.

"Better'n hangin'," Towerly replied. His voice was soft, like a child's, and he sounded somehow relieved.

"So it was you killed Frank Dalton last week?"

"Yeah."

"How come?"

Towerly squeezed his eyes shut for a moment as pain wracked his body, then relaxed again and spoke. "Dave Smith shot him first. Then the other marshal, Cole? He shot Dave, so I started shootin' at him. Dave Smith was my friend. Cole shot Lee and Mrs. Dixon, then he took off. Dalton, he was dyin', so I just finished him off. Thought I was doin' him a favor."

Moody pondered that for moment, then said, "Well, I don't think I'm going to do you the same favor." Towerly managed a weak nod of understanding. Moody turned and sagged against one of the posts supporting the porch roof. A few feet away lay the still form that had once been his best friend. It had been a bad day, and it wasn't even over yet.

Author's Notes

Chapter 1

Two days after Frank Dalton's death a preliminary hearing was held in Fort Smith for Leander Dixon and James Pearson, who had both been charged with murder. Thirty-six pages of witness testimony were taken in this and subsequent hearings, and these documents are on file at the National Archives in Fort Worth, Texas. Pearson was released, but Dixon was held over for a trial scheduled for May. For some reason this trial was postponed until August, and there is no further record of it. The National Archives also have a copy of the long telegram Marshal Carroll sent to the Attorney General describing the incident and requesting the reward for Will Towerly be doubled.

Frank's murder was extensively reported in the *Coffeyville Journal* of December 1, 1887, the Fort Smith *Elevator* of December 2, 1887, and the Vinita *Indian Chieftain* of December 1, 1887. In his book *Beyond the Law*, Emmett gave yet another account of the incident, apparently based on what Jim Cole had told Bob Dalton. Cole's rather self-serving version of events differed significantly from that provided by the many other witnesses.

The newspapers mentioned above also described the return of Frank's body to Coffeyville. Bob's and Emmet's discussion after the burial was derived from Emmett's book.

Stockley's shoot-out with Towerly was described in an article in the Vinita *Indian Chieftain* on December 8, 1887, and was also mentioned by Emmett in *Beyond the Law*.

CHAPTER 2

Saturday, August 11, 1888

At a horseshoe bend in the Caney River, about 28 miles southwest of Coffeyville, was the small town of Bartlesville, Cherokee Nation. After marrying the daughter of the chief of the Delaware Indians, Jacob Bartles had moved to the area and set up a trading post inside the bend in 1874. Purchasing and expanding a grist mill nearby, Bartles gave free seed to the local farmers so they could grow grain to have ground at his mill. In just a few years his settlement was the economic and political center of that part of Indian Territory. In 1888 Jake's general store was a huge two-story building with a wide covered veranda all the way around it, and next to it he had built barns, stables, and a boarding house. At first other businesses and homes had been built in the bend near Jake's, but in 1884 two of Jake Bartles' former employees had established their own store on the south side of the Caney. With easier access and room to expand, that area was now flourishing, much to Jake's chagrin.

When Grat and Bob Dalton rode into town that Saturday morning, following behind Billy Rogers in his mail hack, the vicinity around Jake's store was a beehive of activity. Threading their way through the other riders, wagons, and pedestrians, the two lawmen made their way to the hitching rail alongside the store. It had been a dry summer, and their boots raised small puffs of dust as they dismounted. It wasn't even noon yet, and already the heat was stifling.

The broad wooden porch was cluttered with farm implements, wagon wheels, feed sacks, and wooden chairs occupied by the town loafers. Bob and Grat waited as Billy Rogers climbed down from his buggy and joined them on the porch, and then all three shirt-sleeved men strode into the great emporium. It was stuffy and not much cooler inside, even with all the windows open, since there was no wind to move the air. Billy, a pudgy young man who dressed like a clerk, led the two brothers down the aisles of the spacious general store. It was crowded with people, men and women, whites, blacks, and Indians, all doing their weekly shopping.

As they neared the back, they were met by Jake Bartles himself, a short stocky man whose only concession to the heat had been to remove the jacket of his three-piece suit. His thick sandy hair was brushed straight back, and a bushy walrus mustache hid his mouth completely. With his portly body in tailored clothes, he looked just the way Bob always pictured when someone was described as prosperous.

"How are you, boys?" Jake greeted them with a practiced smile, reaching out to shake their hands with an unnecessarily firm grip. "Glad you could come so quickly. Let's go back into my office." As he led them through a door behind the counter, Bartles said over his shoulder, "Billy, go get Fry." Rogers, who had been about to follow the other three men into the office, immediately spun and scurried out the front door.

"Fry works for me out in the barn," Bartles explained to Bob and Grat while he went behind his desk and sat down. There were no other chairs in the room, so the two Daltons just stood loosely against a wall. Bob hooked his thumbs in his pistol belt; next to him Grat removed his hat and wiped his forehead with a handkerchief.

"What's this all about, Mr. Bartles," Bob asked.

The Daltons and their posse had come down to the Bartlesville area the day before and set up camp on Post Oak Creek. There was to be a big Smoke between the Osage and the Delaware tribes, and the lawmen hoped to catch some of the whiskey peddlers who would inevitably arrive to exploit this opportunity to sell their illegal wares. As Bob and Grat had prepared to leave their camp that morning, however, Billy Rogers had shown up and told them Mr. Bartles wanted to see them right away. Bartles pulled a lot of weight in that neighborhood, so Grat and Bob had quickly responded to the summons, asking Billy what the problem was. Young Rogers wasn't sure, but he thought it was about Charley Montgomery, who had stolen a couple of pistols, one belonging to Billy himself, and one owned by Eli Ramsey at the livery stable.

"I understand that Charley Montgomery is working for you," Bartles said to them. "Is that correct?" He leaned back and looked at Grat with what Bob interpreted as reproach. Bob started to answer this charge with a heated denial, but Grat was too quick for him.

"Not exactly, sir," he said, stuffing the handkerchief back in his pocket with measured movements. Grat was several inches shorter than Bob, and his legs had a distinctive bow in them. All of the Dalton boys had large ears, but on Grat they protruded like handles on a jug, emphasizing the walnut shape of his skull. In recent weeks Grat had grown a thin mustache that he dyed black in the current fashion. Unfortunately, Bob thought, on Grat it looked more sinister than dashing. Grat put his hat back on and addressed Bartles with no more than minimal respect.

"A few weeks ago he told me he had some information about some crimes, and I told him I'd appreciate any help he could give me, just as I would accept assistance from any citizen. He told me about some whiskey peddlers and robbers he claimed to know about, but when we checked out his story, there wasn't anything to it. Guess he just made it up. Haven't had anything to do with him since then."

Bartles nodded in understanding. "You know he's been going around claiming to be a marshal, don't you?"

"No, I didn't," Grat said, "but I'm not real surprised. He seems to have a real active imagination. Is that why you sent for us?"

"No, no," Bartles said hastily, motioning dismissively with his hand. "I didn't think anyone would really make him a marshal. No, I'm afraid this is more serious. Montgomery is a thief, and I have heard that he is about to rob me and steal my horses. But I believe I better let Fry tell it." At that moment Billy Rogers returned with another man in tow.

"Gentlemen," Bartles said without rising from his chair, "this is Jim Fry. Jim, this is Bob and Grat Dalton, deputy marshals." Bob didn't bother to correct Bartles' introduction; he was only a posseman, not a deputy, but he saw no harm in these people believing otherwise. As they shook with him, Bob felt the calluses on Fry's strong hands. The man was wearing overalls with bits of straw stuck to them, and he smelled of human sweat and horse droppings. Remembering his manners, Fry abruptly pulled off his battered straw hat and held it in front of him, staring expectantly at Jake Bartles with his mouth hanging open.

"Jim," Bartles prompted, "tell the deputies about Charley Montgomery."

"He's gonna rob Mr. Bartles tonight," Fry assured them, bobbing his head. "He thinks I'm gonna help him. He's gonna take them two mares, and he's gonna rob the store."

"How do you know?" Bob asked, straightening to his full height and tilting his hat back on his head.

"He tol' me. He's been trying to get me to help him take stuff since the Fourth of July. He said we could make money easy, easier than work for it. I told him I wouldn't do nothing that was wrong, but he kept after me. I told Mr. Bartles, and he said that if I could help catch Charley doing it, he'd give me fifty dollars."

"So what's his plan?" Grat asked, with little apparent interest.

"Plan?" Fry asked blankly.

"What exactly is he going to do? How are you supposed to help him?"

"Oh. Well, I'm 'posed to go to Old Man Defoe's out on Corn Creek and yell out 'Hello' three times, so he'll know it's me. Then we'll go take them two mares, and we'll break into the store here.

"How are you supposed to break in?" Bob asked, privately wondering why Montgomery would want help from such a slow-witted man as Fry. "Have you got a key?"

"A key? No, sir. Charley, he's got some burglar tools, five boxes of 'em. He showed me. He keeps them in his coat pocket."

"Is he armed?" Grat asked. Before Fry could answer, Billy Rogers chimed in.

"He's got two pistols, mine and Mr. Ramsey's, like I told you before."

"How'd he get them?" Bob enquired.

"I loaned mine to him a few weeks ago," Billy said, fidgeting and anxious to help, "because he said he needed it to go arrest this man named Lew in Coffeyville. But then he wouldn't give it back, and he said he'd shoot me if I didn't stop asking him for it. Then, the other day, I was in Coffeyville, and he gave it back, so I put it under the seat of my buggy while I was still in town. After I was out on the road back here, I went to get it, and it was gone. Next time I seen it, Charley had it again."

"What about the other one?"

"He stole that one from Mr. Ramsey. Mr. Ramsey had hung it up in the office over at the stable, Charley reached through the window and took it. Mr. Ramsey says he'll give you five dollars if you can get it back. It's a black-handled Smith & Wesson. Mine's a Colt with ivory handles.

"What I thought we could do," Bartles interrupted, "is perhaps catch Mr. Montgomery in the act. If you boys were waiting for him when Jim went to meet him tonight, then you could arrest him right then."

"We don't have a writ, Mr. Bartles," Grat said. Bob knew Grat was just making excuses because he did not want to fool with Montgomery. "We'd have to send to Fort Smith and get one, and we wouldn't get it before tonight for sure."

"A writ? But he's planning to steal my horses and ride up into the States."

"He's leaving the country?" Bob asked, seeing a possible solution.

"Yes, sir," Fry said. "Said he was going to Kansas City, I think."

“If he might leave the area,” Bob pointed out, more to his brother than to anyone else, “then we could go ahead and arrest him and hold him till the writ got here.”

“Yeah,” Grat grudgingly agreed, “I guess we could do that. But we’d need more men to waylay the road. Can’t do it with just the two of us.”

“Of course,” Bartles said generously. “I’m sure Billy here will help you, and we can get Sheriff Sanders and Wooster Wiley of the Indian Police, and maybe a couple of others. Will that be sufficient?”

As it turned out, that was more than sufficient. After dark that evening the group set out from Bartlesville, heading north to Corn Creek, about twelve miles away. Fry left first, followed by the two Daltons, Billy Rogers, Ed Sanders, the town sheriff, Wooster Wiley of the Indian Police, and two men named Couch and Davis. The plan called for Fry to meet Montgomery and lead him to where the others would be waiting along the road.

Bob later realized he should have expected it, knowing how dim Fry was. Somehow the stablehand wandered off the road in the dark and became lost. He did not link back up with the others until after they had already passed the place where Fry had been instructed to meet Montgomery. With the ambush already botched, the group rode on up to Old Man Defoe’s house, where Defoe told them Charley had stopped by for a late supper and then gone off to sleep somewhere on the prairie. Bob, Couch, and Davis stayed at Defoe’s in case Montgomery returned there, and the others went back to wait along the road where the original meeting was to have taken place. By morning it was obvious that Charley was not going to show, so everyone went home to get some sleep.

After sleeping most of Sunday, on Monday Bob and Grat moved their camp back northeast to Possum Creek, five miles from Coffeyville. In addition to Bob, Grat’s posse included Allen J. Landis and Jeff Griggs, two out-of-work cowboys just glad to have a job. Leaving these two men at the camp, Grat and Bob rode around the area, asking folks if they had seen Charley Montgomery. Fry had told them that Charley divided his time between Bartlesville, where he stayed at a boarding house run by a man named Dan Griggs, and Coffeyville, where he worked as a farm hand for an old man named Barringer. They determined that he had not been seen at either location since Saturday. A couple people said they had heard he was staying with Negroes in the Timber Hills area. At dusk the Dalton boys rode to their family's home near Coffeyville to spend the night.

Tuesday morning Bob arose early and started in on the chores around the farm. Although their father was home more often now, having sold most of his race horses, he was still not much help in maintaining the place. Emmett had gone down into the Nations to work as a cowboy on the Halsell ranch near Vinita, and Bob's older sister Eva had married a man named Whipple and moved to Meade, Kansas. That left Leona, Nannie, and Simon still living at home, but they were too young for heavy labor, so only Grat and Bob were still around occasionally to do the necessary farm work that their father never seemed to get around to doing. This morning, however, Grat had slept in, and when he finally did get up, he saddled his horse and rode into town, leaving Bob to do all the work.

Sweating profusely in the Kansas summer sun, Bob was repairing the corral fence when his father sauntered over to watch him.

"Where's Grat?" Lewis Dalton asked with mild curiosity.

"Said he was going to town," Bob answered through gritted teeth as he lifted a wooden fence rail.

"What for?"

Bob pounded the rail into place and turned to face his father, brushing his hands on his pants. "Said he was going to ask around about Charley Montgomery, see if anybody's seen him lately. Probably do most of his asking in places that serve whiskey and have card games."

"Bobby!" his father gently reproached him. "He's your brother."

"Well, it's true," Bob grumbled petulantly. "He leaves me here to do all the work while he's out having fun."

"Now, Bobby, you don't have to be doing this stuff. Just leave it for me and I'll get to it pretty soon."

"I know, Dad, but some of this just can't wait." Bob looked away as he heard a disturbance behind the house. His twelve-year-old sister Nannie was feeding the chickens, and inside the wire enclosure with her was Simon, who had just turned eight. Simon was chasing and kicking at the chickens, who were flapping and squawking like crazy, and Nannie was angrily yelling at him to stop. Shaking his head, Bob strode off toward the coop to discipline his little brother, leaving his father standing by the corral with his hands in his pockets.

By noon Bob had completed all the chores he had set for himself. After eating a quick lunch his mother had prepared for him, he rode away from the farm in search of Charley Montgomery. Traveling southwest from Coffeyville, he went from farm to farm, asking anyone he saw if they knew Charley's whereabouts. Several people in the Timber Hills area north of Corn Creek reported that they had seen Charley earlier in the day. They told Bob that Charley had been walking around looking for his pony, which he said had wandered away. These same people also warned Bob that Charley was armed with two pistols and was swearing vengeance on Jake Bartles and the Dalton boys. Two men who were out in the fields making hay had informed Bob that Charley had told them he intended to leave the country and go up into the State where the Daltons couldn't find him.

When Bob returned to the Possum Creek camp that evening, Grat and the other two possemen were just finishing their supper. Bob told them what he had found out, and set out his plan for the next day. Timber Hills was west of their camp, so Bob told Grat to circle around to the south and work his way north through the area, while Bob would come in from the opposite direction. Grat suggested it might be better if Landis or Griggs searched the Timber Hills with Bob, while he went back to Coffeyville in case Charley showed up there again. Reminding Grat that Charley was on foot, so he was hardly likely to have made it to Coffeyville, Bob insisted on his original plan. Grudgingly Grat agreed.

Wednesday, August 15, 1888

It was late afternoon when Bob Dalton trotted his horse back into the camp on Possum Creek. Al Landis, leaning against a tree and smoking a small cigar, was clearly bored with all the waiting. Dark-haired and wiry, Landis was the image of a rugged cowboy. Jeff Griggs was squatting by a small campfire in the middle of the dusty clearing, stirring a pot of stew he had suspended over the flames. With the fire adding to the searing summer heat, beads of sweat were rolling down his face in a steady stream.

"Get your horses," Bob ordered as he halted his mount between the two men.

"What's up?" Landis asked, quickly stubbing out his cigar on the tree trunk. He had visibly perked up at the prospect of some action. Griggs straightened up and wiped his face with a towel he had been using as an apron.

"Charley Montgomery's over at June Brown's place," Bob explained impatiently. "We got to go get him before he takes off." Bob's horse, sensing his rider's mood, lightly pranced around in agitation.

"What about Grat?" Griggs asked, lifting the pot off the fire and setting it on a flat rock.

"Where is he?"

"Coffeyville," Landis answered over his shoulder as he walked to where his horse was tied. "Came through here a couple hours ago. Said he hadn't found anything in Timber Hills, so he was going to town to check there."

Bob clenched his fist in exasperation, but then shook his head with resignation. "We'll just go without him. We haven't got much daylight left. Get movin'."

"But Grat's the deputy, not us," Griggs complained while he scuffed dirt over the fire with his boot. Tall and gangly, with curly blond hair, Griggs was always complaining. He dropped his towel over the stew pot and squinted up at Bob. "And what about a writ?"

Landis was already throwing a saddle over his horse. Bob took a deep breath, then spoke in the measured tones of a grade school teacher. "Shelley Keyes says Charley's talking about leaving the country. We can't wait for Grat, or a writ, either. We've got to move *now*. So come on, Jeff, hurry up."

"Okay, okay," Griggs said grumpily, turning to go saddle his horse. Still he dawdled, and it was ten minutes before all three were finally ready. Heading directly into the blinding glare of the afternoon sun, the posse rode out of camp to go arrest Charley Montgomery.

The men had first gone to Shelley Keye's farm, where Shelley and his friend William Ellington told Bob that Charley had just been there. According to them, Charley had walked up and again complained about the Daltons and Jake Bartles, asked if they had seen his missing pony, and then tried to borrow Ellington's horse so he could ride to Kansas. When Ellington refused, Charley had muttered that he would just walk, then, and had trudged off toward the Brown farm to collect his blankets and kit. Thanking Keyes and Ellington for their help, Bob led the posse off in the same direction.

Bob knew the Brown family, and remembered that their cabin faced east, so he decided to approach it from the west. The area was heavily wooded, so they were easily able to ride within a few hundred yards of the house undetected. At a small clearing they dismounted, tied up their horses, and checked their weapons. The sun was almost on the horizon now, and the woods were deeply shadowed.

"When we get to the cabin," Bob told the others, "you two go around the north side, and I'll come around the south side. Remember, we ain't got a writ, so don't shoot him if he runs. I don't know if the Brown family's at home, so watch out for them, too. Okay?" Griggs and Landis nodded their understanding, and the three lawmen began walking cautiously down a narrow trail through the trees. Bob led, carrying an old long-barreled shotgun he had bought second hand, and he had his Colt .45 in a holster on his hip. Landis, directly behind him, also had a holstered pistol, and in the rear trailed Griggs, tightly gripping Bob's Winchester.

In the trees the cicadas, which locals always called locusts, were in full cry. The grating scream of their mating song echoed rhythmically, cloaking the sound of the posse's boots crushing sticks and dead leaves on the parched ground. The setting of the sun and the fading light did little to relieve the suffocating heat, and Bob's body was drenched with sweat, although he realized that some of it might have been caused by excitement.

The gloom of the woods lightened perceptibly ahead, and Bob made out the angular outline of a small cabin through the leaves. Motioning with his free hand, Bob directed the other two men to the left along the low wooden fence that bordered the yard of the cabin. Meanwhile Bob approached the southwest corner of the fence just to his right. Across the small yard was the rough wooden cabin; the back of the building was featureless, and the south end had only a small window. Pausing to consider his next move, Bob glanced over at his two companions, who were approaching the northwest corner of the fence.

Landis, his lanky frame hunched over like a question mark, was in the lead, with Griggs a few feet behind him. Bob waved them forward, but his movement caught the attention of an old coon dog that had been snoozing in the shade of a bush. Raising his massive head and flaring his nostrils, he stared suspiciously at Bob a moment, then let out a single loud "Whoof!" Bob saw Landis duck down behind the fence, and immediately thereafter a shot rang out from the far side of the cabin. Grigg's straw hat flew from his head, and the startled young man threw himself to the ground as well.

Landis cautiously stood back up, his hand poised over his pistol. "Hold it, Charley," he yelled in warning. "Throw up your hands!" From Al's posture, Bob surmised that Charley was at the northeast corner of the house directly opposite from Bob. With a sudden movement Landis drew his gun, flinched as Charley shot at him, and quickly fired in return.

With his blood pumping, Bob leaped over the fence and ran toward the southeastern corner of the house, cocking his shotgun as he ran. The dog followed his movement with his head, but made no move to intercept. There were two more shots close together, a pistol and a rifle, just before Bob rounded the front corner of the cabin.

As he burst into the front yard, Bob found himself face to face with Charley Montgomery, who was racing toward Bob with his pistol raised and cocked. "Stop!" Bob shouted hastily. He intended to then order Charley to drop the gun and throw up his hands, but he never had the chance. Charley ran right up to Bob and fired. With a deafening roar the gun went off in Bob's face, the smoke temporarily blinding him. At the sound of the shot Bob instinctively pulled the first trigger of the shotgun he was still holding at his waist, and the gun bucked in his hands as it blasted into Charley's midsection.

When the smoke cleared, Bob was standing over Charley, who was down on his hands and knees. With a face filled with pain and hatred, he glared up at Bob. The ivory-handled pistol Charley had been using lay on the ground a couple feet away. Wordlessly Charley struggled to reach for the gun, but Bob quickly stepped forward and grabbed it away. Landis had just run up behind Charley, his own pistol held ready. Still swaying on his hands and knees, Montgomery reached back with his left hand for the black-handled Smith & Wesson holstered on his hip. Landis sprang forward and wrapped his left hand around the cylinder of the gun as it came out of the holster and wrenched it from Charley's grasp.

"Throw up your hands!" Bob and Landis commanded almost simultaneously.

Montgomery turned his head to look up at Bob with narrowed eyes, and through clenched teeth he bitterly swore, "God damn you, I can't!" With that he collapsed on his face and lay still.

"Turn him over," Bob said. Landis put his own gun back in its holster and jammed Charley's in his belt, then pulled on Charley's empty gunbelts until he rolled over on his back. There was a gaping wound in the right side of Charley's stomach, and he stared hatefully up at the two men, his breath shallow and hoarse. Griggs ran up to the group and stopped, looking squeamishly at the blood oozing from the ragged hole in Charley's side.

Bob glanced up as Griggs arrived and noticed out of the corner of his eye that there was a black man standing half-hidden behind a tree down toward the barn.

"Mr. Brown?" Bob called out. The man nodded and stepped out into full view. "It's all over. You can come on up now." Nodding, the man complied.

"Here," Bob said to Al Landis, handing him Charley's white-handled Colt. "What do you see?"

Landis, understanding what Bob was getting at, pointed the gun over his shoulder so that her could look at the front of the cylinder, then spun the cylinder slowly. "Four hulls, two wads," he said succinctly. In other words, four rounds had been fired, and two were not yet fired. "It's still warm," he added as he sniffed the barrel.

Junius Brown, a bear of a man, had approached with a few feet of the group and stopped, waiting respectfully. As Landis handed the pistol to Griggs to examine, Bob walked over to Brown. "Mr. Brown," he said politely, "could you please get Charley a pillow, and then hitch up your team. We'll need to borrow your wagon to take him to Coffeyville."

"Yes, sir," Brown said. Purposefully he strode into the cabin. Only then did Bob realize that he had been hearing a child cry inside the cabin since the shooting had ended. A few moments later Brown emerged with an old striped pillow and handed it to Al Landis, who bent down to slide it under Charley's head.

"Marshal," Brown said to Bob, "my wife is pretty upset by all this, so I think I better take her and my boy over to Mr. Johnson's house before we go to Coffeyville. His tone was apologetic, but firm. Bob, who was not unsympathetic, agreed to the condition, and let the man go off to the barn to hitch up his team.

When he rejoined his partners, Bob noticed for the first time that there was a trickle of blood coming from Jeff Griggs' right ear. "What happened to your ear, Jeff?" he asked, looking pointedly at the right side of Griggs' head. Griggs looked puzzled and reached up to feel his ear. When he touched the wound, he winced with pain and jerked his hand away, then looked wonderingly at the blood on his fingers.

"I don't know," he said, pulling a handkerchief from his hip pocket to wipe up the blood. "Guess it happened when Charley shot off my hat."

Griggs' wounded ear reminded Bob that he had felt the blast of Charley's shot at him, and he too might be wounded and not know it. "My face is burning," Bob told Landis, tilting his face up- to catch the fading light. "You see anything?"

Landis leaned forward and examined Bob's beardless young cheeks. "You got some powder burns," he confirmed. "You must a been *real* close when Charley shot at you. You're damn lucky he didn't kill you."

"Yeah, I reckon so," Bob agreed. "Course, having this shotgun didn't hurt none."

The possemen watched silently as June Brown brought up his wagon to the house and helped his wife and child onto the seat. As he drove the team out of the yard and down the small dirt road to the east, Bob turned and squatted down next to Montgomery. Charley's expression had changed to one of fear and desperation, but defiance flared in his eyes as he recognized Bob's face.

"What's your name?" Bob asked gently. He already knew, but it was required in such circumstances to confirm the criminal's identity. Charley blinked away a tear, but offered no reply. "Are you hurt bad?" Bob ask solicitously. "Would you like some water?" Charley refused to talk, seeming to concentrate on his gasping breath, and soon Bob gave up. He stood and joined the other two, who, with exaggerated gestures, were describing to each other repeatedly what they had done during the shoot-out.

By the time June Brown returned a half hour later, night had fallen and Charley Montgomery had quietly passed away. His lifeless body lay where it had fallen. Brown had his neighbor, Mr. Johnson, with him, and both men insisted to Bob that Brown's wagon was "out of fix" and could not be used to haul Charley's body to Coffeyville. Bob sent Griggs with Brown and Johnson to go over to Shelley Keye's farm and borrow a wagon, and he had Landis go fetch the horses they had left in the woods. Griggs and the two farmers returned with a wagon and Bill Ellington, who explained that Keyes didn't have a wagon, so Ellington had offered his.

After Charley's body was wrapped in one of his own blankets and loaded in the back of the farm wagon, Bob had Landis show the three farmers Montgomery's pistols. Brown went inside his cabin and lit a lantern so that they could see the guns better, and the three men passed them around. They all noted that four rounds have been fired from the ivory-handled gun, and assured Bob that they would recognize both guns if they saw them again. Bob was concerned about establishing the facts because he, unlike Grat, was not a sworn deputy, and there had been no warrant for Charley's arrest. In effect, then, Bob was simply a citizen who had killed another citizen, and it was incumbent on him to prove the shooting was justified. By organizing his defense now, Bob hoped to avoid a long inquiry later. It was a forlorn hope.

With Johnson and Ellington driving the wagon, Bob and his partners returned to their camp on Possum Creek around nine that night. Grat was there waiting for them, with no idea where they had gone, and there were heated words between the two brothers after Bob told Grat about the evening's events. Grat was furious because he knew he would be held responsible Charley's death as much as Bob was. Bob worked for Grat, and Grat knew better than Bob how much bureaucratic and legal mess would result from the shooting. Nonetheless, he quickly saddled up and joined them as they took the body into Coffeyville and delivered it to the funeral home.

They all spent the night at the Dalton family home, and the next morning Grat wired Marshal Carroll in Fort Smith about what had occurred, while Bob took care of arranging Charley's burial. As was the policy in the marshal service, Bob had to pay for the burial, since he had killed Charley without a warrant. If Bob thought that was unfair, the preliminary hearing that began two weeks later was even more frustrating.

Consistent with the official policy when peace officers killed a suspect for whom there was no writ or warrant, all four members of the posse were charged with murder, and a hearing was held the first week of September. On September 1 testimony was taken from Jake Bartles, Billy Rogers, Jim Fry, June Brown and his wife, Bill Ellington, and all four members of Grat's posse. All basically confirmed Bob's version of the incident, and Bob assumed he would be exonerated and all charges would be dropped. Three days later, however, the court was reconvened and several witnesses were recalled. Bob was puzzled when each witness was asked if they knew of any conspiracy to murder Charley Montgomery, but kept thinking it was simply a perfunctory requirement for this sort of hearing. When the hearing was continued until November, Bob began to worry.

Proceedings resumed on November 26, and suddenly the problem became clear. Dan Griggs, the man who ran the boarding house where Charley had stayed in Bartlesville, testified that he thought Jake Bartles had conspired to have Charley murdered. According to him, Charley had told him he had a "cinch" on Bartles, since he knew that twelve years ago Jake had hired someone to kill three men, an Osage, a Cherokee, and a white man. Other than some ambiguous statements he claimed to have heard from Bartles and Fry, Griggs had nothing solid to back up his claim, nor could he positively implicate the Daltons in this conspiracy. He swore that William Kerr would back up his story.

Kerr had since moved from Bartlesville and was not available to testify, but a deposition from another friend of Charley's was read into evidence. This man, a Coffeyville resident named A. P. Lynam, told how Charley had come to his house the night of the failed ambush and sworn he would kill Fry, Bartles, and the Daltons. When Lynam had advised Charley to surrender to the Daltons, Montgomery had declared, "If you ever see me in their hands, it will be when I am dead."

The next morning, Sunday, Lynam had gone into town to find the Dalton boys, and had instead run into Bill Kerr. Sitting on salt barrels in front of Bump's General Store, the two men had discussed Charley Montgomery at length. Kerr claimed that Charley was innocent of any crime, and that Jake Bartles was behind the whole thing. Kerr told Lynam that he himself wouldn't think any more about killing Jake Bartles than about killing a damned dog, and Montgomery could kill Bartles and nobody would ever know where it came from. Bob, who was both bewildered and infuriated by these wild accusations, was especially irritated by the next statement.

According to Lynam, Kerr had said, "I don't have the money to give to Montgomery to help him out of the country, but I am a Free Mason, and I could get it right over at that bank." So saying, he had pointed across the street at the First National Bank of Coffeyville. Lewis Dalton had always claimed that banks were not to be trusted, and in Bob's mind Kerr's declaration confirmed his father's opinion. Kerr had also emphasized to Lynam that if Charley were to kill Jake Bartles, then he, Kerr, would give him money to leave the country.

Why Kerr and Griggs leveled these charges against Jake Bartles was never made clear, but Bob suspected it was mostly done out of petty jealously. Jake had been very successful, but he often antagonized his competitors with his high-handed ways. Perhaps these two men had blamed their own lack of prosperity on Jake, and hoped to bring him down to their level. At any rate, the accusations were obviously unfounded, and finally Bob and the others were officially cleared.

Unfortunately the rumors had already been spread, and they would follow Bob wherever he went. Bob blamed Griggs and Kerr for his unjust reputation as a reckless killer, but he also began to see the First National Bank of Coffeyville as an accomplice in this smear campaign. This animosity would fester for years.

Wednesday, January 8, 1989

Bob felt a drop of sweat run down his temple onto his neck. Dressed for the winter weather outside, and now sitting only three feet from a glowing metal stove, he felt like he was being baked for Sunday dinner. Next to him on the hard wooden bench sat Grat, bored and irritable, but not apparently in as much discomfort as Bob. Maybe, Bob thought, it was not just the heat that had him sweating.

They were in the outer office of Marshal W. C. Jones, who headed the Southern District of Kansas. From here in Wichita, Jones directed the activities of deputy marshals in the north central and northwestern parts of Indian Territory, and Grat and Bob had come here hoping to sign on. At a small desk across from them, guarding the door to the marshal's inner office, was one of the office deputies, a thin older man wearing an eyeshade on his head and sleeve protectors on his forearms. When they had come in, he had not bothered to introduce himself; he told them to have a seat, and went back to his paperwork.

"How much longer is it gonna be?" Grat asked the man, breaking the silence of the room. His tone was polite, but just barely. The clerk, who had been scratching away with a pen, paused and looked up.

"Can't say," he replied, annoyed at the interruption. "He's got someone else in there right now. Soon as they're done, he'll see you."

"Thank you," Bob said sincerely, trying to smooth any feathers that Grat might have ruffled. "We're just excited about working for the marshal, and can hardly wait to get started. How long have you been working here?"

"Too long," the man grumbled, and went back to his writing. It was clear he did not think much of field deputies.

Bob unbuttoned his new suit jacket and flapped the lapels gently to try and cool his body. He had bought the black suit just for this occasion, and was proud of his dapper appearance. Grat, however, was in his usual brown jacket and checked pants, both of which had obvious signs of repair. On the coat rack by the door were their hats, Grat's wool overcoat that he had inherited from Frank, and Bob's new gray duster. Grat sat very still, staring stonily at the closed door to the marshal's office, while Bob kept shifting position on the bench, crossing and uncrossing his legs.

They were here for their final interview before being hired as deputies. Grat had been a deputy in the Fort Smith district for a year, so this was nothing special to him, but Bob was finally getting the chance to be a full-fledged sworn deputy himself, rather than just a posseman or guard. They had sent their written qualifications and letters of recommendation to Marshal Jones weeks earlier, and finally they had been summoned for interviews. For Bob it was the culmination of a desire he had held ever since Frank had gone into the service, to actually serve as a Deputy United States Marshal. He smiled just thinking about it.

Grat leaned back and rubbed his cheek. "Who are you gonna use for a posse?" he asked Bob without taking his gaze from the marshal's door.

"Emmett wants to do it real bad, so I figure he'll be one. Other than him, I'll have to see who I can find. Maybe Johnston, or Steve Bellieu.

"Mom's not going to like you taking Emmett with you," Grat warned, turning to look at Bob. "She don't want him getting into any scrapes."

"I know," Bob said, motioning vaguely with his hand, "but who else am I gonna get? Besides, he good with a gun, he'll do what I say, and he works cheap."

"He'll have to," Grat chuckled. Possemen were even more poorly paid than deputies.

"Hey," Bob said, lowering his voice and leaning over to his brother. "I talked to Emmett yesterday. He says Mom and Dad have been fighting."

Grat shrugged. "So? They're always fighting about something."

"No, this is serious," Bob insisted, shaking his head. "Emmett says Mom went into town to see Colonel Elliott about a divorce."

"What do you mean?" Grat whispered sharply, his face clouding like a sudden summer storm.

"I mean she's thinking about divorcing Dad."

"They can't get divorced."

"Why not?"

"They just can't." Grat's hushed voice was getting petulant. "And why'd she go to Elliott? He's a newspaper man." David Stewart Elliott was the editor and publisher of the *Coffeyville Journal*, and a well-known individual in their home town.

"He's a lawyer, too," Bob explained patiently. "He isn't going to tell anybody or put it in the paper."

"Well, why does she want a divorce for, anyway?" Grat's initial anger was changing to confusion, and his voice began to take on a whine.

"I don't know. The usual stuff, I guess. You know how Dad is."

"Still," Grat said, starting to pick his teeth with a fingernail, "he's always been like that. Why now?"

"Who knows? Maybe it's because he's home all the time now."

Grat took a moment to consider that. "How's Emmett know all this?"

"Eva told him. She took Mom into Coffeyville when she was there visiting. Mom told her not to tell anyone, so don't let on you know." Bob was not surprised that his sister had told Emmett despite her promise to their mother not to say anything. Eva was a bossy woman who wanted to be in charge of everything, even her parents' marriage.

Grat leaned forward with his forearms on his knees and stared at the floor. "Hell!" he muttered dejectedly.

"We got to do something," Bob said.

"Like what?" Grat mumbled.

"I don't know. I'll talk to Mom, try to find out what's going on. Why don't you talk to Dad?"

"What good will that do?"

"You never know. He listens to you more'n anyone else in the family." Grat just grunted and continued picking his teeth with his fingernails. Bob saw that his brother did not want to discuss the issue further, so he leaned back and folded his arms across his chest. He was now sorry he had brought it up, since it had ruined his previously elated mood. He tried to think of something more cheerful, and then he remembered what he had been thinking about earlier that morning.

"What do you think our cousins would think about this?" Bob asked with a sly grin.

"Cousins?" With one eyebrow raised, Grat turned his head to look at his little brother.

"The Youngers. Cole and Bob and Jim." Mrs. Dalton's maiden name was Younger, and she was the aunt of the infamous Younger brothers who had ridden with Jesse James twenty years earlier. Although their mother preferred not to discuss her notorious kin, Bob had always taken perverse pride in his relationship to the famous outlaws.

"What about them?"

"Well, here we are, deputy marshals and all. What would they think?"

"They're in prison," Grat pointed out.

"That's what I mean. Kind of funny, isn't it? We're lawmen, and we got family that's famous outlaws."

"I wouldn't go bragging about it if I was you," Grat warned. He sat back up straight and gave Bob a mock serious look. "People might think we got bad blood," he said ominously. Bob nodded and chuckled.

At that moment the door to the marshal's office opened with a creak and a tall, heavy-set man walked out, nodded to the clerk, and brushed past the Daltons on his way out to the hall. Without looking at Bob and Grat, the unfriendly office deputy stood and went into the marshal's office, closing the door behind him. A couple minutes later the door swung open again and the clerk motioned for them to come in., He held the door as they trooped into the smaller room, and then closed it behind them, leaving them alone with the marshal.

Marshal Jones, a solidly built man with thinning hair and drooping mustache, ignored the Daltons for a minute as he sat at his desk reading some papers. When he looked up and saw them standing in front of him, it almost seemed as if he were surprised by their presence.

"Sit down, boys," he said, waving at the two office chairs that sat against the wall on either side of the door. Bob and Grat backed up and lowered themselves into the chairs while the marshal straightened a stack of papers. Jones studied the two men intently, making Bob a little uncomfortable, then glanced down at his papers again.

"Which one of you is Grant?" he asked brusquely.

"It's Grat, sir. Short for Gratton." Grat tried, with moderate success, to hide the irritation he always felt when people mispronounced his name. The marshal nodded, then looked at Bob.

"And you must be Robert."

"Yes, sir," Bob answered eagerly. He sat up as straight as he could and folded his hands in his lap.

"How old are you, Robert?"

"I'll be twenty in May, sir."

"That's pretty young to be a deputy marshal." Jones' tone and expression were neutral, and they gave Bob no clue as to what the marshal wanted him to say.

"Yes, sir, but I've been a guard and a posseman for almost two years now, first with my brother Frank, and then with Grat here."

"Yes, so I see. It's too bad about Frank Dalton. I heard he was one of the best. I hope you learned something from him."

"Yes, sir. He taught me a lot."

"Says here you killed a man last summer over near Coffeyville."

"It was self-defense, sir. He fired first, and he had already wounded another man."

"Hmm." The marshal was looking at his papers again. Bob began to get worried, since the interview was not going the way he had expected. Under the impression that the interview was a mere formality, Bob had come in expecting a welcoming speech, but now it felt more like an inquisition.

"And Grat," the marshal said the name carefully, "you're twenty-seven?"

"That's right."

Jones laid the papers on the desk and leaned back in his chair. "So why do you want to be deputies here in this district. What was wrong with the Fort Smith district?"

"Nothing was wrong, sir," Bob rushed to reassure him. "Our folks live in Coffeyville, and we like to see them ever' once in a while, so we figured we'd have more chance to do that working here out of Wichita." What he did not tell Jones was that Grat's drinking had offended some of the people at the Fort Smith office, and the marshal there would not make Bob a deputy because of his age.

"So you're saying you'd prefer to work the Osage Nation."

"If we could, yes, sir."

"Hmm. Well, we could probably work that out."

Bob's anxiety subsided when he realized that Marshal Jones was indeed going to hire them. He struggled to keep from grinning like an idiot. "But we'll do whatever you want," Bob added, not wanting to sound pushy. "We heard you were a good man to work for, so that's another reason we came over here." Grat cleared his throat, which Bob knew meant that he thought Bob had gone a little too far with his brown-nosing.

Marshal Jones did not notice. He picked up a pen, dipped it in an inkwell, and began making notes on one of the papers. "Which pay system do you want, fees or expenses?" He asked the question without looking up.

"Fees," Bob and Grat answered at the same time. Neither method paid well, but the fee system was easier. Under the expense method, the deputy was required to submit receipts for all expenses incurred, with the chance that some might not be approved. The fee system, on the other hand, granted the deputy a set amount of money for each type of task, so less paperwork was needed. The problem was that the fees were very small. A deputy received ten cents a mile for official travel, $2.50 for reading a warrant or bringing in a prisoner, and forty cents a day for feeding a prisoner. Guards and possemen, such as Bob had been and Emmett soon would be, were paid at a flat rate of two dollars a day when actively employed. The deputy usually could not collect on any rewards offered by the government, although that did not apply to rewards posted by individuals or corporations.

What made the low wages even worse was the bureaucratic tangle required to collect this pay. The deputies had to fill out detailed vouchers and submit them to the marshal, whose office deputies would then total these and prepare claims to be sent to the Justice Department in Washington. There the Attorney General's office would process the claims, allocate funds, and then forward the money to the marshal for disbursement to the deputies. Months would often pass before the deputies would receive the money they had earned, so they were often forced to depend on credit from friendly merchants to survive.

After making some more marks on the papers before him, Marshal Jones put the pen away and gave the boys a forced smile. "Well, that's it," he said. "You two can ride the Osage Nation. When you get to Pawhuska, see the commissioner there, Mr. Dodson, and he'll have your oath of office to sign and your badges. Good luck. You'll need it." Jones looked back down at some other forms on his desk in a clear signal of dismissal.

Wondering if there wasn't something else, Bob remained in his seat with a puzzled expression on his face. Grat, however, immediately rose and signaled for Bob to follow him. Bob pushed himself up from the chair and hurried out of the marshal's office behind Grat. Jones paid no further attention to either of them.

In the outer office the clerk gave them brief letters to give to the U. S. Commissioner at Pawhuska and a small booklet outlining the duties and responsibilities of a deputy marshal. Grabbing their coats and hats, the Daltons left the courthouse and hurried to the train station to catch the last train back to Coffeyville. Bob was disappointed at the lack of ceremony, but he kept reminding himself that he was now a real deputy marshal, and that made up for it. He was sure there were exciting times ahead.

Friday, January 18, 1889

On the tenth of January Grat and Bob had ridden to Pawhuska, a small encampment west of Bartlesville that served as the capital of the Osage Nation, and were sworn in by the commissioner, J. E. Dodson. A few days later they were back in Coffeyville, in a small office on Ninth Street. The weak winter sun streaming in through the large plate glass window warned the waiting area, and the shadows of the letters painted on the window were easily readable on the bare wooden floor: "Gold Room Loan Agency." Grat and Bob sat in straight-backed wooden chairs along the west wall, waiting as George Pfister filled out various loan forms and documents behind the high counter that divided the room.

Grat unbuttoned the heavy, rust-colored wool overcoat his mother had originally made for Frank. The chill he had felt outside was rapidly melting away in the heat of the small building. Sticking his thumb in his vest pockets, he spoke quietly to Bob, as if they were in church.

"You sure this will be enough?"

"Uh-huh." Bob pulled a slip of paper from his vest pocket and consulted the pencil markings on it. "I added up the figures twice to be sure. Seventy-two dollars and ten cents."

"And that will cover you and Emmett both?"

"Yep. Wagon, mule team, rifle for Emmett, blankets, food. Everything we need."

"I hope to hell you're right. Hacks me off that I have to sign your loan." Actually Grat was pleased to help his little brother, but he wanted to impress Bob with the seriousness of what they were doing.

"I'm sorry, Grat, but they say I'm too young to get a loan on my own. Don't worry, I'll pay it back."

"You damn well better. How much did you put on credit over at Barndollar's?"

"About twenty-eight bucks." Bob had bought some clothes for himself, mostly underwear, so he could keep warm on the windy trail.

Grat just shook his head. "Think you're going to do enough marshalling to pay all that back?"

"I'm going to work hard at it," Bob promised earnestly. "I'm thinking about joining the Indian Police, too."

"Well," Grat drawled, "the problem isn't earning the money, it's getting paid that's hard." Grat reached into his coat pocket and drew out a block of tobacco. He gnawed off a corner and began chewing the bitter leaf. "Talked to Dad yesterday," he mumbled around the wad in his mouth.

"What'd he have to say?"

"Not much. Said it wasn't any of our business. Said they'd work it out."

"I hope so. It just isn't right, Mom and Dad getting divorced after all these years."

"Aw, they aren't going to. Mom just wanted to scare him, is what I think."

"I don't know," Bob said doubtfully. "When I talked to Mom, she seemed pretty upset with him. Still wouldn't tell me about what, though."

Grat's response was limited to a grunt through his nose. With his cheek bulging and brown spittle starting to leak from the corner of his mouth, he needed to find a place to spit. A quick scan of the room detected no spittoon. He glanced down at the floor beside his chair, but noticed Pfister watching him from under his eyebrows. Resigned to the inevitable, he stood up and went to the door, opened it, and spit across the sidewalk into the street. Wiping his mouth on his coat sleeve, he closed the door with a bang and returned to his seat. No sooner had he sat down, though, than Pfister motioned them to the counter. Both Daltons rose and went to sign for the loan.

Friday, March 15, 1889

"There he was, bleeding like a stuck pig. Told me all about killing Frank. Guess he knew he was gonna die." Shortly after he had killed Will Towerly, William A. Moody had been promoted to deputy marshal and assigned to work in the Creek Nation. Today, over a year later, he was describing that defining moment in his life to Grat for what seemed like the fortieth time. Grat was tired of hearing it, but Moody wasn't tired of telling it. They were riding together along the Arkansas River northwest of Tulsa, on their way to arrest Jeff Berryhill on some minor charge or other. Grat didn't know the charge, and did not really care. This was Moody's arrest, and Grat was along only because the fugitive was in the Kansas District's jurisdiction, while Moody worked for the Arkansas court in Fort Smith.

"If it was me," Grat declared, trying to hold up his end of the conversation, "I would have kicked the shit out of him anyway." Actually, Grat knew, he would have done no such thing, but he was in a foul mood this morning, primarily because of his hangover.

"Yeah, well," Moody replied. He twisted in his saddle to look back at the prisoner wagon following them. On the wagon were his three guards, young men whom Grat had met the day before, but whose names he could not now recall. He was pretty sure the tallest one was named George something-or-other. The guards were needed because Jeff Berryhill was only the first of several men they planned to take prisoner today; all would be shackled in the wagon and eventually delivered to the jail in Fort Smith. Grat would be with them only while they were in the Osage Nation, however; after they went back to the Creek Nation they were on their own.

The wagon trail they were following apparently got little use; the grass was high between the ruts, and rivulets from the spring rains had washed out parts of the track. Overhead a hawk hung almost motionless in the azure sky, riding the air currents with little effort as his eyes scanned the ground for the tell-tale movement of field mice. The trees were filling out, their new leaves still that lighter shade of spring green that would darken as summer arrived, and the trilling of songbirds floated on the breeze. It was a beautiful spring day in the Osage country, but Grat hardly noticed as he guided his horse over the gently rolling hills. He was preoccupied with the pounding in his head that echoed every step his horse took.

"So how come you were so late this morning?" Moody asked.

"Slept in," Grat said, ignoring the implied reprimand. "Played cards until three."

"Win anything?"

"Twenty-two dollars playing cribbage. That old boy just couldn't stop losing."

"Sounds like you were pretty lucky."

"Lucky, hell! I'm good." Both men chuckled at this. Grat's mood lightened as he remembered his previous night's success, and as his hangover eased, he began to enjoy the fine weather and pleasant company. With the rhythmic plodding of the horses and the cool gentle breeze on their faces, it was almost impossible not to feel a sense of contentment.

The land was heavily wooded this close to the river, but about two hours out of Tulsa they broke out into a clearing. At one time the open area had been plowed and planted, but now it was choked with weeds. Across the small sloping clearing, along the far tree line, were a ramshackle barn and a small cabin cut into the hillside. Built from split logs that were now weathered almost black, the cabin had a few wooden shingles missing from its roof, and the chimney at one end, made of flat chunks of sandstone stacked high in the air, was leaning precariously. The door was closed, but the shutters on the single front window were open, revealing that one of the panes of glass was missing.

"That's the Berryhill house," Moody said as they approached it. "He shouldn't give us any trouble. "

No sooner had Moody spoken than a rifle barrel appeared in the broken window, and with a bang a puff of smoke appeared at the end of it. Reacting instantly, Moody and Grat both wheeled their horses and raced back to the cover of the woods from which they had just emerged. Grat heard the crack of the rifle firing again, and at the same moment felt the hammer-blow of a bullet smashing into his left bicep. He hunched lower in the saddle as he urged his horse into the trees. Ahead of him he could see the three guards tumbling from the wagon, which had halted while still in the woods, and to his right he saw Moody pull up just inside the woods and drop from his horse in a kneeling position, his pistol in his hand.

Grat, who was left-handed, felt helpless. He drew his Winchester from its scabbard with his right hand as he galloped over to Moody and clumsily dismounted.

"Here," he called to the other deputy, "use my rifle." He scrambled over to Moody and nudged him with the stock of the gun. Grat was dumb-founded when Moody responded by slowly tottering over onto his side to lie motionless in the dead leaves.

"Bill?" Grat called to him. He dropped the rifle and pulled on Moody's shoulder until the man rolled onto his back. Only then did he see the red stain on Moody's shirt, and the small hole centered over his chest. Moody's eyes stared blankly at the branches overhead. Since there had been only two shots fired, and one had hit Grat, Moody must have been hit by the first round fired. Somehow he had not reacted to the mortal would until several seconds later. Grat cursed to himself.

Picking up his Winchester, Grat left Moody for the time being and stumbled through the brush and trees to where the three guards had gone to ground. The three young men, only two of whom had pistols, were all huddled in a shallow depression, warily watching the no silent cabin. They looked up expectantly as Grat took cover behind a thick tree trunk near them, leaning his back against the rough bark.

"Moody's dead," Grat told them bluntly. He tossed the Winchester to the taller guard, the one whose name might be George, since the young man had no other weapon. "Take this," he told George, "but don't shoot till I tell you." George caught the rifle by its barrel and quickly familiarized himself with its operation.

Grat probed his wounded arm, which was fortunately still numb, with his right hand, then scowled at the blood on his fingers and wiped them on his pants. Cautiously peering around the tree trunk at the cabin, he inhaled deeply and yelled. "Berryhill! Come on out of there with your hands up! We got you surrounded."

It then occurred to Grat that the cabin was not in fact surrounded, so he pointed at the two guards who had pistols and spoke quietly but firmly. "You two circle around through the woods on either side, make sure he don't escape out the back way." Despite the doubt and fear evident on their faces, the two guards jumped up and took off at a crouching run through the woods.

Grat angrily yelled at the cabin again. "You hear me? Put that gun down and come out of there!" There was no sound or sign of movement from the squat little building.

"You got some kerosene in the wagon?" he asked George, who had taken up a prone firing position on the edge of the depression.

"About half a can," George replied.

"Get it," Grat ordered curtly. George jumped up and scampered over to the wagon, quickly returning with the round metal can. Grat idly observed that blood was dripping from the fingertips of his limp left arm, but decided to worry about it later.

"Berryhill!" he hollered one more time. "This is Marshal Dalton. You better get your ass out of that cabin, or we're gonna burn you out." Grat had just motioned for George to take the kerosene around to the rear of the house when there was a shout from inside the building.

"Okay," a voice called from the window. "I'm coming' out. Don't shoot." The cabin's make-shift door creaked slowly open, and a figure hesitantly stepped into the doorway. The man was wearing blue jeans, long underwear, and a vest. He had no shoes, and his dark hair hung down past his shoulders. He had his hands raised, and one of them gripped an old rifle by the barrel. As he came out into the sunlight, the man lowered the rifle's butt to the ground and let the barrel fall back against the wall of the cabin.

Grat came around the tree and walked unsteadily toward the man, who was obviously an Indian. George rose from the depression and walked beside Grat, keeping the Winchester aimed at the stranger. Off to his left and right, Grat saw, the other two guards came out of the trees, their pistols also trained on the Indian. Keeping his hands high, the Indian strolled forward to meet Grat. Distracted by the throbbing pain he was now feeling in his arm, Grat was directly in front of the man before he recognized him.

"Bruner?" he barked incredulously. Billy Bruner was a Creek who had turned himself in to Grat only a few days before. Wanted in connection with a year-old murder case, Billy had sworn he was not involved, but he might know who was. Since the trial was not for several more weeks, Grat had told Bruner to go back home and wait until they came for him. Now, inexplicably, he was here at the Berryhill house, and he had killed Moody without provocation. With his hands raised and his eyes downcast, Bruner just nodded miserably.

"Check the house," Grat told George, while he glared furiously at Bruner from only a foot away. "God DAMN you!" Grat shouted in Billy's face, making him flinch. Grat slammed his right fist into Bruner's stomach, which had little effect on the well-muscled man, and then kicked him in the shin with all the force he could muster. Billy staggered a step, but kept his hands up. His weathered brown face was contorted with pain and contrition.

"Why'd you shoot at us, you stupid son of a bitch?" With his face flushed and his body trembling, Grat vented his pain and rage at the man, and flicks of his spittle showered Billy's face.

"I thought you were someone else," Bruner offered, tensing for another blow that did not come.

"Someone else? Are you crazy? You killed Bill Moody because you thought we were someone else?" Grat drew back his clenched fist to strike again, but grimaced as pain from his wounded arm shot through his shoulder. Reluctantly he lowered his right arm and reached across his chest to hold his left arm steady. At this

Bruner relaxed a little, dropping his arms a few inches, but he worriedly glanced at the two young guards who were nervously fingering their pistols.

"I'm real sorry Marshal Dalton," Bruner said sincerely. "It was a accident."

"Accident, hell! You shot two U. S. deputy marshals for no goddamn reason."

"I thought you were Southern Creeks coming to kill me."

"Why the hell would you think that?"

They been after me lately." The northern and southern Creeks had been warring for over a year, and tribal policemen, called "lighthorse," had been known to settle clan disputes with gunfire.

"And you think me and Moody look like Indians," Grat said sarcastically.

"No," Bruner admitted, "not now. But when you first come out of the woods, with the sun behind you, I couldn't tell. You might have been Southern Creeks. I didn't want to wait to find out."

"Well you damn well should've." Grat shook his head with disgust, then nodded at one of the guards. "Lock him up in the wagon." The two guards waved their guns at Billy, and he submissively trudged toward the wagon. Then two men emerged from the cabin, an older man with wild gray hair and plaid flannel shirt, followed by George, who had Grat's rifle pressed against the old man's back.

"Who's this?" Grat asked weakly, unhappy with any further surprises.

"Says he's Jeff Berryhill's father," George answered as the two men came to a stop in front of Grat.

"Well, lock him up, too. Must have had something to do with all this." While George prodded the old man in the direction of the wagon, Grat noticed that his field of vision was narrowing. It was like looking through a knothole that was steadily getting smaller, and he realized he was suffering from shock and loss of blood. Suddenly weak in the knees, he staggered over to a nearby tree stump and sat down heavily. Swaying slightly, he closed his eyes and tried to ignore the fiery streaks of agony that were now shooting up and down his left arm and into his chest. All of his strength and concentration were focused on not losing consciousness.

After what seemed to be only a few minutes, Grat forced his eyes open. When his vision cleared, he was amazed to see two of the guards loading Moody's body into the wagon next to the two prisoners. Kneeling beside Grat was George, who was binding the wounded arm with a clean bandanna. In Grat's right hand was an open canteen. Marveling at the amount of time that had obviously passed, he took a long drink of water.

Suddenly a thought occurred to him, and he put the canteen between his knees and screwed on the cap. Reaching inside his jacket, he pulled out a flat metal flask, smiling in anticipation. Momentarily unsure how to get the cap off, he first considered asking George to do the honors, and then cursed his own stupidity. He let the canteen drop from between his legs and then replaced it with the flask, squeezing his knees together to hold it steady as he twisted the cap off. Finally he was able to lift the flask to his mouth and pour the whiskey down his throat. He began feeling better almost at once.

"Think you can ride, Marshal?" George asked as he finished with Grat's arm and stood up.

"I sure hope so," Grat said, one corner of his mouth tilting up in a weak approximation of a grin. "I'd hate to have to walk back from here."

Author's Notes

Chapter 2

The court hearings concerning Charley Montgomery's death resulted in 44 hand-written pages of testimony that are preserved in the National Archives in Fort Worth. Montgomery's shooting was also described in detail in the August 16, 1888, issue of the *Coffeyville Journal*, and a brief account appeared in Emmett's book, *Beyond the Law*. Background information about Bartlesville and Jacob Bartles came from the book *Bartlesville* by Joe Williams. In 1898 Bartles became so disgruntled by the way the town had moved away from him on the south side of the Caney River that he jacked up his huge store, put it on log rollers, and used block and tackle to move it five miles north to a wheat field he owned. The relocation took almost a year, during which time the store remained open for business. Jake named the new town he had thus founded Dewey, in honor of the Spanish-American war hero.

The oaths of office that Bob and Grat signed on January 10, 1889, are preserved in the National Archives in Kansas City. The marital problems of their parents were mentioned in several newspaper accounts after the Coffeyville raid in 1892, and David Stewart Elliott's part in it was mentioned in the foreword to his book, *Last Raid of the Daltons*, published a few weeks after the event. There is reliable evidence that the divorce was never finalized, but the marriage was clearly in trouble, as the next chapter shows.

After Bob and Grat were killed at Coffeyville, a probate judge ruled on claims filed against their estates, and these claims included the loan and purchases on credit mentioned here, which had never been repaid. These estate documents are on file at the Kansas State Historical Society in Wichita.

The Vinita *Indian Chieftain* of March 21, 1889, carried an article about the shooting at the Berryhill house, and Emmett also mentioned it in his book, although he had some minor facts wrong.

CHAPTER 3

Tuesday, May 7, 1889

Bob Dalton should have been worn out when he rode back into the little settlement of Pawhuska that afternoon. The day before he had ridden thirty miles to bring in a whiskey peddler named John Darnall, and this morning the commissioner had given him another arrest warrant. In serving this one he had ridden another twenty-five miles to bring back a man named George Chadwell, also charged with introducing liquor into the Indian Territory. Despite all the hard riding, or perhaps because of it, Bob was in a good mood, pleased with a job well done. He would not turn twenty years of age for another six days, and already he was a respected deputy U. S. marshal, possibly the youngest in the service. That was something he could be proud of.

The morning's sunshine had been replaced by mottled gray clouds, and in early afternoon a spring rain storm had blown through, soaking everything in the area. The rain had eased to a light but steady drizzle by the time Bob brought Chadwell to the commissioner's office. Although it was only a two-story frame house with a wide front porch, the commissioner's office and residence was the most imposing building in town. Pawhuska was the center, both geographically and politically, of the Osage Nation, a roughly triangular area about sixty miles on a side. Bordered on the north by Kansas, and on the east by the Cherokee Nation, the Osage Nation's southern corner was at Tulsa and its northwest corner near Wichita. Pawhuska, a ragged collection of cabins and tents in the middle of a sparsely-populated area of wooded hills, was not only the largest town in the Osage reserve, it was just about the only one.

Bob and Chadwell tied their horses in the muddy street in front of the commissioner's office, scraped the mud from their boots on the edge of the wooden porch, and went inside. The lower floor was where the U. S. Commissioner for the Osage Nation, Mr. J. E. Dodson, did all of his official duties. Upstairs was his residence. The back part of the first floor was a spacious room where the commissioner held court, and it was there that Bob led his compliant prisoner. Behind a large desk near the back wall sat Dodson, studying some ledgers. At a smaller desk on a side wall sat his clerk, a mission-educated Osage wearing a suit and tie.

Bob left Chadwell standing in front of Dodson's desk while he sat down in the back of the room. Contrary to established policy, Bob had not handcuffed the man, feeling it was too demeaning for a man who was not charged with a violent crime. Chadwell stood meekly hunched over, abjectly clutching his hands in front of him.

The arraignment was brief; Dodson read the charges and listened to Chadwell's weak explanation, then held him over for a hearing the next day. Chadwell was released on his own recognizance, and Dodson told Bob to come back in the morning to get the subpoenas for the case.

From the commissioner's office Bob rode over to the camp he and Emmett had set up on the edge of town. Bob was gratified to see that Emmett had fixed their tent as Bob had instructed, tightening up the ropes so that it stood straight and square, with military precision. Next to the tent was their wagon, and it had a square of canvas pulled taut from one side of it down to the ground. Under the canvas, shackled to the wagon wheels, were two scruffy-looking men hunkered down on their heels to keep from sitting on the wet ground. Bob gave them only a passing glance as he climbed down from his horse and went into the tent.

"Hi, Bob," Emmett greeted him cheerfully. Sitting cross-legged on a blanket, Emmett had his Winchester in pieces around him as he carefully wiped each metal part with gun oil.

Bob shrugged out of his slicker and hung it on a nail sticking out of the tent pole. "Tent looks good," he commented, taking off his dripping hat and laying it on a supply box.

"Thanks." With his rounded face and short chubby body, Emmett looked more like Grat than Bob. It seemed to Bob that he and his brothers fell into two groups: short and chunky like Grat and Emmett, or tall and lanky like Bob and Frank. Although Grat and Emmett looked somewhat alike, they fortunately did not share a common disposition. Unlike dour and cynical Grat, Emmett was always friendly and happy, if perhaps a little naïve. Bob enjoyed having him around, and Emmett was appreciative that Bob had hired him as a guard.

"Who's that out with the wagon?" Bob asked, taking a seat on a small folding camp stool.

"Dan Modine and Nat Burt," Emmett said while be began reassembling his rifle. "Henry Roberts brought 'em in yesterday, and Dodson held 'em over for trial in Wichita. I gotta guard 'em until he can take 'em there."

"When's that?"

Emmett shrugged. "Don't know. Henry said it'll be at least a week.

"Huh," Bob grunted. He watched his younger brother tighten the last screw on the Winchester and then started feeding bullets into the magazine. He waited until Emmett had finished, and then remarked, as if he had just thought of it, "Hey, Emmett, do me a favor."

"Sure, Bobby. What?"

"Take care of my horse. Bring my saddle in out of the rain. I'd sure appreciate it."

"Okay," Emmett said willingly, reaching for his own slicker and hat. "I guess you're real tired after all that riding you been doing."

Bob just nodded. When Emmett had gone outside, he reached down and took Emmett's oily rag to wipe down his own pistol.

Thursday, May 9, 1889

After returning the buggy to the livery stable following their ride in the country, Bob Dalton and Eugenia Moore strolled arm in arm down the wooden sidewalks of Vinita, Cherokee Nation. Except for the blustery wind, it was a beautiful late spring day, with a cloudless sky and pleasantly warm temperatures. Vinita was full of activity; farmers, drummers, housewives, and laborers bustled about running their errands and conducting their business. School was out for the summer, so countless children were running around, calling to each other in shrill voices and generally getting underfoot. With money in his pocket and an attractive woman hanging on his arm, Bob was in an expansive mood. There were few writs waiting to be served, and Emmett was still guarding prisoners back at their camp in Pawhuska, so Bob allowed himself to enjoy a well-deserved day off.

When the couple came to Steve Bluejacket's restaurant, Bob paused to read the carefully hand-lettered sign in the window. Eugenia joined him, standing closer to him than the church women of the town would have thought proper. The sign advertised the availability of fresh ice cream, milk shakes, lemonade, and strawberries. Bob nodded toward the sign and raised an eyebrow inquiringly at Eugenia.

"Would you like to go in?" he asked.

She tilted her head to one side as she considered his offer, gazing directly into Bob's eyes. "It does sound refreshing," she said with a smile, "but I wouldn't want you to spend your money needlessly."

"Don't worry about that," Bob assured here, squeezing her arm affectionately. "Besides, I enjoy spending money on my girl."

Eugenia's smile widened as she modestly looked down, and she kept smiling as Bob escorted her into the restaurant and to a table near the back. He held the chair for her as she sat down, and then took a seat across from her, with his back against the wall.

"What can I do for you?" the proprietor said when he came over to their table. He was a tall man with a dark complexion and a prominent nose. Bob assumed he was Steve Bluejacket himself, and probably a full-blooded Cherokee. Except for a drummer reading a newspaper by the front window, Bob and Eugenia were the only customers. It was, after all, the middle of the afternoon.

"Eugenia?" Bob said, consciously watching his manners. "What would you like?"

"I think I'd like to have some ice cream with strawberries," she replied demurely, "if that's all right."

"Certainly, anything you want." Bob tore his adoring gaze away from her face and looked up at Steve Bluejacket. "Ice cream and strawberries for the lady, and a milk shake for me." He realized after he said it that it had sounded a little pretentious, so he smiled ingratiatingly at the man to make up for it.

"Yes, sir," Bluejacket said with practiced humility, and went into the back room.

With the silly half-smile of a young man in love, Bob sat with his forearms on the table and stared at the young woman across from him. "That was a wonderful picnic lunch you made," he said. In fact, he had eaten little of it, and could not now remember exactly what it had included, since his mind had been on other things than food at the time.

"I'm glad you enjoyed it," Eugenia said sweetly, reaching across the table to cover his right hand with her left. Bob thrilled to the touch of her soft fingertips on the back of his hand, and for a minute they just gazed into each other's eyes.

"Here you are," Bluejacket announced as he set their dishes in front of them. Eugenia pulled her hand away with a guilty start, but gave Bob a sly look. "That will be ninety-five cents, please."

Bob reached into his pants pocket and withdrew a silver dollar. Placing it in the man's outstretched palm, he generously said, "Keep the change." Bluejacket grinned knowingly as he walked away.

Bob took a big swig of his milkshake, then set the glass back down and admired how Eugenia carefully sliced a strawberry with her spoon and then scooped it up with a tiny portion of ice cream. Finally she daintily slipped the morsel into her mouth without seeming to open her lips, laid the spoon down in the bowl, and almost imperceptibly chewed and swallowed. Bob was entranced by the gentility of the action.

Eugenia raised her eyebrows at Bob and lightly brushed her upper lip with her little finger. Bob was momentarily confused, then touched his own upper lip and realized it was covered with milk. Embarrassed, he quickly rubbed the milk off with his fingers, then belatedly reached for the napkin to wipe his fingers on. Coyly suppressing a smile, Eugenia prepared another spoonful of her dessert.

"When do you have to leave?" she asked before she took another small bite.

"I'm riding out first thing in the morning. I have to go over near Tulsa and serve some subpoenas."

"Is that dangerous?"

"Naw. It's more trouble than it's worth, though."

"Are these subpoenas for Indians?" Bob had earlier told Eugenia that he had recently become a member of the Osage Indian Police, in addition to his role as a deputy marshal.

"An Osage named Little Coon and an interpreter. Little Coon's a witness in an introducing case." In March, to augment his force in preparation for the big land rush in the Unassigned Lands, Marshal Jones had hired twenty more deputies. This had meant less work for the deputies already on the force, and since he was paid by the job, Bob had sought to supplement his meager income by joining the Indian Police. This was allowed by the marshals service, and even encouraged, since it gave those deputies the authority to arrest both Indians and white men, resolving a frequent jurisdictional problem.

"That should be interesting," Eugenia remarked. Bob took another drink of his milkshake, and this time remembered to wipe his mouth with his napkin.

"Marshal Jones is in hot water now," Bob told her somewhat gleefully.

"Why is that?"

"People are saying that him and the special deputies in the Unassigned Lands staked claims before the rush started." Everyone was talking about the major issue of the day, the opening of the Unassigned Lands to white settlement on April 22, 1889. The offer of free land had lured thousands, and those who had missed out on the prime lots were now pointing accusing fingers.

"How could they do that?" Eugenia had a quizzical expression on her face, and Bob was happy to explain things to her.

"Well, they got to go into the area before the rush to keep out the sooners, and I reckon some of the saw the chance to stake out the best parcels for themselves, and took it."

"That hardly seems fair."

Bob shrugged. "Fair or not, they were there legally. Besides, as poorly paid as we are, us deputies ought to get some compensation. If I'd a been there, I'd probably done the same thing."

"Well, I'm glad you weren't there. I'm not sure I'd be interested in seeing a dirt farmer." Her eyes twinkled with amusement, and Bob proudly straightened his shoulders as he took a long swallow of milkshake.

"You know, I like being a deputy marshal," Bob said earnestly. "I just wish it paid better. Heck, if I just got the money already coming to me, it wouldn't be half bad, but the Marshal's always running way behind in paying fees. Course, it could be worse, I guess. Red Isbell, the deputy who lives here in Vinita, he told me he went over to Muskogee to see about working for the new marshal's office there. You know, it's only a civil court, so you wouldn't be bringing in dangerous prisoners or anything. Anyway, he said they're only paying six cents a mile, one way, to serve papers. One way! Shoot, you can't make living on that kind of money."

"I guess not," Eugenia agreed. She took another small bit of strawberry and rapidly-melting ice cream.

"Said he was going to stick with the Fort Smith court," Bob continued. "Can't blame him. Marshal Carroll's a better man to work for. Marshal Jones isn't bad, but somehow I just don't trust him."

"That's not a very nice thing to say about your boss," Eugenia chided him playfully.

"Maybe. But that's why I joined up with the Indian Police. They pay a regular salary, every month. Something you can depend on."

"That is important," she agreed.

"So what do you think about the picture?" Bob asked, abruptly changing the subject.

"Picture?"

"What we talked about before. Getting our picture made."

"Oh. Well, yes, I think I'd like to do that."

"Okay. Soon as you finish your ice cream, we'll go on over to the photographer's studio." Bob tiled his glass to his mouth and rained the last of his milkshake.

"You mean now?" Eugenia said with alarm. "Oh, I couldn't. Not wearing this old dress, and my hair must be a fright."

Bob set the empty glass down and wiped his mouth carefully with the napkin. "Your hair looks fine, Eugenia, and you are as beautiful as ever."

"Thank you, Bob, but I still would rather not be photographed in this old dress that I wore on our picnic. I mean, when we have our picture taken together, I want it to be something special."

"Then we'll just go and buy you a new dress," Bob suggested.

Eugenia stammered with embarrassment. "Bob, dear, I don't earn all that much as a school teacher, that I can be buying a new dress at the drop of a hat."

"Oh, no," Bob hastened to reassure her, "you don't have to buy it. I'll pay for it."

"I couldn't let you do that, Bob, with you not getting paid and all."

"Hey, I just got my first month's pay from the Indian police, so I've got plenty, and there's nothing I would like to do more than buy you a new dress. Come on, Eugenia, please?"

"Are you sure about this?" she asked doubtfully. Bob smiled as he recognized her acquiescence.

"I'm sure. We can go over to G. W. Green's. I saw in the paper where he's having a big sale. Heck, I might even get me a new suit to pose in."

"Oh, yes," she said enthusiastically, "maybe one of those new double-breasted coats that are so stylish. I'm sure it would make you look even more handsome than you do now."

"You think so?" Bob lifted his chin and turned his head slightly in a mock pose.

"Oh, stop it!" Eugenia said, laughing. Bob laughed as well, then took her hand in his and smiled into her eyes.

"You're wonderful," he said in a low, hushed tone.

"Thank you," she answered shyly. "We'd better go now."

G. W. Green was closing out his winter merchandise, so Bob and Eugenia found some real bargains, although the clothes were a bit heavy and warm for the summer season that had just begun. To hide her hair, Eugenia bought a hat with a large feathered plume. While she was trying on dresses, Bob went next door to the barber shop and had his boots polished. He had already found a coat that buttoned nearly to the top, letting the sides sweep away at the bottom. He suspected it was a little too fashionable for his conservative tastes, but since it seemed to please Eugenia, he bought it anyway. They had been unable to find a matching pair of pants to fit his lanky frame, so he had settled for some sturdy pin-stripes.

At the photographer's studio they were carefully posed in a very artificial garden setting, with Bob sitting on a chair covered with crumple brown paper to make it look like natural stone. Because Bob was so tall, the photographer placed a brick on the arm of the chair so that Bob's elbow would rest more naturally on it. Eugenia stood next to Bob, her hands on his shoulders in a possessive gesture. When the flash powder went off, Bob was staring seriously at a point in space off to the left of the camera, but Eugenia looked directly into the lens with grim determination.

Monday, May 20, 1889

Dodson's courtroom and office was crowded that morning. The commissioner had taken the weekend off, and the backlog of cases had swelled. Bob leaned against the back wall of the room near the door, struggling to keep awake as a series of whiskey peddlers, petty thieves, and assault cases were brought before the commissioner's desk for hearings. With half-closed eyes he watched the shafts of sunlight crawl across the dirty wooden floor and wished the occasional breath of spring breeze floating through the open windows would come a lot more often. To entertain himself he day-dreamed about Eugenia and the wonderful time they had spent together in Vinita a few days ago.

Finally the case Bob was waiting on was called. Dodson, a small, thin, bookish man in his thirties, looked briefly at the legal papers his clerk handed him.

"Albert Dobbs?" he called out, looking around the room.

"Here." Dobbs, a skinny young man in well-worn overalls, was standing just in front of Bob. Bob had arrested him on Friday, and he and Emmet had guarded him over the weekend. Dodson motioned for Dobbs to come forward, waiting impatiently as the gawky man shuffled through the crowded room to a spot in front of the desk.

"You're accused of stealing a horse from Mr. W. A. Wright," Dodson pronounced in a bored tone. "How do you plead?"

"I didn't do it," Dobbs said truculently.

"Mr. Wright, are you here?" Dodson asked, addressing the room.

"Yes, sir, your honor," a well-dressed man said, stepping forward.

"What can you tell us about this?"

"Well, sir, I have a contract to haul supplies to Mr. Barndollar's store here, and I hired Albert here to assist me. Thursday, after we had unloaded the wagons, he stole one of my horses, a roan mare. While I was inside settling my accounts, Albert unhitched the mare and rode off with it."

"Did not," Dobbs grumbled.

"Did you see him take it?" Dodson asked Wright.

"Well, no, but it must have been him. Weren't no one else around."

Dodson glanced down at the arrest warrant on his desk. "Deputy Marshal Dalton?" he said, looking up and zeroing in on where Bob stood.

"Yes, your honor," Bob answered, pushing away from the wall and trying to look official.

"Did Mr. Dobbs have a horse in his possession when you found him?"

"He did."

"What kind of horse was it?"

"A roan mare without a saddle."

"Mr. Dobbs," Dodson said quietly as he began to fill in blanks on the commitment form with quill pen, "I find that there is sufficient evidence to hold you over for trial at the circuit court in Wichita. I am setting your bail at seven hundred and fifty dollars. Do you have this amount, or anyone who can post bond for you?

"Seven hundred and fifty dollars?" Dobbs snorted. "Not hardly."

"Then I shall remand you to the custody of the jail in Wichita until the court is ready for you. Marshal Dalton will escort you to the jail as soon as it is convenient. Next case."

Bob took Dobbs by the arm and led him out of the building. Back at their camp, he shackled Dobbs to the wagon wheel and told Emmett the outcome of the hearing.

"I gotta take him to Wichita," Bob said. "You want to go with me?"

"Naw, not unless you need me." Emmett had been washing out some of their clothes and was draping the wet articles over the tent ropes to dry. "I think I'll go home for a couple days. See how Mom and Dad are getting along." Henry Roberts had left Saturday with the prisoners Emmett had been guarding for him, and once Bob left with Dobbs, Emmett would not be needed in Pawhuska for a while. "When you leaving?" Emmett asked.

"That's a long ride. Think I'll leave first thing tomorrow, get him there by Wednesday night. That way I'll be back here by Friday. You be back by then?"

"Probably," Emmet said. "think there'll be something for us to do then?"

"There's always plenty of whiskey peddlers," Bob answered with a nod. "I figure we'll keep busy."

What had been a busy spring became an even more active summer. Since the opening of the Unassigned Lands in April, the traffic through the Osage Nation had increased tremendously. As the most direct route to the new Oklahoma Territory from railheads in eastern Kansas, the Osage lands saw a surging flow of settlers, tradesmen, and drummers, all on their way to the new Promised Land. Although the law against alcoholic beverages continued in force in both territories, the demand among the thousands of white settlers in Oklahoma encouraged an increased level of smuggling. The deputies had quickly learned that all the wagons traveling through their area were suspect.

Bob and the other deputies worked constantly to stem the flow of illegal liquor, but it was like trying to hold back the tide. On June 10 Emmett swore out yet another complaint against bootleggers, this time listing two men named Clement Denoya and Frank Prudom. It was normal practice for a posse member or another deputy to swear out the complaint that became a warrant given to the arresting officer. This was done primarily to minimize the appearance that a deputy, who was paid for each arrest, was drumming up his own business. Steve Bellieu, one of Bob's guards, had filed the complaint against Chadwell in April, and deputy Henry Roberts had filed the one against Dobbs in May. Based on Emmett's complaint, Bob was immediately issued a warrant to arrest Prudom and Denoya.

By the end of the same day that Emmett had filed the complaint, Bob had already arrested the two men and served several subpoenas for witnesses in the case. On the following day a preliminary hearing was held, and Dodson found sufficient evidence to bind them over for trial at Wichita. Bail was set at five hundred dollars. Louis Del Orier and Frank Denoya stepped forward and posted bond for the two suspects, and all four walked out of the courtroom together.

Bob seethed with resentment as the bootleggers strolled away laughing and joking with their friends. He knew they would probably never show up for trial. The profits from selling whiskey in the territory were so great that it was easy to forfeit the five hundred dollar bail money. The men would just change their names and resume their illicit business in a different location, violating a law that few people really cared about.

Sunday, June 30, 1889

Outside the courthouse church bells were joyously summoning Wichita's residents to reaffirm their faith in the Lord. Inside, however, the mood was more somber. Today was W. C. Jones' last day in office, and dozens of deputies and possemen had gathered to wish him farewell, and, more importantly, collect the fees he owed them.

The political scandal about his special deputies grabbing property in the Land Rush in April had refused to die, and the newspapers had hounded him unmercifully. The official explanation for Jones' departure was that he had chosen to take a more lucrative position elsewhere, but his subordinates knew that he had been forced to resign by the political hacks in Washington, who were more concerned with the next election than with discovering the truth of the matter.

The deputies and possemen were all standing around in the hallway and the marshal's outer office, talking quietly among themselves as they awaited their turn with Jones. Bob and Emmett were among those out in the hall, and they fanned themselves with their hats to ease the oppressive heat of a Kansas summer.

"Think he'll have enough money to pay us all?" Emmett asked worriedly.

Henry Roberts, who also worked out of Pawhuska, nodded. "One of the office deputies told me that Jones is using his own money to pay us off. He hasn't gotten all the disbursements from Washington that he was supposed to, and he'll probably have to sue to get them."

Bob waggled his head back and forth. "That kind of makes me feel bad for taking his money," he said.

"Bad enough to let him keep it?" Roberts asked with a sly grin.

Bob pretended to ponder this question for moment. "Nope," he replied decisively. He had never particularly liked Jones, and while he admired the marshal's effort to take care of his troops, his admiration was not enough to overcome his desire to have what was rightfully his. He needed that money, not only for himself, but for his family. That though triggered a question for Emmett.

"When's Mom leaving Coffeyville?"

"Soon as I get there, I guess," Emmett answered. "You sure you won't need the wagon and mules for a while?"

"Henry here said I can use his if I need to."

"I'm sure we can share," Roberts confirmed, brushing back his wavy black hair. "You just go on and help your family move. Where is it they're going? Guthrie?"

“Kingfisher,” Emmett corrected. “Our sister Eva and her family got some land there in the Rush. Mom and the little kids are going down there to live with them.”

“What about your dad?” Roberts asked. Bob scowled at Emmett in warning, and Emmett’s face showed a brief flash of guilt for the secret he had almost spilled.

“Oh, he’s staying at the farm in Coffeyville,” Emmett temporized. “After the crops are in and he sells the land, he’ll move down with them.” Bob regretted the lie, but the family’s problems were none of Roberts’ business. Adeline Dalton was leaving her husband Lewis for good. He had refused to agree to a divorce, so she was taking the children and moving in with her daughter. There was a strong social stigma attached to divorce, and at their mother’s request, the boys were publicly denying any type of marital discord. Bob still held on to the faint hope that his parents would somehow settle their differences and resume living together. He had claimed that his official duties prevented him from helping his mother move out, but in reality it was his way of refusing to condone or even acknowledge the breakup.

Emmett, with no legitimate excuses, was going to aid the move, using the wagon and team that he and Bob usually utilized to haul prisoners. Once Emmett had delivered his mother and younger siblings to Kingfisher, he would stay a few weeks to help his brother-in-law, John Whipple, expand his cabin to make room for the additional family members. When that was completed and everyone settled in, Emmett would rejoin Bob in Pawhuska.

“Emmett Dalton,” a voice rang out over the murmuring of the men in the hall. Someone inside the office was calling for him.

“Guess it’s my turn,” Emmett remarked to his companions. Politely he wended his way through the crowd of burly lawmen and into the marshal’s office. In his hand he clutched the voucher he had filled out previously, the one stating that he had guarded two prisoners for nine days.

After Emmett had disappeared behind the closed door of the office, Bob turned to Roberts. “Have you heard anything about the new marshal?”

"Walker? Not really. Used to be a deputy, so at least he ain't a politician."

"Well, that's good. He'll know what we have to put up with, anyway, and maybe he can get us our money a little faster."

"Maybe," Roberts agreed doubtfully. "I just hope he's better about keeping the deputies in line. Jones let too many of them get away with stuff." Bob just nodded at that. He and Roberts were not close friends. Roberts was a stickler for the rules, and saw everything in black and white. Bob was more willing to accept the faults of others. Bob considered Roberts to be a stiff-necked, intolerant prig, but he realized that Roberts in turn probably believed Bob to be a soft-hearted fool with no real respect for the law. Still, they had to work together, so they let their differences go unchallenged, at least for now.

When Emmett returned he proudly showed Bob the eighteen dollars he had received, while Roberts was called into the office for his turn. Bob was the next to go in, but he received only a portion of what he believed was owed him. Grumbling to himself, he stalked out of the courthouse, Emmett at his heels. He gave most of his money to Emmett to take to their mother. She was going to need all they could provide to complete this move and set up a new household in Kingfisher.

Bob pushed himself hard in July and August, arresting criminals and serving subpoenas as fast as he could to earn more fees. Almost every day he would ride out of Pawhuska on official missions, patrolling the Osage Nation and looking for lawbreakers. With the duties of both a deputy U. S. marshal and an Indian policeman, Bob had plenty to do, and he prided himself in all that he accomplished.

As Bob had expected, the new marshal, R. L. Walker, took his time in paying the deputies at first. Fully aware of the bureaucratic red tape the marshal was required to deal with in order to get funds from the government, Bob was initially unconcerned about the lack of income. The general store in Pawhuska was owned by a consortium consisting of Jake Bartles, Coffeyville's Barndollar, and a man named Gibson, and because of their past relationship with the Daltons, the owners had gladly given them a credit account. Bob and Grat both frequently stopped in to pick up supplies, signing for the goods with a promise to pay when their wages finally arrived.

Whenever he had some spare time, which wasn't often, Bob would take his rifle down to the river and target shoot. With cartridges he had purchased on credit at the Pawhuska store, he would blaze away at sticks and empty bottles that he tossed into the water, shattering them as they slowly floated away. Local people with nothing better to do would often come watch him, commenting favorably on his skill with the weapon. In no time the word had spread that Marshal Bob Dalton was the finest hand with a Winchester in the Indian Territory.

Even though many of the stories of his prowess were wildly exaggerated, Bob never denied them, telling himself that these stories would make outlaws more cooperative in their dealings with him. It was an exciting and gratifying time for Bob, and he had ample reason to be pleased with himself. Not yet voting age, he was already a highly respected lawman, and he was widely known and liked throughout the northeast corner of Indian Territory. He had a good job, a beautiful girlfriend, and endless possibilities ahead of him. He realized that he had already experienced life more fully than most men did in their entire lives, and the knowledge was intoxicating. It seemed there was no place to go but up.

Friday, August 23, 1889

Bob picked up the cards Emmett had dealt him and added them to the ones in his hand. The summer sun was getting lower, and the shade was retreating across the floor of the tent. Emmett had opened both ends of the tent and rolled up the sides to let some air through as the two young men sat on either side of a small wooden barrel that served as a card table.

"Two pair, tens and eights," Emmett announced, showing Bob his hand.

“Beats me,” Bob signed, plopping his cards down on top of the deck. Emmett added his cards to the stack, then carefully scooped up the “pot,” a pile of wooden matchsticks. While Emmett began shuffling the deck again, Bob stood up and went outside to stretch.

“Here comes Grat,” Bob said, grateful for anything to break the boredom. “He’s got a prisoner for you.” Emmett put down the cards and joined Bob outside the tent.

A dirty, hungry-looking man with a ten-day beard stumbled towards them, his hands cuffed and shackles on his legs. Behind him, prodding him with the barrel of his Winchester, walked a grim-faced Grat Dalton. When the two men reach the tent, Grat tossed some keys to Emmett and said, “Lock him up to the wagon.”

Emmett took the man’s arm and led him gently to the wagon, while Grat ducked inside the tent. Bob followed his older brother in under the canvas and sat down on a stool to watch Grat dig through his bedroll.

“Couldn’t make bail, huh?” Bob said, referring to the man outside. Grat had arrested John Poore the day before on a larceny charge. An old, muzzle-loading shotgun had been stolen from Bill Andrews, and several people had seen Poore, obviously drunk, break into Andrews’ house and take the gun. Grat had just come from Poore’s preliminary hearing with the commissioner.

Grat found the canteen he had been looking for and unscrewed the lid. “Nah, I have to take him to Wichita tomorrow.” Grat took a long swallow from the canteen, then exhaled loudly with satisfaction.

“We got some cool well water Emmett just brought back,” Bob offered, thinking it would be better than what was in the warm canteen.

“Thanks, but this ‘water’ will be just fine,” Grat answered with a knowing grin. He took another swig, and Bob finally detected the distinctive odor of alcohol. He briefly entertained the idea of again lecturing Grat about the propriety of a marshal having illegal whiskey here in the nations, but gave it up as a lost cause. Bob knew it was hypocritical for a lawman who carried illegal whiskey to daily arrest the very men who smuggled it in, but he was becoming used to hypocrisy. The law had originally been passed to protect the Indians, who were notorious for their rapid and dramatic reaction to alcohol, but the growing number of white men in the territory meant that the law was honored only in the breach.

There was money to be made selling whiskey, either to Indians or white men, and that money talked at all levels. More than once Bob had been offered a bribe to let a whiskey peddler go, and at first he had been greatly offended. Now he just considered it part of the job. While he did not fully agree with the law, feeling it was unfair and patronizing to the Indians, as well as impossible to effectively enforce, he was sworn to uphold it, and so he would. It was a matter of honor.

"When you're in Wichita," Bob said, changing the subject, "how about checking on my fees?" Emmett came in, sticking the keys in his pants pocket, and sat down on his bedroll.

"Sure," Grat replied without enthusiasm. "Won't do any good, but I'll ask." Marshal Walker was being very elusive about paying his deputies what they were owed. Bob and Grat had received almost nothing so far, and only Bob's pay from the Indian Police had gotten them through August. It seemed that all they got from the marshal were excuses.

"Check on Emmett's, too," Bob added as an after-thought, patting his younger brother on the back. "He's been working hard since he got back from Mom's."

"Okay." Grat took another drink from his canteen, then wiped his mouth and stroked the thin mustache on his upper lip. "How long you think that's going to last?"

"What?" Bob asked with a puzzled frown.

"Mom being down there at Eva's. I think old John's going to get real tired of her and the kids, and send them all back to Coffeyville."

"I don't know," Emmett said, rubbing the back of his neck. "They seemed to be getting along okay when I was there."

"Yeah, but you know your sister Eva." Grat made a prissy face that caused Bob and Emmett to chuckle. "She has to have everything her way. I just can't see it."

"Maybe," Emmett admitted. "But while I was there, there was a rumor going around that they were going to open up the school quarters, too. If they do, Mom's going to get her own place." During the Land Rush, two quarter-sections out of every township had been set aside for schools, with no one allowed to settle on them. Most people felt that this was too much valuable land going to waste, and there was pressure on the territorial governor to change the law.

"You don't think she'll go back to Dad?" Bob asked hopefully.

"Not hardly, the way she was talking."

"Fudge!" Bob muttered. His parents' separation had been eating at him for months, and he kept nurturing the forlorn hope that they would somehow resolve their differences. He had tried so hard to make his parents proud of him, and now they were too caught up in their own problems to notice.

Grat tilted the canteen up to his mouth again, then screwed the cap back on. "Let's play some poker," he suggested, reaching for the cards. Bob and Emmett exchanged glances, then took their places around the barrel. There was not much else to do.

Monday, September 9, 1889

He had just stepped out of the judge's office at the federal courthouse when Bob saw Marshal Walker entering his own office down the hall. Bob quickly straightened his suit jacket and made sure his appearance was acceptable, then hurried after the marshal, wanting to catch him before he went into a meeting or something.

It had taken several days for Bob to get up the nerve to come to Wichita and confront Walker. Neither Bob nor Grat had received any pay from the new marshal, and Bob had talked himself into a furor over the issue, but until now he had avoided actually going to

Wichita to press his claim. He did not like to argue, and he was still somewhat in awe of his superiors, so it had been easier to just stay in Pawhuska and complain to his brothers rather than risk the possible negative outcome of demanding his pay in a face-to-face confrontation.

A couple days previously, however, as Bob had patrolled his area, he had stopped to talk to some of the full-bloods that were out hunting. One of them had asked Bob if he remembered hearing about a white man who was murdered the previous November. Although Bob had been working farther east in the Cherokee Nation at the time, Henry Roberts had mentioned the case to him sometime last spring. A man named Byron Devris had been killed near Pawhuska, and although it was strongly suspected that his assailant had been an Indian, no witnesses had ever come forward.

Now, ten months later, one of the hunters informed Bob that the killer was indeed an Osage, and gave Bob the man's name. With this knowledge Bob finally had a legitimate reason to travel to Wichita. A murder complaint had to be sworn out at the federal courthouse, since the Pawhuska commissioner had no jurisdiction over capital crimes. To get the warrant, Bob had to ride the sixty-five miles to Wichita. Now he no longer could put off his meeting with the marshal.

Bob had just signed the complaint before J. C. Wilson, the U. S. Circuit Court Commissioner at Wichita, when he saw the marshal. Hurrying into the marshal's outer office, he found Walker talking amiably with his office deputy.

"Sir," Bob interrupted, "could I speak with you?" Walker, a tall, rangy man with thick brown hair, turned and looked at Bob without recognition.

"And you are. . .?" The marshal's eyes glanced up and down Bob's slim figure.

"Robert Dalton, deputy in Pawhuska."

"Oh, yeah," Walker said in a tone that indicated to Bob that the man still did not remember him. "What can I do for you?"

“I wanted to ask you about my pay, sir.” Bob held his hat in front of him with both hands, his fingers nervously tapping the brim.

Walker cleared his throat. With a jerk of his head, he said, “Come on into my office.” Bob followed him in and came to a stop in front of the desk while the marshal settled into the large rotating wooden office chair behind it.

“Close the door,” the marshal ordered, and Bob hurriedly complied. When Bob turned back to face him, Walker said, “Now what’s the problem?”

“Well, sir,” Bob began, taking a deep breath, “my brothers and I haven’t been paid for quite a while, and we were just kind of wondering when we’d get our money.”

“Now, is this money that Marshal Jones owed you?” Walker leaned back in his chair, making it squeak, and tapped his desk with a pencil while maintaining an expression of deep interest in Bob’s question.

“No, sir, we’ve already got most of that. I’m talking about the fees we’ve earned since July.” Bob wisely refrained from mentioning that July was when Walker had taken office.

“Uh-huh,” Walker said with a barely perceptible nod. “And how much would that be?”

“I don’t know for sure, but between the three of us, it’s probably close to a hundred dollars. And I’ve talked to some other deputies, and they ain’t been paid either.”

“No one else has complained to me,” Walker said mildly.

“I’m not complaining,” Bob assured him. “I’m just asking when we’ll get our money.”

“Well, deputy, I honestly can’t tell you right now. You have to understand, I am waiting for the funds to arrive from Washington. If I don’t have the money, then I can’t give you any of it.”

“But it’s been over two months,” Bob pressed. “How are we supposed to pay our debts?”

“I’m truly sorry, but that’s just not my problem. Perhaps you shouldn’t have run up those debts, knowing how undependable a deputy’s pay can be. I’ve got over forty deputies, some of them with wives and kids, and I can’t be held responsible if one young man spends more than he makes. If you have turned your papers in on time and properly filled them out, then your pay should be arriving at any time. Other than that, I don’t know what else I can tell you. You’ll just have to wait like everyone else.”

“For how long?” Bob felt his temper starting to flare, and heard his own voice rising in pitch. “We didn’t have to wait this long with Marshal Jones.” This was not a completely true statement, but Bob’s anger was getting the best of him. Jones had been equally slow about making disbursements, but his final issuing of back pay in a lump sum last June had colored Bob’s perception of previous months.

Walker’s eyes narrowed at the mention of his predecessor, and he immediately sat up straight. “I don’t give a damn what Jones did. I’m marshal now, and I’ll run this office any way I see fit. I told you, as soon as I get the money, I’ll send it to you. If that isn’t satisfactory, then I don’t know what else I can do?”

“But why is it taking so long?” Bob persisted, starting to quiver with nervous rage. “Can’t we even get some of our money?”

“Look, Dalton, I remember you now. You’re too young and obviously too hot-headed to be a deputy marshal, but I kept you on anyway. I did you a favor, but I’m beginning to think it was a mistake. If you want to be a deputy marshal, then, fine, act like one. Otherwise get the hell out of my office!” The two men glared at each other, both with their jaws firmly set.

Finally Bob exhaled slowly and put on his hat. “Yes, sir,” he said sarcastically, bringing his hand up to his hat brim in a salute that was just short of mocking. Spinning on one heel, he forcefully opened the office door and marched out.

Author's Notes

Chapter 3

Over 60 pages of documents from 1889 that mention or were signed by the Daltons are preserved in the National Archives in Kansas City. These documents include sworn complaints, arrest warrants, court records, and subpoenas involving one or more of the Daltons in their capacities as deputy marshals, usually listing Bob Dalton as the arresting or serving officer. Only one document mentions Grat, and three have Emmett's name on them. The events in this chapter were derived from these records.

Since Emmett undoubtedly gave Eugenia Moore a fictitious name when describing her in his book, *Beyond the Law*, there is no way to independently verify any facts about her. The photograph taken of Bob and an unidentified young woman in Vinita in May, 1889, is assumed to be a likeness of Eugenia. Bob's and Eugenia's actions and conversation were based on articles and advertisements in the Vinita newspaper for the months of April and May.

According to land records and her obituary, Eva Dalton Whipple and her family took part in the April 22, 1889, land rush, acquiring property near Kingfisher. Exactly when Adeline Dalton and the younger Dalton children moved to Kingfisher is not certain. In her obituary, Adeline was reported to have moved in July, 1890, after her husband had died, but this story has several logical flaws, and may have been concocted by the family to disguise the fact that she had left her husband, a socially unacceptable act at the time. The *History of Montgomery County, Kansas*, published in in 1904, states that Adeline left Coffeyville in 1889, a year before Lewis Dalton died in nearby Dearing. Since this book was written nearer in time to the actual events than were the later obituaries, and since the authors of this book had no motive for distorting the truth in this matter, I have accepted this version. Because the land Adeline eventually settled on could not have been legally occupied until 1890, since it was a school quarter, I surmised that she went to live with her daughter Eva for a year.

As stated earlier, probate records of claims against Bob's and Grat's estates after their deaths include purchases they had made on credit while serving as deputies. These records include a detailed list of supplies purchased in Pawhuska in July and August of 1889. Bob's expertise with a rifle was widely reported after he became a criminal, and later events would confirm that skill.

The complaint Bob swore out in Wichita on September 9, 1889, is on file in the National Archives. I have assumed that this was the date on which he confronted Marshal Walker about his back pay. Records in the National Archives in Washington show that R. L. Walker was constantly in arrears in his payments to his deputies, and that several deputies later sued him for the back pay that he owed them. Walker contended that the federal government had failed to send him the necessary funds, and that he had been forced to hire a lawyer to investigate the shortage. At any rate, there are no warrants, subpoenas, or other legal documents after this date that list Bob as a deputy marshal, and Walker later wrote that he had let Bob go in the fall of 1889, without being more specific. Subsequent documents show that the people of the Osage Nation remained unaware that Bob had been fired, and Emmett apparently believed that Bob continued as a deputy until the summer of 1890.

CHAPTER 4

When Bob returned from Wichita he did not tell Emmett and Grat the full story of his meeting with Marshal Walker. Instead he spun them a tale of having accosted Walker in the hall, demanding their back pay forthwith. He described Walker's response as a meek admission of fault and a promise to send the money to them as soon as possible. Bob said nothing about how the meeting had ended, in part because he himself was not sure what the outcome had been.

Initially Bob believed that the discussion had ended with his quitting the marshals service, but on the long ride back to Pawhuska he had replayed the conversation in his mind, and began to wonder if he had been fired. Then, the more he thought about it, and the more he realized what his family's reaction would be, the more he tried to convince himself that it had been merely a minor disagreement, and that he was still a deputy. He still had his badge and commission, after all, although that might simply be an oversight on the marshal's part. For now, at least, he could still justifiably claim to be a deputy marshal, and so he would. He would retain his badge and commission until he was paid the money owed him—or until the people in Pawhuska discovered the truth.

Upon arrival at the Pawhuska camp, Bob had asked Emmett, with feigned indifference, if there had been any messages from Wichita. Emmett's reply in the negative, along with the normal treatment he received from the local citizens, calmed Bob's immediate fears, but left him in a state of nervous anticipation, contemplating what he felt was the inevitable humiliation of a public dismissal. Anxious to avoid this impending embarrassment, Bob informed Emmett the day after his return that they were going "on the scout," and together they rode out of Pawhuska to patrol the farther reaches of the Osage Nation. As far as Emmett knew, Bob was just doing his duty as a deputy marshal, and Bob saw no reason to disillusion his little brother.

For the next few months the two brothers were always on the trail, rarely returning to Pawhuska. Bob would stop any suspicious-looking wagon and demand that it be searched, and frequently he would find hidden supplies of illegal liquor. Rather than take the culprits in to Pawhuska for trial, which would result in lengthy paperwork, Bob now chose to fine them on the spot. After collecting the fine, he would usually then have Emmett pour out the whiskey on the ground, and send the bootleggers on their way empty-handed. He felt reasonably confident that these criminals would not complain to the authorities about his treatment of them.

It took a while to do it, but Bob finally convinced Emmett that what they were doing was within the spirit of the law, if not the letter of it. He pointed out that the normal procedure of arresting the whiskey runners, taking them to court, and then having them pay a fine or jump bail, was tedious and ineffective. The fines and forfeited bail money collected from these men eventually went to pay the deputies' wages, so Bob had simply found a shortcut in the system. With this new procedure, the whiskey peddlers were punished, the whiskey destroyed, and Bob and Emmett got paid immediately.

Although Emmett still expressed some doubt, he finally agreed that this method had its merits, influenced, no doubt, by his unwavering faith in his brother's judgement.

Wednesday, December 25, 1889

A gusty north wind chased scattered brown leaves down the road ahead of them as they leisurely rode south in an empty corner of the Osage Nation. It was Christmas Day, and Bob and Emmett were alone, far from their family and friends. The sky was cloudless, and the mid-day sun, although low in the southern sky, gently warmed their chests as the wind cooled their backs.

The day before they had gone to see their father, who was now living in Dearing, Kansas, but he had drunkenly refused to talk about apologizing to his wife for whatever he had done. When Bob had pressed him, he had turned on them as well, swearing and calling them worthless mama's boys. Finally they got fed up and left.

Earlier that month, after endless hounding from Bob, Grat had agreed to go with Bob to Fort Smith and ask to be put on the payroll there as deputies. Marshal Carroll had been replaced in May by a man named Jacob Yoes, and Bob hoped the new marshal would hire him despite his age and problems with Marshal Walker in Wichita. While Grat was hired immediately on the strength of his previous record with Judge Parker's court, Bob was turned away again. Like his predecessor, Marshal Yoes felt that Bob, who could not yet even vote, was far too young to be a responsible deputy.

Bob was crushed by this disappointment, and he began to feel a growing resentment toward the marshals and other appointed officials. He had never received the back pay owed him by Marshal Walker, and it was only the "fines" that he and Emmett were collecting that kept them going. He owed money in Coffeyville and Pawhuska both, but he made no attempt to make good on these debts. To his way of thinking, these debts had been incurred as necessary expenses for his work as a deputy, and therefore they would have to wait until Bob was paid for that work by the marshal.

A few days ago Emmett had suggested going to Kingfisher to spend Christmas with their mother, but Bob had insisted their duty was here in the Osage country. The true reason, Bob admitted only to himself, was that he could not face his mother right now. He was embarrassed about losing his position as a marshal, and a little ashamed of how he had hidden that fact from his brothers, not to mention feeling a little guilty about extorting money from whiskey peddlers. Bob was pretty sure Emmett had guessed the truth about his dismissal from the service, but both young men had carefully avoided the topic in order to maintain the fiction. His mother, however, would undoubtedly squeeze the truth out of him, for she always could detect when he was telling a lie. He was just not ready for that.

Adeline Dalton was a devout Presbyterian and a strict disciplinarian, and as a child Bob had always been impressed by the way she would know when he had misbehaved even before one of his siblings had inevitably told on him. By now Grat had probably discovered the true state of affairs, and he might have already dropped hints to her about Bob's firing. There had been rumors floating around the territory, too, about the bribes being paid to certain lawmen by bootleggers, and if Mother Dalton had heard them, she would certainly disapprove. Either way, Bob felt he could not face a family argument, so he had chosen to remain in the Osage Hills for the holidays. Besides, the traffic in illegal whiskey—and the opportunity to profit from it—was sure to increase during this time of celebration and relaxed law enforcement. Emmett, ever loyal, had elected to stay with Bob.

The only bright spot in Bob's bleak personal life had been Eugenia. On his infrequent visits to Vinita he had confessed to her, bit by bit, how he was circumventing the law, and had been pleasantly surprised by her lack of condemnation. On the contrary, she had praised his enterprise and resourcefulness, while commiserating with his rejection and bad luck. Her support had been essential in maintaining his belief in himself, and it encouraged him to keep trying. Now all he needed was an opportunity.

These thoughts and memories preoccupied Bob as they rode along, but he was brought from his reverie by Emmett's sudden remark.

"Who you reckon that is?" Emmett asked, nodding toward a wagon stopped in the road ahead. There was a boy sitting in front holding the reins, with his back to the Daltons. He had not yet noticed their presence.

"Let's find out," Bob answered, chucking his reins to bring his horse to a trot. When they got closer, Bob saw an older man coming out of a clump of bushes, buttoning up his trousers.

"Merry Christmas, Harry," Bob said cordially, bringing his horse to a halt between the man and his wagon. Harry Callahan was a skinny man in his thirties with long greasy black hair and the blunt hands of a laborer. He was wearing an old patched overcoat as the top layer of a mismatched set of ill-fitting clothes. Bob and Emmett had met him several times in the area, and had "fined" him once.

"Same to you, Marshal," Harry replied without enthusiasm.

"What are you doing out here?" Bob asked pleasantly.

"Taking a crap. What's it look like?" Callahan's tone was testy, but not really angry. He scowled as Bob blocked him from climbing back on his wagon.

"Howdy, Bob, Emmett," the young man on the buckboard said, his friendly smile revealing a couple of missing teeth. Jasper Riddle was about Emmett's age, maybe younger, and was Callahan's assistant. He wore jeans and two plaid shirts, and his sandy hair was ruffled by the wind. Bob and Emmett both returned his greeting warmly.

"Got another load of whiskey?" Bob asked Harry mildly, raising his eyebrows. Callahan's shoulders slumped and he shook his head slowly from side to side, a pained look on his face.

"Bob," he pleased, "don't do this to me. Ever cent I got is tied up in this load. I cain't pay no fine, and if I don't sell this stuff, I'll be flat broke. How about lettin' me slide this time?"

"Where you taking it?"

"Over to Bird Creek. A bunch of Osages is camped there at Chi-sho-wah-hah's for Christmas."

"Now that's what we need to celebrate the birth of the Lord," Bob scolded him, "a bunch of drunk Indians."

"Hey," Callahan objected with righteous indignation, "it's Christmas. Even Indians ought to be able to get drunk on Christmas."

Bob paused to consider this idea. He had made many friends among the Indians, who called him the Little Marshal, and sometimes he thought the government's treatment of them was patronizing, if not downright degrading. Letting them enjoy this great holiday was perhaps not so terrible a sin.

"Let's let 'em go, Bobby," Emmett urged, echoing Bob's own feelings.

"Tell you what," Bob said to Callahan, "I won't fine you this time. But we're coming along, to make sure there isn't any trouble."

"Well, sure, Bob," Callahan agreed with a smile of relief. "That'd be just great." Bob backed his horse up to let Callahan scramble up the wagon wheel and plop into the seat of the wagon. "Come on, Jasper, let's go."

Chi-sho-wah-hah was an Osage chieftain who had built a small log cabin in a field near Bird Creek, a couple hundred yards from the road to Pawhuska. To celebrate the holiday, the chief had invited several Osage families to join him, and they had set up their teepees around his cabin. While Jasper Riddle turned the wagon team off the main road and down the path toward the encampment, Bob signaled for Emmett to wait with him a moment.

"Why don't you stay here at the road," Bob suggested.

"How come?" Emmett asked, creasing his forehead in puzzled disappointment. Emmett always enjoyed the Indian social gatherings.

"We have to guard this camp," Bob intoned seriously. "You'll be our outer line of defense. If you see anybody coming, you call out. I'll be busy maintaining order at the camp, so I'll be depending on you."

"Okay," Emmett grudgingly agreed. "How long we gonna be here?"

"Till sunset, I imagine." Bob lifted his reins in preparation for following the wagon, but then another thought came to him. "And if anyone tries to leave this camp before we do. . ." Bob paused as he pondered what was feasible. "Well, you just try to talk them into staying. You know how Indians get when they're drunk. We don't want anyone taking off and getting into trouble. Okay?"

Harry Callahan jumped down from the wagon and reached up to take the first couple jugs of whiskey from Jasper Riddle. While

Harry negotiated the first sale, Bob rode slowly around the camp, greeting the Indians that he recognized with his limited command of the Osage language, and pointing to the wagon while he said the universally understood word, "whiskey." He pretended not to notice that some of the women were glaring at him angrily while they called for their children and hustled them inside the teepees. Behind the cabin was a small corral in which were two of the finest mules Bob had ever seen. Bob figured that being a chief had its advantages, if Chi-sho-wah-hah could afford good animals like those.

After his first tour through the camp, Bob rode back over to the wagon, which was now surrounded by men shouting and waving cups and money.

"Jasper," Bob called out over the din, "hand me one of them jugs." Riddle looked down at Callahan, who gave him a nod of permission, then passed a jug over to Bob. Bob pulled the cork with his teeth, spat it on the ground, and then rested the jug in the crook of his arm and tilted it up to his mouth. Bob rarely drank, and this rotgut was like liquid fire coursing down his throat. He coughed violently, and finally took several deep breaths as he wiped the tears from his eyes. "Good stuff," he croaked to Jasper, who was trying hard not to laugh.

Bob managed a couple more small swigs of the liquor, then motioned to one of the Indians.

"Hey, Big Road," Bob said. The Osage smiled at the sound of his English name and waved cheerfully at Bob.

"Little Marshal!" he roared jovially, followed by something incomprehensible in his native tongue. Bob held out the jug with one hand while he made an offering gesture with the other. Big Road, who was holding a tin cup, smiled even more broadly and pushed through the crowd to Bob's side, holding the cup high in the air. Leaning over in his saddle, Bob poured some whiskey into the cup. Even more whiskey splashed on the Indian's hand and the ground, for the noise was making Bob's horse dance nervously.

Big Road immediately took a big drink from the cup, and suddenly he was doubled over in a coughing fit, hanging on to Bob's stirrup for support. When his spasms subsided, he took a deep breath and straightened up, giving Bob a huge grin of gratitude. Bob smiled back, glad that he was not the only one who had trouble drinking the stuff. "Merry Christmas," he said warmly.

"Merry Christmas!" Big Road bellowed back at him. "Merry Christmas! Merry Christmas!" He took another drink, this time without coughing, and wandered away, yelling "Merry Christmas!" at everyone he met.

Bob was now surrounding by men clamoring for his attention and holding up a variety of cups and glasses. They had quickly realized that Bob was giving away whiskey for free, while Callahan was selling it for a dollar a cup. Bob filled as many cups as he could, still spilling more than got into the containers, until the jug was empty. He held the jug upside down to show that Indians that he had no more, and the crowd dejectedly flowed back over to where Callahan was standing.

The whiskey he had drunk was now having an effect on Bob. His body was suffused with a gentle warmth, and he felt a flowing good will toward everyone in the area. He rode around the camp again, smiling benignly at his many Indian friends and enjoying the holiday spirit that prevailed. Once he passed close to the front of the cabin, and Chi-sho-wah-hah was standing on the front porch with a worried expression.

He gestured to Bob and said something, but his English was broken and hard to hear over the uproar around the wagon. Bob smiled, assuming the chief was giving him a Christmas greeting, and then gave a merry "Whoop!" and rode on through the camp.

Bob saw another face he recognized, and rode over to the tall Indian carrying a jug.

"Hlu-ah-shu-tse," Bob said loudly, "how in the hell are you?"

"I am fine, Marshal Bob," Hlu-ah-shu-tse answered in halting English. "I have happy Christmas. How are you?"

"I'm having a happy Christmas, too, thank you." Bob reached down to shake the man's hand, then straightened up and continued his rounds with a parting wave.

After a while Bob noticed that the crowd around the wagon had ebbed away, and his own slight inebriation had mostly worn off. Like a splash of ice water in his face, he realized what a precarious position he had placed himself in. His collecting of "fines" from the peddlers had been relatively safe, as those criminals were unlikely to report him to the authorities. This party, on the other hand, was a much different situation, since there were many witnesses who knew him well and who themselves had committed no crime. He could only hope that their friendship would keep them silent.

With worry nagging at him like a woodpecker at a tree trunk, Bob rode back over to the wagon where Callahan was unloading his last two jugs of whiskey. The sun was hanging low in the southwest, throwing long shadows across the trampled brown grass.

"I think it's time to go," Bob told the two bootleggers. Harry pulled a wad of crumped dollar bills mixed with coins from his coat pocket and began sorting and counting it.

"What's my fine today?" Callahan asked as he smoothed the bills on the tailgate.

"Nothin'," Bob said, shaking his head emphatically. "Just pack up and get out of here."

Callahan looked up at Bob with consternation, then shrugged. "Sure thing, Bob. Be on our way in just a minute." He scooped up the money and stuffed it back into his coat, then raised the tailgate to latch it in place.

Bob trotted his horse out to the road, where Emmett still stood watch, his horse peacefully munching at some grass.

"Let's go," Bob said curtly, starting down the road at a canter without looking back. He heard Emmett obediently goad his own horse into movement behind him.

Sunday, March 2, 1890

Grat had felt worse before, but at the moment he could not recall when it might have been. His stomach was churning and gurgling alarmingly, and his head was spinning and screeching like a train wheel with a bad bearing. He pushed himself away from the table and concentrated on the effort required to stand up. As he lurched to his feet, the wooden chair tipped over backwards and smacked the floor with a loud crack. The man Grat had been playing cards with, his head cradled on his arms as he sprawled half across the table, gave no reaction to the noise. He was passed out, unaware even that his shirt sleeve was soaking up the puddle of spilled whiskey next to his overturned glass.

They had played cards all night long, and drank all night long, and smoked and chewed tobacco all night long. When the evening had begun there had been more men present, but as the night progressed the others had drifted off to home and to bed, leaving only Grat and the other man, whose name Grat had already forgotten. Grat worked his tongue around in his mouth, which felt like slimy cotton, and grimaced in disgust. Stretching to work out the kinks in his back from sitting so long, he wondered idly what time it was. They had been playing cards in the windowless back room of a small store, and it was like being trapped in a mine shaft. A smoky, stuffy, cluttered mine shaft that stank of human sweat and stale liquor.

A pile of money lay by the sleeping man's head, and Grat contemplated it for a long minute. Before he had collapsed into unconsciousness, the other man had won virtually every cent Grat had, and Grat thought about taking some of it back, knowing the man would probably not have a clear enough memory of the evening to notice the shortage when he woke up. But the man had won it fair and square, so Grat just heaved a sigh of resignation and turned to the door. It was time to go make camp somewhere and sleep off this drunken hangover. The act of turning his body had made his head spin even faster, and Grat reached back and clutched the edge of the table for support. He would need something to steady him, he decided. Twisting around slowly this time, he searched through the clutter of bottles on the table until he found one that still contained a few swallows of brown liquid at the bottom. With exaggerated deliberation he lifted the bottle up to his lips and tilted his head back until the whiskey poured down his open throat. He closed his eyes and waited for the liquor to have its intended effect, letting the empty bottle drop and clatter on the table. Now he could face the world.

When he stumbled into the front part of the store, Grat noticed that it was daytime. Although the blinds were down on the windows and door, the light was seeping through and around them, stabbing at Grat's eyes with a painful brilliance. He squeezed his eyelids to a narrow slit and moved toward the door, weaving from side to side and staggering as his limited view of the room tilted and rotated. He felt like he just had to get outside, where maybe the fresh air would help, and he tried to walk faster, closing his eyes completely to block out the image of the spinning room. That was when his shin made contact with a protruding shelf, and the blinding pain made Grat roar and stumble backwards. He collided with a barrel full of rakes and hoes, and both he and tools toppled over with a crash.

Cursing at the top of his lungs, Grat kicked the barrel and implements away and struggled to his feet again, pausing to rub his bruised leg. This was too much. He had lost all his money, he felt like death warmed over anyway, and now this damned store had attacked him. Furious, Grat stomped to the door and jerked at the door knob, but the door was locked and only rattled as Grat pushed and pulled the knob spastically. His anger now totally out of control, Grat screamed and kicked the door, then finally found the lock and twisted it forcefully until it unlatched. Throwing the door open until it slammed against the wall, Grat pushed through the opening and lurched onto the wooden sidewalk.

It was early morning in Tulsa, and the glare of the bright sun struck Grat's face like a whip. He covered his eyes with his hands as he filled his lungs with the cool fresh air. Gradually he lowered his hands and opened one eye just a crack. The daylight was piercing through his eyeball, but he forced himself to look around so that he could get his bearings. Tulsa was a small town, but already people were out and about, strolling the sidewalks and riding their wagons and buggies through the streets. Most of the people seemed to be dressed up, and belatedly Grat remembered that it was Sunday.

Still keeping one eye closed, Grat swiveled his head around, looking for the horse he had left tied up somewhere around here the night before. The head movement was ill advised, however, as his brain screamed in protest and the wooden sidewalk began to tilt and slip away from him. Grat shut his eye and tried to regain his equilibrium, staggering around with an outstretched arm in hope of finding something to hold on to. His hand encountered something soft and cloth-covered, and he clutched at it in desperation.

"What are you doing?" It was a man's voice, and it carried a tone of annoyance. Grat cracked open one eye again, to see that he was grasping the shoulder of a stout man in an expensive suit, and the man's face was twisted with anger and distaste.

"Let go of me, you drunken lout!" the man ordered, glaring at Grat as he tried to pry Grat's hand from his shoulder.

"Lout?" Grat said hoarsely "Who are you callin' a lout?" He gripped the man's shoulder more tightly and scowled at him in what he hoped was a menacing way. He recognized the man from somewhere. He had seen him around Tulsa, showing off how rich he was and looking down on people. His name was Delonsdale—a stupid name, as far as Grat was concerned. Things had been bad enough this morning; he did not need to be taking any crap from this high-falutin idiot.

Delonsdale stopped struggling and stared directly into Grat's one open eye, putting on a mask of reasonableness. "Please," he said firmly but politely, "let go of my shoulder." Even in his drunken state, Grat knew he was being talked down to, that Delonsdale was condescending to treat him politely only because of the circumstances, and that in reality he considered Grat the scum of the earth. Grat's fury exploded, and with his free hand he drew his pistol and shoved it into the fat man's face, pushing his nose aside with the barrel. Delonsdale's expression melted into abject fear, and he began whimpering and shaking like a whipped puppy. For some reason this just infuriated Grat more, and with mindless, uncontrolled anger he began beating Delonsdale over the head with his pistol.

Delonsdale crumpled to the sidewalk, trying to shield his head with his arms, as Grat clumsily swung the pistol up and down, releasing all his frustration on the despised man who knelt at his feet.

There was no thinking, no reason in his actions; Grat simply felt a need to hurt someone.

Suddenly someone was grabbing Grat's arms, and although he struggled, his gun was pried from his fingers and his arms were twisted behind his back. Two men had come up behind him, and they quickly subdued him and pulled him away, while others gathered around Delonsdale and offered him their assistance. As quickly as it had arrived, Grat's anger dissipated, and he willingly allowed himself to be led to his horse and pushed up into the saddle.

"You can have your gun back when you sober up," one of the men said, handing Grat the reins. He slapped the horse's rump, and Grat grabbed at the pommel to keep from falling out of the saddle as his horse bolted down the street. When he regained his balance, he slowed the horse down to a walk, but kept it moving out of town. A sense of shame was settling over him, and he needed to get away from the accusing stares that he was sure were now being aimed at him by the people of Tulsa. Embarrassed by his own behavior, Grat sought the emptiness and privacy of the country. He had to find a place to sleep, as well, for he was overcome with lethargy. Maybe after he had slept off this hangover he could think of a way to redeem himself.

Wednesday, March 26, 1889

The commissioner's courtroom in Pawhuska was much the same as it had been the last time Bob was there, but now he was looking at it from a totally different perspective. Stripped of their gunbelts, Bob and Emmett had been ushered into the room by their old friend, Deputy Lafe Shadley, and seated at the defendant's table near the front. So far they were the only people in the room, which suited Bob just fine. Although he pretended to be unconcerned, inside he was emotionally distraught by the reversal in his status from respected lawman to criminal defendant. He was also just a little frightened by the potential outcome of the upcoming hearing. Beside him Emmett slumped in his chair, his head hanging low in a pose of abject disgrace. Bob gave him a reassuring pat on the shoulder and a grin of confidence that he did not truly feel.

Someone, probably Chi-sho-wah-hah, had told Henry Roberts about the Christmas Day incident, and the sanctimonious Roberts had lost no time in swearing out a complaint against Bob and Emmett. The warrant had been issued to Lafe Shadley on January 7, but he had made little effort to serve it on the Daltons, in deference to their long association. Perhaps, Bob thought, Shadley had also occasionally stepped over the line between right and wrong, like most of the deputies, and for that reason sympathized with their plight. Whatever his motive, Shadley had quietly spread the word that Bob and Emmett should stay out of sight, and this they had done for three months.

Even though friends and relatives had provided food and shelter for the two young fugitives, Bob hated imposing on them and possibly implicating them, so he and Emmett had spent most of their time on the scout. Counting on the lack of communication between the Wichita and Fort Smith marshals, they had also worked as possemen for Grat and Deputy Floyd Wilson, who were at that time based in Tulsa.

Tired of the hiding and uncertainty of his future, Bob finally allowed Grat and Floyd to talk him into surrendering himself. Thus, last Friday, Bob and Emmett had ridden into Pawhuska and turned themselves over to a surprised Lafe Shadley. Arraigned on Saturday by the new commissioner, Bob and Emmett were ordered to return for their hearing on Wednesday, in order to give Shadley time to round up the witnesses and an interpreter. Humbled by the experience, but hopeful that his past service would be taken into consideration, Bob had camped just outside Pawhuska to await his fate. As always, Emmett followed his brother's lead.

Strong March winds rattled the windows of the courtroom, through which Bob could see the low, fast-moving clouds that dimmed the sky. It was tornado season, but Bob judged that the conditions were not right today for such a storm. In a way that was unfortunate, for a tornado would keep him from having to endure this hearing.

The door at the back of the courtroom opened, and Bob looked around quickly to see who had come in. It was the court clerk, the same Indian who had held the job for years. Bob waved to him with a weak smile. The man's stoic expression did not change, but he nodded to Bob as he walked by. After laying some papers on the commissioner's desk, he took a seat at his own little table and waited with patient boredom.

A moment later the commissioner himself walked in and briskly strode to his desk. After he had seated himself and adjusted his suit coat and tie, he picked up the papers his clerk had left, straightened them, and then laid them back down in front of him. W. S. Fitzpatrick was a short, wiry Irishman with bristling dark red hair and a sprinkle of freckles across his up-turned nose. As Fitzpatrick made miniscule adjustments to the inkwell and blotter on his desk, Bob had a sinking feeling that this hearing was not going to go in his favor. At his arraignment on Saturday, Bob's initial impression of the new commissioner had not been encouraging. The man seemed to be a perfectionist, a self-righteous prude who suspected the worst of everyone, but in the days since that first meeting Bob had convinced himself that the man was simply new and trying to establish an aura of authority. Watching him now, though, made Bob believe that his first impression had been entirely accurate. Bob began to feel a tightness in his chest.

"Mr. Shadley," Fitzpatrick said suddenly, still looking at the papers on his desk, "bring in the witnesses."

"Yes, sir," Shadley answered. He strode out of the court room, and minute later came back in leading six Osage Indians and a white man, pointing out the chairs they were to sit in.

Bob recognized most of the Indians, and held up the palm of his hand to them in greeting. "Chi-sho-wah-hah, how are you?" he said warmly. "Shah-pe-hah-she, Big Road, Hlu-ah-shu-tse, Pah-hah-ne-gah-hle." As he called out their names, each raised their hand in response. Some smiled at Bob, but others, including Chi-sho-wah-hah, maintained a stone face. Paul Akeu, the interpreter, did not sit down; instead he took a standing position behind the Osages.

"How are you doing, Paul" Bob asked. Before Akeu could answer Fitzpatrick slammed down the gavel he had brought with him to Pawhuska, and Bob sensed Emmett jerk upright at the sudden bang of wood on wood. Fitzpatrick's expression was grim, and he clearly felt that Bob's talking to the witnesses was out of order.

"Defendant is reminded that he will speak only when spoken to," the commissioner barked with repressed anger, his watery blue eyes glaring directly at Bob. Bob placed his hands in his lap and stared back at the judge with what he hoped was pleasant cooperation. Their gazes locked for a moment, then Fitzpatrick lowered his eyes to the papers on his desk again.

"Is. . ." Fitzpatrick paused as he struggled with the unfamiliar pronunciation, "She-so-wah here?" He glanced up at the seated Indians.

"That's Chi-sho-wah-hah, your honor," the interpreter corrected. "He's right here." Akeu moved to position himself behind the chieftain.

"Does he speak English?"

"He speaks some, your honor, but he has asked me to interpret for him to be sure his words are understood."

"Very well. Would you please ask him to come forward and be sworn in." The Osage rose and was sworn in by the clerk, then took a seat in the chair beside the judge's desk. Paul Akeu stood beside him.

Waiting until his clerk was back at his table and ready to take notes, Fitzpatrick spoke over Chi-sho-wah-hah's head to the interpreter. After some preliminary questions about where Chi-sho-wah-hah lived and if he knew the defendants, the commissioner said, "Would you please ask him to describe what happened on December twenty-fifth of last year."

Without waiting for Akeu to translate the question, the Osage chief began speaking in his clicking, guttural native language, and Paul Akeu struggled to keep up with his translation.

"I saw Bob at my house Christmas Day. I did not see Emmett. There were two men with Dalton. They had a wagon loaded with jugs of whiskey. One of the men was in the wagon, and one on the ground. Bob was on horseback, riding around the wagon and through the camp. A lot of Indians were camped at my place for several days about Christmas. I though Bob was a marshal, and I asked him to take those men away from my place. He made me no answer, but gave a whoop and rode away. I think he was under the influence of liquor. The Indians all got drunk."

There were a few more questions about Bob's involvement in actually selling the whiskey, and then the next witness was called. Bob's posture sagged as the damning evidence mounted against him. Some of the Indians were his friends, and they shaded their stories to make Bob's participation seem more innocent, but others did not really know Bob, or were too honest to lie on his behalf.

Finally it was over. All the witnesses had testified, and their statements were written down by the court clerk. The room was quiet as Fitzpatrick filled out the transcript form, the scratching of his pen clearly audible over the whistling of the wind outside. When he had finished, Fitzpatrick carefully set his pen in its holder, methodically rolled the blotter over the long form, and then looked around the room to make sure everyone was listening.

"Upon hearing all the evidence," he announced officiously, "I find that there is not probable cause sufficient to warrant the belief that Emmett Dalton is guilty of the charges."

Next to Bob Emmett wiggled in his chair with excitement and relief, and Bob felt a ray of hope shine through the clouds that had enveloped him. If Emmett's charges were dropped, then maybe his would be, too. His brief elation was immediately crushed.

"However," Fitzpatrick continued, "I do find that there is probable cause to believe that defendant Robert Dalton is guilty. I hereby order that Emmett Dalton be discharged, and that Robert Dalton be held to appear at the next regular time of the District Court at Wichita, on September first, 1890. Bail is set at one thousand dollars. This court is adjourned." He rapped the gavel again, then gathered up his papers and left the room.

While the other people filed out of the court room, Bob sat unmoving, stunned by the judge's pronouncement even though it had been expected. Emmett jumped out of his chair and fidgeted in front of Bob, obviously torn by conflicting emotions. On one hand he was ecstatic that he had been exonerated, but on the other hand he was distressed that Bob had been held over for trial.

"What now, Bob?" he asked apprehensively. Bob just shook his head and stared at the commissioner's empty desk, fighting back tears of disappointment and anger.

Lafe Shadley came over and put his hand on Bob's shoulder. "I was afraid this'd happen," he said. "I got somebody who'll post bond for you."

"Who?" Bob asked, looking up at Shadley with a spark of hope.

"Hoots and Ririe. They'll put up their cattle as security."

"Why would they do that?" Bob pushed himself up from his chair and stood beside Emmett.

"You got friends," Shadley assured him. "Of course, they probably expect you'll pay them for their trouble later."

"Well, sure," Bob said sincerely. He held his hand out to Shadley. "Thanks, Lafe. You've done a lot. I owe you."

Gripping Bob's hand firmly, Shadley said, "You're welcome. Maybe I'll need your help sometime. Come on, let's go get you bailed out."

The three men left the court room and went to the front office where the clerk worked. Through the open front door of the building Bob saw Chi-sho-wah-hah getting into his wagon, and again he noted what a fine pair of mules the Indian owned. Incensed by the chieftain's testimony against him, Bob briefly thought to himself that the Indian did not deserve to have such quality animals. Then Bob was distracted by the bail bond process, and his mind flew on to other things.

Friday, April 11, 1890

The train shuddered to a stop, and Bob Cox jumped lightly down to the platform, a valise in one hand and a Winchester in the other. Behind him Deputy Floyd Wilson climbed down more slowly, his face flushed and his movements labored. Cox was Wilson's posseman, and the two had come to Claremore searching for two prisoners who had escaped from the Little Rock penitentiary, but Wilson's illness was hindering their pursuit.

Wilson had received a telegram at Tulsa the day before from Marshal Yoes in Fort Smith, notifying him that Bud Maxfield and a man named Halm had escaped from Little Rock and were suspected to be in the Claremore area. Wilson, suffering from a severe ague chill, had been in bed when the telegram came, and he had delayed acting on it for one day in the hope he would feel better after a good night's sleep. This morning his condition had indeed seem improved, and he and Cox had packed and boarded the train for the short ride to Claremore. By the time they arrived, however, Floyd Wilson was again feeling sicker than a dog.

The two men checked into a hotel, and Wilson immediately flopped onto the bed, too exhausted to even take off his boots. Cox, an ambitious and energetic young man, left him there while he went out and began asking questions around town, looking for leads on the escaped convicts. Two hours later he returned with what he considered exciting news. He found Wilson still in bed, propped up on a pillow and covered with a blanket. On the floor lay Wilson's boots, which he had finally managed to remove.

"Maxfield and Halm been seen out at Hightman's place," Cox told him earnestly, running his fingers up and down the lapels of his suit jacket as he stood beside Wilson's bed. "There's going to be a big party out there tonight. I figure we could go out there and join the party, not saying who we are, and when we get a chance, just grab those two and bring 'em in."

Wilson coughed and shook his head wearily. "I'm too sick, Bob. I can barely make it to the outhouse. I wouldn't do you no good tonight. Besides, lots of them folks know me."

"I know," Cox said. "I thought of that. You just stay here and get better. I ran into Charley Canon, and he said he'd help us. He's been invited to the party, and he'll tell 'em I'm a friend of his. They won't know we're lawmen until we put the cuffs on 'em."

"It's too dangerous, Bob," Wilson protested weakly. "Those men are hardened criminals. You better wait until I can go with you. Maybe tomorrow I'll be up to it."

Cox looked down at Wilson, who was shivering with a chill at the same time that sweat was dribbling down his forehead, and knew the deputy was a long way from recovery. "They might be gone tomorrow, Floyd. We gotta get while the gettin' is good. Don't worry, Charley and me can handle it.

Wilson was still opposed to the plan, but he was too ill to argue any more. With mumbled assent he sank back into the pillow and closed his eyes, falling asleep even before Cox had left the room. Cox went downstairs to claim his Winchester from the front desk, and then went in search of Charley Canon. It looked like it was going to be an exciting night.

Hightman's farm was just outside Claremore, and the farmhouse was unusually large for the area. It was a two-story frame house, and the party was taking place mainly on the second floor, which was not partitioned into rooms. Like the other guests, Cox and Canon left their weapons in a downstairs closet and went upstairs to join in the festivities.

Within a few minutes of their arrival, the two men were approached by a boy named Ed Louthers, who looked to be around thirteen or fourteen years old, and he offered them the opportunity to buy some whiskey. Charley Canon gave the boy some money, and five minutes later Louthers returned with a pint of whiskey. With little prompting the boy proudly explained that a man named Halm was running a saloon in the loft of the barn, and he was paying Louthers a commission to make sales and deliver the liquor to the party guests.

It was an excellent party, and Cox and Canon were enjoying themselves and the illegal liquor, so they convinced each other that it would be best to wait until the party was over and most of the guests were gone before they made their arrest. Besides, they had still not located Maxfield, the other fugitive. Around three in the morning most of the party-goers had gone home, and there had been no sign of Maxfield. Cox decided it was time to make their move on Halm, but first they had to take care of Louthers.

The two undercover lawmen went downstairs and waited in the front hall for the boy to return from another trip to the barn. When he came back into the house carrying a bottle, Canon grabbed him in a bear hug and held him while Cox put a pair of handcuffs on him. The whiskey had had its effect, though, and Cox had not thought this all the way through. Louthers began yelling for help and struggling to get away, while Canon wrestled with the boy and tried to make him shut up. Cox jerked open the hall closet door to retrieve his rifle, when two men rushed into the hall in answer to Louthers' cries. Both men had dark hair and swarthy skin, evidence of their Cherokee heritage, and they looked very much alike, despite their difference in ages. The older man, Cox knew, was Alex Cochran, a prosperous local farmer with the reputation of being a mean drunk. With him was his teenage son Jesse Cochran Jr., who was known to be a trouble-maker and hell-raiser.

Alex Cochran had a pistol in his hand and fire in his eyes, and everyone froze when he and his son entered the large foyer. Young Jesse quickly sized up the situation.

"Let's take him away from them," he goaded his father, starting toward Louthers. Bob Cox grabbed his Winchester from the closet and swung around to face the two Cochrans, but he was too slow. Alex Cochran's pistol blasted at him, and the force of the bullet striking his neck flung Cox back against the wall. Straining to remain upright, supported by the wall, Cox managed somehow to return the fire, cocking and firing the Winchester wildly at the Cochrans, who had dived for cover beyond the doorway into the parlor.

Cox was peripherally aware that Louthers and Canon had both run out the front door into the night, but his attention was focused on Cochran, who was firing blindly around the door frame, his bullets punching holes in the wall several feet from Cox. Edging toward the front door, Cox shot back at Cochran, and he had just about made it to the front porch when Cochran took a more careful aim and put a round through Cox's thigh. Cox fell through the doorway and crashed to the front porch floor. Fighting off the pain and shock, he forced himself to roll across the porch and down the front steps, out of the line of fire. No shots followed his desperate escape; perhaps Cochran had emptied his pistol and had to reload.

Out of the darkness Charley Canon appeared, leading two horses he had found somewhere, and he hastily helped Cox mount one of them. As soon as Cox was secure in the saddle, Canon quickly climbed on to the other and they galloped away, heading back toward town. There was no further attack from within the house.

They had gone only a mile or so when Cox, weakened by shock and the loss of blood, swore he could go no farther. Canon led them to the next farmhouse he saw and pounded on the door to wake up the occupants. While the farm family made Cox comfortable and tended to his wounds, Canon dashed into town for the doctor, who hitched up his hack and came out to carry Cox back into Claremore.

As soon as Bob Cox was carried into the doctor's office and was being treated, Charley Canon went over to the hotel and reported to Floyd Wilson what had occurred. Wilson, still too sick to get around, dictated a telegram for Canon to send to Fort Smith. The message outlined what had happened and implied that Cox was fatally wounded, for so Canon had described Cox's condition to Wilson. The message also requested help from all available deputies in the area. As Wilson knew, this meant primarily the Daltons.

In response to the disheartening result of his hearing in Pawhuska, Bob had resolved to start over and prove himself worthy of wearing a badge again. He felt he had disgraced the memory of his brother Frank and tarnished the reputation of his entire family, and so he was determined to now work hard to restore the good name of the Daltons. He and Emmett had resumed working as possemen for their brother Grat and for Floyd Wilson, and Bob hoped to show Marshal Yoes in Fort Smith that he should again be made a deputy, since his twenty-first birthday was only a month away. His pending trial in Wichita was conveniently forgotten.

When Bob and Emmett arrived in Claremore on the train from Tulsa Saturday afternoon, Grat was already there waiting for them. He had arrived from Vinita an hour earlier, and the three brothers greeted each other warmly. Bob, still enthusiastic about his resolution to be a better peace office, was aroused by the prospect of a gunfight between the Daltons and the Cochrans. To him it took on the mythic proportions of the gunfight at the OK Corral between the Earps and the Clantons, and he could hardly wait for the showdown.

From the train station the boys went to the hotel, checking their weapons at the front desk as required. While Grat and Emmett went upstairs to visit with Floyd Wilson and get the latest information, Bob walked out on the street to have a look around. As he strolled down the wooden sidewalk, he met Davis Hill, a local merchant Bob had done business with a few times. He did not really care for Hill, but he nodded in recognition.

"Hello, Bob," Hill greeted him with a wry smile. "Looking for Alex, I suppose."

"Yep," Bob replied as he carefully eyed the other people on the street that pleasant spring afternoon. He turned and looked at Hill. "If he'll come in peaceably and surrender, I might not even lock him up." Bob suspected Hill was a friend of Alex Cochran, and thought his message might be relayed.

"Not much chance of him surrendering," Hill said, "at least until he hears how Cox comes out."

A young man who had been lounging near the hitching rail and listening to this conversation offered his own opinion. "Old Alex'll shoot anyone comes near his place."

"That's right," another man chimed in. An old-timer in shirtsleeves who had been leaning against the wall of a store, he now shuffled over to join Bob and Hill. "I wouldn't want to be the man who tried to arrest old Alex Cochran. Him and his folks would not take kindly to that."

"We'll get him," Bob promised. "He broke the law, and the Daltons will see to it that he pays."

"Well, Bob," Hill said, craning his neck to look down the street, "Cochran was just in my store a few minutes ago buying cartridges. That's him riding off down the road right now. If you want him so bad, why don't you just go and get him?"

"Are you sure that's him?" Bob asked, his hand reaching for the pistol that was no longer on his hip. He had never met the Cochrans before, and wanted to be sure who he was arresting.

"Well, that sure it his horse," the young man at the hitching post confirmed, "so I reckon that's him."

Without a further word Bob ran back to the hotel and demanded his Winchester from the clerk. As the man handed him the rifle, Grat and Emmett came down the stairs. "It's Cochran!" Bob shouted to them as he rushed out the front door. "Get some horses and come on!"

In front of the hotel Bob spied a saddle horse tied to the rail, and with no hesitation he untied the reins and leaped into the saddle. Wheeling the strange horse around and spurring its flanks, he galloped out of town in pursuit of the fleeing Cochran.

With his rifle in one hand and the reins in his other, Bob sped after the other rider, the wind whipping his coat tails and tugging at his hat. Cochran, unaware of being chased, had his horse at a trot, and Bob quickly caught up with him. Knowing Cochran's reputation for violence, Bob wanted to take no chances, so when he was within a hundred yards of the man he reined in his horse and jumped to the ground.

"Hold it, Cochran!" he yelled. "U. S. Marshal."

The other rider took a quick glance back at Bob, then spurred his horse and took off at a dead run, crouching low across the pommel. Swiftly Bob brought the rifle up to his shoulder and fired a warning shot right over the man's head. In response Cochran's horse abruptly veered to the right and pounded toward some nearby trees.

Concentrating on his aim this time, Bob rapidly pulled off two more shots. The first had no noticeable effect, but at the second shot the horse stumbled and collapsed on its neck, throwing the rider over its head to the ground, where the man lay in an unmoving heap.

Carefully Bob approached the fallen horse and rider. Behind him he heard two horses come up, and he glanced back to see that it was Grat and Emmett. Bob continued to walk forward to where Cochran lay, his rifle held ready. The horse, lying on its side, was snorting wildly and heaving its chest; then, with a final shudder, it died. Next to the horse its rider, a younger man than Bob had expected, was clutching his thigh and moaning piteously.

"That ain't Alex Cochran," Grat observed, riding up beside Bob. "That's Jesse Cochran Jr."

"His son?" Bob asked with surprise.

"Sort of," Grat replied cryptically.

"Well, hell, them people in town told me it was Alex."

"Is he hurt bad?" Emmett asked. He had maneuvered his horse over close to the wounded young man, and was leaning out of his saddle to be a better look.

"Hey, boy," Grat called to him, "you hurt bad?"

"My leg!" Cochran cried. "You shot my leg!"

"Pretty good shootin', Bobby," Grat remarked, estimating the distance from where Bob had left his horse to where Cochran had fallen. Bob nodded.

"Emmett," Bob said, crouching down by young Jesse Cochran to inspect the wound, "you better go get a doctor and a buggy or something. I don't think he can walk." Emmett obediently brought his horse around and galloped off back in the direction of Claremore. Bob rolled Cochran over on his back and retrieved the boy's hat to put under his head as a pillow. Grat climbed down from his horse and motioned with his head for Bob to join him a few feet away. He lowered his voice so Cochran could not hear.

"This might be a problem, Bobby."

"How come? He was probably an accomplice anyway."

"Don't matter. Did you ever wonder why Alex's son's name is Jesse Cochran *Junior*?"

"Is kinda odd," Bob admitted.

"The District Solicitor's name is Jesse Cochran. Junior here might have been named for him, or they might be related somehow. I don't know exactly what the story is, but two years ago Jesse Junior and his cousin George Cochran were caught stealing horses. George, being almost full blood, was tried and convicted by the Cherokee tribal court, but Junior here was released and the charges were dropped. What I'm saying is, Jesse Junior seems to have some political strings he can pull."

"What do we do, then?"

Grat shrugged. "Not much we can do. Just have to wait and see." They did not have to wait long.

Bob Cox's wounds proved to be relatively minor, and in a month he was again fit for duty. The doctor who treated Jesse Cochran Junior declared that Bob's bullet had passed through the boy's thigh and saddle to kill the horse he had been riding.

Because Bob Cox was not a sworn deputy at the time of the shooting at Hightman's, and because there had been no warrant for the arrest of either Louthers or Alex Cochran at that time, charges against the elder Cochran were dropped. Since Bob Dalton had been acting under orders from the U. S. Marshal, and because he had good reason to believe that he was shooting at an escaping felon, no charges were filed against him for wounding Jesse Junior.

Nonetheless, a few days later Grat was informed that his services were no longer required by the U. S. Marshals Service. Ostensibly he was fired because of the incident with Delonsdale in Tulsa, but he and Bob believed the dismissal was more likely caused by political pressure resulting from the Cochran shooting. For whatever reason, for the first time in six years there was no Dalton serving as a deputy U. S. Marshal.

Author's Notes

Chapter 4

Numerous newspaper articles, most written after the Coffeyville raid, mentioned the rumors of the Daltons accepting bribes from bootleggers during this period. An interview with their older brother, Ben Dalton, was published in the October 27, 1892, issue of the *San Francisco Chronicle*, in which he confirmed that the boys had accepted money to let whiskey peddlers go free.

The events at the Osage camp on Christmas Day of 1889 are well documented, with several pages of testimony from witnesses on file at the Kansas City branch of the National Archives. The Archives also contain the arrest warrants for Bob and Emmett, the hearing transcript, Bob's bail bond documents, and a letter from Commissioner Fitzpatrick to the district attorney in Wichita explaining his actions against the Daltons.

A letter from Marshal Jacob Yoes in the National Archives in Washington mentioned that he had hired Grat as a deputy, but had felt Bob was too young, although Bob and Emmett had been allowed to work as possemen and guards for Deputy Floyd Wilson.

Grat's beating of Delonsdale was mentioned in the March 6, 1890, issue of the Vinita *Indian Chieftain*. The April 17, 1890 issue of this same newspaper carried a detailed account of the shooting of Bob Cox at Claremore, and Bob's subsequent wounding of Jesse Cochran Jr. This incident was also described in Emmett's book, *Beyond the Law*. Information about Jesse Cochran Jr. and his previous brush with the law came from the *Indian Chieftain* of May 31 and June 6, 1888, which also contained unrelated articles about District Solicitor Jesse Cochran.

The letter from Jacob Yoes mentioned above also stated that he had fired Grat for drunkenness and because of his conduct in Tulsa, but the timing suggests that the Cochran incident may have been the final straw.

CHAPTER 5

Eighteen-Ninety was turning out ot be a bad year for the Daltons. After Grat was fired from the marshals service, it became obvious to Bob that he and Emmett were no longer welcome either. They continued working for Deputy Floyd Wilson, but things Floyd said—or didn't say—left Bob with the impression that Floyd was uncomfortable with their continued employment. The upcoming trial on the introducing charge, along with the Jesse Cochran incident, had badly tarnished the Daltons' reputation, and Bob suspected Wilson was under pressure from community leaders to distance himself from the boys.

To save his friend from a difficult situation, Bob went to Wilson on June 20, 1890, and told him that he and Emmett were quitting. Citing his frustration over the withholding of his back pay, Bob declared his disgust with government service and its lack of support for its employees. Wilson, clearly relieved by Bob's action, quickly paid Bob and Emmett the money he owed them and wished them success in any future endeavor.

With these meager funds in their pockets, Bob and Emmett left Tulsa and rode a few miles northeast to Claremore. They spend the next two weeks hanging around this small railroad town, spending what little money they had and debating what they should do next.

On the Fourth of July, Bob made his decision. He and Emmett were sitting on a large rock near the top of the hill at the west end of Claremore, waiting for the fireworks to begin. Each had a glass of lemonade they had purchased at the town celebration, and Emmett was fanning himself lazily with his hat. The sun had just set behind them, but the still air remained suffocatingly hot and humid, and the twilight was not yet dark enough for the fireworks. There was an occasional pop or whiz-bang from close by as local boys set off their firecrackers, and Emmett secretly wished he wasn't too old and responsible to go join them.

"I been thinking," Bob announced quietly.

"Mm?" Emmett grunted when Bob didn't immediately continue his thought.

"This is all Chi-sho-wah-hah's fault. If he hadn't told Henry Roberts about Christmas Day, and then testified against me, then I'll bet Yoes would have made me a deputy again."

"Maybe," Emmett said dubiously.

"The way I figure it, he owes me."

"What do you mean?"

Bob turned his head and looked at Emmett intently, almost fiercely. "I mean I intend to collect. We've lost a lot of wages 'cause of him, so it's only right that he pay us back."

Emmett's forehead was wrinkled in confusion. "He ain't going to pay us anything. Why should he?"

"Why shouldn't he?" Bob countered. He scooted over closer to Emmett and lowered his voice. "We can make him pay."

"How? He'll just send for Roberts or one of the other deputies and have us arrested again."

"Not if he doesn't know who did it."

"Did what?"

"Took those two mules of his and sold 'em."

"You want to steal his mules?" Emmett's voice went up an octave and his eyes opened wide in disbelief.

"Sure. Why not? We can go in there real quiet at night, while everyone's asleep, and then take 'em down to Fort Smith or somewhere and sell 'em. They ought to bring a pretty good price, as nice as they are."

"But that's against the law," Emmett argued, his fingers fluttering around the lemonade glass. "That'd make us criminals."

"Hell," Bob muttered dejectedly, "I already am, according to them. Remember? I got to go to trial in September."

"But you said you were sure you'd be found innocent."

"Yeah, but what if I'm not? Besides, everyone thinks I'm guilty anyway. Might as well get some money for it."

Emmett set the glass down and twisted his body to face Bob squarely, his shock and misgiving apparent even in the semi-darkness. "Bob, you're talking about us becoming outlaws."

"So?" Bob said defensively. "Our cousins were outlaws, and had books written about 'em."

"Yeah, and they went to prison, too."

"Well, we won't. We used to be marshals, so we know the law and how it works. We won't get caught like the Youngers did."

"Are you sure?" Bob could tell from the way Emmett asked that he was wavering in his opposition to the plan. Deciding that he needed to offer Emmett a compromise, he used his back-up ploy.

"Look, Emmett, we'll just take them mules and sell them to get us a stake. We can use the money to go to California, maybe, and start us up a ranch or something. Bill would help us." Their older brother Bill worked a ranch owned by his father-in-law near San Miguel, California.

There was a long silence between them as Emmett mulled over Bob's proposal. Although, at nineteen, Emmett was only two years younger than Bob, he respected Bob's opinion and admired his intelligence and innate leadership ability. On the other hand, both boys had been raised in a very religious home; their mother, a devout Presbyterian, had insisted on proper behavior and constantly warned them not to become like their cousins, the Youngers. Finally Bob's power of persuasion won over, and Emmett grimly nodded his head.

"Okay," Emmett agreed, "but just to raise a stake."

Bob smiled with satisfaction as the first rocket rose up in the dark summer sky on a trail of sparks. He watched as it climbed higher and higher in an arc, then burst into glowing stars that faded into nothing as they fell back toward the earth.

Tuesday, July 22, 1890

"There it is," Bob said unnecessarily as the farm house came into view. He had his head tilted to the right so that his hat brim sheltered his eyes from the harsh glare of the late afternoon sun, and his suit jacket was draped across the pack tied behind his saddle.

"I see it," Grat answered grumpily. They had just crested a low hill, and across the rolling prairie ahead of them was the line of trees and bushes that marked the course of California Creek. Near the creek was the cluster of farm buildings—house, barn, stable—that belonged to John and Zue Mitchell.

Zue was a cousin of the Daltons, and they had visited there many times before, back when they were deputy marshals and had needed a place to spend the night and get a meal. Zue and her husband had always welcomed the boys, but it had been almost a year since their last visit, and their reputation had suffered in the interim. Relatives were relatives, however, and frontier hospitality dictated that they would be offered a meal and shelter for the night.

A short distance away they could also see the Ravelle home, where Zue's sister and her husband lived. While Mrs. Ravelle was just as related to the Daltons as Zue, her husband had discouraged the boys from visiting there as often, and consequently they had grown closer to Zue and her more friendly husband, John.

Grat twisted in his saddle to look behind him again, checking on the two horses that he and Bob were leading. Seeing that they were all right, he turned back around, scowling momentarily as his gaze brushed over the beautiful big bay horse Bob was riding. Bob ignored the look, having grown tired of arguing about the horse. He wondered again what the horse would bring up in Kansas, and how he could keep Grat from finding out if he sold it.

His recent experiences with stolen livestock, combined with what his father had taught him, had convinced Bob that he was an expert in horse trading now. Granted, things had not gone too smoothly at first, but he had just been learning the ropes. After stealing Chi-sho-wah-hah's two mules, Bob and Emmett had gathered up a few horses they found unguarded as well, all in Osage country. Then they had driven the stock southeast into the Cherokee Nation, hoping to find a buyer in Fort Smith. When the Arkansas stock buyers starting asking too many questions, they left and took the animals north toward Kansas. Along the way they had sold the two mules to a man named Emmett Vann near Vinita. The horses were finally sold in Columbus, Kansas. When they arrived back in Tulsa, Grat had told them the bad news.

John Mitchell and his young son were standing on the front porch waiting for them as they rode up to the house and dismounted.

"Hi, Bobby! Hi, Grat!" the boy chirped and waved, thrilled to have company.

"Hey, boys," John Mitchell greeted them with a nod. "How you all been?"

"Pretty good, John," Bob said, holding his horse's reins in his left hand as he reached out with right to shake John's hand. "How about yourself?"

"Oh, I been worse," Mitchell said with a smile. As he stepped off the porch to shake Grat's hand, Zue came out through the front door, wiping her hands on her apron. When she saw the two Daltons, she smiled broadly and opened her arms to Bob.

"Bobby! Come give your cousin a hug. It's been a long time."

"Howdy, Zue," Bob said happily, giving her a brief but affectionate hug. Bob knelt down to hug Zue's boy as Zue hugged Grat in turn, and then he asked if they could put their horses in the stable for the night.

"Of course you can," Zue said. "And you'll stay for supper, too. I made plenty. I kind of had a feeling we might have company tonight. We'll make up beds for you in the parlor. It's so good to see you. How are your folks?"

Before Bob or Grat could answer her, John, who had been examining the horse that Bob had been riding, interrupted. "That is one fine looking horse you got there, Bobby. Where'd you get him?"

"It was my Dad's," Bob replied quietly, his expression suddenly serious.

Mitchell, still admiring the horse and oblivious to Bob's tone, said, "How much would you take for him? I been looking for a good horse like that."

"John!" Zue admonished her husband, motioning with her head to look at the two visitors. Unlike him, she had immediately picked up on the change in atmosphere, and knew that there was something wrong.

"Dad passed on last week," Bob stated sadly, looking down at the ground.

"Oh, no!" Zue cried. "How terrible!" She wrapped an arm around Bob's shoulder sympathetically. "How did it happen?"

"Cholera morbis," Grat answered grimly. "Came on real sudden, and he passed away last Wednesday before any of us could get there."

"Oh, Lord, I'm sorry, boys," John said, coming over to put a hand on Grat's shoulder. "How's your mother taking it?

"It hit her kinda hard," Bob said, slowly shaking his head. He did not think the Mitchells knew about his folks' separation, and now was not the time to tell them. In fact, he realized, it was now a moot point, and there was no need to ever mention it.

"Emmett's helping her move the furniture and stuff to Kingfisher," Grat said. "She's staying with Eva until she gets a cabin built. She's leased a section on a school quarter there in Kingfisher. That way she'll be close to family if she needs help or anything."

"Well, that's good," Zue said. "How are you boys holding up?"

Bob sniffed before he spoke. "Okay, I guess. Had a nice little funeral there in Dearing. . ."

"Dearing?" John cut in. "I thought your folks lived in Coffeyville."

"Oh, they did," Bob hastily clarified, "but Dad was in Dearing when he took sick. It's only five miles from Coffeyville."

"That bay and the horse I'm leading were Dad's," Grat said to change the subject. "That's why we don't want to sell them." Bob kept quiet, knowing the real problem was Grat's annoyance that Bob had claimed the big bay first.

"I can understand that," John said. "Come on, let me help you put these horses up, and then we'll have supper."

"That's right," Zue said, patting Bob on his back as he stepped back off the porch. "I better go check on my roast. By the time you boys get those horses taken care of and wash up, supper should be on the table."

"Thanks, Zue," Bob said as he followed Grat and John toward the stable, "we really appreciate it." As they stabled the horses, Bob went over in his mind what he would tell the Mitchells over supper. He was sure they would ask a thousand questions about his family, and he had to come up with a consistent story that would not reveal his parents' marital problems. The home-cooked meal he had so been looking forward to earlier now augered to be an excruciating inquisition.

Wednesday, July 30, 1890

Bob reined in his horse and raised his body up straight until all his weight was carried by his boots in the stirrups, both to stretch his tired muscles and to give him a better vantage point as he surveyed the area. The yellows and greens and browns of the prairie grasses undulated gently around him, interspersed with the darker greens and browns of trees in small copses and along stream beds. Off to his right, in the shade of a small stand of oak, were about a dozen horses peacefully munching the lush grass and lazing about in the noonday heat.

“What do you think?” Bob asked as Emmett halted his mount next to Bob’s. Without waiting for his brother’s answer, Bob sat back down in his saddle and chucked the reins to move his horse forward. “Let’s go check ‘em out,” he said as he moved away. Emmett compliantly followed behind Bob as they rode closer to the small herd, riding along slowly to avoid spooking them.

“Branded ‘AR’,” Emmett observed as they got nearer and Bob stopped again.

“Uh-huh,” Bob agreed thoughtfully. With squinted eyes he carefully scanned the surrounding terrain to see if they were being observed.

“You know that brand?” Emmett asked, scratching his cheek. A few days earlier he had gotten into some poison ivy, and had spread it from his hands to his face. Liberal application of calamine lotion had mostly cleared up the resulting rashes, but his five-day growth of beard was now almost white from the medicine, and his face still itched occasionally.

Bob shook his head. “Not for sure. Might belong to some relative of Clem Rogers.” Rogers was a wealthy and very influential rancher in the area north of Claremore, with a big house in Oolagah and property extending north to Talala. He had enough money that he had sent his young son Will off to a military academy. Bob had recently learned that it was not wise to arouse the anger of the politically well-connected, and if these horses belonged to Clem Rogers, Bob intended to leave them alone. “Come on,” he said, and he and Emmett rode down the slope toward the line of trees marking a creek’s course to the north.

As they rounded a grove of trees a small unpainted cabin came into view, with a large barn only a few hundred feet behind it. Bob smiled as he recognized the buildings.

“You hungry?” he asked Emmett.

“Sure,” Emmett replied. At nineteen years of age, he was always hungry.

"A Negro family lives there," Bob said. "Me and Bud Heady had supper there once. Lady fixes a pretty good meal for a fair price."

"I thought we didn't have any money."

"I got a quarter. That ought to be enough."

"What if it ain't?" Emmett tried to be the voice of reason whenever he could.

"Don't worry about it. But let me do all the talking. She don't know you, and it'd be better if we keep it that way. Okay?"

"If you say so, Bobby."

After a simple but filling meal of chicken-fried steak, biscuits and gravy, and collard greens, Bob and Emmett went out onto the front porch of the cabin to rest awhile. Bob sat in the only chair, a rickety wooden kitchen chair with one arm missing, while Emmett sat on the wooden porch floor with his back against the wall. After putting the dishes to soak in a basin, Rhoda Rogers came out and stood on the porch with them, leaning against one of the roof supports.

"What you doin' out here, Mr. Dalton?" she asked conversationally. She had remembered Bob from his earlier visit with Bud Heady, and another time when he had come by alone. She was a young woman in her twenties, slim, with her hair covered by a bandana, and as she talked she kept an eye on her three children playing out in the yard.

"Just looking for a horse," Bob said, searching his pockets for a toothpick. When he found one he politely covered his mouth with one hand as he picked at his teeth with the other. "Have you seen a roan mare running around loose? Got a bar D brand on it."

"No, sir," she said with a slow shake of her head. "Ain't seen nothing like that."

"That's too bad. We been looking all over for that horse." Bob sucked at his teeth as he slipped the toothpick back into his vest pocket. "Say, do you know who owns them horses up on the prairie south of here? Saw about ten or twelve head up there branded 'AR'."

"Those would be my old man's."

"I thought your husband's name was Bob," Bob said with a puzzled look.

"'Tis," Rhoda said. "Least that's what he goes by. Real name's Alonzo, but he don't like that, so he calls himself Bob."

"So his brand is 'AR'?"

"That's right."

"Could I see your branding iron?" Bob asked, as if this was a normal request.

"I guess so," Rhoda said, shrugging. "Kids!" she yelled toward the three dark-skinned children across the yard. "Run down to the barn and get the branding iron. Hurry up, now." The three children, a boy about seven and two younger girls, all barefoot, ran yelling and laughing down the dusty path to the barn. While they were gone, the adults remained silent, staring out at the shimmering heat of mid-day in July.

Soon the children returned, the boy glancing shyly at Bob as he handed the heavy iron rod to his mother. As the children stood out in the sun curiously staring at the two white men on the porch, Rhoda Rogers passed the iron over to Bob. Carefully he examined the end of the iron rod, where flat strips of metal had been bent into the shapes of letters and welded to the rod.

Bob pressed the business end of the iron against his flattened palm and nodded knowingly as he examined the quickly fading impression it left on his skin.

"Yep, AR," he said. "Now we'll know that brand whenever we see it." With a smile he held the branding iron out to the little boy who had brought it. "You can take it back now, son," he said encouragingly. With a grin the boy took it and ran back toward the barn.

"Well, we better get moving," Bob said, slapping his hands on the front of his thighs. He stood up, his rangy body towering over the black woman, and stretched his shoulder and back muscles. Behind him Emmett scrambled to his feet as well.

"What do we owe you for that fine dinner, Mrs. Roger?" Bob asked, reaching into his pants pocket.

"That'll be fifty cents, Mr. Dalton, for the two of you."

Bob frowned as he examined the quarter he had drawn from his pocket. "You don't have change for a five dollar bill, do you?" he asked, placing a hand on his vest pocket.

"No, sir, I don't," Rhoda replied, in a tone that indicated how silly she thought the question was.

"Well, all I've got otherwise is this here quarter. Tell you what, I'll give you twenty-five cents now, and I'll bring the rest back tomorrow, after I've had a chance to break this five dollar bill I got. We'll be coming back this way, and I'll just give the other twenty-five cents to your husband when I see him out in the fields. Would that be okay?"

"I guess it'll have to be," she said with resignation.

"We really appreciate it, Mrs. Rogers, and I'll make sure you get your money. Thanks again for the meal." Hurriedly Bob walked over to his horse, untied the reins from the hitching post, and mounted up, waiting impatiently for Emmett to do likewise. He felt uncomfortable about lying to the woman, suspecting, correctly, that she knew he was lying. He smiled and waved at her as they spurred their horses into motion and moved east down the creek, but noted with chagrin that she did not return the gesture.

"The hell with her, then," Bob said to Emmett when they were out of her hearing. "I told her I'd pay her."

"Do you really have a five dollar bill?" Emmet asked suspiciously.

"Of course not," Bob said. "I just told her that so she wouldn't think we were trying to cheat her. Still doesn't give her the right to be unfriendly with us."

"Seemed friendly enough to me," Emmett said, rubbing his chin. "But why'd you want to see her branding iron?"

"I wanted to make sure those were her husband's horses we saw and not Clem Rogers'. I like to be sure whose horses I'm dealing with, if you know what I mean."

"Oh. So we're going to take them?"

"Yep. Them and some others. I think tonight would be a good night to find a bunch of horses and round 'em up. There was a dozen or so back there, so let's see if we can find a few more this afternoon that we can come back for after it gets dark."

"Where we going to take them this time?"

"Back up to Columbus. Those folks up there don't ask too many questions. I like that." Bob flicked his reins and kicked his heels against his horse's flank to goad it into a trot. "Come on, Emmett, we got work to do."

The bright moon was just above the horizon when Bob and Emmett brought the herd of horses into the farmyard of their cousin Zue Mitchell. The bluish light threw long shadows across the dusty ground as Bob rode up to the front porch of the house and dismounted, while Emmett circled the herd to keep them bunched together. It was well past midnight, but the day's arid heat still lingered. Bob went up to the front door and rapped on it with his knuckles, trying to make it loud enough to wake those sleeping inside, but no so loud as to alarm them.

Since they had left Rhoda Rogers the two young men had ridden hard, scouting out all the horses in the rolling hills between Claremore and Bartlesville. Each time they saw a few head grazing, they carefully evaluated the nearness of occupied buildings, the quality of the animals, and the routes of approach and retreat. By the time the sun finally set, Bob had made a mental shopping list, planning the operation so that the horses in the southwest were rounded up first, and then others as the steadily growing herd moved northeast.

It would hardly have been possible without the moonlight to reveal the horses and to help the riders avoid obstacles in the terrain. As it was, they made very good time, and by 1:00 a.m. had accumulated over thirty head of prime stock, all moving north-northeast at a steady rate. The long hours of riding and the mental stress of their activities as they worried about discovery eventually took their toll, however, and Bob concluded they had to stop for the night and get some rest. Trusting in the bonds of blood relationships, Bob had brought Emmett and the stolen horses here to the Mitchells.

The front door rattled and swung open, and the orange light of a kerosene lamp spilled out onto the porch. Standing there in long cotton nightgown and a puffy nightcap was Zue Mitchell, squinting at Bob blearily from one eye as she rubbed the other with her fist.

"Bobby?" she croaked, looking up at his face in the flickering lamplight.

"Hi, Zue," he said cheerfully in a low voice.

"What are you doing here at this hour?"

"Just stopping by. Me and Emmett got some horses with us, and I was wondering if we could put them in your pasture for the night. If we leave 'em out on the prairie, we'll lose some of them for sure."

Zue looked past Bob into the yard, struggling to make out Emmett and the horses that restlessly shuffled in the dirt. Crossing her hands over her chest, she rubbed her upper arms and frowned.

"It's awful late, Bobby," she said.

"I know, and I'm sorry. We just need a place to put the horses for a while."

"All right," she agreed grudgingly. "Put 'em in the north pasture. But keep 'em out of the millet, you hear?"

"Yes, ma'am."

"I guess I'll see about making up some beds for you."

"Oh, no," Bob quickly assured her, "you don't need to do that." We'll just sleep out on the ground with the horses. You just go on back to bed, and we'll see you in the morning."

"You sure?" Zue asked, clearly relieved.

"I'm sure. Don't you worry about us, we'll be just fine. And we really appreciate you letting us use your pasture."

"Well, just don't let them horses get into the millet. I mean it, now."

"We won't, Zue, I promise." Bob stepped off the porch and mounted his horse.

"Emmett," he called softly, "let's move 'em into the north pasture." The triangle of orange light that had dimly illuminated the yard slowly narrowed and disappeared as Zue closed the door and returned to bed.

Zue put a plate of fried eggs in front of Bob, then returned to the stove where more eggs were cooking for Emmett.

"We're taking them to Fort Scott," Bob was explaining to John Mitchell, who had just come in from the barn where he had been doing his early morning chores. "Mr. George Williams hired us to drive this herd north for him from Tulsa. He's going to meet us at Lenapah Station, then we'll all ride up there together."

"What are you going to do with them in Kansas?" John asked, reaching across the table to get a slice of bacon from a platter in the middle. Bob also took a couple slices of bacon and began cutting up his eggs with the side of his fork. Emmett, sitting opposite Bob, looked longingly at Bob's eggs, and turned to see how Zue was coming with his.

"Oh, Mr. Williams is going to sell them. He knows a man up there who buys stock."

"And he hired you to drive them up there?" Zue asked, as if to clarify some confusion.

"That's right. He's paying us sixty dollars. See, he had some business back in Tulsa, so we brought the herd up yesterday, and he's taking the train to Lenapah today."

"I thought you said he was going to ride up to Fort Scott with you" John said, chewing on his bacon.

Bob paused to take a bite of egg and to work out his story in his head. He was getting more questions than he expected, and it was hard to keep his lies consistent. "Well, he is," Bob finally said. "He's bringing a saddle with him, and he'll ride one of the stock horses up there. Then, after he's sold them, he'll take the train back.

"Oh," John said.

"That's why we got in so late last night. It took us longer than we thought to get up here, but we had to be here to meet the train."

Zue slid some eggs out of the skillet onto two plates, and then put the plates in front of Emmett and John.

"That sure looks good, Zue," Emmett said enthusiastically, picking up his fork. "We ain't had a good meal in days."

"Eat up, then," Zue said with a smile. "I can make some more if you want it." She watched with satisfaction as Emmett began stuffing food into his face.

Bob took a slice of bread from a cutting board next to the bacon platter and began sopping up egg yolk with it. "You all going to the big picnic on Gooseneck Creek Monday?" Bob asked, wanting to avoid further discussion of the horses.

"Yeah, I thought we would," John answered around a mouthful of egg. "Zue and Little John need to get out and see people. Looks like it's going to be really something."

"That's what I hear," Bob agreed. "As soon as we get rid of them horses up in Kansas, Emmett and me are coming back here for the celebration. Ought to be real fun."

For a variety of reasons, including the weather, Emancipation Day was celebrated on August 4 in Indian Territory in the years following the Civil War. While technically a Negro holiday, all the residents of the territory joined in the festivities—black, white, and Indian. There was not much that passed for entertainment in that rugged frontier area, and any excuse to get together and relax was welcomed by one and all.

Emmett took a drink of water to wash down his food and then said, "What all is gonna be going on there, you reckon?"

"Everybody is bringing a covered dish," Zue said, bending forward to slice some more bread, "and the men are going to cook up some sides of beef and some chickens over campfires. There'll be watermelon and cakes and pies, I imagine. Some of the church ladies are making up some lemonade and iced tea, and there's going to be a baseball game between Vinita and Bartlesville. There might even be some fireworks."

"But you'll have to watch out," John warned with a sly grin, "'cause I heard there might be some of the demon whiskey brought in, too. You wouldn't want to accidentally drink none of that, now, would you?"

"Oh, certainly not," Bob said with a laugh, "that stuff's illegal, you know."

"Yeah," John agreed, laughing too. Still chuckling, Bob finished his breakfast.

While Emmett continued eating, Bob walked across the road to visit Zue's sister, Mrs. Ravelle, having instructed Emmett to get their horses ready as soon as he was done with breakfast. When Bob came back about fifteen minutes later, the kitchen was empty, so he wandered into the parlor. He was standing by the piano plinking on the keys with one finger when Zue walked into the room.

"Where's Emmett?" she asked.

"Out getting the horses saddled."

"So you're leaving now?"

Bob turned from the piano and faced his cousin. "Yeah, pretty quick. Zue, would it be all right if we leave our Winchesters here at your house? We won't need them up in Kansas. We'll pick 'em up when we come back for the picnic."

"I guess that'd be okay," she said. "Just put them in the front closet."

"Thanks." Bob paused, nervously stuffing his hands into his pants pockets. "Zue? Could I ask you another favor?"

“Sure, Bobby, if I can. What is it?”

“Well, we won’t get paid until after them horses get sold, and, well, we’re flat broke. Could I borrow five dollars? I’ll pay you back in a few days, when we come back for the picnic.”

Zue looked at Bob’s face for a moment, then sighed and shook her head slowly. “I guess,” she said with resignation. She walked over to the sideboard and reached into a silver pitcher that sat in the middle of it. She withdrew a five dollar bill and handed it to Bob.

“Thank you,” Bob said sincerely. “You don’t know how much I appreciate this. I’ll pay you back next week, I promise.”

“I know you will, Bobby.” She patted his arm, then turned away and left the room. Bob pocketed the money and went outside.

Emmett was down at the gate to the pasture, holding the reins to both their saddle horses. Bob strode down to meet him. After explaining about the Winchesters, Bob had Emmett take the two rifles up to the house and put them in the front closet while he climbed up into the saddle and waited.

When Emmett had returned and mounted, they opened the gate and went in to get the herd. It was still a long ride to Columbus.

August 4, 1890

It was around three in the afternoon when Grat arrived at the Gooseneck Creek celebration. The shade of the trees where he tied his horse was a welcome relief from the burning summer sun, and the sound of children splashing in the river began to lift his spirits. It had been a hard summer for Grat since he had lost his position as a deputy, and he had been forced to depend on odd jobs and the hospitality of friends to survive. This picnic would at least temporarily take him away from his problems, and provide some free food as well.

The picnic had started several hours earlier, and it was now in full swing. Hundreds of people from all the surrounding communities had gathered at the bend in the Verdigris River to share food and have a good time, and there was a lot going on. As he walked over to the main picnic area, Grat saw that sawhorse tables had been set up under the trees, and on them were a variety of bowls and pans from which people were dishing up food onto plates. In a sunbaked open area nearby large fires had been built, and sweating men turned spits that were jammed with huge hunks of beef and whole chickens.

Groups of men and women sat eating, while others strolled about greeting friends or gathered in bunches to share the latest gossip. Children chased each other around the tables and trees, occasionally stopping to gobble down some food before returning to their games. Grat waved and spoke to several people he recognized, but some of them only nodded to him in acknowledgement, while others pointedly turned their backs on him. Grat normally did not care what people thought of him, but this community ostracism was starting to get to him.

When Grat saw Jon and Zue Mitchell, his disposition immediately improved. Here, at last, were some people who would not shun him.

"Hey, John, Zue," Grat said as he walked up to them, holding out his hand for John to shake. "How you been?"

"Pretty good, Grat," John said with a welcome smile. "How about yourself?"

"Could be better," Grat said, also smiling, "but I ain't complaining. You all enjoying the picnic?"

"We certainly are," Zue said with what seemed to be a forced smile. Grat saw her eyes flicker from side to side as if she were checking to see who was watching them. "Did you just get here?"

"Yep," Grat said, brushing some dust from his clothes. "Rode in from Tulsa a few minutes ago. You been here long?"

"We got here before noon," John said. "Little John couldn't hardly keep his britches on, he was so excited about it. He's over swimming in the river with the Ravelle kids right now."

"You gonna stay all night?" Grat asked. The picnic had been planned to last until breakfast the next morning, for those who so desired.

"No," Zue said firmly, shaking her head, "we'll have to leave before dark. Little John's got to get his sleep, and Big John here has work to do tomorrow." John's pained expression told Grat that if it were up to him, they would stay much later.

"That's too bad," Grat said. He stretched his neck to look around the area. "You haven't seen Bob and Emmett here, have you?"

"Not yet," John said, also looking around, "but they ought to be here soon."

"Oh, yeah?"

"They were at the house the other day," Zue explained. "Said they'd be here at the picnic. They left their rifles at the house, so if they don't come here, I'm sure they'll come there."

"Are you going to stay all night here at the picnic?" John asked.

"Don't know," Grat said, rubbing his chin. "I kind of want to talk to my brothers."

"Well, if you don't run into them here," John said, "why don't you just come over to our house and spend the night. They're bound to show up there some time."

"Aw, I don't want to put you out any," Grat politely demurred. He could see the negative looks that Zue was throwing at her husband, who was totally oblivious to them.

"You won't put us out," John assured him. "Just be quiet if you come in late."

"We'll see. I appreciate the offer, John."

"You better go get you some of the food before it's all gone," Zue told Grat. Although she said it with a smile, Grat sensed that it was almost an order, intended to get rid of him. He took the hint, and wandered over to the tables to get a plate.

A half hour later, after Grat had polished off a chicken breast, a thick slice of roasted beef, and several helpings of baked beans and potato salad, he was approached by two men he recognized. One was Jess Heald, a cowboy Grat had often played cards with, and F. R. Burnett, who had occasionally worked as a guard for various deputy marshals in the area.

They greeted each other jovially, vigorously shaking hands and jokingly arguing about how long it had been since they last saw each other. Heald reached into his pocket and pulled out some coins, carefully counting out several before handing them to Grat.

"Here's that two-fifty I owe you," he said. "Don't want you thinkin' I'm a welcher."

"Hell, Jesse," Grat grinned, "I knew you'd pay me. Otherwise I'd have beat it out of you."

"Sure," Heald chuckled, "you and who else?" They all laughed at this witty exchange.

"Say," Grat said, "you all seen Bob and Emmett lately?"

Burnett closed one eye and appeared to think hard about the question. "Not for several weeks," he finally said, pulling on his ear lobe.

"Me neither," Heald said. "What happened? Them boys run away from home again?"

Grat ignored the attempt at humor. "My cousin said they were supposed to be here at the picnic. I need to talk to them about something."

"Ain't seen 'em today," Burnett assured Grat, "but if I do, I'll tell 'em you're looking for 'em."

"Me, too," Heald said, nodding.

"Thanks," Grat said, looking over Burnett's shoulder at what was being brought in by a recent arrival. "I think I'll go have a piece of that pie. You boys take care, now."

By nine that evening Bob and Emmett had still not shown up, and Grat had grown tired of pretending not to notice how many people were ignoring him. Despite the quiet arrival of a wagon loaded with beer and whiskey, Grat mounted up and took a slow ride over to the Mitchell's house. All the lamps were extinguished when he arrived, so Grat led his horse into the stable, took off the saddle, and made a bed for himself in the hay. After eating so much food at the picnic, he had no trouble going to sleep.

The sun had been up for almost two hours when Bob and Emmett crossed the railroad tracks at Lenapah Station. Tired and hung over, the two young men were both slumped over in their saddles, and Bob felt each time his horse's hooves hit the ground as if it were a whack on his head with a wooden ruler. It had been late in the evening when they had made it to the Gooseneck Creek celebration, but they had made up for it by consuming as much food and drink as they could during the seemingly short night. After a cold breakfast of left-overs, they had left just as the sun topped the trees.

The sale of the stolen horses had not gone exactly as planned. They had arrived in Columbus on Friday Afternoon, but had been unable to locate W. W. Scott, the man to whom they hoped to make the sale. He had gone to Baxter Springs, where his home was, and would not return to Columbus before Saturday. After a nervous night camped outside of town, Bob and Emmett had brought the horses in to the stockyards the next morning, where they had to fend off curious questions about the various brands on their stock.

Finally, around noon, Scott showed up and began looking over the herd. His initial offer to Bab was way below market value, and Bob knew he should haggle with the man to get a more reasonable price. He made a feeble demand for more money, but when Scott suggested that Bob might try another buyer, Bob caved in and accepted the original amount. They had been herding thirty head of stolen horses for three days, and Bob just wanted to be rid of them and on his way, before someone called the law.

Expecting the $367.50 in cash, Bob was dismayed to be handed a check instead. Explaining that he would certainly never carry that much money in cash, Scott shrugged off Bob's pleas, telling him to take it or leave it. With no other option immediately apparent to him, Bob took the check, only to find that the Columbus bank it was drawn on was closed, and would not reopen until Monday.

With only the five dollars Bob had borrowed from Zue to sustain them, he and Emmett camped outside of town, laying low until Monday morning rolled around. At the bank an overly cautious teller delayed them by sending a messenger to Scott to confirm the validity of the check, which Bob had already counter-signed. Frustrated and angered by the delays, Bob took the money that was finally presented and went to the nearest saloon to buy drinks. Emmett followed him quietly, and after Bob had become a little more mellow, he talked his older brother into buying a good lunch at a restaurant.

With money in his pocket, and food and drink in his stomach, Bob became much more cheerful, and with high spirits they begun the ride back to Indian Territory. The late start delayed their arrival at the picnic, but the successful completion of their latest crime had made everything else seem unimportant.

At Lenapah Station the two boys turned south, the morning air gradually clearing Bob's head of the fuzziness left over from the liquor he had drunk at the picnic. It was going to be another hot one, and Bob shrugged out of his suit coat, draping it across the pack tied to the saddle behind him. As Bob turned his head forward again, he saw another rider coming up the road towards them. Emmett, removing his coat in imitation of his brother, had not yet noticed the other man.

With a sudden tightness in his chest, Bob recognized the approaching rider as Sam Wycoff, the deputy marshal at Lenapah. Bob hissed at Emmett, warning his with his eyes about the coming encounter. Bob had not talked to Wycoff for several months, and he was unsure what kind of reception Wycoff would give them. Assuming a casualness he did not really possess, Bob rode on as if nothing were out of the ordinary.

"Morning, Sam," Bob called cheerily as he brought his mount to a stop a few feet away,

“Morning, Bob,” Wycoff replied as he halted his own mount. “Emmett,” he added with a nod in the younger Dalton’s direction. “What are you all up to these days?”

“Not much,” Bob answered. “How about you?”

“Oh, you know,” Wycoff said, taking off his hat. “The usual—serving subpoenas and chasing whiskey peddlers.” With a handkerchief he wiped off his forehead, then ran the cloth around the inside brim of his hat. “Where you been? I haven’t seen you lately.”

“Up in Kansas,” Bob replied, vaguely but honestly. “We’re headed down to the Mitchell place now.”

“Yeah?” Wycoff replaced his hat on his head and picked up the reins. “Well, say hi to John for me, okay?” He urged his horse forward, continuing on toward Lenapah.

“Sure thing, Sam. See ya.” Bob jerked his head at Emmett, and both spurred their mounts into motion as well. Bob felt a sense of reprieve wash over him as the distance between him and the deputy began to widen. He was finding that being a criminal was even more tense and exciting than being a deputy marshal had been.

Grat was sitting on the front porch when Bob and Emmett rode up to the Mitchell’s house. As they came within a few yards of the house and reined in their horses, Grat stood and stepped off the porch toward them, his frown even darker than usual. Ignoring Emmett’s cheerful greeting, Grat strode over to Bob, who had just dismounted and stood waiting by his horse. His thin mustache was twitching and his eyes glared with anger as he rapidly switched his gaze between Bob and the ordinary-looking bay animal he had been riding.

“Where’s the big bay we got from Dad?” Grat demanded, tilting his head back to look up at his taller brother with narrowed eyes.

Bob shrugged innocently as he looked over Grat’s shoulder at the open door of the house, through which he could see John and Zue Mitchell pretending not to listen to the confrontation.

“What do you mean?” Bob temporized.

"You know damn well what I mean," Grat insisted belligerently. "Where's my horse?"

Bob assumed an apologetic expression with downcast eyes. "He ran off."

"Ran off?" Grat exclaimed.

"Yeah. I, uh, I had him staked out, you know, and, well, somehow he got loose and took off. I'm real sorry, Grat." Bob hated lying to his brother, but he was sure it was better than the truth in this instance. He had, in fact, sold the horse several weeks ago, along with other horses that he and Emmett had stolen. The buyer had insisted that the beautiful bay horse be part of the deal, or he would not take any of the animals. Desperate to finish the sale and get back to the territory, Bob had reluctantly agreed. Since he had not told Grat about his and Emmett's new occupation, he had to make up a story to account for the horse's loss.

"Why didn't you keep an eye on him?" Grat asked, lightly pounding on his gunbelt with a closed fist.

"Bill McElhanie was supposed to be watching him," Bob said, "but he had to go to town for something."

"McElhanie? That idiot?" Grat snorted in disgust. "He probably stole the damn horse himself. You know he's a lying thief."

"I don't think so, Grat. I'm pretty sure the horse just pulled up the stake and wandered off." As he said this, Bob again looked toward the house, and Grat, noticing the gesture, looked back as well. Seeing the Mitchells trying to look busy at something else, Grat grabbed Bob's elbow and pulled him toward the stable.

"Let's get these horses taken care of," Grat said, louder than was necessary. Their conversation temporarily halted, the three Dalton brothers walked across the yard and down the gradual slope to the stable. Not until they were in the building and out of earshot of the Mitchells did they resume their talk.

"I can't believe you lost my horse," Grat said as Bob removed the saddle and bridle from his mount.

"It was *our* horse, Grat," Bob corrected him. Dad left him to all of us."

"Yeah, but *you* had to ride him back from Coffeyville, and *you* had to take care of him, and now he's gone."

"I said I'm sorry."

"Sorry, hell! Fat lot of good that does."

"What do you want me to do, Grat? The horse is gone." Bob almost believed his own lie now, and was getting irritated that Grat wouldn't let the matter drop. Emmett stayed out of the discussion entirely, concentrating on getting food and water for his horse and for Bob's.

"I was going to sell that horse and get us some money," Grat explained, on the verge of whining. "I'm tired of being broke."

"We've got a little money," Bob said cautiously. "I could let you have some of it. Sort of pay you for your share of the horse I lost."

"Where'd you get any money?" Grat asked, his curious tone tinged with suspicion.

"Me and Emmet drove some horses to Kansas for this guy. He paid us sixty dollars." Bob reached into his pants pocket and rummaged around, then pulled out a few bills, hoping that in doing so he would not reveal that he in fact had much more than sixty in his pants. As he straightened the crumpled bills, he saw that he had brought out two tens and a five.

"Here. You take this twenty dollars. I owe Zue five dollars, so I got to give this to her, but you can have the rest." Bob held his hand out to Grat, offering him the two tens. Grat shook his head.

"Aw, I can't take your last money, Bobby. You'll need it as much as me."

Bob kept his hand extended. "That's okay, Emmett will loan me some of his share. Go ahead, take it."

"Naw, it just wouldn't be right."

“Well how about this, then,” Bob said, passing one of the tens to his other hand. “You take ten, and I’ll keep ten. We’ll be even.”

Grat chewed on his lower lip a moment as he considered the offer, then nodded and took the money. “Thanks,” he said gruffly.

“I better go pay Zue back while I’m thinking about it,” Bob said, ending the discussion. Without looking back he walked out of the stable into the morning sunlight and strolled up to the house.

Bob found Zue in the kitchen washing dishes, and presented the five dollar bill to her with sincere expressions of gratitude. He followed her into the parlor as she replaced the money in her silver pitcher, still thanking her for both the loan and her hospitality. She accepted the money and thanks graciously, but insisted she had lots of work to do, getting their dinner ready.

When Bob went back to the stable, Grat and Emmett were both perched on the top rail of one of the stalls, the heels of their boots hooked on a lower rail to steady them. Bob noted to himself, not for the first time, how much they looked alike. Even though Grat was ten years older than Emmett, he still looked fairly young, and Emmett, with his fast-growing heavy beard, looked more than his nineteen years. It was mainly Grat’s narrow, black-dyed mustache and prominent ears that distinguished the two.

Bob told the other two that Zue was fixing them dinner, and suggested they go into the house and relax. Grat, bored and open to suggestions, agreed, but Emmett said he would stay with the horses and maybe take a little nap. He was still feeling the after-effects of the picnic celebration.

While Bob went into the parlor and made himself comfortable on the horse-hair couch, Grat found Zue out back rinsing out some clothes and asked if she could wash his shirt for him while she was at it. With a sigh she agreed, and waited while Grat went back inside to take it off, replacing his suit jacket over his bare chest for the sake of decorum.

When Grat returned to the parlor, he took a seat at the upright piano, and after doing a few scales to limber up his fingers, began to play. After a halting but accurate rendition of “Holy, Holy, Holy,”

Grat's favorite hymn, he segued into "Oh, Susanna," which flowed more smoothly.

After the final bar, Grat rotated around on the piano stool and looked at Bob with brotherly affection. "Want to accompany me on something?" he asked.

"With what?" Bob said, his tone indicating he was not opposed to the idea.

"I got a harp out in my saddle bags. I'll be right back." Grat hurried out of the room, brushing by Little John, who had come to stand in the door to the parlor and listen to the music. While Grat was gone, Bob talked to the boy, enthralling him with the story of Charley Montgomery.

Grat tossed Bob the harmonica when he returned, and soon they were playing together, first a lively jig, and then another hymn. After a few minutes, however, they had exhausted their repertoire, so they wandered down to the stable to see what Emmett was doing.

It was after noon when dinner was finally ready, and the three Dalton boys ate like it was their last meal. Grat took his clean shirt, still damp despite hanging for two hours in the hot August sun, and went into the parlor alone to put it on. Then, again expressing their gratitude, they said good-bye to the Mitchells and rode out, headed south for Tulsa. Later, in court, John and Zue Mitchell would recall this visit in vivid detail.

Friday, September 5, 1890

"Oh, shit!" Bob moaned, reining in his horse abruptly. The twenty head of horses behind him, trailed by Emmett and Bill McElhanie, slowed to a stop around him, milling about in confusion. It was late morning, and they had just reached the outskirts of Baxter Springs, Kansas, intending to skirt the train station to go to the stockyards.

"What is it?" Emmett asked as he rode up beside Bob. McElhanie, with a puzzled look, came up on the opposite side.

"Over there at the depot," Bob said, nodding in that direction. "Frank Musgrove and Clem Rogers."

"So?" McElhanie asked.

"That's Scott they're talking to. By now they probably know we stole their horses." No sooner had Bob spoken these words than he saw the three men turn to look directly at them. With a shout Musgrove raised his arm and pointed, while Rogers looked around anxiously, as if seeking assistance.

"Boys," Bob said ominously as he slowly turned his horse back toward Indian Territory, "I think it's time to leave."

"What about the horses?" McElhanie asked.

"Leave 'em," Bob advised, "unless you want to stay and explain where you got 'em." By now he and Emmett were both pushing south, keeping their horses to a walk to avoid drawing any more attention to themselves than there already was. The stolen horses, no longer controlled, began to scatter and graze. McElhanie looked at the horses longingly, then looked back at the ruckus at the depot, and finally made a decision. With a shouted "Hyah!" he spurred his horse into a gallop toward the west.

Risking a glance back over his shoulder, Bob saw men running and saddling horses near the depot, with Rogers and Musgrave waving their arms and gesturing toward the Daltons.

"Come on, Emmett," he said grimly, "they're getting up a posse." He spurred his mount into a gallop, with Emmett close behind him, and together they raced down the road to Indian Territory. Their only chance was to out-distance the posse and hide out in the hills they knew so well. Legally, only a deputy U. S. marshal with a warrant could arrest them in the Territory, but citizen posses such as the one currently forming behind them were not always known for following the letter of the law.

The rush of wind and the pounding of the hooves filled their ears as they rushed southward across the countryside. The low hills of the area were heavily wooded in most places, forcing them to stay on the dusty road to make any time. Bob's mind was also racing, as he strove to think of where they could leave the road and lose their pursuers. It had to be someplace where they would not be seen, and where they would leave no noticeable trail.

"Bobby!" Bob heard Emmett yell from behind him, and looked back to see that Emmett was rapidly falling behind. He pulled up and allowed Emmett to catch him, as he anxiously scanned the road behind them.

"What's the matter?" Bob demanded curtly. His heart was pounding and his muscles were as taught as bowstrings.

"My horse is giving out." Bob could see that it was true. The horse was panting and bug-eyed, foamy sweat mottling its coat.

"Hell!" he swore. "Well, we can't stop here. Let's keep moving at a slower pace while I try to think of something." Keeping the horses as a trot, the two continued their escape, as Bob furiously considered and dismissed various alternate plans of action. There was still no sign of the posse behind them, but Bob knew its arrival was inevitable.

A few minutes later they came out of the woods through which they had been riding, as the road began to wind across a couple miles of open country, gently rolling hills carpeted with yellow and brown prairie grass. As they crested one of the hills, Bob saw a man driving a wagon toward them with two fine horses in the harness.

"There's our answer," he told Emmett as they rode up to meet the wagon. Bob held up a hand to the man, indicating he would like the man to stop and talk for a moment. He was an older man in overalls and a straw hat, and he smiled as he pulled his team to a stop next to Bob.

"Mornin'," he said genially.

"Morning, sir," Bob said politely. "I was wondering if maybe you could do us a favor."

"If I can." The old man appraised Emmett's horse. "Son, that horse needs a rest."

"That's what I want to ask you about. How about we trade you that horse for one of your team. He's a fine horse when he's rested, worth more than either of yours."

"Not my horses," the old man explained. "They belong to Mr. Moore, lives in that house over there." He gestured toward a house about two hundred yards off to their southwest. "You'd have to ask him about any tradin'."

"Bobby!" Emmett yelped with alarm. Bob turned and saw a group of riders come out of the woods about a mile behind them, clouds of dust billowing behind them as they galloped. They were clearly on a mission.

Bob drew his pistol and pointed it at the old man on the wagon. "Unhitch that horse. Now!" Emmett jumped down to help, and Bob kept his gun in his hand as he kept glancing back at the approaching riders, gauging how much time they had. "Hurry!" he admonished them.

There were a couple puffs of smoke at the front of the posse, and a split second later Bob heard the report of the guns. Although the range was still too great, they had opened fire on the Daltons, confirming Bob's belief that they would show no concern for the niceties of the law.

Finally the wagon horse was free of its traces, retaining only its bridle and horse collar. Emmett pulled the animal over next to his own winded mount and reached for the saddle hitch.

"Leave it!" Bob said in a strained, high pitched voice. "We haven't got time. Just get your rifle."

Following Bob's orders, Emmett pulled the Winchester from its scabbard and leaped onto the back of the wagon horse, clutching the horse collar for support. Digging his heels into the steed's flanks, Emmett urged the animal into a gallop. With one last look behind him, Bob holstered his pistol and lit out after Emmett. As far as Bob was concerned, this was cutting things entirely too close.

Two hours later, as they crossed the Katy railroad tracks near the town of Bluejacket, Cherokee Nation, Bob finally allowed his muscles to relax a little. They had outrun the posse, and it should be a couple days before writs were issued and deputy marshals alerted to look for them. The chase had been thrilling, and though he would never admit it to Emmett, he had in some way enjoyed the excitement and danger.

“They almost got us, Bobby,” Emmett said, almost in reproach.

“But they didn’t,” Bob noted, “and that’s what counts.”

“What if they had? We’d be in jail now.”

“Yeah, but we’re not. But I know what you mean. It’s getting too dangerous around here. Maybe we ought to go somewhere else, try something different.”

“Like where?”

“Oh, I don’t know. I’ll think of something.”

Author's Notes

Chapter 5

Bob's leaving the marshals service and initial foray into horse theft was described in a recap of the Dalton's career published in the May 8, 1891, issue of the Fort Smith *Elevator*. The theft by the Daltons of the Osage chief's mules and other horses was mentioned in the August 7, 1890 issue of the Vinita *Indian Chieftain*.

Hearings were held in September 1890 regarding the Dalton's activities in the previous two months. Testimony was taken from Clem Rogers, John and Zue Mitchell, Rhoda Rogers, F. R. Burnett, and S. T. Wycoff, who described in detail their encounters with the three brothers during this period. This testimony, along with related telegrams, writs, and other official documents, is on file at the National Archives in Fort Worth, Texas.

Bob and Emmett's escape from Baxter Springs was reported in the September 11, 1890, issue of the Vinita *Indian Chieftain*, as well as in the above-mentioned issue of the Fort Smith newspaper.

An interesting historical footnote is the fact that Clem Rogers, who would take a major part in seeking the arrest of the Daltons, was the father of the famous humorist Will Rogers, who was eleven years old at the time.

CHAPTER 6

Saturday, September 6, 1890

The Osage Hills, between Bartlesville and Pawhuska, were a rugged and heavily forested area criss-crossed by a maze of narrow gullies and rocky ravines that made them an ideal place to get lost. That was Bob's intention: to go where no one would find them.

The thick canopy of leaves overhead blocked out all the direct sunlight, making it difficult to judge how high the sun was, but Bob knew it had to be getting late in the day. It had been a long hard ride from Bluejacket, since they had been forced to stay off the main roads and circle around populated areas. Now, within the relative safety of the Hills, Bob could finally allow himself to relax a little, although he felt like he would fall asleep right there in the saddle if he relaxed too much. When he occasionally looked back at Emmett, whose stolen horse was wearily following Bob's, he saw Emmett's head droop until his chin touched his chest, then jerk back up, only to start falling again.

They were following a dry creek bed, the horses' metal shoes echoing loudly on the smooth round stones, when Bob saw the familiar fallen tree trunk. He allowed his horse to stop, its head hanging low; Emmett's horse, as tired as its rider, almost bumped into Bob's.

"What?" Emmet said groggily, looking around in bleary alarm.

"Sh!" Bob ordered. Then he took a deep breath and whistled, but his lips were so dry it came out as only a high-pitched whoosh. Running his tongue around his lips, he tried again, and this time managed a fair imitation of the two-note call of a quail. The birds were called bob-whites around there, since their call sounded as if they were trying to say the name Bob White. Bob gave the whistle twice more, and then waited alertly. In a moment he heard two hoots, a poor rendition of an owl's cry, and smiled in recognition.

"He's here," Bob said to Emmett. "Come on."

A few feet farther up the creek bed they turned down a narrow but very deep ravine. Vines and branches hung so low that Bob and Emmett had to brush them aside to make their way along. Finally the ravine widened and they found themselves in an almost circular clearing with steep banks of earth and stone marking its perimeter. Three unsaddled horses grazed near the left side of the natural amphitheater, and straight across from where they had entered a huge slab of auburn rock jutted out over a dark grotto. Just under the edge of the overhang a small campfire was smoking, tended by a wiry young man without a hat. Farther back, lounging against a rock but keeping a wary eye on the new arrivals, was another man, this one with a large nose and a thick black mustache. Neither man rose to come meet them.

Bob was almost to the center of the clearing when he heard rustling to his right as someone pushed carelessly through the underbrush.

"Glad you could make it," McElhanie said as he half slid and half stumbled down the slope of the surrounding bank and out onto the level floor of the clearing. In his left hand was his Winchester. "We was beginning to think you'd been caught."

"Damn near," Bob admitted, grinning at his friend. "How the hell did you get here so quick?" With slow movements to ease his aching muscles, Bob climbed down from his horse to shake Will's hand.

"Took a short cut," McElhanie said, his wide smile revealing missing teeth. "Wake up, Emmett," he joked, before turning back to Bob with a more serious expression. "Come on, I want you to meet a couple fellas."

The two strangers stood up and cautiously shook Bob's and Emmett's hands as McElhanie introduced them. The wiry young man who had been tending the fire was Charley Bryant. It was readily apparent why he was nicknamed "Blackface Charley"—his cheeks and forehead were speckled with hundreds of black dots of various sizes, the result of an accident with gunpowder that blew up in his face. Bob sympathized, having had powder burns on his own face once.

The other man, a tall, darkly handsome cowboy with an air of self-assurance, was introduced as George Newcomb, the Slaughter Kid. McElhanie explained that the seemingly ferocious nickname was actually a result of Newcomb's once having apprenticed to Sheriff John Slaughter in Arizona. Now, however, he was more commonly called "Bitter Creek," due to his frequent singing of a popular song whose main refrain was "I'm a lone wolf from Bitter Creek, and tonight is my night to howl!"

Despite McElhanie's attempts at establishing an immediate camaraderie, Newcomb and Bryant remained aloof at first. It had only been a few months earlier that Bob and Emmett had been on the other side of the law, and trust would take time. For now they would let the Daltons do all the talking, while they carefully evaluated these new criminals to ensure they were what they claimed.

Bryant had been preparing supper when Bob and Emmett showed up, and he invited them to share, albeit with little enthusiasm. The Daltons had had little opportunity to eat on their flight from Baxter Springs, and immediately dug in to the simple meal with gratitude. As they ate the greasy rabbit meat and dug the centers out of charred baked potatoes, the men soon began to talk with more familiarity, initially limiting the conversation to impersonal topics such as politics and weather.

Later, as the sky darkened and the mosquitoes came out, Bob told the others an embellished account of his and Emmett's narrow escape from the posse, and McElhanie bragged about their joint efforts at stealing horses. By the time the stars appeared, Emmett was asleep, but the rest of the men were laughing and telling lies like they had been friends for years.

In the morning, after a breakfast of stale bread and bitter coffee, Bob broached the idea that had occurred to him during the night. In Indian Territory and in Kansas they were all wanted men, so it made sense that they leave the area, preferably to somewhere that was still wild and lawless. Newcomb had told them stories about his days in Arizona and New Mexico, and these had sounded very appealing to Bob. The logical conclusion was that they should all go to New Mexico; they could ride to Silver City, stake claims, and get rich mining silver.

Except for Newcomb, the other young men were enthused about the idea from the beginning. As the only one who had ever actually been to New Mexico, Bitter Creek had a more realistic picture of the difficulties involved and the problems they would encounter, but he was trapped by his own stories. Rather than admit his exaggerations, Newcomb offered a few cautions, then reluctantly agreed to go along, with some minor provisos.

They would need a good stock of provisions for the long and arduous journey, he told them, and he needed to go to Guthrie on the way west. Newcomb had staked a claim there during the Land Rush the year before, and he wanted to stop there long enough to make sure it hadn't been jumped, and to do some minor improvements necessary to meet the requirements of the Homestead Act. Bob readily agreed, because he had his own reasons for going to Guthrie—Eugenia was there.

Monday, September 8, 1890

Having grown bored with Tulsa, Grat had ridden northeast the day before and camped just outside of Claremore. The golden light of the early morning sun was still casting long dark shadows between the buildings as he rode into town, leading the other horse he had gotten from his father's estate. What he wanted most right then was some breakfast, followed by a drink of whiskey, if he could find an illicit source for it.

Despite the early hour, there were several townspeople on the street that morning, and Grat was disturbed to note that some of them reacted to his appearance with alarm. As his horse steadfastly plodded down the dusty street, Grat ran his hands over his face and examined his clothes to try and detect what was causing the stir among the residents. Finding nothing amiss, he shrugged and guided his mount to a halt in front of a restaurant that was already open. As he climbed down and tied his horses to the hitching rack, he heard someone sharply call out his name.

On the wooden sidewalk to his left Grat saw Burril Cox facing him. Cox had his legs spread slightly and his hand on the butt of his pistol; his expression was anxiously solemn.

"Hey, Burril," Grat greeted him neutrally. Cox was a deputy marshal, but Grat had never considered him a friend. Cox was even lazier than Grat, but was always ready to take credit for the accomplishments of others. He had become a deputy, Grat suspected, only so he could brag and sponge off people. Even now he was striking a pose, trying to look braver than he was. Grat finished tying his horses and stepped on the sidewalk toward the door of the restaurant.

"I'm placing you under arrest!" Cox blurted, his voice cracking at the last word.

Grat paused and gave the man an exasperated look. "Arrest? What for?"

"Horse stealin'. Hand me your gun."

Grat opened his jacket to the deputy, saying, "My gun's in my pack, and these are both my horses. What in the hell are you talking about?"

A crowd was starting to gather, and Cox was gaining courage from their support. He swaggered over closer to Grat, searching the surrounding faces for looks of admiration.

"You and your brothers been stealing horses and selling them up in Kansas. We know all about it. Now you just come along to the jail so I can wire the marshal."

Cox held out his arm to Grat, who ignored the gesture, staring into Cox's eyes with a glare that caused him to visibly wilt and lower his arm again.

"You want to show me the writ?" Grat challenged him.

Cox glanced nervously at the people that circled them, seeking assistance. "Don't worry, I'll get one. We already got one on your brothers, and that'll do to hold you until we get another one."

Grat knew Cox was right. He could be held for questioning until a writ had been issued, and the expressions on the faces of the townfolk showed he could expect little sympathy from them. Grat's shoulders slumped with resignation.

"All right, Cox, you dumb son of a bitch," Grat muttered angrily, "but when I find out who's responsible for this, they're going to be real sorry."

"Are you threatenin' us?" Cox said belligerently, including the onlookers with a circular nod.

"Take it however you want," Grat said with disgust, pushing past Cox and walking toward the jail. Members of the crowd scuffled with each other trying to get out of his way, while Cox hastily scampered after him, trying to grab Grat's elbow to show who was in charge, Grat just shook him off.

After locking Grat in the single jail cell, Cox had scurried out, leaving Grat to be stared at by the endless line of young men and boys who paraded by his cell in silent wonder. Grat felt like a lion in a circus wagon, and occasionally would roar at his spectators and watch in amusement as they jumped backwards. He was surprised at how glad he was when Cox finally returned around noon. Cox shooed away the last of the gawkers to make room for two other men who had come with him. Grat recognized them both.

The tall man with an aquiline nose and an expensive suit was Clem Rogers, the wealthy rancher from Oolagah, and Cox treated him with nauseating obsequiousness. The other man, wearing a cheap, badly-fitted suit and looking like a weathered farmer on his monthly visit to town, was deputy marshal W. B. Killian, who worked out of Baxter Springs. Both men came over and looked down at Grat through the bars; Grat was sitting on the cell's cot with his back against the wall. He raised one eyebrow at them, but said nothing.

"Where's your brothers?" Killian asked in the slow cadence of a country hick.

"Damned if I know," Grat answered pleasantly.

"Why'd you take them horses?"

"Didn't," Grat said with a shrug.

"We have witnesses," Rogers intoned, "that say otherwise."

"You have witnesses that are mistaken," Grat corrected him. "Or they're lying."

"I saw Bob and Emmett myself," Rogers said, gripping his lapels. "Are you calling me a liar?"

"Did you see me?"

"No, but they're your brothers."

"That's an interesting legal concept," Grat said, rubbing his chin. "Guilt by blood relationship. I don't remember seeing that in the federal statutes."

"Bein' smart-alecky ain't gonna help none," Killian warned, scratching his crotch.

"He's right," Rogers concurred, his tone now more accommodating. "If you are innocent, as you say, then you could help yourself by telling us where your brothers are. That way we can get this whole thing cleared up."

"I don't think my brothers stole any horses either," Grat explained patiently, "and even if I knew where they were, I sure as hell wouldn't tell you people. Why don't you all just go piss up a rope."

"This is a waste of time," Rogers conceded, turning away from the cell. "Mr. Cox, do you have something to write with?"

"Yes, sir," Cox said, rushing over to the desk to pick up a pencil, then frantically searching the drawers for a piece of paper. When he was finally ready, he looked up at Rogers expectantly.

"Send a telegram to the W. H. H. Clayton Brothers law office in Fort Smith." Rogers paused as Cox scribbled this down. "Tell them, 'Grat, Bob, and Emmett Dalton are stealing horses here by the drove. Grat is here under arrest. Have the writ sent here to W. B. Killian, U. S. Marshal, for the three Daltons,' You got that?"

Cox scratched furiously with the pencil, then looked up again. "Sign your name, sir?" he asked.

"Of course."

As he wrote Rogers' name, Cox made a studiously off-hand suggestion. "You know, maybe they should send the writ to me, since I'm the deputy here in Claremore."

Grat saw the fleeting look of disdain on Rogers' face before he answered. It was obvious that the rancher's opinion of Cox was not much different than Grat's.

"I don't believe that will be necessary, Mr. Cox," Rogers said with a hint of condescension. "Marshal Killian was the original officer involved in this case, and it would be better if he continues to be in charge."

"Yes, sir," Cox replied with disappointment. "I guess I'll go take this over to the telegraph office."

"Yes, thank you," Rogers replied. Reaching into his vest pocket, he pulled out a coin and handed it to Cox. "Here, this should cover the cost of the wire." Cox nodded and left. Grat smiled at Cox's petty theft; official telegrams such as that were charged to the government, so Rogers' money would go directly into Cox's pocket.

With feigned indifference, Grat stretched out on the lumpy cot and placed his hat over his face as if going to sleep. In fact, he had a lot of thinking to do. These people seemed extremely convinced that Bob and Emmet had been stealing horses, and in retrospect, that would go a long way toward explaining their recent behavior. He had only talked to them a couple times in the last few months, and there had been no reason not to accept Bob's account of their erstwhile activities. Now, however, certain oddities took on a new light, and Grat was forced to admit to himself that his two younger brothers had become thieves.

Not only had Bob and Emmett become criminals, they had somehow implicated Grat in their schemes. As a former lawman himself, Grat knew how easy it was to assume that breaking the law ran in the family, especially in their case, since the three Daltons had a long and well-known history of working together. His arrest, therefore, was not unusual, but Grat was relatively confident that his innocence would soon be established. He had seen too many guilty men go free not to believe that the courts were tilted in favor of the defendants, so a truly innocent man, such as himself, should have no problems. Or so he wanted to believe.

The next day Killian came in and put handcuffs and leg shackles on Grat before escorting him to the train station. After a short train ride up the line to Lenapah Station, Grat was taken into the station's waiting room, where the U. S. Commissioner from Claremore had set up an impromptu court to take testimony against Grat. Grat was tremendously surprised when the first witness called was John Mitchell.

Mitchell refused to meet Grat's gaze as he testified, even though nothing he said directly implicated Grat in any thefts. He told about Bob and Grat coming by after their father died, and about Bob and Emmett stopping there with a herd of horses a couple weeks later. He recounted Grat's appearance at their house after the Gooseneck Bend picnic, and how he waited for Bob and Emmett to arrive. When the testimony ended and Mitchell left the room, Grat felt relieved. So far the prosecutor had only established that Grat had met with his brothers on two occasions, neither of which occurred when there were possibly stolen horses around.

As Grat now expected, the next witness was Zue Mitchell. Her version of events closely paralleled her husband's, but Grat was disheartened by her barely concealed anger. She indirectly accused Grat of stealing the five dollars Bob had repaid her on their last visit, citing the letter Grat had written her as evidence.

When Zue had written Grat about the missing money shortly after they had been at her house, he had been unaware of what she was talking about. At the time he had had no reason to suspect Bob, so he wrote back to her and sympathized with her loss, but denied any involvement in it. Perhaps his suggestion that her son, Little John, might have taken it, had offended her maternal instincts.

Although he was charged with horse theft, and Zue had made no statements that linked him with this crime, the accusations of petty theft from a relative certainly did not help his case any. Grat looked questioningly at his cousin, but she steadfastly refused to return his gaze, leaving no clue as to why she had spoken against him. There was little comfort in the knowledge that she had not specifically accused him of stealing horses, nor explicitly linked him to any such thefts.

No other witness were called at this time, but a deposition taken earlier from Deputy S. T. Wycoff was introduced into evidence. The sworn statement was read to the commissioner, but it only described a brief encounter between Wycoff and Bob and Emmett the morning after the picnic as they were on their way to the Mitchells'.

Commissioner Wheeler ended the proceedings abruptly, declaring that he found there was sufficient evidence of Grat Dalton's guilt to retain him in custody, and directed that Burril Cox should escort the defendant to Fort Smith immediately. At Fort Smith Grat would be brought before Judge Brizzolara for a further hearing to determine whether he should be held over for trial. Grat glared at Wheeler, who was obviously more concerned about public opinion than justice, and silently cursed his luck. He had almost convinced himself that the charges would be dropped that day when it became clear that there was no evidence linking him to the crimes, but now he was doomed to spend at least a few more days in jail. It was not a pleasant prospect.

Still in cuffs and shackles, Grat stared out the train window at the passing countryside. Beside him Burril Cox rooted through an old leather briefcase, sorting the papers within and occasionally looking up briefly to see if anyone was watching him carry out his important official duties. Even though it was periodically laced with sooty smoke from the engine, the air blowing in through the window felt good to Grat as it provided some welcome coolness. He was also trying to absorb and retain the freshness and freedom it symbolized, knowing he would spend the next few days, at least, in the Fort Smith jail.

"Know what I got in here?" Cox asked tauntingly, jabbing his elbow into Grat's side to get his attention. Grat ignored him. Cox pulled some long light-green ledger pages out of the briefcase and made a show of straightening them. From the corner of his eye, Grat could see it was a letter of some kind.

"It's a letter," Cox confirmed, "that Clem and me got up." Grat noted the unwarranted familiarity Cox expressed, implying that he and Clem Rogers were friends and equals, when Rogers would probably rather eat a live toad than associate with Cox.

"You want to know what it says?" Cox prodded. Grat scratched his mustache and continued to look out the window. Cox needed no encouragement from him. "It's a letter to the United States Attorney, the Honorable William H. Clayton, and it's signed by a hundred and one citizens of Claremore. You ought to read it. It's about you." Cox held it out in front of Grat, who glanced at it, sighed, and slowly raised his hands to grasp it. With a malicious snicker Cox jerked it back away from him.

"I better read it to you," Cox said patronizingly. "Wouldn't want the letter to get dirty or nothin'."

Cox theatrically cleared his throat twice, and then began reading the letter aloud. His rendition was halting and labored as he struggled with unfamiliar words, and he paused at the end of each written line, rather than at commas and periods, giving it a sing-song cadence.

"'We the undersigned citizens of Claremore and vicinity most humbly petition and request of you and the Honorable Court to hold Grat Dalton without bail until his two brothers, Emmett and Robert, can be caught. They have been implicated in the theft of about one hundred head more or less of horses within the last thirty days. From their actions we feel satisfied that Grat Dalton is the chief mover in this affair and lays plans for their movements.

"'We would like for him to be held without bail so as to keep him from communicating with his brothers until further developments as we feel sure that if he is let out on bail that he will jump it. His two brothers have both jumped a $1,000 Bond each this last week to appear in Wichita, Kansas. He has also threatened in case he gets out to kill several parties in this vicinity who took actions in arresting him.' It's signed by a whole bunch of people, but I won't tell you who, 'cause you might try to kill 'em."

Cox waited for some reaction, but Grat returned to watching the passing scenery as he considered the contents of the letter. From what was said, Grat deduced that they had no solid evidence against him, and were in effect holding him hostage in the hopes of smoking out Bob and Emmett. By holding him without bail or communication, the Claremore people hoped that Grat's brothers would either turn themselves in as a show of brotherly affection, or expose themselves in an attempt to break Grat out of jail. Grat knew the chances of either occurrence were small.

Unlike Clem Rogers, Grat was well versed in the law, and knew that he could not be restricted from communicating with his relatives. As for being held without bail, Grat knew this was unlikely in a case of horse theft, especially where the evidence was so shaky. The letter also lost some credibility by claiming that both Bob and Emmett had jumped bail at Wichita, since it was a matter of record that charges against Emmett had been dismissed. Besides, Grat could not legally be held responsible for the actions of his brothers.

It was ironic. Cox's effort to goad Grat and make him miserable had instead had the opposite effect. By knowing how weak was the case against him, Grat felt more confident about the upcoming hearing, and was almost looking forward to the come-uppance his tormentors would get when he was inevitably set free. In the meantime, however, he would have to work on keeping Bob and Emmett out of jail, since their guilt appeared to be a foregone conclusion.

Although Grat was disappointed by his brothers' turning to crime, he was not terribly surprised. Bob had always been reckless and headstrong, and Emmett had become Bob's permanent shadow. While he had never gone as far as Bob and Emmett, Grat himself had not been averse to bending the law on occasion, so he could sympathize to some degree. At any rate, they were his brothers, when all was said and done, and he was obligated to help them all he could.

Bob hesitated before he knocked on the door of the small log cabin. He hoped that Emmett, standing beside him in the dark, could not detect the uncertainty he felt at that moment. It was late, but lamplight still showed through the cracks around the door, and when he finally rapped his knuckles on the rough-hewn boards, he heard the scuffle of a chair being moved inside.

When the door swung open, Bob had to blink at the sudden burst of light. Behind him was the lonely blackness of a prairie night, and in front of him was the welcome brightness of a friendly cabin. He smiled at the thin woman who stood there in the doorway and held out his arms.

"Hi, Mom!" he said.

"Robert!" she exclaimed, giving him a brief hug. Bob stepped into the cabin as his mother greeted Emmett in the same manner. From the other room of the small cabin came some yelps, and in rushed the three youngest Daltons--Leona, Nannie, and Simon—all dressed in their nightclothes. There was much hugging and teasing among the siblings, until finally Mrs. Dalton ordered the younger ones back to bed. She filled some glasses with water for her two sons, and they sat down at the dinner table to talk.

"Do you know about Grat?" Mrs. Dalton asked. From the look on her face, Bob feared that Grat had died.

"What? The last we knew, he was in Tulsa."

"He's been arrested. They took him to Fort Smith, put him in jail."

"What for?" Bob couldn't imagine his brother doing anything that would get him locked up.

"Stealing horses. They say the three of you are in it together."

Bob saw the guilty look flash across Emmett's face, and hoped that his mother had not. He shook his head slowly as if amazed by this news, while he tried to come up with a plausible explanation.

"That's crazy, Mom," Bob said. "We've hardly seen Grat lately. And he wouldn't steal horses."

"That's what he says. He wrote me a letter from Fort Smith. He says they don't have any real evidence on him, so he should get out after the hearing next week."

"That's good," Emmett remarked, nodding with satisfaction.

"Yeah," Bob agreed, "they must have made some kind of mistake."

Mrs. Dalton reached across the table and took Bob's hand as she looked into his eyes with maternal concern. "Robert, he says they're after you and Emmett. He says they have evidence that you stole some horses. Is that the truth?"

Bob looked down at the table top, unable to meet his mother's eyes. "How can you say that, Mom? You know I wouldn't do anything like that."

"Then why do they think you did?"

"I don't know. Wait! I'll bet it's those horses we took to Columbus. Me and Emmett drove some horses up there for a guy, and he had us sell them. They must have been stolen horses, and we didn't know it. That's what it is!" Bob looked up at his mother, trying to gauge her reaction. Inwardly he was very pleased with himself for having skillfully diverted suspicion.

His mother stared at him and Emmett for a moment with a penetrating gaze, but Bob could not tell if she believed him. Finally she patted his hand and got up from the table, going over to the kitchen cabinet to straighten some dishes.

"You missed your trial at Wichita last week," she said with her back to him. Although she spoke in a conversational tone, Bob could hear the underlying accusation.

"I know, Mom, but I had to. They were railroading me. They would have sent me to jail for sure, and I didn't do anything wrong."

"Okay," she said, still not facing them. "But now they're looking for you. There were some marshals out here to the house yesterday. Grat thinks you ought to disappear for a while." She paused, and Bob heard the catch in her voice as she added, "And I think you should, too."

“You want us to go right now, Mom? Bob asked, fearing the answer.

“Uh-huh,” she said in a tiny, strained voice. She noisily put some dishes in the sink, never turning around to face her embarrassed and ashamed sons.

Bob sniffed and looked at the ceiling, then pushed his chair back and stood up, motioning for Emmett to do the same. Putting their hats on, they shuffled outside. Just before Bob closed and latched the front door, he quietly said, “Bye, Mom.” There was no reply.

Friday, September 19, 1890

“The defendant will rise and face the court,” the judge said in the bored tone of someone who had spoken those words countless times before. Having expected this command, Grat had already quietly scooted his chair back from the table, and now he rose to a standing position, his pose neither abject nor defiant. With his head erect, he put on a poker face as he regarded James Brizzolara, a commissioner of the District Court of the United States, in and for the Western District of Arkansas. Since yesterday Brizzolara had been listening to testimony against Grat to determine if there was sufficient evidence to hold him over for trial. Grat was much less sure of the outcome than he had been when the hearing started.

Clem Rogers had been the first witness called, in deference, no doubt, to his political importance, and he had testified at great length. Explaining that he and Frank Musgrove ran their horses in the same pasture, he told how they had gone out to brand colts in August and had discovered several head were missing. Responding to rumors of stolen stock appearing in Kansas, they had traveled to Columbus on September 4, where they were informed that a man named W. W. Scott had bought some horses there and taken them back to Baxter Springs.

On the following day Rogers and Musgrove had gone to Baxter Springs and questioned Scott, and Scott had allowed them to look at his horses, which were located in various barns and pastures in the area. In the next few hours Rogers and Musgrove found several horses with Musgrove's brand, Clem Rogers' missing filly, and a sorrel colt in the brand of Bob Rogers, a black man who lived near Clem. Just after returning to the Baxter Springs train depot, the two ranchers had spotted Bob and Emmett Dalton, along with a man they could not identify, bringing in another herd of stolen horses.

A posse had been formed to chase the escaping thieves, but they had managed to elude the volunteer lawmen. Meanwhile Rogers and Musgrove had tracked down Deputy Marshal Killian and sworn out a complaint against Bob and Emmett. Scott had provided a canceled check made out to Bob Dalton, proving he had bought the horses from him.

The commissioner pressed Rogers about the third man who had been with Bob and Emmett, and Grat had felt a surge of hope and satisfaction when Rogers stated that while he could not identify the man, he would swear that it was not Grat Dalton.

Significantly, W. W. Scott, the horse dealer in Baxter Springs, had not appeared for the hearing, despite the subpoena having been issued. Grat guessed that Scott wanted to avoid any testimony that might incriminate himself as having knowingly purchased stolen property. Grat allowed himself to relax a little at this stage of the proceedings, thinking the worst was over, and sat back to hear the rest of the testimony.

The next to be called was Zue Mitchell, whose testimony was almost identical to what she had given ten days earlier in Lenapah. Under cross examination, she claimed she had not invited Grat back to her house after the Gooseneck Creek picnic, due to the community censure she had experienced as a result of previous visits by the Daltons. Further questioning revealed that she had not specifically told Grat not to come, either, nor had she mentioned to him the prejudice of the community. Although his feelings were hurt by his cousin's lack of whole-hearted support, Grat was still pleased that she had said nothing new that linked him to any theft of horses.

Zue's husband, John, followed her to the stand, and basically repeated his earlier statements. As it was getting late in the day, the hearing was continued before John's testimony was complete. When court reconvened the next morning he answered a few more questions, but for the most part claimed ignorance, since he had not been present when many of the activities reported by his wife had occurred.

Two more witnesses were called, and the first of the two left Grat shaking his head in bafflement. Rhoda Rogers was a young black woman that Grat had never seen before, and she testified that Bob and his brother had come to her house for dinner one day in July. Bob had done all the talking, and he had asked to see her husband's branding iron, after commenting on some of her husband's horses he had seen earlier. When Rhoda had told Bob she couldn't change a five dollar bill, Bob had given her a quarter, half of what they owed her for the dinner, and promised to pay her husband the rest the next day. He had not done so, and later the Rogers family noticed that eight head of their horses were missing.

What was most devastating for Grat was Rhoda's statement that Grat was the man accompanying Bob that day. At first she seemed vague about the identification, since she had never seen Bob's partner before, and Bob had never spoken his name, but under subsequent questioning she firmed up her conviction and swore that Grat was the man. Grat knew it had to have been Emmett, but he had no way to prove it unless Emmett were there with him for comparison, and that would only get Emmett thrown in jail instead of Grat. He and Emmett bore a close family resemblance, more so than any of the other Dalton siblings, despite their ten year difference in ages. Rhoda's confusing them, after seeing one of them two months after seeing the other, was understandable. Unfortunately, it meant that the weight of evidence against Grat was growing.

The last to testify was F. R. Burnett, and his statement only concerned what had happened at the Gooseneck Creek picnic. What he had to say only confirmed that Grat had been looking for his brothers that day, and otherwise was irrelevant. Grat interpreted this lack of bad news as encouraging, and for a few moments convinced himself that he would soon be released. Now, however, as he stood and awaited Jude Brizzolara's ruling, he felt his confidence drain out of him like water out of a split bucket. Forcing himself to remain steady, he listened as the judge began to speak.

"Grat Dalton, the court finds that the foregoing evidence satisfies me the offense with which you are charged has been committed, and there is probably cause to believe that you are guilty thereof. In light of your previous record of service to this court, I will not comply with the request of the citizens of Claremore to deny you bail. That bail is set at one thousand dollars, and you are ordered to appear at the United States Court Room here at Fort Smith on the fifteenth day of October, 1890. Do you have sufficient funds for your bail, or someone who will post bond for you?"

"No, sir," Grat said miserably, his worst fears realized.

"Then the deputy will escort you back to jail to wait until your trial. Court is adjourned."

Grat barely noticed the scuffling and murmuring as people filed out of the court room, and went along meekly when Cox took him by the elbow and guided him back to jail. Later, in his cell, his depression slowly transformed into anger—anger at the witnesses who had testified against him, anger at Cox, the man who had arrested him, anger at the judge who had jailed him, and anger at himself for getting into such a mess. Grat knew it was illogical, but for some strange reason he felt no resentment toward his brothers, even though they were the true cause of his predicament. As he lay on his cot and stared at the ceiling, he wondered what they were doing now.

Tuesday, September 23, 1890

It was just a small town, with one hotel, a few stores and saloons, and a train depot, but to Emmett it was like an oasis in the desert. They had been riding for two weeks, most of it across a flat barren prairie under a blistering sun. The last couple days the terrain had risen into low hills and then actual mountains, with scrub oak and manzanita bushes interspersed with cholla cactus, and cottonwood trees along the stream beds. Finally they had arrived at this outpost of civilization. Emmett didn't know if this was the fabled Silver City that they had set out for, and at this point he didn't even care. As long as he could get a bath, a good meal, and a soft bed, it could be the gateway to Hell and he wouldn't mind a bit.

New Mexico, or at least this part of the territory, was not quite what Emmett had expected. The altitude made the air thinner, but also fresher and crisper than he was used to. The orange sun setting over the distant mountains gave the town's natural colors of brown and tan a more reddish tint, but the stretching shadows at least promised relief from the incessant baking heat. While most of the buildings were of the wood frame construction common throughout the West, others were flat-roofed adobe structures with small windows and protruding roof beams.

Emmett scratched his chest and stomach, uncomfortably aware of the sweat-caked dirt that coated his entire body, then smiled to himself as he was able to pick out the word "Baths" on the side of the hotel as they rode down the wide main street.

"There's the livery stable," Bob announced, nodding toward a weathered barn to the left. "We'll get the horses taken care of, then check into the hotel." No one argued, as all had tacitly agreed to Bob's leadership on the long ride out. Emmett would have preferred to have dinner and a bath first, but he admitted to himself that Bob was right, as usual. They depended on the horses, and it was proper to take care of them first.

A few minutes later, as the five men walked across the street from the stable to the hotel, Emmett looked around in wonder at the foreign sights of the town. In addition to the pueblo-style buildings of adobe, there was a Spanish mission church down the road with lofty architecture unlike any he had seen before. The people were different, too. More than half the population appeared to be Mexican, with dark eyes and strange, decorated clothing. There were also Chinese and Indians, although these Indians looked different than those of the Five Civilized Tribes Emmett had known back in Indian Territory.

The hotel was large, and it had obviously seen better times. Now it was getting a little seedy, but the remnants of its former glory were still enough to impress Emmett, after staring at sand and sagebrush for so long. Bob checked himself and Emmett into a single room; Newcomb, Bryant, and McElhanie pooled their money to pay for another. After dropping off their bedrolls and packs in their rooms, all five returned downstairs and took seats at a large table in the dining room.

A short round Mexican woman took their orders, and Emmett was charmed by her pleasant accent. As soon as she left to turn in their orders to the cook, a stranger came over and sat down at the table with them.

"You fellows mind if I join you," he asked jovially, smiling and nodding to each of them. He was a large older man, tending toward fat, with pomaded hair brushed straight back and a brown suit that was showing signs of age.

"Help yourself," Bob answered for the group.

"Name's Canty, Ben Canty," the stranger said, and looked at the others expectantly.

"George Newcomb," Bitter Creek introduced himself, half rising from the chair to shake Canty's hand. Bryant and McElhanie quickly followed suit. Emmett was surprised when Bob, who had constantly drummed into Emmett the need to maintain security, stood up to reach across the table.

"I'm Bob Dalton, and this here's my brother Emmett."

Emmett leaned forward and gave Canty a perfunctory shake as well.

"Dalton, huh?" Canty said curiously, and Emmett felt a low surge of fear, thinking this man already knew of their status as wanted men. "Where you boys from?"

"Missouri," Bob answered, more or less truthfully, since both of them had been born in that state before moving to Kansas.

"Is that right? Well, I'm from Missouri, too. I thought that name sounded familiar. What's your Daddy's name?"

"Lewis Dalton," Bob answered, then lowered his voice and eyes. "He passed away two months ago."

"Oh, that's a shame. I knew a Lewis Dalton once. Good old boy. Used to do something, what was it?" Canty scratched his sideburn and squinted at the ceiling as if trying to remember.

"He raced horses a lot," Emmett said helpfully.

"That's right," Canty said, shaking his finger at Bob and Emmett. "Now I remember. Used to see him all the time down at the race track. And you say he's passed on. Terrible thing. Still, imagine meeting his boys here in this God-forsaken place."

The waitress brought over the drinks the boys had ordered and placed them in front of each.

"Ma'am," Bob said to here, "would you bring Mr. Canty here a drink, too. It's on me."

"Oh, I couldn't," Canty protested weakly.

"Please," Bob encouraged him.

"Well, all right, I'll have a whiskey. But you'll have to let me buy a round later." The woman looked at Canty and sighed, then went to get his drink. She seemed to know Canty well, Emmett noticed, but concluded that was to be expected in such a small town.

"So what are you boys doing way out here?" Canty asked, glancing at the bar to watch the waitress's progress.

"Going to Silver City," McElhanie piped up, having already downed his entire drink.

"See if we can't make some money," Bob continued for him. "Maybe mine some of that silver."

"You don't want to do that," Canty said. He paused as the waitress brought him his drink, taking the glass from her hand and pouring half of it down his throat. "Ahh! Just what the doctor ordered."

"Why not?" McElhanie prompted, since Canty had apparently forgotten what he had been saying.

"Why not?" Canty repeated, directing most of his attention to Bob. "Because there's no more silver there, that's why not. Leastways, not enough to worry about. See, that's the trouble with gold and silver strikes. By the time you hear about them, all the good stuff is gone. Trust me, I've seen it happen before. No, you boys'd be wasting your time going to Silver City."

Emmett saw a look pass between Newcomb and Bob, but wasn't sure what it meant. Canty finished his drink and asked, "So what did you boys do before you came out here to New Mexico?"

"We were deputy marshals," Bob answered.

"Well, isn't that a coincidence!" Cant said a little too loudly. "I was the deputy marshal here for a long time. I reckon we got a hell of a lot in common. Son of a bitch. We all used to be marshals."

The waitress brought steaming plates of food over to the table and set them in front of the boys. Newcomb lifted his glass to show her it was empty, then said "Charley?" Bryant held his empty glass up as well, nodding, and the others did the same, including Canty. As the waitress left to get more drinks, Canty turned to Newcomb and slapped him on the shoulder.

"Thanks, George. I'll get the next one."

Emmett dug into his food with both hands, and was so intent on his eating that he barely noticed when the second round of drinks was brought, and he paid scant attention to the conversation that followed. He did notice that Ben Canty did most of the talking, but this seemed reasonable, since he was the only one who was not stuffing food in his mouth. Because of the warm glow brought on by the whiskey and food, Emmett also gave little heed to the fact that Charley Bryant bought the next round. While Emmett was wiping the last bit of gravy from his plate with a chunk of bread, Canty reached into his vest and pulled out a large gold watch. It was a beautiful watch on a gold chain, and with the press of a button Canty opened the flip-top cover that was embossed with the figure of a leaping stag. Emmett admired it enviously.

"Look at the time," Canty said. He snapped the watch closed and slipped it back into his pocket. "Well, boys, I've got things I have to do. Are you going to be around?"

“We might stay here a couple days and rest up,” Bob said judiciously. Canty pushed his chair back and stood up.

“Then maybe I’ll see you tomorrow. I could show you around, give you the nickel tour. I have lots of friends here, maybe I can find you a better opportunity than Silver City.”

“Thank you, Mr. Canty,” Bob said. “You have a good evening.”

“You, too,” Canty replied as he walked out of the hotel.

When Canty was gone, Newcomb rolled his eyes and guffawed.

“What?” Emmett asked, not getting the joke.

“Never mind,” Bob said. “You look tired, Emmett.”

“I can hardly keep my eyes open,” Emmett admitted. With his hunger sated, and relaxed by the whiskey, weariness had engulfed him like a shroud, and he knew that the bath he had so longed for earlier would now how to wait until morning.

“Why don’t you go on to bed, then,” Bob told him. “I’m gonna go see if the telegraph office is still open, so I can wire Mom and tell her we’re okay.”

“Okay,” Emmett mumbled, forcing himself to his feet. Fighting his own lethargy, he struggled up to their room, pulled off his boots, and collapsed on the bed with his clothes on. He was asleep as soon as his head hit the pillow.

Sitting in the huge overstuffed chair, Emmett felt more relaxed than he had in months. Beside him sat Bob and Bill McElhanie, who were slouched back on a brocade couch lazily arguing the relative merits of a Colt revolver as compared to a Smith & Wesson. They were the only ones in the hotel lobby this afternoon, other than the desk clerk, who wandered around with a feather duster doing desultory cleaning. Newcomb and Bryant, after borrowing money from Bob, had gone down the street to find a saloon with a decent card game going. Emmett leaned his head back against the crocheted antimacassar and let his mind wander, enjoying the fact that there was nothing he needed to do right then, nowhere he needed to go, and no danger lurking around the corner. Off in the distance, through the open front door of the hotel, he heard the whistle of an approaching train.

"Back in a few minutes," Bob said suddenly, grabbing his hat and jumping to his feet. As he rushed out the door, Emmett and McElhanie exchanged puzzled looks, then settled back into indolence. Both were familiar with Bob's restlessness and occasional acts on impulse, and they knew it would do no good to question him about it. When he was ready, he would explain it to them.

A half hour later, as Emmett listened to McElhanie tell about a mean horse he used to own, Bob walked back into the hotel carrying a carpet bag and a suitcase, his face flushed and happy. Beside him was a beautiful young lady with brown hair and flashing green eyes. She wore a simple traveling dress, gray with black trim, and she was the prettiest thing Emmett had seen since they arrived in town two days ago.

"Emmet, Will, I want you to meet someone," Bob said cheerfully as he set the bags down beside Emmett's chair. Emmett immediately stood and faced the woman, who held her hand out daintily for Emmett to gently grasp as she gave him a warm smile that showed perfect teeth.

"Eugenia, this is my brother Emmett," Bob said formally. "Emmett, this is Miss Eugenia Moore. You may remember that I have spoken to you about her before."

"Pleased to meet you, Miss Moore," Emmett stammered. Bob had frequently talked about the girl he had met in Vinita, but until now Emmett had assumed his brother had exaggerated her beauty. He marveled at her poise and genuine friendliness as she was introduced to McElhanie, a rough and rowdy character at best, then blushed as she caught him staring. She smiled to show she took no offense as she patted at her hair.

"Eugenia has brought us news," Bob announced gravely, waving with his arm to show that everyone should be seated. As he sat back down, Emmett suppressed a grin at the stilted form of speech Bob had adopted in the lady's presence. Once all were comfortable, Bob nodded to her to begin.

"Your brother Grat needs your help," she said, the corners of her mouth turning down to underscore the seriousness of what she was telling them. "He's in jail at Fort Smith, and he needs a thousand dollars bail to get out."

"But he didn't do anything," Emmett protested. "How can they hold him without evidence?"

"Easily," Bob said. "Rogers probably paid someone to lie in court about it."

"But, why?" Emmett could hear the whine in his own voice, but he was helpless to control it.

"What I heard," Eugenia said quietly, glancing around to make sure no one else could hear, "was that they couldn't catch you two, so they arrested Grat instead. I suppose they thought that one Dalton was as good as another."

"But that's not fair," Emmett said, realizing how childish that sounded as soon as he said it.

"No," Bob agreed, "so we've got to do something about it." He turned his head toward Eugenia. "When is the trial?"

"It's set for October 15."

"Then we don't have much time." Bob's eyebrows were furrowed in thought for a moment, and then he straightened and took on his most authoritative demeanor. "Emmett, you and Will go find Charley and Bitter Creek. Tell 'em we're riding out first thing in the morning. We've got to get back and get Grat out of jail." As Emmett and McElhanie stood up and put on their hats, Emmett heard Bob tell Eugenia, "I'll get you a room for tonight. Tomorrow I'd like you to take the train back to Guthrie and wait for me there. By then I'll have a plan worked out."

Emmett was hurrying out the door of the hotel before Eugenia had the chance to reply, but her expression seemed receptive to Bob's commands. As he and McElhanie split up to search the saloons, Emmett felt a rising excitement in his chest. They were going back into danger on an important mission, and he was surprised to find that he was looking forward to it.

Saturday, September 27, 1890

The steak was over-cooked and tough as shoe leather, and Emmett struggled to cut it into chunks small enough to put in his mouth. Even as hungry as he was, it was hard to appreciate the food in this run-down Chinese restaurant. Bob, who had adventurously ordered mysterious oriental dishes, had pushed them to the center of the table after only sampling them. Newcomb and Bryant, like Emmett, forced down the steaks and baked potatoes they had ordered, but McElhanie was smiling as he wolfed down Bob's Chinese food, having already devoured his own. It had been late when they rode into the small town, and by the time they had the horses put away for the night, the Chinese restaurant—the only eatery in town—was just about to close. Not one to turn away any business, the owner had welcomed them anyway.

While the others finished eating, Bob tilted his chair back, reached into his front pants pocket, and withdrew a large gold pocket watch, snapping open the cover to look at the time. Emmett immediately recognized the jumping stag on the cover, and blurted out accusingly, "What are you doing with Mr. Canty's watch?"

Bob closed the cover and began winding the stem. "He gave it to me," he said, keeping his eyes down.

"When?" Emmett asked. He barely noticed that the other three men had focused their attention on their food.

"The night before we left, after you went to bed," Bob answered mildly, putting the watch back in his pocket. Without looking at Emmett, he picked up his glass and took a drink of water.

"Why would he want to give you his gold watch?" Before Bob could frame an answer, their conversation was interrupted.

The proprietor of the restaurant was a small Chinese man of indeterminate age, and he wore a black oriental tunic over a pair of blue jeans that were far too large and sagged over his wooden sandals. After cooking and serving their meals, he had hovered nearby, nodding and grinning at the five men who were his only customers, and now he rushed over with a pitcher to refill their water glasses.

Ignoring Emmett's question, Bob took the opportunity to ask the restaurant owner, "How much do we owe you, partner?"

"Fi' dollah," the man said without hesitation. Emmett frowned at the price, as it seemed way too high for the quality of the meal, but Bob simply nodded and pulled out a wad of bills, counting out five ones as he placed them in the owner's outstretched hand.

The money quickly disappeared under the man's tunic, and he asked, "You boys like play cards?"

Bryant had earlier joked and laughed about the man's accent, but Emmett had been proud when Bob reprimanded Bryant for his lack of compassion. Now Bob looked up at the little man and nodded, saying, "I guess we've played a little poker now and then."

"There is big game in saloon. Plenty cowboys in town tonight. Maybe you win much money." The owner bobbed his head and smiled in encouragement.

"What do you think, boys?" Bob asked the others. "You up for a little poker?"

"Why not?" Newcomb said. The others shrugged and nodded in agreement.

"Come. I show you," the Chinaman said as they stood up from the table. With his wooden sandals clacking as he shuffled along, he led the group out of the restaurant and across the street to a weathered sagging building with a sign tilted over the door that simply said, "Saloon."

It was a small place, but crowded and lively, even for a Saturday night. Along the left wall was a dark carved oak bar with a brass foot rail, and behind it was a huge mirror framed in plaster filigree painted gold. The mirror was cracked, and the gold paint was flaking off the frame. Oblivious to his once-elegant surroundings, a thin Mexican behind the bar filled glasses and took money with utter boredom.

At the back of the room was a small empty stage that look seldom used, and the rest of the saloon was furnished with tables and chairs of random shape and size, all of which were cheap and worn. In addition to three dance-hall women, the room was packed with men. They were about evenly divided between white and Mexican, and most had the rugged look and sturdy clothes of cowboys. Of the three women, one was a blonde, and the other two were Mexican; all three were homely and hardened. Just after Bob and the others entered the saloon, Emmett saw a young cowboy hand one of the Mexican women some coins before following her out the back door.

When they entered the saloon, Emmett and the others paused to get their bearings. The room was filled with the sound of clinking glasses and deep male voices, and the smoke from cigars and poorly trimmed kerosene lamps made Emmett's eyes sting. When he gradually adjusted to this overload on his senses, Emmett saw the Chinese man insistently motioning to them. Nudging Bob with his elbow, Emmett threaded his way through the crowd, with Bob following close behind. Bryant and McElhanie made a beeline for the bar, and Emmett saw Newcomb saunter over to the blonde woman and begin a conversation.

"You sit here," the Chinaman told Emmett, pointing to an empty chair at a large round table. The oriental took the seat next to him. There were no other vacant chairs, so Bob stood behind Emmett. Of the three other men at the table, two were cowboys and the third was a large Mexican man in an expensive suit who was dealing the cards. All of them nodded at Bob and Emmett in silent greeting. The restaurant owner laid the money Bob had given him on the table, and Bob handed Emmett some money to play with as well. The game was called monte, and it took several labored explanations from the Chinese man before Emmett understood the rules, which mostly consisted of the players betting against the dealer on what color the next card turned up would be.

At first Emmett and the Chinaman were both winning more than they lost, and Emmett was really enjoying himself. Then his luck changed, or so it seemed, and Emmett lost all he had in only a few hands. The restaurant owner, however, continued to win, as did the dealer. The other players did not do so well. Depressed by his failure, Emmett got up from the table and gave his seat to Bob. As they changed places, Bob leaned close and in a low voice told Emmett to stand guard. Emmett understood, for Bob had always insisted that somebody be a lookout or watchman whenever there was potential danger. It was an old, almost military habit he had picked up as a deputy marshal.

While Bob began to play cards, Emmett edged through the crowd and found a wall to lean against, scanning the room through slitted eyes. Occasionally he would brush his hand against the butt of his pistol to make sure it was still there and ready. McElhanie and Bryant were still at the bar, talking and laughing with some stranger, and Newcomb and the blonde woman were nowhere to be seen. A player piano back by the stage had been fed some nickels, and as it tinkled a tune the two Mexican women danced with a succession of lonely cowboys.

When Emmett looked back at the monte game, he was pleased to see that Bob had increased his take by several dollars. As he watch the game more intently, however, he noticed that the Chinese man had developed a strange tic in his right eye, and soon Bob was losing steadily. From his vantage point to the side, Emmett could tell that the little oriental was sneaking a peek at Bob's cards as he picked them up and was then signaling to the dealer with his eye blinks. Pushing away from the wall, Emmett caught Bob's eye and tossed his head to one side, indicating they needed to talk in private.

Bob told the dealer he would be right back, then picked up his money and came over to Emmett, scowling at the interruption. "What?" he asked in a testy tone.

"That's a crooked game," Emmett told him. "The Chinese is giving signals to the dealer about your cards."

"Are you sure?" Bob looked back at the table, as if judging the possibility.

"Positive," Emmett answered. Bob pondered this news, scanned the room, and quickly came to a decision.

"Well, if you're sure," Bob said, "then we'll teach these greasers a lesson. Go saddle up the horses and bring them here. When you get back, just stand inside the door there and nod, so I'll know you're ready. I'll go tell the others."

Emmett did as he was told, and twenty minutes later he had all their horses tied to the hitching rail in front of the saloon. With his heart pounding, he stepped inside the door of the saloon with his hand on his pistol. No one seemed to notice. Scanning the room, he saw Newcomb, Bryant, and McElhanie standing alertly on each wall, and Bob lounging with feigned casualness near the gambling table. Bob raised an eyebrow at Emmett, and Emmett nodded.

With lightning quickness Bob drew his pistol and shouted "Hands up!" over the din of the crowd. A second later Emmett and their three friends did the same, their simultaneous commands instantly catching the attention of the saloon's customers. Only the sound of glasses being placed on the table could be heard as arms slowly were raised around the room. Like his friends, Emmet swung the barrel of his Colt slowly left and right, covering all the occupants, and wondered what Bob would do next.

There was a screech and clatter as a chair was pushed back and over, and suddenly the Chinese man was running toward the door in a crouch. Caught off guard, Emmett could only spread his legs to block the exit, but the little oriental was not to be deterred. With the skill of an acrobat he dove between Emmett's legs, nearly knocking Emmett down in the process.

When Emmett regained his balance, he spun and stepped out into the darkness, firing his pistol wildly at the fleeing man, but to no avail. With surprising swiftness the man had disappeared into the night. Emmett stepped back into the saloon just as Bob began to speak.

"You people don't know how to treat strangers, so we're gonna teach you a lesson." Keeping his gun trained on the dealer, Bob scooped up all the money on the table and stuffed it into his jacket pocket. He looked pointedly at Newcomb, Bryant, and McElhanie in turn, and then all four of them began to back and edge toward the door, keeping their guns trained on the crowd. By the time they had reached the entrance, Emmett had already backed out of the saloon and untied their horses, tossing them the reins as they ran across the wooden sidewalk. With wild whoops and laughter they all mounted and galloped out of town into the desert darkness, teasing each other about who had been the most scared. Emmett was just glad that no one seemed to blame him for the escape of the Chinaman.

Since it was too dangerous to ride across unfamiliar country at night, and because they and their horses were all tired, Bob found a rocky hilltop where they camped until dawn. In the morning they made a quick breakfast of jerky and hardtack, then started out on their journey again, heading north. Bob said they would eventually come upon the old Santa Fe Trail, which they could then follow back to No Man's Land, as the Oklahoma Panhandle was then known. Emmett was reassured by Bob's confident knowledge of New Mexican geography, and while they rode he daydreamed about the exciting adventures that still awaited them.

Newcomb asked how much money Bob had gotten from the Mexican card dealer, but Bob said he didn't know, they would count it later. The issue was dropped.

By late afternoon they were riding abreast across a wide, mostly barren plateau, but just ahead of them stretched some relatively lush green foliage that marked the course of a river. The horses, energized by the smell of water, began to pick up their pace.

"Oh, hell!" McElhanie cursed, looking behind them, and Emmett joined the others in following McElhanie's gaze. Across the plateau, approaching at a gallop, were seven rides, all wearing broad sombreros, and all waving guns. Emmett was pretty sure he recognized the card dealer they had robbed leading the charge.

"Let's get 'em," Newcomb said, drawing his Winchester from its scabbard.

"Yeah!" Emmett exclaimed, drawing his own rifle and turning his horse to face their pursuers.

"No, wait," Bob said. "It's too open here. We'll cross the river, make 'em think we're running, then hit 'em when they cross. Come on!" Bob kicked his horse into a gallop, and Emmett and the others followed. Dodging through the bushes and small trees, they quickly came to a small stream and looked for a place to cross. The banks of the river were steep and treacherous, but just to their right they saw a small waterfall. Downstream from the falls the river was in a small but deep canyon where it would be impossible to cross, and above the falls the water had backed up into a wide pool of unknown depth.

Without hesitation Bob led them down the rocky slope to the head of the falls, and in single file they carefully picked their way across. Emmett tried not to think about the twenty-foot drop on his right side as his horse cautiously stepped through the shallow rushing water to find a purchase on the slab of stone beneath. On the far side they scrambled to the top of the bank, found some bushes to take cover behind, drew their guns, and waited.

Emmett heard the posse long before he saw it. Crashing through the underbrush and talking loudly in Spanish, they made no attempt at stealth, apparently believing that their prey was still on the run. Or maybe, Emmett thought, they made so much noise in order to scare away their prey. If so, he tried to convince himself, it wasn't working.

One by one the Mexicans emerged from the trees and began guiding their horses down the opposite bank, unaware of what awaited them. Bob raised his rifle to his shoulder, and as soon as all the riders were visible, he fired. At the sound of Bob's rifle, Emmett and the others opened up as well. The lead horse of the posse, with the card dealer in the saddle, reared up and whirled around in fright. The car dealer struggled to control his mount, while the other posse members drew their pistols and returned fire. After one quick volley they turned and followed their leader, who had managed to direct his horse back up the bank into the brush.

"I'm hit!" McElhanie cried, staring at the widening red stain on his sleeve. Bob didn't seem to notice.

“Let’s charge ‘em!” Bob yelled, spurring his horse into motion. Yelping and hollering, Emmett, Newcomb, and Bryant followed him back down the slope and across the falls. McElhanie just shook his head and poked at his wounded arm, letting them leave him behind.

At the top of the south side of the river bank they pushed through the brush and paused as they came to a large open area. Three hundred yards away, galloping for the protection of another line of trees, the Mexican posse was on the run. Bob leaped from his saddle, brought his Winchester up, took careful aim, and fired a single shot. The trailing horse of the posse stumbled and fell, its rider deftly jumping as it collapsed. The rider hit the ground running, and lost no time in joining his companions in the brush.

“I don’t think they’ll be chasing us anymore,” Bob remarked as he got back up in the saddle.

McElhanie’s wound turned out to be minor. Emmett helped him wash it in the river, while Newcomb chewed up some tobacco. The wad of chewed tobacco was then pressed against the wound and bound there with a handkerchief. Only slightly worse for wear, they resumed their journey back to Oklahoma Territory.

Even though it took no longer than the trip out, the trip back seemed to last forever. Through desert country with sparse population, the ride was monotonous and uncomfortable, and they were constantly searching for a new water source. Emmett was glad when they finally left the Santa Fe Trail, for then they were no longer in New Mexico, and that meant they were making measurable progress. Now they had entered No Man’s Land, the narrow strip of territory that separated Kansas from the Texas panhandle. It was called that because federal law prohibited anyone from settling there until the ongoing dispute over which state owned it was settled. An area of desolate high plains savagely cut by gullies and canyons, it seemed improbable to Emmett that anyone would even want to live there, yet they occasionally saw signs of habitation anyway.

Whenever they came across a cabin or sod house, Bob would let them stop there and ask for water, a place to rest, and offer to pay for food. As was the custom of the frontier, they were never refused. Bob told Emmett that since these settlers were there illegally themselves, he was not worried about them reporting the Daltons to the law. Still, he usually paid them far more than they asked for the meals they provided, privately commenting to Emmett that money could buy a lot of silence.

Near the town of Woodward they crossed from No Man's Land into the Cherokee Strip, although there were no signs to mark the change. The Strip, or Cherokee Outlet as it was more properly named, was a sixty-mile-wide band of territory than ran east from No Man's Land to the western edge of the Osage Nation. Its northern border was Kansas, and on the south edge was the newly formed Oklahoma Territory in the east, and the Cheyenne and Arapahoe lands here in the west. It was nominally owned by the Cherokee tribe, originally granted to them by the federal government as a route for expansion, but the tribe had never occupied it. Instead they had leased it out to cattle ranchers, but now there was growing political pressure from boomers to open the Strip for settlement as well.

Turning southeast, Bob led his band down the old military road that connected the old Army post at Camp Supply, just northwest of Woodward, with Fort Reno, south of Kingfisher. This road took them into the Cheyenne and Arapahoe lands, where there were few white men and the law was enforced, if at all, by the Army. It was here that they met Jim Riley.

Riley ran cattle in the area southeast of Woodward with the tacit permission of the Cheyennes, who were not very concerned about property rights. He provided the five weary travelers with rest and a meal one night, obviously welcoming their company. From the questions that Riley asked and remarks that he made that evening, Emmett became convinced that Riley knew they were fugitives from the law and did not mind at all. In fact, he seemed to take pleasure from their stories of action and high adventure, and when they left, he insisted they come back any time there were in the area.

Sunday, October 12, 1890

After a month on the trail, a month that had seemed to last a year, they were back in Oklahoma. They set up camp along a creek northwest of Kingfisher, and Bob and Emmett waited until dusk to ride over to their mother's cabin. It was a short visit, and the others were still awake when they returned. Joining them at the campfire, Bob told them what he had found out, while Emmett felt miserable because of the worry and disappointment he had seen in his mother's face.

"Grat's out of jail," Bob told them as the flames crackled and sparks rose in the cool night air. "Prosecutor finally admitted he didn't have sufficient evidence, and they dropped the charges. Mom says he was in Muskogee, last she heard."

"That's good," McElhanie said. "So what're we gonna do now?"

"Me and Emmett were talking," Bob said, "and I think we're gonna go out to California. We got some kin out there, and Mom says they're still looking for us around here."

"What about us?" Bryant asked, his speckled face frowning in the flickering firelight.

"I don't know. What do you want to do?"

Newcomb poked at the fire with a long stick. "I think I'll go back to my farm," he said. "Don't imagine anyone is still looking for me, and I need to build a cabin before winter."

"You know," McElhanie said speculatively, "that Jim Riley fella was nice enough. Maybe I could go work for him. He said he always needs cowboys. How about you, Charley?"

Bryant considered the idea for a minute, and then shrugged. "I guess." He looked over at Bob. "You two planning on staying out there?"

"For a while, anyway," Bob said. "See how things look in a few months. Why?"

“Well, it’s been kinda fun lately, and . . .” His voice trailed off as he failed to find a way to express his feelings.

Emmett saw Bob smile, and knew that Bob was pleased that Charley didn’t want them to leave. “I know,” Bob said, “I know. It has been fun. Tell you what. You two go to Riley’s, and Bitter Creek, you go to your farm. Come spring, me and Emmett will probably be back, and we’ll know where to find you. Maybe then we can get up some business together.”

This plan met with general approval, and in the morning the group split up and went their separate ways. Bob and Emmett went to their sister Eva’s house and left their horses and rifles in her reluctant care, then cautiously boarded a train for the two-day trip to California. Before they left, they had promised their mother that they would stay out of any more trouble. Emmett fervently hoped they could keep that promise.

Author's Notes

Chapter 6

The National Archives in Fort Worth, Texas, contain numerous documents concerning Grat's arrest and subsequent hearings. These documents include arrest warrants, telegrams, letters, a deposition, and many pages of testimony, all of which were incorporated into this aspect of the story.

The only known record of Bob's and Emmett's activities during this period is contained in Emmett's two books, written more than twenty-five years later. Emmett's account contains statements that are provably false, and others that seem highly implausible. It is possible that the entire trip to New Mexico was a figment of Emmett's imagination. On the other hand, there is no evidence that they were anywhere else at this time, and there is no obvious motivation for Emmett to have totally fabricated the story.

Emmett claimed they rode to Silver City, in the far southwestern corner of New Mexico, but the distance to that location could not possibly have been covered on horseback within the time they had available. He may have been confused, or possibly misled by Bob; they probably only made as far west as Las Vegas, New Mexico, a thriving railroad town at the time, or some other town in the area northeast of Santa Fe. Emmett claimed that Bob met Eugenia for the first time in New Mexico, and immediately instructed her to go to Guthrie, Oklahoma, and wait for him there. This unlikely scenario was probably Emmett's way of protecting her identity.

In his books, Emmett never admitted or even referred to either the "introducing" charges or to the horse stealing and Grat's arrest, claiming that the robbing of the card dealer was their "first crime." Consequently he avoided giving any compelling reason for going to New Mexico, nor any reason for their abrupt decision to return, but in light of their escape from Baxter Springs and Grat's arrest, their motivation seems fairly clear.

The card dealer and his posse were referred to by Emmett as Mexicans, and so were portrayed in this book. In all likelihood, however, they were Hispanic men descended from the Spanish conquistadors of the sixteenth and seventeenth centuries, and had never even been to Mexico. The majority of the Spanish-speaking residents of northern New Mexico were, and are, such descendants, and they rightfully resent being referred to as Mexicans.

Incidentally, Emmett claimed in his books that it was Bill McElhanie that went to California with Bob instead of him, but there is abundant evidence to the contrary. Apparently Emmett was trying to distance himself, literally, from the crimes committed there, even though he wrote that Bob and "McElhanie" were wrongly accused, and totally innocent anyway.

CHAPTER 7

Wednesday, January 28, 1891

It was a typical winter day in central California. The late afternoon sun had brought some welcome warmth to the crisp cool day, and Bob Dalton was covered with a thin sheen of honest sweat. Flicking the reins to keep the team of mules moving, he carefully guided the plow they were pulling to ensure a straight and even furrow. Behind and to the left of him he could hear the snorting and creaking of his brother Emmett's plow team doing the next row. They had been working hard the last few days, hurrying to get the fields plowed and the seed in before the next rains. Since last October, when they had arrived at their brother Bill's ranch between Paso Robles and San Miguel, Bob had insisted that he and Emmett earn their keep by helping out.

"Hey, Bob!" Emmett called out. Bob stopped his team and turned to look in the direction his younger brother was pointing. In the distance a cloud of dust plumed up behind a buggy with two men in it, and the buggy was coming their way. Bob's hand went to the butt of the pistol he had worn constantly since they arrived in California, despite the unfavorable attention this had drawn from people in the area. His caution had been vindicated, in his mind, when Grat had arrived two weeks before.

"Mom sent me," Grat had explained as they sat around the table in Bill's kitchen that evening. "You know there's a reward posted for you two, don't you?"

"I was afraid of that," Bob answered with a sigh. "How much?"

"Don't know for sure. One guy said it was a thousand dollars, but I think he was talking through his hat." Although he maintained a solemn expression, inwardly Bob was in some ways pleased that a reward of that magnitude had been placed on his apprehension. It made him feel important, and affirmed his new self-image as a celebrated outlaw.

"For me, too?" Emmett asked, his eyes wide with awe and concern.

"Probably," Grat acknowledged. "Bobby's still wanted on that introducing charge and jumping bail, along with the horse stealing. I'd guess you're only wanted on the horse stealing, if anything."

"Horse stealing?" Bill broke in, his blue eyes shooting an accusatory look at Bob. He had just joined them at the table after helping his wife with the dishes. "You never told me anything about stealing any horses."

"That's because we didn't do it," Bob lied smoothly. "We were just selling some horses for a man in Tulsa, and these other people said we stole them. It was a put-up deal; they just wanted to get us in trouble because we used to be marshals. Heck, they even arrested poor Grat and put him in jail for it, but they had to let him go 'cause there wasn't any evidence. Ain't that right, Grat?"

"That's a fact," Grat agreed, letting Bob's version go unchallenged. Bob almost believed it himself now.

"So now we got a reward out on us, and we didn't even do anything. That's pretty bad, if you ask me." Bob did not even have to feign the righteous indignation he felt at that moment.

Grat took a sip of whiskey from the glass he had been cradling in his hands. His pencil-thin mustache, dyed black in the current style, gave him the look of a villain in a melodrama. "There's more," he said. "Mom says there's been men asking around about you, and she thinks someone told them you were here."

"They wouldn't come all the way out here to arrest us, would they?" Bob asked, leaning forward. Grat shrugged.

"Might, for the reward. I'd stay low, if I was you, just in case."

Bob noticed that Bill was nervously running his hand through his sandy hair and glancing frequently at the front door. Bill's wife, Jennie, had gone out to sit on the front porch, and he was clearly worried that she might overhear what real trouble Bob and Emmett were in. As far as she knew, Bob and Emmett had come west simply because they had tired of being deputy marshals. Grat's unwelcome news had now placed Bill in a more precarious position, both with the law and with his wife. Bob regretted putting his brother on the spot, but unease about his own plight outweighed any concern he had for Bill. Already cautious, Bob and Emmett had gone to full alert that evening, and in the following two weeks they had stayed close to the ranch, suspicious of any strangers who happened by.

"Who you reckon it is?" Emmett said as he joined Bob behind the lead plow. With his brown checked pants and vest over his wheat-colored shirt, Emmett was over-dressed for the work he was doing. Although he had shaved the day before, his face was already darkened by his heavy beard, in marked contrast to Bob, whose boyish beard rarely needed shaving. In imitation of the "Arizona cowboy suit" that Bitter Creek Newcomb had often worn, Bob had put on a pair of blue denim overalls over his black suit pants, vest, and white shirt, with the cuffs of the overalls rolled up a few inches. Bob squinted his eyes as he studied the approaching buggy, then relaxed.

"It's Cole and Clark Bliven," he said, letting his heartbeat settle down. "I wonder what they're in such a hurry for." Henry Coleman Dalton, the second oldest of the many Dalton brothers, was a perpetually unemployed mechanic who was currently living with Bill. Robert Clark Bliven was Bill's brother-in-law; he worked the ranch next to Bill's, both of which were actually owned by Clark's father.

"Cole's waving at us," Emmett noted.

"We better go see what they want," Bob said, and he started walking toward the edge of the field. He knew Emmett would follow, and he saw Bill come out of the barn and stride over to meet them. Cole stopped the buggy at the border of the field, and stayed in the seat under the shade of the fringed top. He and Bliven exchanged greetings with Bob and Emmett as they came up to stand beside the tall spindly buggy wheels. When Bill had joined his younger brothers beside the buggy, Cole broke the news.

"We got trouble, boys," Cole said seriously. "Tell 'em, Clark."

"I was in San Miguel this morning," Bliven told them. "Went in to get some feed. Stopped by the barber shop to get a shave, and while I was waiting I got to talking to a man said he just arrived from Ohio. He told me that on the train ride out, he met some sort of lawman. Said he'd never met a real western marshal before, and was real impressed. Said the man was looking for some notorious outlaws named Dalton, was gonna bring 'em in for the big reward." Bliven paused to let the significance sink in before he continued. "Real casual-like, I asked him where this lawman thought these Daltons were, and he said he thought the man said they were probably somewhere around here. I tell you what, boys, it probably won't be long before he shows up here at the ranch. The Dalton name's too well known around here."

"He's right," Cole said, looking around as if he suspected someone might be listening to them, even though they were surrounded by miles of open land. "Bobby, you and Emmett need to hide out for a while, till this fellow gets tired of looking and goes home."

"I guess so," Bob said, quickly weighing all the possibilities. "But where?"

"I got a friend up north," Bill offered. "He'd probably give you a job on his ranch. We could tell him you're my cousins and your name is Wilson or something, so no one would ever look for you there."

"Who's that, Bill?" Clark asked curiously.

"Davis, up at Firebaugh's Ferry."

"Yeah, I remember meeting him. Sure, he'd probably do that for you."

Bob stared at the ground a moment as he considered the plan. He did not particularly like the idea of staying with strangers, but he could not come up with a better plan on such short notice. He looked up and squared his shoulders. "Okay, when do we leave?"

"Right away, I'd say," Cole advised. "The sooner the better."

"I'll still have to write a letter to Davis," Bill said, "and you'll have to get your stuff together. And I've only got one saddle."

"You can borrow mine," Bliven offered. "Then express it back after you get to Davis's."

"It'll be late before we can get everything ready," Bill continued, "too late to start tonight. You can start out at first light tomorrow."

"I don't know, Bill," Cole said with a worried frown. "What if that guy shows up here tonight? I mean, everyone knows where you live, so it won't take him long to find you. I think they need to get out of here right away."

"He's got a point," Bob agreed. "I don't want to get you and your family involved in our troubles. We ought to take off right now."

Having respectfully remained silent while his elders talked, Emmett now spoke up with his own suggestion. "I could ride bareback," he said quietly. Bob patted him on the shoulder, and the others ignored him.

"No," Bill said with a shake of his head, "let's don't go off half-cocked. There's some haystacks over in the northeast pasture. Bob and Emmett can stay there tonight, while we get everything ready, then leave in the morning. Probably ought to have Grat go with them, since he knows the area." Grat had spent several years in California in the eighties, and Bob recognized the wisdom in Bill's suggestion. He and Emmett had never traveled more than a few miles from Bill's ranch since their arrival, and without a guide they would have to stop and ask directions a lot more than would be prudent.

"Good idea," Bliven agreed. "I'll go get that saddle. Cole, you stayin' here or coming with me?"

"I'll stay here for now, I reckon." Cole climbed down from the buggy and let Bliven turn the buggy around.

After Bliven drove off, Bill said, "Bob, you and Emmett better get those teams put away. I'll go tell Grat what's going on and get started on that letter."

"Come on, Emmett," Bob ordered unnecessarily, "let's get it done." The two young men loped across the plowed field to the stationary teams, while Bill and Cole hurried back to the ranch house. Energized by the changing situation, Bob was anxious to complete the preparations and hit the road.

By the time Bob and Emmett had brought their plow teams into the yard, Grat was standing there in front of the barn waiting for them, his hands on his hips and chaw of tobacco in his mouth.

"Gonna be sleeping in a haystack," Grat chided them with a grin as they began removing the harnesses, "just like Little Boy Blue."

"So?" Bob challenged, struggling with a difficult buckle.

"Just sayin'," Grat replied nonchalantly. "And then I got to baby-sit you over to Davis's ranch. At least it'll be a change from hanging around here."

"Well, I don't want to put you out none," Bob said sarcastically as he let one mule's harness drop to the ground. Since Grat had arrived on the fifteenth, he had done little to help out. At Jennie's insistence he had helped cook some of the meals and deliver them to the boys working in the fields, but otherwise he had just loafed around and complained about being bored. "We could probably find it on our own," Bob added as he went to work on the second mule.

"Naw, that's okay," Grat said, then paused to spit of stream of tobacco juice into the grass. "It's a couple days ride, maybe we can have some fun along the way. Think maybe I'll go on to Fresno after I drop you off at Davis's, see what's happening there, go see Litt." Littleton Dalton was yet another of their many brothers, between Grat and Cole in age, and who lived near Fresno.

When Bob had unfastened the last of the harness straps and let the tangle of leather straps fall to the ground, he led the two mules into the corral and latched the gate behind them. Emmett, who had already corralled his team, was carrying his harnesses into the barn when suddenly Bob saw a flaw in the plan. He broke into a run toward the ranch house, shouting back over his shoulder, "Would you put that stuff away for me, Grat? I got to talk to Bill." Without waiting for an answer, he kept running until he burst through the back door of the house.

"Bill!" he said anxiously when he found his brother seated at the kitchen table with pen and paper. "We're going to need another saddle. We've got yours and Clark's, but Grat'll need one, too."

Bill finished writing a sentence before looking up at his younger brother with a calm expression. "I know, Bob," he said. "In a little bit I'll ride over to Brewster's place and see if I can borrow his. It's under control, don't worry about it."

"Oh," Bob said sheepishly. He watched Bill return to his writing, then wandered over to the bucket on the kitchen counter and dipped himself a drink of well water. In a moment Emmett came in, wiping his face with a handkerchief, and right behind him was Grat. Emmett took the ladle from Bob and dipped himself a drink, then joined Bob and Grat in loitering around the kitchen waiting as Bill scratched away at the table. Through the kitchen window they could see Bill's wife hanging up clothes on the line in the back yard. Cole was sitting on a box talking to her as she worked. Finally Bill signed his name and looked up, just as they heard a buggy drive into the yard.

"It's Mr. Bliven," Emmett told them, craning his neck to look out the window.

"Okay," Bill said to get their attention. "Bob, you and Emmett go pack up your stuff and get ready. Grat, you take the saddle from Clark and put it on the sorrel, and put my saddle on the large bay. We'll take the boys out to the haystack, and then I'll run over to Brewster's and borrow a saddle for you. In the morning Grat will meet you two at the haystack and you can take off from there. All right?"

Thursday, January 29, 1891

Bob and Emmett had been on the road for half an hour when Grat caught up with them. The sun had not yet risen over the distant Sierra Nevada Mountains, but the eastern sky in front of them was already turning a pinkish gold, and the surrounding hills were steadily becoming more visible as the stars faded away. They had heard the hoofbeats of Grat's horse long before they could see him, and at first Bob had feared that it might be the mysterious lawman hot on their trail. Since there was no time to hide, he had chosen to try and bluff it out, hastily concocting a suitable story and resolving to fight if he had to. He checked his holstered pistol as excitement surged through his body. Disappointment was mixed with relief when he recognized the distinctive shape of Grat's head, capped by the flat-crowned hat he always wore. Bob relaxed his grip on the Colt .45 and gave his brother a friendly wave.

"Mornin', Grat," Bob greeted him amiably as his brother came abreast of them and slowed his horse's pace to match theirs. Because of the early morning chill, Grat wore Frank's old overcoat, complete with bullet holes. Bob had on a more stylish gray canvas duster, complemented by a white slouch hat dipped in the front; he thought this outfit gave him the look of a dime-novel hero. Emmett huddled in his snuff-colored overcoat, making his resemblance to Grat even more striking, despite the tall black hat he wore.

"How come you left without me?" Grat demanded with irritation. "It ain't even sun-up yet."

"The early bird gets the worm," Bob replied cheerfully. He knew how much Grat hated to get up early in the morning, and enjoyed teasing him about it.

"We wanted to get a head start on any pursuit," Emmett added importantly, repeating something Bob had told him when they had left the haystacks.

"Nobody but you two fools would be up this early," Grat grumbled. "Besides, you don't know where you're going. Only reason I'm going along is to show you two how to get there."

"We know how to get to Cholame," Bob pointed out reasonably. "We've been there a couple times. We figured we'd wait for you there. We just didn't see much point in waiting around at Bill's while you got your sorry ass out of bed."

"What if I wasn't going by way of Cholame?"

"You said you were last night. Besides, how else would you go?

"That's not the point," Grat argued. "You were supposed to wait for me."

"Well, we didn't," Bob said with finality. "Say, that's a fancy looking saddle you got there."

Grat nodded morosely. "Brewster needed his saddle, so Bill had to go borrow this one from some guy named Halter." It was a Spanish saddle, made from fine tooled leather and adorned with nickel medallions and leather fringe. Over the stirrups were tooled leather tapaderos, conical embellishments that covered the toes of the rider's boots. Bob thought it was one of the prettiest saddles he had ever seen, and he immediately coveted it.

The road they were following angled toward the northeast, and the sky off to the right was now shading into a a bright golden blue. The morning light brought color to their surroundings, suffusing everything with a soft yellow glow. Grat looked over at his two brothers and raised one eyebrow in puzzlement.

"I thought Emmett was riding the sorrel," Grat said.

"We decided to trade," Bob said, feeling that was sufficient explanation.

Emmett added helpfully, "Bob said I should take the bay because it'd be faster if we have to run for it." What Bob hadn't said to Emmett, however, was that the sorrel was a better-looking horse, and much taller, so it was more appropriate that Bob rode it.

The three Dalton boys rode in silence for a while, watching the sun flare up in the east and cast long shadows across the empty fields. During the night the temperature had dropped to almost freezing, but with the sun would come the usual California warmth. By afternoon it would be in the seventies if the sky stayed clear. Rains a few weeks earlier had transformed the land into a swelling green sea of grass sprinkled with whitecaps of wildflowers, and the air was fresh and invigorating.

"Firebaugh's Ferry," Bob mused aloud, his head bobbing in time with the horse's gait. "What's it like?"

"The town?" Grat said. "'Tain't much. Just a store and a couple houses, last time I was there."

"And that's where Davis's ranch is. Any other towns nearby?"

"Nothing big. Fresno's the closest town of any size."

"How big's Fresno?"

Grat shrugged. "Big enough. Got a couple hotels, lots of saloons."

Bob digested this information before he spoke again. "I don't know about us going to Davis's," Bob said doubtfully. "Seems like we'd be letting ourselves get cornered."

"How do you figure that?" Grat asked.

"You know, just sitting in one place, waiting for them to find us."

"How are they gonna find you? Change your names, keep out of sight, who'll know you're there?"

"Yeah, but what if somebody talks?"

"Who? Bill?" Grat's voice dripped with sarcasm.

"Bill wouldn't tell on us," Emmett insisted with certainty.

"No," Bob said, "not Bill. But what about Clark, or this Davis guy?"

"Why would they?" Grat asked, showing annoyance. "Bliven's related, and Davis will think you're the Wilson brothers. Now what's your problem, Bobby?"

"I'm just sayin'," Bob said obstinately. "I don't like hiding and waiting, is all." He was also not enthused about working on a ranch indefinitely. He considered such employment demeaning and tedious, not to mention a lot of hard work, but he kept that to himself.

"So what do you think we should do, Bob?" Emmett asked.

"What I'm thinking," Bob ventured, rubbing his nose, "is maybe we ought to go to Fresno with Grat. Check things out. Ask around, see if anyone is looking for us. Maybe come up with a better plan."

"Like what?" Grat asked.

"I don't know. Maybe we'll go on to Davis's later. I just want to go into town there, relax a little, think things out."

"Fresno ain't cheap," Grat pointed out. "You got any money?"

"Bill gave me twenty-two dollars, and we had a few bucks left over from before. How much you got?"

"Billy gave me twenty-five just before I left. That's all I got."

"Twenty-five?" Bob's voice rose in consternation. "He told me this twenty-two he gave me was the last he had."

"He borrowed it off Jennie," Grat explained with a look of disgust. Bob knew that Grat disapproved of a man having to ask his wife for money, but Grat had never been married, so what did he know?

"That means we got about fifty dollars between us," Bob said enthusiastically. Right then it seemed like a fortune.

"That money's got to last us a while," Grat warned. "Things can get kind of expensive around here." Bob noted with pleasure that Grat had not actually refused, and thus tacitly agreed with the plan.

"Oh, we'll be careful," Bob assured him, "but I'm sure we'll have an opportunity to make some more. Maybe make a little playing cards or something. Meanwhile we can have a good old time. Don't you think so, Emmett?"

"I guess," Emmett said, although he did not sound convinced.

"Then it's settled. We'll go to Fresno for a few days, then decide what to do next." Bob pretended not to notice the looks that Grat and Emmett gave each other, and urged his horse into a trot, in a hurry to get to Cholame.

It was around 8:30 in the morning when they rode into the small town. Cholame consisted of only a few buildings, including one general store and one saloon. While Grat and Emmett went over to the saloon, Bob tied his horse in front of the store and dismounted. Sweeping the front porch of the store was Albert Lander, a young man who had worked with Bob and Emmett on Bill's ranch for two weeks right before Christmas.

When Bob stepped up onto the wooden porch, Lander, wearing a long black apron over his clothes, stopped sweeping. "Good mornin'," he greeted Bob.

"Albert," Bob said with a friendly smile, "how are you?"

"Not bad, not bad. Where you headed?" Lander gripped the top of the broom handle with both hands and leaned on it.

"Going to Fresno," Bob replied. "See the big city." Lander chuckled at the small joke. "Albert," Bob said more seriously, "can you change a twenty dollar gold piece for me?"

"I can't," Lander answered, "but Mr. Sittenfeld probably can. Come on in." Lander leaned the broom against the wall and led Bob inside the store. "Mr. Sittenfeld?" he called toward the back. "Got a fellow here needs to change a twenty dollar gold piece."

A short husky man came out of the back room. He wore a striped brown suit, and his thinning black hair was plastered across his scalp with hair oil. His face seemed permanently creased in a frown. "You buying something?" he asked Bob with a deep rumbling voice.

"Not exactly," Bob admitted.

"He's bought stuff here before," Albert interjected. "Won't hurt none to give him change."

Sittenfeld grunted and stared at Bob through narrowed eyes for a moment, then sighed and sent to his cash drawer. "What do you want?" he asked with resignation.

"Whatever you can spare," Bob answered gratefully, laying the gold coin from his pocket on the counter. "Fives, ones, quarters, don't matter." The store owner counted out some bills and coins and grudgingly placed them in Bob's hand, after first scooping up the gold piece and putting it in his own pocket. Bob thanked him sincerely, said good-bye to Lander, and went back out to his horse. He remounted and sauntered the big sorrel down the short street to join Grat and Emmett, who sat on their horses in front of the saloon talking to a man who Bob assumed was the bartender. Standing by the hitching rail, the bartender was holding a small flat whiskey flask in his left hand, and had his right hand held out, palm up. The bottle was about one-third full of amber liquid. As Bob came up, Grat turned to him.

"You got two bits, Bobby?" he asked.

"For that?" Bob questioned. "Why isn't it full?"

"It's a six-bit flask," the bartended said, "but this gentleman said he only wanted two bits worth.

"Oh, go ahead and fill it up," Bob said with a magnanimous wave of his hand. "I think we can afford six bits." The corners of Grat's mouth drooped slightly, but Bob felt sure Grat wouldn't argue about spending money on whiskey. When the bartender returned with a full flask, Bob paid him and they all rode out of town. Once they were back on the trail, Grat opened the bottle and took a healthy swallow, letting out an exaggerated sigh of gratification. He offered the flask to Bob and Emmett, but Bob passed, saying it was too early in the morning. Emmett dutifully followed his brother's cue.

By mid-afternoon they had seen the last of the rolling coastal hills and had ridden out onto the flat plain of California's central valley. Its wide expanse of pastures, scattered farms, and occasional small trees reminded Bob of the area around his mother's home in Kingfisher, and he had to quell a brief spell of homesickness. Unlike Oklahoma, however, there was a distant indigo line of mountains on the eastern horizon, and the weather here was milder, without the extremes of head and cold he was used to.

Around three o'clock they rode into the small town of Huron, which was really not much more than a stage stop on the way to Fresno. Since it was about midway on their trip, and since they had begun their journey so early in the morning, they agreed to stop the night there. They checked into Mrs. Martin's small hotel, took care of their horses, and then spent the evening on the hotel's front porch passing the whiskey flask around and telling each other stories they had all heard before. The next day they went to Fresno.

Monday, February 2, 1891

Bob pulled out his gold pocket watch and checked the time. It was two o'clock, and the afternoon train carrying Emmett wasn't due for another half hour. He snapped the watch's cover shut and slipped it back into his vest pocket. He had to maneuver it under the bib of the overalls he still wore over his suit.

"About thirty minutes," he said to Grat, and took another sip of whiskey. The two of them were standing at the bar of George Michael's saloon in Traver, a small town south of Fresno, having a drink and killing time until Emmett's train arrived.

Just as Grat had predicted, Fresno had been an expensive place to visit, and they had soon run out of money. Unable to resist the lure of drinking, gambling, and dance-hall entertainment, Bob had quickly squandered their funds, despite Grat's admonitions to go easy. Bob belatedly decided there were no great opportunities awaiting them in Fresno, and told Grat that he was now certain that he had no desire to waste away working on Davis's ranch. Therefore, he concluded, he and Emmett would leave California.

Maybe they would go to Arizona, which Bitter Creek Newcomb had always described in glowing terms.

Grat attempted to convince Bob to stick with Bill's original plan, but with no success. He had pointed out to Bob that they had no money, which made leaving California a difficult proposition, but Bob had quickly formulated a plan to rectify the situation. Grat would sell the sorrel horse, and then they would head south to some of the smaller towns along the railroad, where they would have a better chance of winning money at cards. After a long argument, Grat finally conceded.

"What are you going to tell Bill about that horse?" Grat asked, staring morosely at his empty whiskey glass.

"We'll get him another one," Bob replied simplistically. He swept his gaze around the saloon, which was mostly empty at that time of day; Michaels, the saloon keeper, was down at the end of the bar washing glasses. "These small town farmers and railroad workers will be easy pickin's. In a couple days we'll have the money to buy a horse, and have enough left over for me and Emmett to ride to Arizona. Don't worry about it."

"You better be right," Grat warned.

Bob drained the last of his own whiskey, then took his foot off the bar's foot-rail and turned toward the door. "Come on, let's go meet Emmett."

Together they left the saloon and slowly strolled down the dusty street to the train station. With only two horses, it had been necessary for one of the three brothers to take the train from Fresno, and Emmett, as the youngest, was selected. Grat and Bob had ridden out of Fresno early that morning, leaving Emmett there to wait for the afternoon train, so that they would be in Traver in time to meet him.

By Bob's watch the Southern Pacific passenger train arrived twenty minutes late. Emmett smiled and waved from the window as the train pulled in, then struggled with the bulky saddle and pack as he climbed down onto the platform. Emmett was carrying Clark Bliven's saddle, while Grat used Bill's and Bob had ended up with Halter's fancy Spanish saddle. When they won enough cash to buy another horse, Grat would use Bill's saddle on that one and return both to their brother's ranch. Bob was a little vague about how the other two saddles would eventually be returned.

When Bob and Grat had first ridden into Traver, they had scouted around the area to find a likely campsite. They now led Emmett there, to a grove of trees west of town, and helped him set up camp. Bob instructed Emmett to stay out of sight, keep a sharp lookout, and avoid talking to strangers. Then he and Grat walked back into town. There was a barber shop next door to the saloon, and Bob suggested they go in and take a shave.

"Afternoon, gentlemen," the barber greeted them with a friendly smile. "What'll it be today? Haircut? Shave?"

"Shave," Bob said, tossing his hat onto the hat rack by the door and plopping himself down into the barber's chair. Grat patiently took a seat in one of the wooden chairs that lined the opposite wall and placed his hat in the empty chair next to him. The barber, a tall bony man with a high forehead, shook out his chair cloth and with a flourish swept it over Bob and fastened it around his neck.

"Ed Brown's the name," he said as he started whipping up some lather in a mug. "Don't believe I've seen you two around before."

"We're just passing through," Bob said. "We been up at Moore & Smith's mill doing some work, but the work ran out." They had passed the mill on the trip down from Fresno, and Bob hoped the man didn't know someone else who worked there. He was glad when the barber began smearing the soap suds on his face, since it gave him an excuse for not saying anything further. Grat picked up an old newspaper to read, and after a few standard remarks about the weather, Brown quietly concentrated on his work. Bob's beard was still so light and wispy that he could easily have gone another week without shaving, but he kept hoping that frequent shaves would increase the coarseness of his beard and give him a more manly face.

When Bob's shave was done, he got up so Grat could take his place. While Bob admired himself in the big mirror behind the chair, Grat settled in and moodily waited for the lather.

"How much to dye my mustache?" Grat asked as Brown came up next to him with the shaving brush and mug.

"Four bits," Brown answered as he dabbed suds on Grat's stubbly cheek.

"Four bits?" Grat repeated in a grumpy tone. "It usually only costs me two bits."

Brown shrugged as he continued to lather up Grat's frowning face. "Well, here it costs four bits. I do a real good job, get it nice and dark. Guaranteed to last at least a month. I can fix you right up if you want."

"Nah," Grat said. "I ain't paying four bits for it."

"Suit yourself." The barber picked up his razor and began stropping it with a rhythmic swing. Bob went over and took a seat along the wall to watch as Brown expertly scraped Grat's beard away, leaving only the thin mustache that was now a dark auburn color. When he was done, Bob paid the barber, and he and Grat returned to Michael's saloon.

Bob was back at the barber shop as soon as it opened the next morning, entering as soon as Ed Brown unlocked the front door.

"Good to see you again," Brown said while Bob slipped off his canvas duster and hung it and his hat by the door. As Bob climbed into the barber chair, the barber asked, "You ready for another shave?"

"Nope," Bob said, "I think I'll have a haircut today." He was flattered that the barber thought he might need another shave so soon. "I feel like sprucing up a little."

Brown wrapped the chair cloth around Bob's neck and clipped it tight. "Where's your friend this morning?" Brown asked as he prepared his clippers.

"Sleepin' in," Bob answered with a wry grin. "He was up real late gambling. Well, we both were, but he just doesn't like to get up early."

"How'd you do, if you don't mind my asking?"

"Not bad," Bob said, trying not to nod, since the barber was now attacking his hair with the clippers. Bob could see clumps of dark brown hair falling onto his shoulders. "In fact," Bob boasted, "I did real well. Won me a good sum of money playing poker over at Michaels' saloon. Now, George—that's my friend you saw yesterday—he didn't do so good at poker, but he made out all right playing cribbage later. All in all, we had a pretty good night."

"It does sound like it," the barber said, snipping away at Bob's locks. "Maybe your friend can afford to get that mustache dyed now."

Bob laughed and said, "I don't know. He's pretty tight with his money." Brown chuckled and worked on the haircut.

Bob was in an excellent mood that morning, even though he had gotten little sleep himself. His plan to come south and gamble to raise a stake was paying off already. If he and Grat kept winning at the rate they had last night, they would soon have more than enough to buy another horse and finance Bob's and Emmett's trip to Arizona. This was a lot more profitable than working at Davis's ranch, and a lot more fun as well. Bob and Grat Dalton, expert card players, would take these small town yokels for every cent they had.

As he sat there in the barber chair staring at the hair oil advertisement on the far wall, Bob decided they had probably got all the good out of Traver they were going to. It was a small town, and word would get around about how good he and Grat were. Then folks would refuse to play cards with them, or bet really conservatively, and it would end up taking all night just to get a few dollars. No, they ought to ride on today, hit the next town, clean up there, and keep on moving. They needed to keep ahead of the officers pursuing them as well, so as soon as they had Emmett on the train again, they would take off and find the next town on down the railroad line. Bob congratulated himself for his wise thinking, and settled back to fantasize about future adventures as Brown finished his haircut.

After the barber had oiled his hair, brushed him off, and helped him out of the chair, Bob pulled out the wad of bills he carried in the pocket of his overalls. Proudly explaining that this was the stake he had won playing poker the night before, he peeled off a dollar bill and gave it to Brown, then gave him another one as a tip. Pulling on his overcoat, he thanked Brown for the haircut, then put on his hat and left.

Next door, Grat was just then going into Michaels' saloon, so Bob followed him in and playfully punched his arm. "Getting up kinda late, aren't you, old man?" Bob joked. Grat glared at him and curled his lip, uttering a low growl. Then he went over to the bar and ordered a drink. Bob shook his head at Michaels' questioning glance, and led his brother over to a table as soon as Grat had the glass of whiskey in his hand.

"What's the next town down the line?" Bob asked earnestly. Grat took a drink as he paused to think.

"Tulare," he croaked, rubbing his eyes with both hands. "Damn, I'm tired."

"I been thinking," Bob said, ignoring Grat's complaint. "We probably got all we can here. Let's move on south and try our luck in Tulare."

"What about Emmett?"

"We'll put him on the train again. I figure we can make enough in Tulare and maybe the next town to buy another horse, and then Emmett and me will take off for Arizona, 'less you want to go with us."

"All I want to do right now is go back to sleep," Grat muttered, tilting his head back as he drained his glass. "Look, you go find out what time the train leaves and get Emmett a ticket, and then go get Emmett. Once you get him taken care of, meet me at the stables. I'll be there taking a nap." Grat shoved the chair back, creakily pushed himself erect, and walked out of the saloon. A little resentful that Grat had given him orders, Bob waited a minute before he followed his older brother out the door and went to the train station.

Thursday, February 5, 1891

Bob Dalton wandered the quiet streets of Tulare, enjoying the brisk morning air and nodding politely to the few people he met. Grat and Emmett were still asleep back at their camp on the edge of town, but Bob, with his usual restlessness, had risen early. The morning sun reflected invigorating warmth and brightness off the wooden walls of the small town's buildings, and Bob was feeling quite pleased with himself. On the western horizon, however, was a line of steel-gray clouds that hinted at the approach of a storm.

They had arrived in Tulare late Tuesday evening, and because Emmett complained about always having to stay with the horses, Bob had decided to board their mounts at the local stable. All three had then gone to Hevrin's saloon and played cards until three in the morning. There were few people in the saloon that night, and the Daltons had often found themselves playing cards only with each other, so their opportunity to increase their stake had been limited. Still, Bob and Emmett had both come out slightly ahead for the night, although Grat's luck had turned sour and he had lost steadily.

Bob had been careful to always refer to Grat as George and Emmett as Thomas in whatever conversations they engaged in, But Grat, either through contrariness, forgetfulness, or drunkenness, continued to call his brother "Bobby" instead of "Pete," as they had earlier agreed upon. Grat had at least managed to avoid giving their correct last names, so Bob was not particularly concerned about the lapse.

On Wednesday Emmett had used his winnings to buy some fancy new nickel-plated spurs and had elaborate black spur leathers attached to them. Bob had been amused by how proud Emmett was of his purchase. That night they played cards again, this time in P. J. Conway's saloon, and again they achieved mixed results. By eight o'clock Emmett had lost what little money he had left, and after watching the other two for a while, he told Bob he was going back to the camp and disappeared into the night. Bob's luck was erratic. He bet heavily on dubious hands, losing big almost as often as he won big, but overall he came out ahead. Grat, on the other hand, played conservatively and lost consistently in small increments. By midnight he was broke. Disgusted, he had stomped out of the saloon, with Bob following along to jokingly taunt him as they walked back to camp.

Today, idly wondering when his brothers would be up and moving again, Bob wandered to the Tulare train depot, where he spied a black boy in patched and worn clothes operating a one-chair shoe-shine stand. Bob had bought new boots in Fresno, and they already showed wear from the ride south, so he decided to get a good coat of polish on them. With a friendly greeting to the boy, who looked to be around twelve years old, Bob climbed into the tall chair and put his boots on the foot rests so the boy could work on them. As the boy knelt down and began smearing polish on the boots with a rag, Bob heard the screech of a train whistle and turned his head to watch the arrival of the morning train. With metallic squeals and clanking, and the hiss of escaping steam, the four-car passenger train eased to a stop at the platform. Immediately porters jumped down and placed stools below the steps for the passengers to use when disembarking.

Distracted by an attractive young lady being assisted by a porter in carrying her luggage into the station, Bob did not notice the two men who followed her off the train until they had been standing on the platform for almost a minute. Both men were tall, and their suits fit snugly over their muscular bodies. Each had short hair and a well-trimmed walrus mustache; one was blond, and the other had hair as black as coal. Their faces were tanned and leathery, and their eyes seemed to be in perpetual squint. They had to be lawmen; Bob had been one himself, and he knew the type. When the blond turned to look in Bob's direction, Bob quickly ducked his head so that his hat brim shielded his face. They might not be looking for him, but there was no sense in taking chances.

Quelling the impulse to jump and run, Bob kept his head down and pretended to observe the work of the shoe-shine boy, who was now briskly buffing his boots with a pair of soft brushes.

Surreptitiously peeking out from under his hat brim, he observed the two men pick up their carpet bags and walk down the platform to the express office. When they disappeared inside, he raised his head again, and as he did so he realized how tense all the muscles in his shoulders and neck had become. Drawing a deep breath, he forced himself to relax, and smiled approvingly at the shoe-shine boy as he straightened and stepped back to show Bob he was done.

"That'll be a dime, mister," the boy said, holding out his hand. Bob fished around in his pocket and came out with a half-dollar. He dropped the coin in the boy's palm with one hand as he patted the boy on the head with the other.

"Keep it," he instructed the boy, who grinned in appreciation. With a conscious effort to appear casual, Bob walked away from the station and went directly to Conway's saloon. Maybe, he thought, a drink would help calm him down.

Conway was on the porch sweeping when Bob walked up. "Be right with you," Conway said as he kept sweeping. Bob nodded and went in, pausing as his eyes adjusted from the bright daylight to the dimness of the saloon. There was only one other person in the room, and Bob was glad to see that it was Grat. Slumped against the bar, Grat was taking sips from a glass of whiskey between spasms of short, hacking coughs.

"I think they're here," Bob told him urgently as he came up beside him. Grat looked up at Bob with bleary eyes.

"Who?" he grumbled, and began coughing again. With a final hack, he turned and spit into a spittoon on the floor beside him.

"Lawmen," Bob said, keeping his voice down. He kept glancing around the room and at the entrance to ensure they were alone.

"What are you talking about?" Grat took another sip of liquor, and Bob could see that his face was flushed.

"I was getting my boots shined over at the station just now, and two lawmen came in on the morning train."

"How do you know they're lawmen?"

"They had that look," Bob assured him with a knowing nod. "You can tell."

"Hmmph," Grat grunted, and went into another coughing spell. When it subsided, he asked, "So what do you want to do, have a show-down with them?"

Bob frowned at Grat, irritated that his brother wasn't taking him seriously. "I think we better get out of town. Maybe head in a different direction."

"I feel like shit," Grat said, "and I'm tired of camping out. You and Emmett take the horses and do whatever the hell you want. Me, I'm taking the train back to Fresno." Bob started to argue with him, but at that moment Conway came back inside the saloon, propped the broom in the corner, and asked Bob what he would have to drink. Bob ordered a whiskey, and Conway set it in front of him, and then wiped his hands on his apron.

"So how'd you boys do last night?" Conway asked. "Did you get rich quick?"

"I won twelve bucks," Bob said, "which ain't too bad. Old George here went broke." Grat coughed a couple times, and then drained the last of his drink.

"The Southern Pacific pay car is coming through in a couple days, you know," Conway informed them. "Them workers will have some money then, and you'll probably have better luck."

Grat shook his head, and bent over as his body was racked with more explosive coughing. With an unpleasant noise he leaned over the spittoon and dropped a wad of mucus into it.

"You don't sound too good, partner," Conway said solicitously.

"I'm sicker than a dog," Grat agreed. "I'm getting out of this town, go somewhere to get well." Conway nodded in sympathy as Grat pushed himself from the bar and carefully walked out the door. Bob gulped down his drink and followed his brother onto the porch.

"Let's go get the horses," Bob told him, "and then go get Emmett."

Grat shook his head. "I meant what I said. I'm taking the train back to Fresno. You and Emmett get the horses, do whatever the hell you want."

"Okay," Bob conceded, "you'll take the train to Fresno. But you better go with me to get the horses. It was you and me brought 'em in to the stables, and if Emmett and me pick 'em up, they might get suspicious."

"Who cares?" Grat complained, coughing a couple times. He sighed and shook his head in resignation. "All right, but I ain't carrying that damned saddle. You can just ship it to me."

"Okay," Bob said as they started walking toward the stable. "I'll go get Emmett moving. You sure you don't want to go with us?

"You sure you don't want to go to Davis's ranch like Bill said," Grat countered.

"Guess not," Bob said. "You need money for the stable?"

"Yeah. And for the train and a hotel in Fresno. Can you spare it?"

"Sure." Bob pulled some bills from his pocket and gave them to Grat, then picked up his pace and veered away from his brother. "I'll meet you at the stables," he called as he departed.

By late afternoon the clouds from the west had moved in and blanketed the skies with a dark and threatening cover. A breeze suddenly sprang up, bringing with it the musty smell of impending rain. Bob and Emmett were about twenty-five miles south of Tulare, on the east side of the Alila train station, when the first marble-sized drops of icy water began to hit them. Bob could see the curtain of rain approaching them like a tidal wave. It was time to seek shelter.

Alila wasn't much more than a whistle stop for the Southern Pacific, but across the road from the depot there was a large barn with an open shed on the north side. The Daltons spurred their horses under the overhanging eaves and prepared to wait out the storm. With a sigh of relief Emmett dropped the bulky saddle he was carrying, then climbed down from his horse and stretched his arms and legs. Bob also dismounted, just as the wall of rain caught up with them. In an instant there was a drumbeat of drops smacking against the wooden shingles of the shed's roof, and a counterpoint of thumps as the deluge pelted the dry earth around the barn. The first drops raised incongruous little puffs of dust, but the dirt was quickly transformed into mud. It was the kind of downpour that their father had always said was "like a cow pissing on a flat rock."

For a few minutes the Daltons watched in silent wonder at the fury of nature, but jaded by a life on the prairie, they then went over and sat down on the straw-covered ground with their backs against the wall of the barn.

"Won't last long," Bob predicted, clasping his arms around his drawn-up leg knees. Emmett just nodded and scratched at the dark stubble on his chin; he had not shaved since Fresno, and his beard was getting thick. Off to their left was the train station, its platform empty; Bob watched the water streaming from its roof.

"What a bunch of crooks," Bob remarked, picking up a piece of straw to play with.

"Who?" Emmett asked lethargically.

"The railroad. Southern Pacific."

"Mm," Emmett acknowledged. His eyelids were beginning to droop.

"I been thinking about what Bill told us, about the railroads and the Republicans. I mean, that just ain't right." Their brother Bill had been active in local politics, and was considering a run for the state assembly as a Democrat. He had practiced some of his political speeches on Bob and Emmett, righteously indignant over the way the Southern Pacific controlled the Republican Party and, by extension, the California state and local governments. It was the era of robber barons and monopolies, and Bill did not have to exaggerate the corrupt influence the money men wielded over the state's affairs. In the central valley especially, the railroad's broken promises and high-handed tactics had brought partisan politics to a fever pitch, and the opposing factions had on more than one occasion resorted to violence. Although Bob had rarely paid any attention to politics, nor ever voted for that matter, he was stirred by Bill's populist sentiment, and he envisioned his brother as a David against the Goliath of the railroad.

“Somebody ought to do something, teach those fat bastards a lesson,” Bob said. He lightly pounded on his upraised knees with his left fist. Emmett remained silent. After a few minutes Bob leaned over so he could reach in his pocket and draw out all his cash. As he separated and sorted the bills and coins, he said, “How much money you got, Emmett?”

“I don’t know,” Emmett said sleepily. “Dollar or two.”

Bob counted what he had, then shook his head as he put it back in his pocket. “Not enough,” he said with real concern.

“I thought you said we had plenty.”

“It’s a long way to Arizona.”

“Well, we’ll just keep playing cards until we have enough.” Emmett was obviously not as concerned as Bob.

“Nah,” Bob said with a frown, “that’s just nickel-and-dime stuff. Besides, it’s too chancy. Somebody might recognize us.”

“So what do you think we should do?”

Bob laid out his plan. At first Emmett refused to go along, but Bob wore him down by reminding him how evil the railroad was, by assuring him that no one would get hurt, and by alluding to the story of Robin Hood. By the time the rain stopped, Emmett had reluctantly agreed. They mounted up and continued south toward Delano.

About an hour before sundown they passed a man working in the fields near the road. They exchanged friendly waves, but the man was too far away to talk to. Within half an hour they had arrived at Delano.

Their first stop was the Delano train station, where they hauled Bliven’s saddle into the express office and had it shipped to “George Wilson” in Fresno. Bob had decided not to ship the saddle from Tulare that morning because he had seen the two men he suspected of being officers go into the express office there, and was worried they might have left wanted posters or otherwise warned the express agent about the Daltons. Once the saddle was crated and paid for, they went to the depot waiting area and quickly studied the train schedule posted there. Bob made a mental note of the information he needed, glanced around to see if anyone was watching him, then casually strolled from the station with Emmett in his wake.

After dropping their horses off at the town's only livery stable, the Daltons went to the grocery store, which doubled as a lodging house, and rented a room for the night. From there they went to Tilton's chop house and had a quick supper. They stopped in Valencia's saloon for a few minutes, but there were no card games in progress, so they returned to their room.

Bob pulled off his boots and stretched out on the bed, but Emmett nervously began pacing the small room, stopping every few minutes to open the door a crack and peer out into the hall. They discussed Bob's plan again in hushed voices, and Bob was kept busy coming up with answers for all the potential problems that Emmett foresaw. Tired and fed up with Emmett's anxiety, Bob finally suggested that perhaps Emmett should go outside and stand guard. To Bob's surprise, Emmett readily agreed, and after strapping on his gunbelt, he left the room. Through the thin walls Bob heard Emmett encounter the building's owner, George Dyer, who asked Emmett if he was sick. Emmett assured him that he was fine, but said that Dyer could lock up for the night, as he would not be coming back in.

In the morning Bob found Emmett waiting for him and showing no signs of lost sleep. Perhaps he had slept on the ground in the stables; Bob didn't ask, but he was worried that Emmett might not be up to the task ahead of them. They went to the livery stable to pick up their horses, and Bob also purchased a ten pound bag of barley mixed with wheat to feed their horses over the next few days. Leading their mounts over to Tilton's chop house, they went inside to get some breakfast. Before they could order, however, Emmett jumped up and told Bob he would wait outside. Refusing to allow Emmett's apprehension affect him, Bob ordered a hearty breakfast for himself, and he asked Tilton to make up fifteen ham sandwiches to take with them. While Bob ate and Tilton made the sandwiches, Emmett stood just outside, scanning the street and fingering his pistol.

Tilton wrapped the finished sandwiches in newspaper and, at Bob's direction, handed them to Emmett, who packed them on his horse while Bob paid Tilton for the food. It wasn't until they had mounted and ridden a mile out of town that Emmett seemed to relax a little. They crossed the rail line and stayed off the main roads, following a seldom-used farm road that led generally in a northerly direction on the west side of the railroad tracks. Shortly they came to a small creek, running full with fresh clear water from the previous day's rainfall. Bob told Emmett it was time he shaved, hoping that cleaning up in the cold water would restore his younger brother's usual spunk, and meekly Emmett complied.

The brief pause had its intended effect, and Emmett regained his humor and composure. Refreshed, the two continued their ride back north, joking and talking about many things, but avoiding discussion of what they would do that night.

Bob had taken an old farm road in the hopes of avoiding other people, but about two miles outside of Delano they met a man resting his plow horse. It was the same man they had waved to the day before, a thin bearded man in overalls and shapeless brown hat. As they came up beside him, they halted their horses and nodded to him. Bob decided his best approach was to take the initiative and sow some confusion.

"Good morning, sir," Bob said. "I was wondering if you could help us."

"If I can," the man said warily.

"Could you tell us the way to the lake?" Bob was unfamiliar with the area, but assumed there was some kind of lake somewhere nearby.

"Which one?" the man asked. "The old one, or the new one?"

"The old one," Bob answered, playing it by ear. Emmett hung back and said nothing.

"It's about ten miles in that direction," the man said, pointing toward the northeast. Bob tried to look attentive as the man then gave complicated instructions on which roads to take and what landmarks to watch out for.

When the man finished, Bob nodded as if he had just memorized the directions. Then he asked, "About how far is it from here to Huron?"

"Huron? About fifty, sixty miles, I reckon. Why?"

"There any fences between here and there?" Bob purposely ignored the man's question.

"A few," the man said. "Your best bet is to head straight west till you hit the main road to Pond, then cut north till you get to a big white house with a split rail fence around it. That's Mr. Porter's, and he'll direct you from there. You boys come from Huron?

"Yes, sir," Bob said.

"Well, then, you ought to know the road."

Bob couldn't think of a good answer to that, so he spurred his horse into motion, saying, "Thanks," as he began moving away. Emmett fell in behind him, and Bob glanced back once to see the man still watching them curiously as they rode away.

The day was overcast, and showers moved through during the morning, but Bob and Emmett kept riding, buttoning up their overcoats against the chilling rain. Around noon they came to a shallow wash; thick grass covered the wide gully, which was now flowing with a meandering trickle of water. A low trestle-work bridge carried the rail line across the wash a few hundred yards downstream of them. Farther north up the tracks, less than a mile distant, Bob could just make out the Alila train depot and the roof of the barn where they had taken shelter the day before. He studied the area through squinted eyes, trying to memorize all the landmarks and form a lasting mental image of the terrain. When he was finally satisfied, he turned back south, leading Emmett back to a track he had noticed on their way north.

It had been a wagon road once, but appeared to have not been used in several years. It led straight west, and Bob and Emmett followed it for about three miles until it faded away in a shallow depression surrounded by small trees.

"This will do," Bob announced and dismounted. The rain had stopped, but they were cold and wet, and the winter wind increased their discomfort. Emmett tied his horse to a bush and immediately gathered up fallen limbs to make a campfire. Once they had a blaze going, they huddled around it until their clothes were dry and their bodies warm again. Emmett got out the ham sandwiches and ravenously attacked one after another. Bob ate only one sandwich, having filled up on breakfast that morning.

While Emmett wolfed down the greasy bread and meat, Bob poured out some grain for the horses, and then stood looking at his mount with a furrowed brow. Halter's Spanish saddled was a beautiful piece of work, and that made it a very noticeable and memorable item. With what they were planning, it would not pay to be conspicuous. Reluctantly Bob took out his pocket knife and opened the blade. Feeling like he was desecrating something, he began cutting off the tooled leather tapaderos and other adornments.

Emmett stopped eating long enough to ask what Bob was doing, and Bob explained the necessity for changing their appearance. Emmett got up and tried to alter the saddle he was using, but Bill's saddle was a simple utilitarian one, and there was little he could do to change its appearance other than remove some small straps and sheepskin stirrup covers.

As the afternoon wore on, Bob suggested they try to get some sleep, and both laid out their bedrolls on the soft ground. Emmett was soon dead to the world, snoring gently, but Bob was too restless to sleep. His mind kept churning with plans and possibilities as he contemplated their night's work, and finally he sat up and surrendered any hope of sleep. Acting on one of the ideas that had come to him, he pulled out the white handkerchief he kept in his breast pocket. It was clean, for his mother had always insisted he keep a clean white handkerchief in his pocket. He unfolded it and tried to tie it around his face, but it was too small, the corners barely touching behind his neck. Again he pulled out his pocket knife, and carefully he cut a large square hole in the center of the cloth. He took of his hat, and tilting his head way back, he laid the handkerchief across his face so that his nose and eyes were centered in the hole. Then, keeping his head back and still, he put his hat back on from front to back, trapping the top of the handkerchief between the brim and his forehead. Once he had snugged the hat down, he straightened his neck and moved his head back and forth to test it out. It worked. Witnesses would see only his eyes and nose, not enough to make an identification. He pulled the cloth from his face, carefully folded it, and returned it to his breast pocket. Then he lay down and tried once again to sleep.

Grat sat at a table in the Hughes saloon in Fresno, drinking his third glass of whiskey and trying to stay awake. Charlie Worth, the bartender, looked over at Grat and raised his eyebrows as he touched the bottle sitting on the bar. Grat shook his head, and Charlie went back to doing the books. Another drink, Grat knew, and he would pass out. His illness had abated, but the lack of sleep was dragging him down like a heavy wet blanket. He knew he had to get up and move around.

He finished his drink and stood up unsteadily, bracing himself on the back of the chair. He paused a moment to regain his equilibrium, then shuffled out, telling Charlie he would see him later. Outside, the fresh air partially revived him, and he began to feel almost human again as he strolled the busy sidewalks of town. The morning rain had made the streets a morass of mud, forcing everyone onto the wooden walkways. Grat had to dodge around all the busy folks who, unlike him, had somewhere to go and something to do.

It had been after midnight when he had arrived in Fresno. He had gone to sleep on a bench at the train station in Tulare after Bob and Emmett left, and had missed the afternoon train. He went back to sleep and managed to wake up for the late night train, which brought him to Fresno feeling rested and much healthier than he had been that morning. He had felt so much better, in fact, that he had immediately gone to the Acme saloon and played cards until just before dawn. Since then he had wandered from saloon to saloon, drinking and looking for a card game, and feeling increasingly tired and ill again.

The rain returned with a vengeance, and the wind blew a fine cold spray under the overhanging porches onto the sidewalk. Grat ducked into the first hospitable place he came to, which turned out to be the Grand Central Hotel. Others had done the same, and Grat was surprised to discover his brother Litt among the people taking shelter there. He hadn't seen Litt in over three years, but their reunion was anything but exuberant; Litt was even less warm and demonstrative than Grat, so they just shook hands and greeted each other with barely a smile.

They found an empty bench in the lobby and sat down for a desultory conversation. Litt—full name Littleton—was a thin wiry man with chiseled features and the Dalton jug-handle ears. He asked about their mother, but seemingly more because it was expected than out of any real interest. Much to Grat's relief, Litt did not ask about any of the other family members. Grat did not want to try and explain the actions of his younger brothers.

The long boring conversation with his brother acted like a soporific for Grat, and he dozed off for a moment while sitting on the hard wooden bench. Apologizing for his rudeness, Grat explained that he had not been to bed for two days. Litt asked why he hadn't checked into a hotel, and Grat hinted that he didn't have enough money, hoping the Litt would then invite him to come out and stay at his place. Instead, Litt gave Grat some cash, made clear that it was just a loan, and told him to go get a room. Grat thanked his brother for the unexpected generosity and did as Litt had suggested. It was a small room, but the bet was soft, and Grat was asleep as soon as his head hit the pillow.

When Grat came back downstairs around five that afternoon, Litt was still there, so together they went next door to the Elite saloon to get some supper. Litt left for home an hour later, and Grat joined a card game, the first of many that would occupy him throughout the night. Once Grat fleetingly wondered where his brothers were and how they were doing, but then it was his turn to bet, and thoughts of Bob and Emmett were set aside for the evening.

"There it is," Bob whispered as a light appeared in the distance, reflecting dimly off the shiny steel rails. Because of the heavy cloud cover, it was as dark as the inside of a coal mine, and the lanterns at the Alila depot and the approaching train's headlight were the only sources of illumination. A strong wind from the north brought the smell of smoke and the chugging sound of the engine down to where Bob and Emmett waited, crouched by a telegraph pole just south of the station. As the train pulled into the depot, Bob lay down in the weeds and pulled Emmett down beside him, just in case the headlight might reveal their presence too soon. Rolling over on his back, he put on the handkerchief mask just as he had earlier. Emmett pule a large red bandanna up over his nose in the traditional manner of western outlaws.

They waited a couple minutes after the train had stopped, allowing time for passengers to get on and off, before Bob quietly said, "Let's go." Both men sprang to their feet and began running. Emmett veered away to the right, crossed the tracks, and ran down the east side of the embankment. Bob stayed on the west side, holding the handkerchief against his chin with one hand to keep it from flapping in the wind. Smoke from the engine billowed down the opposite side of the tracks, hiding Emmett's approach, but the headlight's reflection in the swirling gray cloud brightened the west side, leaving Bob feeling very exposed.

Bob dashed past the engine and stopped to rapidly scan the cars behind it, analyzing their silhouettes in the glow from the station on the opposite side of the train. Just as he had figured, the express car was right behind the engine's coal car. He turned and ran back toward the engine's cab.

When Bob reached the cab and started to pull himself up using the steel grab handles, the engineer unexpectedly leaned out and said, "Go back. You can't ride up here."

Bob pushed his way into the cab and drew his pistol. With no further protest the engineer backed away and raised his hands. Meanwhile, Emmett had climbed aboard on the other side, shoving the fireman toward the middle of the cab and drawing his own gun as well.

"You know the trestle a half mile south of here?" Bob asked curtly, keeping the pistol pointed over the engineer's head. The engineer gave him a blank look. "Run this train down to the trestle and stop when I tell you."

"Sure thing, mister," the engineer said in a quavering voice. "You just show me where the trestle is, and I'll stop." Cautiously lowering his hands, he turned to operate the controls, and a moment later the train jerked into motion.

Bob's jury-rigged mask was starting to slip, and the loose threads tickled his nose. Impatiently he pulled it down and stuffed it inside his coat. It was too dark for anyone to recognize him anyway, he reasoned, but no sooner had he removed the mask than the cab was awash in an orange glow. The fireman had opened the door to put more coal in the burner, and the flames flickered hellishly in the tight confines of the engine's cab.

"Shut that door!" Emmett screeched, whacking the butt of his pistol on the fireman's shoulder. "We don't want no light in here!" Hastily the fireman slammed the door with a clang and stood back with his hands again in the air. Gradually gaining speed, the train rolled away from the station.

"Just drive it slowly until the engine's past the trestle," Bob told the engineer.

"Please don't hurt my fireman," the engineer pleaded. "He's a poor man, and he's got a family."

"You don't need to be afraid," Bob reassured him in a calming voice. "We're friends of all the boys on the road." He leaned out of the cab and carefully watched the engine's wheels cross the wooden trestle. "Okay, stop," he said, and the engineer applied the air brakes with a loud whoosh. "Make it stop with the mail car over the trestle," Bob corrected, seeing that was stopping too soon. The engineer release the air brakes and let the train coast forward some more before finally bringing it to a complete halt.

"Get off," Bob ordered, motioning toward the east side of the train, past Emmett.

"And take that pick," Emmett told the engineer, waving toward the long-handled tool leaning against the back of the cab. "We might need it to knock down the express car door." The engineer complied, and the four men dropped from the cab onto the sloping ground next to the engine. The smoky reflection from the headlight provided only enough light to make out the bigger shapes looming in the dark; far to the rear of the train could be seen the twinkling lanterns of the depot. With gentle prodding Bob and Emmet urged the other two men back along the train.

As they passed the coal car, Bob saw a dancing yellow light bouncing between the wheels on the opposite side of the train. Someone with a lantern was approaching from the other end.

"Go back," the engineer called out in a croaking voice.

"Say that again," Emmett hissed ferociously, "and I'll put your lights out."

"Tell him you need a link," Bob whispered to the engineer, proudly displaying his knowledge of railroad terminology. As the engineer did so, Emmett scurried across the platform at the near end of the express car, and soon brought the other man back at gunpoint. It was the brakeman, and at Emmett's instruction he extinguished his lantern and raised his hands, leaving the lantern hanging from his upper arm.

With nudges and shoves Bob and Emmett positioned the three train men around the wide door on the side of the express car. Bob and Emmett stepped about eight feet back from them, spread out on either side of the door.

"Knock on the door and tell him to open up," Bob ordered the engineer. Even in the darkness the engineer's shakiness was readily visible as he raised the handle of the pick and rapped on the wooden door.

"Open the door," he called out, his voice cracking with fear. "It's us. Please, don't shoot!"

The inside of the express car was dark, but Bob could make out the glint of a window in the door, and thought he saw a face briefly appear in the frame. Then the glass shattered and a pistol fired from inside, the flash almost blinding Bob and the blast echoing in his ears. Bob and Emmett both fired shots in return, and then quickly ducked closer to the train. With their backs against the express car, the gunman inside could not bring his weapon to bear on them. Caught in the cross fire, the three train men were rooted in place, trying to crouch while keeping their hands above their heads.

There was another shot from inside, and the fireman abruptly clutched his shoulder and spun to the ground.

"I'm shot!" he cried incredulously, and immediately began moaning and sobbing.

"I'm shot, too," the engineer yelled as he dived to the roadbed under the car.

"Stand up!" Bob shouted at him in annoyance. "You're not hurt." There were two more shots from the window, and Bob fired back, more in frustration than in any real hope of hitting anything. The situation was spiraling out of control, and he was helpless to stop it. In front of Bob, crouching down with his hands still raised, the brakeman was begging the express messenger to stop shooting and open the door. Emmett, also in a crouch, was at the other side of the door, firing wildly at the top of the car and cursing, "Open the god damned door quick, you son of a bitch!"

There was a brief pause in the shooting, and then a shotgun barrel poked out of the window and both barrels were fired in quick succession, the bright flashes illuminating the scene like lightning as the roar shattered the cool night air. Bob fired once more, and Emmett fired back until his hammer clicked on spent casings. There was relative quiet again, while the messenger apparently reloaded. It was then that Bob noticed people looking out of the windows of the passenger cars back across the trestle, and some were starting to climb down to investigate.

The fireman was lying on the ground whimpering softly, and the engineer and brakeman cowered in front of Bob with their hands half raised, the lantern still swinging from the brakeman's arm. Behind Bob the engine huffed and hissed, and from the passenger cars came questioning shouts. Bob clenched his teeth in frustration; it had all gone wrong, and he could think of no way to salvage it. It would take too long to break down the door, and the messenger was showing unexpected bravery, even at the expense of his fellow workers. It was time to cut their losses.

"Come on, let's go," he told Emmett, who had started to fumble at the bullets in his gunbelt. With no hesitation, Emmett ducked down and darted across the bottom of the express car door.

He was right behind Bob as they climbed up on the platform at the front of the express car, crossed, and dropped down on the far side. As a warning not to follow them, Bob fired his last three rounds over the express car, and they sprinted off into the night.

Away from the lights of the train, Bob almost panicked when he could not immediately get his bearings. Then he spotted the telegraph pole where they had left the horses, and relief washed over him. Leaping into their saddles, the two unsuccessful robbers rode off to the west, letting the shouts and clamor from the stopped train recede behind them.

Bob cursed the stubborn messenger as they rode through the night as fast as they dared, wishing he had planned for that as well as he had for the rest of the robbery. Next time, he thought, if there were one, he would know what to do.

Author's Notes

Chapter 7

As will be described later, Grat was arrested and tried for the attempted train robbery at Alila. Over seventy witnesses testified at the trial, which lasted more than two weeks, the longest trial California had seen up to that time. It became what is now called a "media event," and was reported in newspapers across the country, including the *New York Times*. Two local papers, the *Tulare County Times* and the *Visalia Weekly Delta*, carried extensive coverage of the proceedings, summarizing the testimony of each of the witnesses in detail. The statements from the many witnesses, including Grat, Bill, Cole, Litt, and Adeline Dalton, made it possible to reconstruct Bob's and Emmett's movements and actions in February 1891 on almost an hourly basis. The testimony leaves no doubt as to their involvement in the attempted robbery.

CHAPTER 8

Sunday, February 8, 1891

Bob peeked around the window frame, took a brief glance, and ducked his head back.

"Just Bill and Gracie," he informed Emmett in a whisper. They had already looped through the other ranch buildings and around Bill's house, stealthily assuring themselves that there were no lawmen waiting in ambush for them. Bob had just seen Jennie and Chub in the kitchen fixing dinner, so the house appeared to be safe as well. Leaning over in front of the parlor window again, he gently rapped on the glass to get Bill's attention.

When Bill joined them on the front porch, he had his young daughter perched on his hip and a puzzled frown on his face.

"Hi, Bill," Bob greeted him. He winked at Gracie and tickled her chin.

"What are you boys doing back already? Wouldn't Davis hire you?"

"Didn't go to Davis's," Bob admitted. "We were going to go to Arizona, get out of your hair completely, but we ran out of money. Then we saw some officers and thought they were on to us. Has there been anyone coming around here?"

"No, not yet," Bill answered. He pressed his lips together, gazing at Bob appraisingly for a moment. Emmett faded into the background, trying to hide behind his taller brother.

"Someone tried to rob a train at Alila Friday night," Bill said, staring into Bob's eyes. "Did you have anything to do with that?"

Bob looked away, shaking his head. "A train robbery? No, we haven't even heard about it, have we, Emmett?" Bob turned to seek support from Emmett, who also shook his head emphatically.

"Where were you Friday night?" Bill asked. He was still standing stock still, his gaze locked on Bob's face, ignoring the wiggling of his daughter.

"Friday?" Bob looked up at the roof of the porch as if trying to remember. "Let's see, that was day before yesterday. Why, we must have been on our way back here, about halfway to Huron, I reckon." He risked a quick glance at this older brother, assuming a wide-eyed innocence. "Honest, Bill, we didn't rob any train."

Bill kept watching Bob for a moment, then let his shoulders slump and nodded grimly. "Okay. So where are my horses and the saddles?" His eyes searched the farmyard.

"They're out in the pasture," Bob said, glad that the topic of the robbery was past. "We got in late last night, and we camped out there so we wouldn't wake you all up." It was also because he had feared that Bill's house might be under surveillance, and he wanted to sneak in and check things out before he made his presence known.

"You look tired," Bill said with constrained sympathy. He shifted Gracie to his other hip. "Why don't you two come on in the house and have Sunday dinner and rest up. We can go get the horses and saddles tomorrow."

"Okay," Bob agreed gratefully. The last two days had been a strain on Bob, both physically and emotionally, and he knew that it had been even harder on young Emmett. They could worry about their next move later.

Thursday, February 12, 1891

There was a tap on his shoulder, and a timid voice said, "Sir, I am placing you under citizen's arrest." Grat drained his whiskey glass before he turned away from the bar in the Elite saloon to look at the man who had made this ridiculous statement. He was a stocky young man with a square face and black curly hair sticking out from under his small derby hat, and he kept shifting his anxious gaze between Grat and a furtive man lurking by the door.

"You're doing what?" Grat asked him incredulously. Out of the corner of his eye Grat observed the man by the door, a pudgy man with weasel eyes. He had an official look to him.

"I'm P. J. Conway," the curly-haired man announced with all the authority he could muster, "and I am arresting you. Will you accompany me to the police station, sir?"

Conway was stretching to his full height, which was about the same as Grat's, and his shoulders were thrown back in a defiant pose, but the trembling of his knees and the quaver in his voice revealed his true emotional state. He looked vaguely familiar, like someone Grat had met in a bar. The situation was totally ludicrous. Unable to restrain himself, Grat started laughing, cackling like a laying hen. Conway flushed and took on a confused expression. His eyes pleaded with the man by the door for guidance. As his laughter subsided, Grat reached out and patted the young man on the shoulder.

"Okay," Grat chuckled. "Let's go to the police station." Brushing by both Conway and the other man, Grat strode out of the saloon. Conway scurried after him, and the third man fell into step behind them.

The jail was only a few doors down from the saloon, and only an officer named Anderson was on duty. When the three men filed into the front office, he put down the dime novel he was reading and raised his eyebrows in a mute question. Conway took a breath to begin his explanation, but the weasel-eyed man behind him rudely pushed him aside.

"I'm Detective William B. Hickey," he announced pretentiously, "and I want you to put this man in jail."

"Which one?" Anderson asked, slowly unfolding out of his chair.

Grat grinned at the officer. "I think he means me."

“What’d he do?” Anderson asked. He hooked his thumbs in his belt, one hand casually close to his sidearm.

“Yeah,” Grat said, turning toward Hickey, “what did I do?”

“He’s under suspicion,” Hickey replied assertively, as if that were sufficient. “You put him in jail, and then I’ll explain the circumstances to you in private.”

“I don’t suppose you have a warrant, do you?” Grat asked reasonably. Anderson nodded in agreement and looked expectantly at Hickey.

“One will be coming along directly,” Hickey stated, “as soon as I notify my superiors that the suspect is in custody. Officer, I must insist that you lock this man up immediately.”

Anderson looked back and forth between Grat and Hickey for a moment, unsure what to do. Grat took pity on him.

“Go ahead and lock me up,” he told Anderson. “We’ll get it straight later.”

With a shrug Anderson took the jail keys and led Grat back to a cell. After he had locked Grat in, Anderson went back to the front office, and Grat could hear the murmur of voices as Hickey and Anderson talked. Grat sat down on the wooden cot and leaned forward to rest his elbows on his knees. Despite its comic overtones, the arrest troubled him, primarily because it confirmed his suspicions.

When he had heard about the robbery attempt on the Southern Pacific train at Alila, and read the description of the perpetrators, he had immediately suspected that this was another of Bob’s stunts. It had all the earmarks of something Bob would do, and his younger brothers had been headed toward Alila when he last saw them. Because the three Daltons had been seen together at Traver and Tulare, Grat had figured that it would be only a matter of time before someone would connect him with the robbery as well. The thought of Tulare jogged Grat’s memory, and he now placed Conway as the bartender in a saloon there.

Grat wondered how much the authorities really knew. Secure in the knowledge that he himself was truly innocent—of this crime, at least—Grat guessed that the detectives hoped to pressure him into giving up his brothers. Briefly he considered doing just that, in order to teach them a lesson, but the bonds of kinship were too strong. He knew he would have to do all he could to cover for them.

About ten minutes after he had locked Grat up, Anderson returned with the keys and let him out. Telling Grat that Hickey wanted to talk to him, Anderson led him to a small room adjoining the sheriff's office, where Hickey sat at a small writing desk, the only furniture in the room. Anderson left them along and closed the door. Grat leaned back against the wall and waited for Hickey to speak.

Hickey took a small notebook and a pencil out of his inside coat pocket, opened the notebook, and prepared to take notes. "I understand you were at Traver on the second of this month. Is that correct?"

Grat shrugged, but said nothing.

"And you were in Tulare on the third, in Mr. Conway's saloon."

"If you say so," Grat said in a bored tone.

"Mr. Conway has positively identified you as one of the men playing cards in his saloon that day. Now, it appears there was a little crookedness in that game. I would like you to come back to Tulare with me and Mr. Conway and explain it."

"I won that money fair and square," Grat mildly protested. He pretended to believe that was the real reason he was now in custody. "Sure, I'll go back. I did nothing illegal."

"Good," Hickey said, rising from the chair. "We'll go right now. Where have you been rooming? Do you have some clothing or gear there you need to pick up?"

"No," Grat said as they went back into the front office where Anderson and Conway were sitting. "All I have is what I'm wearing."

"He left a coat at the Elite saloon," Conway piped up, rising to meet them. "I can show you." Conway led them back to the saloon and pointed out Grat's old rust-colored overcoat hanging by the door. Grat admitted it was his. Hickey took it from the hook and quickly searched the pockets, then handed it over to Grat.

At the train station Grat, Hickey, and Conway boarded the next southbound express. They were met at Goshen by a tall, heavy-set man who introduced himself as Sheriff Kay of Tulare County. Grat was not really surprised when they took him not to Tulare as promised, but instead to Visalia, the county seat, where Sheriff Kay, with little discussion, locked him up in the county jail. In the evening dimness of the cells, Grat resigned himself to the inevitable. He made himself as comfortable as possible on the thin straw mattress that covered the metal bed frame, and in a few minutes he was asleep.

It was still dark outside when Grat woke up the next morning. In deference to the other prisoners who were still asleep, he quietly caught the attention of the sleepy jailer and asked for soap, water, a razor, and a towel. After bringing the requested materials, the jailer, bored from a long night on duty, lounged around outside Grat's cell and watched him lather up his face. There was only a single bare electric light bulb for the row of cells, and Grat could barely make out his reflection in the small mirror mounted on the back wall. Briefly, and undoubtedly without effect, he stropped the straight razor on his pants leg. Carefully he began scraping off the ten-day growth of beard.

"Kinda hard to shave in the dark," the jailer commiserated. Grat grunted in agreement and made another cautious swipe across his cheek.

"They arrested Haswell yesterday," the jailer told him, relaying the latest bit of news.

"Who?" Grat asked, then puffed out one cheek to stretch the skin taught.

"Haswell. The messenger on that train got robbed down at Alila. Charged him with manslaughter, on account he shot the fireman during the gunfight with the robbers."

Grat paused in his shaving and turned to look at the jailer. "The papers said the robbers killed him," Grat said, puzzled.

"Nope, it was Haswell did it. I heard he fired first, too."

"Hmm," Grat said, turning back to the mirror. That certainly eased his mind a little. When he had first heard of the robbery attempt and began to suspect his brothers, he had been extremely bothered by the claims that they had killed the fireman in cold blood. He knew Bob was reckless, but he did not think Bob would shoot an unarmed man. The truth made Grat much more forgiving of his brothers' actions, which were far less serious than what he had previously thought.

Peering into the mirror, Grat carefully began to trim around his thin mustache, a task made even more difficult by the weak glow from the light bulb. Tilting his head from side to side for comparison, he realized he had cut one side shorter than the other. He applied more soap and attempted to even the two sides. A quick scrape with the razor, and then the opposite side was too short. Giving it up as a lost cause, Grat re-lathered his upper lip and sliced the mustache off completely. At the time it seemed of little importance.

Around ten that morning the day jailer came and took Grat to a barren room at the front of the jail building. A small round table occupied the middle of the room, and sitting at it were three men, all with the arrogant look of hired lawmen. The one on the right was Hickey, the "detective" who had caused Grat's arrest the day before in Fresno, and he motioned for Grat to take the empty chair next to his. With as much nonchalance as he could muster, Grat dropped into the chair and slouched back, staring defiantly at the other three men.

Hickey, his small eyes darting in his soft shapeless face, had his hat off, revealing sparse stringy auburn hair plastered across his forehead with pomade. In the middle, directly across from Grat, was a hard-looking man in a black suit, sitting ram-rod straight with both hands on the table. His face was all angles and shadows, and his brown eyes had a piercing gaze that never wavered, giving him a look of boundless determination. This, Grat realized, was a man to be wary of.

The third man, on Grat's left, was a colorless non-entity, an ordinary young man with mousy hair and the earnest look of someone who is always trying too hard. His hands were folded primly in his lap.

"I'm William Smith," the man in the middle stated without offering his hand, "special officer for the Southern Pacific company. This is Mr. Hume," he inclined his head briefly to his right, "of the Wells, Fargo Company. And I believe you've already met my associate, Mr. Hickey." The other two nodded at Grat, but he ignored them and stared straight back at Smith.

"Sir," Smith intoned, "we would like to ask you some questions about what you were doing last week." Grat glared back at Smith, offering nothing. Hume withdrew a pencil from his vest pocket and held it poised over a pad of paper, ready to take notes.

"I see you shaved this morning," Smith remarked, attempting a smile.

"I thought I needed one," Grat said.

"What happened to your mustache?" Hickey asked accusingly.

"Cut it off too short shaving in the dark," Grat replied, still looking at Smith, "so I had to shave it completely off."

"That's too bad," Smith said, staring right back. "Will you answer some questions for us?"

"I need a drink," Grat said, reaching up to rub the back of his neck. Smith looked at Hickey and jerked his head toward the door. Hickey scrambled to his feet and left the room. Grat and the other two waited in silence. In a couple minutes Hickey was back with a bottle and a glass, which he set down in front of Grat.

Grat looked at the full bottle of whiskey and felt the desire welling up inside him, but he did not reach for it. Instead he said, "I don't like to drink alone." Smith considered this a moment, then gave a short single nod to Hickey, who jumped again and hustled out. This time he returned immediately, bearing three more glasses.

When he had set them down and taken his seat again, Grat pulled the cork from the bottle and poured them all a full glass of whiskey.

Grat picked up his glass and took a long sip, closing his eyes to savor the pleasant burning as it washed down his throat. When he opened his eyes, the three detectives were also sipping from their glasses, although Grat suspected that Smith had only touched the liquid to his lips without actually tasting it.

"Could I ask your name, sir, just for the record?" Smith said politely. Grat took another sip, and already he began to feel much more sociable. He decided to tell these men the truth when possible, and as near to the truth, when necessary, as he could without implicating himself or his brothers.

"Gratton Dalton," he replied. Hume began scribbling furiously.

"Your occupation?"

"Until recently I was a deputy U. S. marshal." Grat saw the flicker of disbelief on Hickey's face, but Smith accepted the statement with a knowing nod.

"And where are you from?"

"Cass County, Missouri." Although born in Kansas, Grat had grown up in Missouri, and he still considered it his home.

"How long have you been in California?"

"About three months."

"And what is your business here, if I might ask?"

"I've got a brother that lives in Fresno county, name of Litt Dalton. I came here to visit him, see if I could find some work."

"Mr. Hickey tells me that you were in Traver on the second, playing cards."

"It might have been the second," Grat admitted.

"Do you remember who you played with?"

"Just some fellows I met there."

"I understand you went to Tulare the next day. Did you see anyone there you recognized?"

"Saw a couple of men on the street there that I had played cards with in Traver. Played cards with them in Tulare, too."

"Do you know who they were?"

"No. They were just strangers I'd met in Traver. I might have seen them somewhere before, but I couldn't say for sure."

"Does this sound like the men you played with?" Smith nodded at Hume, who shuffled through the papers in front of him until he found the sheet he wanted, and began reading aloud. It was a description of two men, and it was a fairly close approximation of Bob and Emmett. When Hume finished reading, Grat shrugged.

"Could have been," he said. "I didn't really pay that much attention to them."

"Did they ever tell you their names?"

"Not so as I would remember."

"You never called one of the 'Bob'?"

Somebody at that game obviously had a good memory. Grat decided to play along. "Well, now that you mention it, I guess one of them was called 'Bob' or 'Bobby'."

"Did they ever mention to you where they were going next?"

"As a matter of fact, I think they said they were going to Bakersfield, since the pay car would be there, and even asked me to meet them there."

"Bakersfield. But you didn't go there?"

"No. Got sick, went back to Fresno."

Smith sat back in his chair and looked at Grat appraisingly. Hickey took the opportunity to ask his own questions.

"Were you in the stable at Traver with these men?"

Grat turned his head to look at Hickey with feigned helpfulness. "I came down on the train from Fresno. I had no reason to be at the stable."

"But you were seen at the stable in Tulare."

"Oh, in Tulare, yeah. In Tulare I went to the stable with one of the men, he wanted to show me his horse. Then I got on the train and went back to Fresno."

There were a few more questions, mostly about where Grat was on the night of the robbery, and then Smith had Hickey get the jailer to take Grat back to his cell. Smith's granite countenance was hard to judge, but Grat did not feel the railroad agent had bought his story. On the other hand, Grat had not told him any lie that could be easily disproved. Most of what he said was true, so Smith was welcome to believe whatever he wanted.

That afternoon, while Grat was sitting in his cell playing solitaire, Hickey showed up, leading two reluctant men to Grat's cell. One man was clearly a farmer, and the other looked like some sort of shopkeeper. Grat had never seen either man before.

"Is this one of the men you saw?" Hickey asked them, waving his hand toward Grat. Grat looked up with a bland expression as the two men peered through the bars at him.

After a moment the farmer shook his head. "Nope, they were both much younger than this man," he said decisively. He continued to stare at Grat, like he was at a circus and Grat was some wild animal.

The shopkeeper seemed less certain. "There's a resemblance," he noted doubtfully. "The shorter man hadn't shaved in a while, and that makes it hard to tell." He squinted at Grat, as if trying to picture him with a beard. "No, I don't think so. Mr. Merry's right, he was a much younger man."

The expression of disgust and disappointment on Hickey's face made Grat grin with gleeful satisfaction. When Hickey had taken the two men back out of the jail, Grat chuckled out loud. If that was their best evidence against him, he would be out of jail in no time.

That afternoon Grat was released from jail, since the railroad detective had been unable to find sufficient evidence against him to swear out a warrant. Although he was glad to be free, Grat was also discouraged. His own situation was bleak, he was worried about Bob and Emmett, and he wondered how he would explain things to his brother Bill. The trickery and false arrest by the special agents had been aggravating, but as a former lawman himself, he recognized that they were just trying to do their job. Wishing he had enough money for a drink, Grat wandered the streets of Visalia trying to decide what he should do.

He had paused in front of the bank, pondering the chances that they might make him a loan, when a stranger approached and asked Grat if he needed any help. Grateful for a sympathetic ear, Grat ruefully admitted he had just been released from jail and had no money. He assured the well-dressed man that he was now looking for work. Introducing himself as John Harris, the stranger told Grat there was plenty of work out in his home town of Hanford for a good able-bodied man like Grat. Grat accepted his offer to loan him the train fare, and together they walked to the station.

While Harris was in line for the tickets, Will Smith showed up again. Grat knew it was no coincidence that the railroad detective would be at the depot the same time as Grat. He was being followed and watched, but there was nothing he could do about it. The stone-faced agent probably hoped Grat would lead him to Bob and Emmett, or perhaps give Smith sufficient grounds to obtain a warrant for Grat's arrest.

When Smith pointedly asked Grat where he was going, Grat honestly told him that he was going to Hanford.

"What's in Hanford?" Smith asked.

"A job," Grat replied succinctly, but then decided to embellish his story. "I'm going to work for Mike White." It was a common enough name, and for all Grat knew, there might actually be a Mike White in Hanford. All Grat wanted to do was to satisfy Smith's curiosity enough that he would leave Grat alone.

"I thought you were going back to Fresno," Smith said, with only a hint of accusation.

"I'm too broke," Grat admitted with a hang-dog expression. "Say," he said, perking up as if a thought had just occurred to him, "do you need any help tracking down those guys I was playing cards with? I'd be glad to help out, you know, if you covered my expenses."

"No, thanks," Smith said with a dead-pan look. As Harris returned with the tickets in his hand, Smith touched the brim of his hat and walked away.

The main railroad line, which ran from Sacramento in the north to Los Angeles in the south, passed through Goshen, about five miles west of Visalia. A spur line connected Visalia to the main line at Goshen, then continued west out to Hanford, another twenty miles beyond. Grat and Harris rode the morning train out to Hanford together, with Harris amiably rattling on about the weather, local affairs, and particularly about the recent train robbery attempt. Grat kept his end of the conversation to a minimum, uttering only grunts of acknowledgement and an occasional, "Is that correct?"

When they arrived in Hanford, Harris led Grat to the lodging house he ran and offered Grat a place to spend the night. Grat made no commitment, saying he would go start looking for work first, and then he headed out into the country. To Grat, Harris's generosity seemed forced and out of character, and this, combined with the man's frequent mention of the train robbery, made Grat suspicious of his motives. The railroad had already offered a reward in connection with the crime, and now amateur detectives would be coming out of the woodwork. Under the circumstances, Grat felt it would be safer to sleep out in the open than to stay the night with Harris.

For the next two days he roamed around the area, hitching rides as far west as Lemoore, and did odd jobs in return for meals. It was strictly a farming community, and he wasn't really interested in doing manual labor; he just wanted to get back to Bills' ranch at San Miguel. On Tuesday he was back in Hanford, still broke, and now desperate enough to talk to John Harris again.

Late in the afternoon he returned to the lodging house, where Harris was just preparing for supper. As Grat had hoped, Harris invited him to eat with him, and during the meal Grat briefly told Harris about his lack of success in finding work. Without being specific, Grat said that he knew a place where he could get a job, but that he would need some money to get there. He estimated it would take about fifteen dollars in travel expenses, and if Harris would loan it to him, he would repay it in only a week's time. When Harris easily agreed to this outrageous request from a total stranger, Grat suspected the man had some kind of a bigger return on his investment in mind.

As Grat was well aware, there was only a morning train from Hanford to Goshen, but he decided to push it and see how far Harris would go to accommodate him. When Harris gave him the loan, Grat thanked him and started to leave, saying he would have to hurry to catch the last train. As expected, Harris explained that there would not be a train to Goshen until the next day. When Grat insisted he was anxious to get started, Harris offered to drive Grat the twenty miles to Goshen in his buggy, even though it was already near sunset. Grat pretended to be appropriately grateful, and made no comment when Harris stopped at the railroad station on the way out of town, telling Grat he had to send a telegram "about a business meeting."

On the drive to Goshen through the gathering darkness, Harris again brought up the Alila robbery, pressing Grat for his opinion about who did it. Grat curtly told him, "There's nothing in it for you or me," and refused to discuss it further. When they finally arrived at the Goshen depot, Grat climbed down from the buggy and walked away, ignoring Harris's farewells.

Grat bought his train ticket and found a space on a bench on the platform. He was puzzled when he noticed that Harris was still sitting there in his buggy, until another man joined Harris in the buggy and the two men huddled with their heads together. A minute later the second man, who wore a dark suit and a tall beige hat, left the buggy and casually walked onto the platform, studiously ignoring Grat. While Grat was watching this stranger, someone plopped himself down next to Grat and nudged him. It was Hickey, the Southern Pacific special agent.

"Haven't seen you for a couple days," Hickey said with a grin. "What have you been up to?"

Grat signed. "I went out to Hanford, looking for work."

“Didn’t find any, I take it.” Hickey was trying to sound sympathetic.

“Nope.”

“So where you headed now?”

“Guess I’ll go back to Fresno, maybe find something there.” There was a mechanical shriek from down the tracks, and the flickering headlamp of an approaching train became visible. “There’s my train,” Grat said, rising to his feet. Without looking back, he walked over to the edge of the platform and waited to board. He noticed from the corner of his eye that the stranger who had met with Harris did the same.

As the train pulled away from the station, Grat made his way to the smoking car, hoping to bum a cigarette or small cigar. He was not surprised to find Hickey there already. They nodded in greeting, and Hickey offered Grat a thin cigar. He lit it for Grat, and both sat down together on one of the upholstered benches.

“You know who those men are who robbed that train, don’t you?” Hickey said, casually looking out the window.

“Huh-uh,” Grat denied, taking a drag of his cigar. “You say it’s those two I was playing cards with down in Tulare?” Hickey lifted his shoulders slightly and nodded. “Well, if you were to make it worth my time,” Grat said speculatively, “I could go down to Bakersfield and probably find them. I think their name was Wilson, Wilkins, something like that.”

“There is a reward being offered by the railroad,” Hickey admitted. “If you were to identify the robbers, then you’d get a part of it, but it’d have to be divided up. But, yeah, you’d get your share.”

“But you all wouldn’t hire me to go look for them?”

“Southern Pacific wouldn’t,” Hickey replied with finality. “I don’t know about Wells Fargo.”

“Tell you what, if Wells Fargo gave me a job, I could guarantee their trains would never get robbed.”

“You’d have to talk to them about that. As for finding the boys that did the job at Alila, I don’t think that will be too hard. The way they went at it, I don’t think they had ever tried anything like that before. Amateurs like that should be easy to find.”

“You don’t think they’ll give me a job, then?”

“I wouldn’t count on it. Why, are you broke?”

“As a matter of fact. . .” Grat left it hanging in the air.

“I guess I could loan you some money,” Hickey said, making it clear that it would be a major sacrifice. He pulled a leather wallet from inside his coat and, turning it so Grat could not see its contents, withdrew a banknote and handed it to him. It was a one dollar bill.

“Thanks,” Grat said, trying to sound grateful. As he pocketed the dollar, he stared out the window, trying to make out the dark shapes that rushed by the train in the night. When he looked back at Hickey, he saw that the chubby man was writing in a small notebook. Hickey ripped the page out and handed it to Grat.

“Here’s my address,” he said. “If you find those two men, or remember anything else about them, let me know.” Grat glanced at the address, then folded the sheet and slipped it into his vest pocket. Hickey looked at Grat with his pencil poised over the notebook. “And where can I reach you if I have any more questions?” Grat gave him Litt’s address, and as Hickey wrote it down, Grat carefully stubbed out the ash on his cigar and put the remainder in his pocket. Yawning theatrically, he stood up.

“Think I’ll go find an empty seat and take a little snooze,” Grat said. Without saying good-bye, he walked away from Hickey.

In the next car there were several empty seats, but Grat also saw a tall beige hat behind a hastily raised newspaper. Swaying with the railcar, he passed on to the next coach, found a seat, and slumped down with his hat over his face. Seconds later he was asleep.

It was a long ride back to Bill’s ranch, and not without incident. In San Jose Grat was arrested yet again, but released within a few hours. He was running out of money, and his attempt to go farther than he had paid for by pretending to sleep through his stop did not fool the conductor. He had to walk the final thirty miles, and most of that tedious journey was done at night. Throughout the long trip back to Paso Robles, Grat caught fleeting glimpses of a man in a beige hat.

Monday, February 23, 1891

It was a cool gray afternoon in San Miguel, and the rain that had fallen intermittently all day was once again coming down in torrents. With his back wet and his shoes heavy with accumulated mud, Grat loaded the last of the supplies in the back of the buggy and climbed into the front seat beside Bill. The buggy's canvas top shielded them from the direct downpour, but the wind-blown spray through the open sides kept them damp and shivering. Grat took off his flat-topped hat and shook the water off it, then set it firmly back on his head. As he did so, he felt the buggy sag on its springs as someone climbed into the back seat.

"Afternoon, gentlemen," the newcomer said pleasantly. "Mind if I sit here out of the rain a minute while I talk to you?"

Grat and Bill both twisted in their seats to look at the man. Wearing a black suit, a black hat, and a black tie around his high white collar, the craggy face of William Smith showed just a trace of a smile. Grat winced as he recognized the Southern Pacific agent, whom he had hoped to never see again.

"I'm Will Smith," he said to Bill, offering his hand. "Special agent for Southern Pacific." Bill shook his hand warily while shooting a questioning glance at Grat.

"He's the one questioned me in Visalia," Grat explained to Bill while scowling at the officer.

"And you, sir?" Smith said to Bill with raised eyebrows.

"William Dalton. I have a ranch near here."

Smith turned his steely gaze to Grat. "I thought you were going to Hanford?"

"I decided I would rather stay with my cousin Billy," Grat said. The tempo of the rain increased, and the drumming of the drops on the buggy's taught cover forced the men to talk louder.

"Uh-huh," Smith said with a nod. "And when did you get to Billy's?"

"He arrived around Christmas," Bill said with a trace of annoyance in his voice. Grat knew that wasn't what Smith meant, but he let it go.

"I thought you said you were staying with your brother Cole," Smith said to Grat, watching him intently.

"Cole lives with me," Bill said.

"And he's not my brother," Grat hastened to add. "He's Billy's brother, my cousin." Grat was anxiously searching his memory, trying to remember what he had actually told Smith, but his memory of the interrogation in Visalia was largely a hazy mish-mash of disconnected phrases.

"But it was Billy here that gave you a horse and saddle to ride to Fresno, right?"

"I never said that," Grat denied as earnestly as he could, quickly before Bill had a chance to say the wrong thing. "Look, why don't you quit pestering me? I'm sick and tired of being arrested everywhere I go. If you don't have a warrant, then just leave me alone."

Smith stated at Grat a moment, his face betraying no emotion, before he spoke. "I'm sorry you feel that way, Mr. Dalton. You said you were willing to help track down these criminals."

"What does that have to do with my cousin Billy?" Grat challenged him.

"I don't know yet. I hear tell there's been a couple other 'cousins' staying out at your place, Mr. Dalton." Smith shifted his gaze to Bill, who paused to wipe some of the spray from his face with his sleeve before he answered.

"Well, yes, there were, but they have gone now. They, uh, went to Seattle to visit some friends. Now, if you will excuse us, Mr. Smith, we have to be going."

"Certainly," Smith said and climbed out of the buggy. "Thank you for your time." Apparently oblivious to the rain now soaking him, Smith stood rigidly in the street and watched as Bill flipped the reins and set the buggy moving away from him. Grat restrained himself from looking back at the lone figure. There was not a shred of doubt in his mind that he would see Smith again.

Tuesday, February 24, 1891

Someone was roughly shaking him awake. Grat cautiously opened one eye and peered up into the troubled face of his brother Bill. "Wake up!" Bill hissed at him. "That Smith guy is here with Sheriff O'Neill. They want to talk to you."

Grat sat up and rubbed his eyes. The angle of the sunlight coming in around the shades told him it was still early morning. The other two cots in the small bedroom were empty, their covers neatly straightened.

"Where's Bob and Emmett?" Grat asked, smacking his lips to clear the gummy film of sleep. Bill stood impatiently in the middle of the room, his hands on his hips.

"Be quiet! They might hear you!" Bill was whispering hoarsely, and his blue eyes flared with rising anger. "They're hiding in the back room. Come on, get dressed."

Grat picked up his pants from the floor and pulled them on, then maneuvered into his shirt and only partially buttoned it. Still barefoot, he made his way through the house and out onto the front porch. Squinting against the bright sunlight, Grat saw Smith and Ed O'Neill sitting in a well-used buggy parked close by the porch. Smith looked the same as always—black suit and hat, and a face like a cigar store Indian. Ed O'Neill, the sheriff of San Luis Obispo County, was an old friend of Bill's, and Grat had met him casually in town a couple times. With a noticeable paunch and graying hair, he looked older than his years, and his fatherly appearance matched his personality.

"Good morning, sleepy-head," O'Neill greeted him with a smile. Smith just nodded at him.

"Morning. What are you all doing out here this early?" Grat scratched himself and leaned against one of the posts supporting the porch roof. Behind him Bill stood in the front door, his arms akimbo, as if blocking the way inside.

"Mr. Smith here was wondering if you'd answer a few questions for him."

"Am I under arrest?"

"No," Smith said, but his tone suggested that it was only a matter of time.

"Well, what do you want to know?" Grat yawned and flexed his shoulders.

O'Neill's expression was more serious now. "Maybe it'd be better if you came into town with us," he said. Smith was watching Grat's every move intently.

Grat was aware of Bill's fidgeting behind him, and knew Bill wanted the two lawmen gone before Bob did something foolish. Grat heaved a big sigh.

"Okay. Let me go finish getting dressed." Making no pretense at hurrying, Grat turned and went back inside. Bill moved aside only long enough for Grat to pass.

They took him to O'Neill's office in Paso Robles and talked to him for hours. Smith sat behind O'Neill's desk with a pad of paper and a pen, taking copious notes, while O'Neill lounged in one of the wooden chairs next to his desk. Smith did almost all of the questioning; O'Neill was only there as a witness and to give the interrogation some legal standing, since Smith was not a government official. Smith asked Grat about his trip to Fresno, his background, and his relatives. The questions came rapid-fire, and jumped back and forth between subjects. Grat wished for a drink as he struggled to keep his story straight.

He tried to remember what he had told Smith in Fresno, and in town yesterday, as well as what Bill had told Smith. He also had to try and guess what other people in the area might have told Smith, and around all of that weave a plausible story that did not implicate himself or his brothers. The railroad detective's tenacity was wearing on Grat's nerves, and he desperately wanted the questioning to end. He was hungry, he wanted a drink, he had not gotten enough sleep, and now he had to suffer through this endless badgering. Soon he gave up on achieving consistency in his lies and just told Smith whatever came to mind, just to get him off his back.

Finally, after what seemed like days, Smith finished writing and handed a sheet of paper to Grat. "Would you look over this statement and see if it is correct?" he told Grat. Grat shrugged and began to read the neat, precise handwriting. It read:

> *Borrowed bay mare and saddle from Billy Dalton. Might have been ten days or two weeks previous to the robbery. Left the ranch alone. Stopped at some ranch between Billy's and Lemoore all night. Reached Fresno and placed mare in a stable near the Grand Central hotel. The following day I sent the mare back by a man, think his name is Nevins; said he lived below Billy's. The saddle I had is the one hanging in Billy's barn, an old saddle, think it is that one; no tapaderos on it. Don't know what day I sent the mare back. Have brothers named Tom and Chris; they live in Covington, Ky.; they have lived in Mount Sterling, Ky. My cousin's names, brothers of Billy Dalton, are: Cole, Litt, John, Charley, and Frank. Can't remember that he has any other brothers. Reached Sacramento just after Christmas, 1890. From Kansas City, from Green County, Mo. From Sacramento went to San Miguel, from which place I went to Billy's; walked there. Remained at Billy's three weeks. Then went to Fresno on Billy Dalton's mare. My last visit to California previous to this visit was four or five years ago. Can't remember exactly, but it is over three years ago. On my way to Fresno from Billy Dalton's I stopped at Lemoore, where I put my horse in a livery stable and stayed in a hotel all night. Don't know the name of the hotel or livery stable. Did not register at the hotel.*

Grat nodded thoughtfully as he finished reading. He laid the paper down on the desk in front of him and paused. "I guess that's about right," Grat finally said.

"Would you sign it please?" Smith requested, although it came across as a command.

"I'd like to add something first," Grat said, reaching for the pen.

"Certainly," Smith agreed.

Under the last line of the statement, with his best penmanship, Grat wrote "This statement is as near as I can remember to dates. Am not sure of dates." Then he signed his name with a flourish. As he handed the pen and paper back to Smith, he silently hoped this was the end of it, and that Smith would finally be satisfied and go away, for a while at least. Smith blew on the page to dry the ink, and slipped it into a leather satchel he lifted from the floor behind the desk.

"Anything else?" Grat asked. Smith looked back at him with an unreadable expression and shook his head.

"I believe that's all I need right now, Mr. Dalton. Thank you for your cooperation." All three men stood.

"Can I give you a lift back to Bill's" O'Neill offered. Something about O'Neill's posture and attitude made Grat believe that the sheriff liked Smith even less than Grat did.

"I'd be much obliged," Grat replied.

Wednesday, February 25, 1891

Grat was just finishing a late breakfast when Bob and Emmett scurried through the kitchen on the way to the back room, warning Grat that a stranger was approaching. Bill was out in the fields, and Jennie had taken the kids over to see her parents. Grat went out onto the porch as a buckboard with one man in it drove into the yard.

After bringing the wagon to a halt, the driver, a young man with an ill-fitting suit, climbed down and nervously approached Grat.

"Are you Grant Dalton?" he asked, stopping at the foot of the steps. Grat didn't bother to correct him, and just frowned at the man. When Grat didn't answer, the young man cleared his throat and continued. "My name's Wilson, and I'm here to arrest you."

"What for?" Grat growled.

"Stealing a gun," Wilson answered, his hands fluttering over his jacket.

"Didn't steal any guns," Grat assured him. "You got a warrant?"

"A warrant?" Wilson almost squeaked.

"Then get the hell out of here!" Grat roared at him. Wilson flinched, then scrambled back on this wagon and shouted the horses into motion, sending bits of mud arcing through the air behind him as he rushed away from the ranch. He swerved around a buggy that was just arriving and disappeared down the road back to town. Grat waited with resignation as Smith and O'Neill drove up and stopped in front of him.

"More questions?" Grat asked hopefully. O'Neill shook his head regretfully.

They placed Grat under arrest and told him to get his things. Smith was especially insistent that Grat bring his old overcoat, the rust-colored wool coat that he had inherited from Frank. O'Neill drove them to San Miguel, where Smith and Grat boarded a train. By evening they were back in Visalia, where Smith turned him over to Sheriff Kay's jailer.

The next morning, when Sheriff Kay came in to work, he released Grat again, but warned him that there would be a grand jury hearing on the train robbery starting March 9. He advised Grat to remain in the area, and to be present for the grand jury, and Grat agreed. Despite Smith's hounding, Grat felt sure that when a grand jury heard all the evidence, they would realize he was not involved and drop the charges against him. Unfortunately, he underestimated the power and determination of the Southern Pacific railroad.

Sunday, March 2, 1891

Bob and his nephew Charles were playing catch with a bean bag. At four years old, Chub, as he was nicknamed, was a precocious child, and Bob enjoyed playing and talking with him. Only a couple yards separated them, and Bob tossed the bean bag gently right into Chub's hands. Chub squealed with delight when he caught it, and threw it awkwardly back toward Bob, who had to stretch to intercept it. The sun hung low over the coastal range to the west, but the air was still warm and the breeze swirled around Bob like a pleasant fragrance. The winter rains had ended, but the grass in front of Bill's house was still lush and green. Although he had removed his jacket and vest, Bob still wore his gunbelt and pistol, a continual source of discord between Bob and Jennie.

"Okay, Chub," Bob said before he tossed the bag again, "if somebody asks you where I am, what do you say?"

Chub squeezed his eyebrows together and looked at the ground a moment before he smiled and chirped, "My Uncle Bobby's gone to Se-at-tle."

"That's right!" Bob praised him, and lobbed the bean bag to his little nephew again. Chub grabbed at it clumsily, sending it flying sideways to the ground. As the boy ran to retrieve it, Bob looked up and saw a flicker of movement far way on the road. Someone was coming. Telling Chub to stay where he was, Bob grabbed up his jacket and vest and ran inside, hollering for Emmett. His younger brother was helping Bill clean up the supper dishes while Jennie fed the baby, but both men reacted quickly when Bob told them what he had seen. Bill rushed to the front door, while Emmet grabbed his jacket from the back of a kitchen chair and followed Bob into the back room, locking the door behind them.

Originally intended as a mud room, where Bill could clean up after working in the fields, the back room was now Bob and Emmett's hide-out. They kept all their possessions there, and there were some blankets for them to sleep on if necessary. Only one small window provided illumination, and the impending sunset would soon leave it totally dark. They couldn't risk having a lantern lit. Bob stood beside the door with his back to the wall, his hand resting on the handle of his pistol. With a jerk of his head he motioned Emmett to take a similar position on the other side of the door. From in front of the house they could hear male voices raised in greeting, but they were unable to distinguish the words.

A few minutes later there were clumping sounds of boots on wood, and Bob could tell that Bill had brought two men into the house. Through the thin wall he could easily make out their words, and his heart raced as he realized that the visitors were William Smith and Sheriff O'Neill. Bill told Bob later that when the two men had first arrived and were still out on the lawn, Smith had squatted down in front of Chub and asked the boy where his Uncle Bobby was. As he had been taught, the boy immediately answered that Bobby had gone to Seattle.

Bob heard Smith tell Bill that he was now convinced that Bob and Emmett had tried to rob that train, and he believed Grat had assisted them. He assured Bill that there would soon be warrants for all three of them. He already had Grat, he said, and he would soon track down Bob and Emmett. He had just made a fruitless trip back east to Oklahoma Territory in search of them, and he would not rest until they were found.

Bill tried to convince Smith that the boys were innocent, claiming Bob and Emmett had never left the ranch during that period. He pointed out that Grat had been in Fresno at the time of the robbery, but Smith was not deterred. He told Bill, honestly enough, that the railroad was determined to make somebody pay for the crime, and the courts would take his word over Bill's any day. Bob became increasingly angry at the railroad detective's arrogance, and briefly considered bursting out of the back room with gun drawn to have it out with him. Telling himself it would be improper to do such a thing in his brother's house, and not wanting to force Ed O'Neill into a showdown, Bob chewed on his lower lip in frustration.

When Bill invited the two officers to spend the night, Bob was at first outraged. Then he saw the wisdom in the move, for by doing so Bill convinced the men that he had nothing to hide. Bob admired

Bill's courage and composure under what had to be trying circumstances for him. He was laying his good name on the line to help his brothers, and Bob felt a tinge of guilt, knowing that he had misled his brother and caused these problems. When Bob heard Smith again insist that he would get Bob and Emmet and send them to prison, he transformed his guilt into indignation and hatred toward the self-confident railroad man. He seethed as he listened to the conversation in the other room, and he resolved that he would never surrender to such a man. In fact, he told himself, if they considered him such a dangerous criminal, then he would show them just how dangerous he could be.

Eventually everyone else went to bed, but Bob and Emmett took turns sleeping throughout the night. One of them was always on guard at the door of the back room, in case Smith decided to do some late night snooping. In the morning the two lawmen rose early and drove away, and as soon as they were gone Emmett burst from the stuffy room where they had been trapped and ran for the outhouse. After Bob had also had his turn, Bill told them to saddle up the horses. Clearly shaken by the experience of the previous night, Bill insisted that they leave the state immediately.

While Bob and Emmett prepared the horses, Bill went off to borrow some cash. When he returned, the three of them started off to the south, riding as hard as they could without ruining their mounts. Bill said he was going along to show them the way through the mountains, but Bob suspected there were other reasons as well. Perhaps remembering what had happened when he sent them to Firebaugh's Ferry, Bill now wanted to ensure that they went where he told them and did not get into trouble along the way. Maybe he didn't trust them with the cash. Whatever the reason, Bob welcomed his brother's escort, for it signified a family involvement that Bob relished.

Fearing pursuit, the three men pushed their horses as hard as they dared, covering over fifty miles a day. Avoiding towns and ranches, where someone might recognize them or become suspicious, they slept only a few hours a night. They ate only what they could scrounge and what little they had brought with them, and refilled their canteens from creeks and rivers.

Toward the end of the third day they began their ascent up Tehachapi Pass, the only route through the Sierra Nevada Mountains to the deserts of southeast California and western Arizona. It was an increasingly steep and winding road, and the daylight warmth of the central valley quickly gave way to the chill of higher altitudes and darkness. The farther they climbed, the more the terrain became nothing but jumbled rocks and scattered pine trees. The road roughly followed a mountain stream, and the gentle roar of the rushing water was a constant companion. Around midnight, when they approached the summit, it began to snow.

After three long days of riding, the Daltons were too exhausted to continue. Gathering pine nuts for the horses to eat, they built a fire and rolled up in blankets to shiver themselves to sleep. Despite the cold and his gnawing hunger, Bob almost passed out as soon as he laid his head down. He was in a deep dreamless sleep when some remote part of his brain nudged him back to wakefulness. It took his groggy mind a moment to remember where he was, but then he noticed the noise from the horses. Whinnying and stomping, all three were tugging at their reins with wild eyes. While they slept the snow had stopped and the sky had cleared. Under the black, star-sprinkled heavens a blanket of crystalline snow bathed everything in a pale blue light. High in the powdered branches of the twisted pine tree to which the horses were tied a dark shape was lurking.

Moving slowly to avoid alerting the intruder, Bob stretched out and picked up Bill's Winchester, gently shaking it to dislodge its accumulation of snow. Still lying on the ground, Bob brought the rifle to his shoulder, aimed at the hulking silhouette, and squeezed off a shot. The blast of the rifle shattered the frigid night air, causing Bill and Emmett to sit up in a panic as the dark figure crashed down through the trees, snapping the branches in crackling succession until it thumped onto the ground with a final growling moan, followed by a shower of disturbed snowflakes.

Emmett grabbed his pistol, and all three cautiously approached the dark mass lying still at the base of the tree. Bill lit a match, and in its feeble flickering glow they saw the tawny coat and sightless eyes of a mountain lion. A small dark hole in its side testified to Bob's shooting skill.

“Do you think you could have done as well if that had been Detective Smith?” Emmett asked, the glitter of his teeth revealing his smile.

“I sure would like to have him in the same place and then try it,” Bob answered with a chuckle.

Bill just grunted and said, “I’m going back to sleep.” Bob and Emmett also lay back down, but found it difficult to doze off again. The shooting of the cougar had gotten his blood flowing, and he was pleased with his own rapid reaction and marksmanship. He replayed the incident over and over in his mind, until exhaustion finally won out and he sank back into a deep slumber.

They were up with the sun, and the trip down the eastern side of the pass naturally went much faster than the previous night’s climb. As the mountains began to level out, they stopped at a small ranch in a valley and asked for food for themselves and their horses. As was the custom, the old Irishman who owned the ranch welcomed them and fixed them a big country breakfast. The old man was obviously lonely, and he talked a blue streak the entire time the boys were there.

Bob mostly listened with only one ear as the man prattled on, but he devoted full attention when the conversation veered onto the recent train robbery at Alila. On February 26 the Southern Pacific had posted a $5000 reward for the robbers, and included a detailed description. The rancher had it on reliable authority that the description matched some boys named Dalton, but he doubted they would be able to catch anyone with a good old Irish name like that.

The old Irishman complained that he, too, had experienced run-ins with the railroad and express companies, and if he were a little younger he would take them on just as well as these Daltons had done. For that matter, he claimed, his son, a former deputy sheriff, was none too good to take a hand in it either.

Rested and refreshed, the brothers thanked the old rancher and mounted their horses. After Bill told the rancher that he would be back through in three or four days, they rode off, still headed east. Beyond the foothills the land became flatter and drier, and the horizon shimmered in the heat. By mid-afternoon they had reached the edge of the Mojave Desert, and the appearance of a sheepherder's camp was accepted as a sign to stop for the night. Availing themselves of the sheepherder's hospitality, they ate and rested in preparation for the grueling trek ahead of them. They were going to try and cross the desert to Needles on horseback, something the sheepherder claimed had never been done.

They started out before sunrise, when the desert air was still cool, but by noon they were baking in a dry stone oven, surrounded by the most lifeless and foreboding scenery they had ever encountered. The ground was hard-packed sand and colorless dust, speckled with scattered brown tufts of weeds and greenish-gray sagebrush, and it seemed to go on forever. In some areas red sandstone bluffs erupted from the surface of the desert, and in others there were piles of brown rocks like a giant's abandoned building materials. The sun beat down on all of it, until everything was too hot to touch, but the Daltons pushed on, the rancher's words about the reward circular echoing in their ears.

That night they camped outside a little town called Daggett, a train stop on the Atlantic and Pacific line. As they sat around the campfire eating their meager supper, Bill talked about how he missed his family, and said he was worried about how this new reward being offered would affect things.

"Are you still planning to try and make it back to Oklahoma?" Bill asked. He had told Bob and Emmett that he would accompany them to Needles, near the Arizona border, but they would be on their own after that.

Chewing on his jerky, Bob just nodded. Between them the small fire cracked and spit, sparks flying up and dying as they floated away in the cool night air.

"That's a hell of a ride," Bob said sympathetically. "I told Eva you'd be there in about two months." Bill had written their sister Eva before they left his house, warning her that Bob and Emmett were returning. Bob had asked Bill to include a request for Eva to contact Bryant and McElhanie out at Riley's ranch and let them know as well. "Are you sure that's what you want to do? They're still looking for you there, too."

“We got friends there,” Bob said. “We’ll be all right.” Bill shrugged, and nothing more was said for a while. Bill’s concern about his family had started Bob thinking again, and the guilt he felt about how his robbery attempt had affected his family reappeared. Gathering his courage, he began to speak in a quietly apologetic tone.

“Bill, we might just as well tell you the truth. Emmett and I robbed the train at Alila, or at least we tried to.” Bill’s expression changed only slightly; this revelation was obviously not unexpected. “Since you have a family, we don’t want you to suffer on our account. You’re liable to have a fight on your hands any minute if you stay with us, and we don’t want to be responsible if you get killed.”

“Bobby,” Bill began, then stopped, holding his hands open in front of him as if trying to grasp the right words. He took a deep breath and tried again. “I am really disappointed in you. I appreciate your concern for me now, but you should have told me about this a long time ago. I’ve been lying to all those people about you because you swore you were innocent. Now what am I going to do? Go home and say, ‘Oops, I was wrong’? What if they arrest me for helping you? Don’t you ever think about the consequences of your actions?”

Bob was taken aback by Bill’s smoldering anger, and abashed as he recognized the truth in what Bill said.

“But you said the railroad was crooked,” Bob argued in a plaintive voice, knowing as he said it that it was a weak defense.

“But that doesn’t give you the right to steal from them,” Bill admonished. “Good Lord, Bobby, Mom taught you better than that.”

“I know,” Bob admitted, looking down at the ground contritely. “It’s just, well. . .”

“Well, nothing.” Bill dug into his pants pockets and brought out his wallet. “Here,” he said fishing out a thin sheaf of money. “Use this money to get to Oklahoma, or wherever. I’m going home in the morning.”

Bob took the money and put it in his own pocket as he tried to make amends. "Look, Bill, I'm real sorry. . . "

"Sorry doesn't cut it. Just let it drop, Bobby. I'm going to go to sleep now." Bill spread out his bedroll and lay down with his back to his brothers. Bob and Emmett looked at each other guiltily while they made their own beds.

In the morning, after a good night's rest, Bill was in a better mood, and he warmly wished Bob and Emmett luck before he departed back toward his home.

Bob and Emmett packed up and continued east across the desert, following the rail line, as the landscape grew progressively more barren and rugged. They had been fortunate so far, but the long, hard ride was taking its toll. By late afternoon Emmett's horse showed signs of severe fatigue and dehydration, and only by slowing their pace to a walk were they able to reach a railroad section house at Ludlow.

The section foreman and his wife, a pleasant young couple inexplicably living in the middle of the desert, welcomed them into their home and fed them. Bob told them they were sheepmen on a buying trip to Arizona, and asked if they could leave their horses with the couple to recuperate. In a few days, Bob said, they would either come back and get them, or arrange for them to be picked up. The nice young couple said they would be pleased to help, and the section foreman then put Bob and Emmett on the next freight train that came through headed east.

At Needles they climbed off the freight and bought tickets on a passenger train leaving that night. They rode the sleeper all the way to Peabody, Kansas, and switched trains there for a southbound to Dover, Oklahoma Territory. From Dover they walked the seven miles to their mother's house in Kingfisher. Bob felt an unexplainable sense of security back here in Oklahoma, among people he knew. Once again, things were looking up.

Author's Notes

Chapter 8

As with the previous chapter, most of the events described here are drawn from the testimony at Grat's trail. Grat's activities after the attempted robbery were gone into at great length, in an attempt to show that his contradictory statements and frequent travel were evidence of his involvement. Grat was followed from Goshen to San Miguel by a former lawman named Frank Griffith, who had been contacted by John Harris and put on Grat's trail with an agreement to split any reward. Grat's written statement was introduced into evidence by William Smith.

Emmett described what happened when Smith and O'Neill spent the night at Bill's ranch in his book, *Beyond the Law*. He also told of their subsequent flight south to Ludlow, although he failed to mention that Bill accompanied them. Bill testified at Grat's trial that he went as far as Daggett with Bob and Emmett, and that it was not until they camped at Daggett that Bob finally admitted his part in the Alila affair.

CHAPTER 9

It was a time of turmoil in the Twin Territories, as people now called the region between Texas and Kansas. The Land Run in April 1889, which opened the Unassigned Lands for settlement, had been more successful than anyone had imagined, and the swelling population had quickly organized, designating the area as Oklahoma Territory. In early 1891, however, this new territory consisted of only a small section of land, about forty mile wide and sixty miles long, shaped like the shield on a coat of arms. Hundreds of cities had sprung up, but the largest were Kingfisher, Guthrie, and Oklahoma City.

To the east and south of Oklahoma Territory was what remained of Indian Territory, a loosely organized collection of tribal nations and agencies with a hodgepodge of local governments and a mixed population of whites, blacks, and Indians. To the west were lands that had been granted to various tribes, including the Cheyenne, Arapahoe, Wichita, Caddo, Comanche, Kiowa, and Apache, but these flat arid sections remained sparsely populated and politically unorganized. The northern border of Oklahoma Territory, however, was the one that most concerned its people: between them and Kansas lay the Cherokee Strip, a sixty-mile-wide band of prime grazing and farming land still owned, but never used, by the Cherokee Tribe.

While the Five Civilized Tribes in the eastern section of Indian Territory had developed sound governments based on democratic principles, most of the remaining tribes had not been as ready to accept the white man's ways. Negotiations were already under way with these politically unsophisticated tribal councils, with the aim of eventually opening all the Indian areas to white settlement. These plans were being pushed by the politicians and businessmen of Oklahoma Territory, locally called Boomers, who mainly wanted to expand their areas of influence and make a profit. The most pressing of these deals was the opening of the Cherokee Strip, which would geographically connect Oklahoma Territory with the United States. Fortunately, the Cherokees were agreeable, and a tentative settlement with the tribe had already been reached; the strip was to be opened by a land run in 1892. Meanwhile, however, the ranchers who had been leasing large parcels of land in the Strip for years were now being forced to close down and move out, in order to make the land available for prospective settlers.

Enforcing the laws in the Twin Territories was becoming increasingly problematic. The Indian areas had their own tribal law enforcement agencies, but they still had no jurisdiction over non-Indians. The new arrivals in Oklahoma Territory had set up their own city police and county sheriff departments, but as yet there was little cooperation between them, and territorial laws were still in the process of being written. The only agency with criminal jurisdiction over the entire region was the U. S. Marshals Service, and even it was becoming fragmented. In a politically motivated effort to reduce Judge Isaac Parker's power in Fort Smith, new district courts had been set up in Muskogee and Guthrie; other parts of the territory had already been made subordinate to the courts in Wichita, Kansas, and Paris, Texas. The marshals were jealous of their regions, and deputies had to seek permission before pursuing a criminal into another marshal's jurisdiction.

Since deputies were paid on a straight fee basis, receiving a set amount for each criminal they apprehended, there was little incentive to waste time searching for an elusive and possibly dangerous fugitive, unless, of course, a large reward was being offered. Instead, they could more easily arrest the hundreds of petty criminals that infested the tumultuous territories. The cowboys who had lost their jobs in the Strip, the settlers who arrived too late to stake a claim, the bootleggers slaking a people's illegal thirst, and the con men drawn to the lawless land of opportunity, all provided the deputies with endless chances to earn their fees. As an ex-deputy himself, Bob Dalton was well aware of the problems his former peers faced, and he took full advantage of this knowledge.

Upon their return from California, Bob and Emmett spent the night at their mother's house. One night was all they dared risk, since the hunt for them was now on in earnest. Charley Bryant and Will McElhanie brought them their horses and rifles from their sister Eva's house, and the four of them rode out to the east, following the

Cimarron River over toward Guthrie. While the others camped along a creek that night, Bob went into town to see Eugenia. Between embraces she brought him up to date on what had been happening and who was chasing him. Southern Pacific and Wells Fargo had offered rewards totaling $3600, and there was still a $1000 reward from the horse-stealing near Claremore. These substantial sums had encouraged all sorts of detectives, both official and amateur, to join the pursuit. She told Bob that his old friend Heck Thomas was leading the search, assisted by a railroad detective named Smith.

When Bob returned to his companions, he was no longer as confident as before. While he had many friends who would help them elude their pursuers, he realized that many of them would undoubtedly be tempted by the rewards, and might sell the Daltons out. Even more worrisome was the knowledge that Heck Thomas was after them. Highly respected by all that knew him, Heck was considered the best deputy marshal in the territory, and he had many years of experience. Bob liked and admired Heck, but he was certain that Thomas would not let their friendship interfere with his attempts to bring Bob to justice. Heck Thomas was honest and incorruptible; this, along with his Democratic Party affiliation, had kept him from ever being appointed Marshal, despite his obvious qualifications for the position.

Anxious to keep on the move, Bob led the gang away from Guthrie before sunrise, heading farther east to Bitter Creek Newcomb's claim. When they first arrived, Bob thought that Newcomb must have abandoned the place, such was the condition of the farm. The fields were choked with weeds, and the ramshackle house looked like it was about to collapse, but they found Newcomb lounging inside in his underwear. Farming had not suited his temperament, Newcomb explained, and he gladly accepted their offer to rejoin the gang. Anything was better than digging in the dirt.

For the next few weeks the five men roamed all across the territories, intentionally skipping from one jurisdiction to another to muddy their trail. First east through the Iowa and the Sac and Fox agencies to the Creek Nation, then north through the Osage Nation and west through the Cherokee Strip, and finally south into the Cheyenne and Arapahoe lands, with occasional forays into

Oklahoma Territory to see Eugenia at Guthrie and their mother at Kingfisher.

Newspapers frequently mentioned that the notorious Dalton boys had been sighted in one place or another, and many unsolved crimes were erroneously attributed to them. Bob enjoyed seeing his name in the papers, but he wished there was also some money in it for him. The cash Bill had given him had run out quickly, as had the little Eugenia was able to provide him. They tried stealing some horses and cattle, but their notoriety made it almost impossible to sell the stock at a reasonable price.

One day, while camped in a hollow in the Osage Hills, a citizen's posse had tracked them down and opened fire on them from the surrounding woods. Bob's well-aimed rifle fire had driven the farmers off, but the incident had a sobering effect on Will McElhanie. Still bothered by the wound he had received in New Mexico, he decided this second brush with death was one too many. The next day he departed, saying he was going to go visit his sister in Arkansas. The Daltons never heard from him again.

Fortunately, the old-timers of the territory were more than willing to give the boys temporary respite. The people who had been there since before the land rush were the outcasts and mavericks of society, folks who had come to Indian Territory to escape the strictures of government and civilization, and they perceived the Daltons as their champions. They warmly welcomed anyone who was willing to poke the establishment in the eye and defy authority, and they readily gave Bob and the gang food and supplies while asking nothing in return. When he had the money to spare, Bob paid them generously. Not only did such largesse enhance his self-image as a Robin Hood character, it also helped buy silence. Still, he was increasingly aware that this life on the run could not last forever, and they would need a large infusion of cash to continue.

While Bob and Emmett roamed the territories evading the law, events in California were coming to a head. On March 17, 1891, Grat and Bill Dalton were indicted by the Tulare County grand jury on charges of attempted robbery and murder, with bail being set at $20,000. When Bob learned of this, he was incensed at the injustice. His older brothers were totally innocent of the charges, and Bob was convinced that the authorities in California were well aware of the fact. Intense pressure from Southern Pacific and Wells Fargo to arrest somebody, anybody, had led to this miscarriage of justice, and Bob's anger festered and grew with each passing day. Short of turning himself and Emmett in, though, the only way Bob could think of to help his brothers was to acquire money for them to use as bail and to pay for their defense at the trial. That, however, would require a large sum, more than Bob had ever seen.

In late April, while visiting Eugenia again, Bob confided his concerns and his feelings of helplessness. When he ranted and cursed the railroads and express company, she made a simple suggestion. Why not take the money from the express company to pay for Bill's and Grat's defense against spurious charges leveled by that same express company? Bob was instantly enthralled with the brilliance and irony of the plan, and soon came to believe that it was actually his own idea. Eugenia, graciously allowing Bob to take credit, then offered to "go on the scout," to travel around the territory on the various railroads to find the best location for the robbery and to gather intelligence about the schedules and money shipments. As an attractive young woman, she would arouse no suspicion, and with her knowledge of Morse code she could listen in on the private communications of the railroads simply by hanging around the telegraph offices.

Although Bob expressed concern about the danger she was placing herself in, he was actually very enthusiastic about Eugenia's idea, and soon they were planning her routes and making arrangements for leaving messages. By the time he returned to the gang's camp, Bob was walking tall again, his mind spinning with the possibilities. He would apply the lessons learned at Alila, and with four men instead of two, he could ensure that the robbery went off successfully.

Saturday, May 9, 1891

"We want to thank you again, Mrs. Hamby. That was an excellent meal." Bob smiled at the old woman with genuine affection. Dressed in a plain black dress with a soiled white apron over it, Mrs. Hamby reminded him of his mother: thin, frail, and widowed. Bob pressed a silver dollar into her hand.

"I wish I could give you more," Bob told her, "but times have been pretty hard lately, what with all the ranches closing up in the strip." Behind him Bryan and Newcomb grunted and nodded in affirmation. Emmett had already gone outside to get the horses ready.

"Well, I was glad to do it," Mrs. Hamby told them, clutching the dollar tightly. "Don't often get a chance to cook for the menfolk any more, and it's always nice to have company. I know you boys must be having a rough time of it lately."

"Thank you for caring, ma'am," Bitter Creek said. He was holding his hat in front of him, and to Bob it seemed that Newcomb was sincerely moved by the woman's compassion.

"That's quite all right, young man," she said. "It's the Christian thing to do. I really enjoyed having you, and you all come back any time you're in the area, you hear?"

"Yes, ma'am," Bob assured her, "we will. And you take care, now." The three men shuffled out of the small farm cabin and mounted the horses that Emmett had brought to the front porch. With a final wave they rode away, heading back to their secluded camp on property owned by Charley Bryant's brother. It was still early afternoon, and they all kept a sharp lookout for other riders. The camp was just outside of Mulhall, a little town in the northeast part of Oklahoma Territory. They were just across the Cimarron River from Guthrie, the territorial capital, and the threat of capture by the authorities was always present.

It had been almost two months since Bob and Emmett had returned from California, and many of the amateur sleuths and opportunistic lawmen had given up on finding the Daltons and gone on to more lucrative pursuits. Others, unfortunately, were more tenacious. Eugenia had told Bob that Heck Thomas, along with his new partner Burril Cox and the hated railroad detective William Smith, were still on their trail, as were several other lawmen. While most of their pursuers were motivated solely by the prospect of collecting the rewards, Bob suspected that Thomas and Smith were driven by other, stronger motives. In a confrontation with the Daltons, the reward-seekers, unwilling to risk their lives for money, would undoubtedly back down. Thomas, on the other hand, with his zeal for justice, and Smith, whose one-track mind was bent on their capture, would be deadly opponents.

The constant state of alert and the ever-present danger of capture or death had worn on all of them, frazzling their nerves and testing their friendship. McElhanie's departure, which Bob felt was a failure on his part as a leader, made him realize that they must do something soon. Some sort of action was needed to restore the confidence of the group, as well as to improve their financial situation, which was now getting desperate.

That night, as they sat around their campfire inside a grove of trees, they heard a single horse approaching. Bob grabbed his Winchester and went into a crouch, then heard an exchange of whistles in the darkness. In a moment Emmett, who had been standing guard, led Eugenia into the clearing. After a brief, demure hug with Bob, she told him her news. Tomorrow night, on the Santa Fe line, the Kansas City—Gainesville express would be carrying $80,000 in cash. She had overheard the message clacking on the telegraph at the Guthrie train station, and had ridden out immediately to tell Bob. This was the opportunity they had been waiting for.

She had copied down the train's schedule, and by the firelight they all went over the list of stops and times, trying to determine the ideal place to strike. Soon it was settled, and Bob sent Eugenia back to Guthrie with a chaste kiss on the cheek. The promise of action rejuvenated the four young men, and they stayed up late into the night discussing how they would pull off this job.

Sunday, May 10, 1891

It was getting close to midnight, and Bob jiggled his foot impatiently. Next to him in the darkness stood Bitter Creek Newcomb, chewing tobacco and quietly spitting every few minutes. They were hiding behind a railroad equipment shed across the tracks from the small depot at Wharton junction, awaiting the arrival of the Santa Fe train from Kansas City. Wharton, a few miles north of Guthrie, was just inside the Cherokee Strip, and it marked the junction of the Santa Fe line with the Saint Louis and San Francisco Railroad which crossed the Strip from east to west.

Although it had cooled off considerably since sundown, the night air was still pleasantly warm, and the south wind had calmed to only a steady breeze. The only lights were those from the station, and Bob and Newcomb kept in the shadows of the shed. Bob peeked around the corner of the small wooden building for what seemed like the hundredth time, and finally he saw what he had been waiting for. Far up the tracks to the north he detected a glimmering pinpoint of light. The train was coming.

Bob nudged Newcomb with his elbow. "Here it comes!" he whispered excitedly. "You ready?"

"Uh-huh," Newcomb muttered, leaning out from the wall of the shed to take a look himself. As the engine pulled into the station with squealing brakes and escaping steam, they flattened themselves against the wall of the shed to keep from being seen. Bob pulled the bandanna he had around his neck up over his nose, and nodded approvingly as Newcomb did the same. As the train shuddered to a halt, Newcomb started to move, but Bob placed his hand on Newcomb's chest to stop him.

"Not yet," he said. "Wait until they're about to leave." Although they were on the far side of the train from the station, they could see enough between the cars to judge what was happening, and as the conductor called out, "All aboard!" Bob pushed away from the shed and sprinted for the engine, with Newcomb close on his heels.

With his boots crunching on the gravel and the smell of damp cotton in his nose, Bob crossed the train yard and clambered into the cab of the engine, his pistol already drawn. "Throw up your hands!" he ordered the two train men, and they quickly complied.

"Get down," Bob told them, stepping aside so they could pass him and climb down to the ground where Newcomb was waiting. Bob jumped down after them and prodded the engineer in the back with his gun. He and Newcomb escorted the train crew back along the side of the train away from the platform. As was usual practice, the express car was right behind the engine, and when they reach the far end of it, Bob halted the group.

"Uncouple it," Bob commanded. Newcomb scampered across the end of the express car and warily stood guard on the far side, both to observe the rest of the train and to prevent the engineer and fireman from escaping in that direction. Responding to Bob's waving pistol, the two crewmen lowered their arms and went to work on the linkage, struggling to free the huge metal coupling. Bob jerked with a start when Newcomb's gun went off.

"Get back in the cars!" Newcomb yelled toward the rear of the train. The shot had also startled the train men and given them added impetus. The coupling broke free, and Bob and Newcomb hustled the two back to the engine.

"Run on down the tracks about two miles to the stockyards," Bob told them when they were all back in the cab. The engine and express car slowly pulled away from the station, leaving the passenger cars behind. Newcomb leaned out from the cab and watched to ensure that no one was following. The station receded in the darkness, and soon the fences of the stockyard were visible in the train's headlight. At Bob's instructions the engineer brought the train to a halt, and through the clouds of escaping steam Bob saw Emmett and Charley Bryant appear out of the gloom.

"Guard these two," Bob shouted down to Emmett, while Bryant took a position on the right side of the train and alertly scanned the darkness. Emmett joined them in the cab of the engine and handed Bob a burlap sack. Leaving Emmett to guard the engineer and fireman, Bob and Newcomb jumped down on the left side and walked back to the express car.

Bob reached up and rapped on the door with his pistol. When there was no response, he pounded again, harder this time. Newcomb, behind him, kept a wary eye back toward the station, in case someone tried to sneak up on them in the dark. Finally there were some metallic clicks, and the big door scraped as it slid open for a few inches. A white face, backlit by the lamps inside the car, appeared in the narrow opening.

"What's the matter?" the man asked in a frightened voice. "What's up?"

Bob jerked the door open farther and climbed up in, his pistol leading the way, "This is a robbery," Bob said by way of introduction. The messenger, a slightly-built man in a striped shirt and vest, raised his eyebrows and hands simultaneously. With a wave of his pistol, Bob motioned the man back to the end of the car, where a small green safe was bolted to the floor. "Open it," Bob directed, nodding his head toward the safe.

"Yes, sir," the messenger said, and knelt down to spin the dial. In a moment the door swung open, and Bob told the man to put the money in the gunny sack he had been carrying draped over his arm. While the messenger bent to this task, Bob picked up the Winchester and pistol that had been lying on a desk and tossed them out the open door. The messenger, shaking with fright, straightened up and held the bag out to Bob. It obviously had little in it. Bob shook his head.

"Now the through safe," he told the man, jerking his head toward the large black steel cabinet in the middle of the car.

"I, I don't have the combination," the man stuttered. "They locked it in Kansas City and wired the combination to Gainesville without telling me." This was the announced policy of Wells Fargo, but Bob had learned as a deputy marshal that it was not actually followed. It was only a ruse to dissuade train robbers and reassure their customers.

"Open the damn safe!" Bob yelled with pretended fury, firing a round from his pistol into the wooden floor at the messenger's feet. At the sound of Bob's pistol, Newcomb also fired a couple times, perhaps from a nervous reaction to the unexpected noise of Bob's shot, or perhaps to frighten the train men and distant passengers. The three shots, whatever their reason, completely shattered the messenger's resistance. With trembling fingers he turned the dial, and after one miscue, he completed the sequence and turned the handle to open the heavy door.

Under Bob's threatening scrutiny, the messenger pulled packets of money and pouches from the safe and stuffed them in the dirty burlap bag. When he finished, Bob took the bag and ordered the man to lie down on his stomach. There had been little cash in the safe, and Bob was suspicious. Several minutes had passed between the time they had uncoupled the train and the moment the messenger had opened the door to the express car, giving him plenty of time to hide some of the money. Bob hastily searched the car, pulling open drawers and dumping out mailbags. He discovered a couple packets of bills and added them to the bag of loot.

Returning to the messenger, Bob knelt down beside him and held his pistol to the man's head while he searched the man's pockets with his other hand. All he found was a watch, which he pulled from its chain and stuffed in his pocket. It would be a good idea for everyone in the gang to have a watch, he thought, so that they could better synchronize their actions. He stood and took one more quick look around the car.

"I guess that's all, young fellow," he told the messenger cheerfully, and then leaped through the door onto the ground, the heavy bag flopping against his leg. "Let's go," he told Newcomb, and together they crossed behind the express car to where Charley Bryant was waiting.

"We got it," Bob told him as Bryant fell in beside them. "Come on!" he called out to Emmett as they came abreast of the engine. With a last warning threat to the engineer and fireman, Emmett jumped down and ran to catch up as the others hurried to where the horses were tied.

Laughing and whooping with pleasure, the four young men galloped away into the night, taking a round-about route back to their camp near Mulhall. Success was theirs, just as Bob had promised. Bob was doubly glad, for not only had they acquired huge sums of money, they had also struck back at the express company. In his own mind, at least, he had wiped out the disgrace of his failure at Alila, and at the same time he had begun a new chapter in the stirring saga of the Dalton boys.

Back at the camp the boys were jubilant, playfully punching each other and making jokes as they retold their night's experiences again and again.

"Did you see that guy's face when. . . ?" one would say.

"I'll tell ya, when I heard that first shot, I thought . . ."

"So I told him, you damn well better. . ."

"Jesus! That was fun!"

Amidst the joshing , Bob carefully counted the stolen money, after first separating it from the useless documents and papers the messenger had slipped into the bag. He gave Newcomb and Bryant about $2000 each, most in small bills and coins. He retained the rest for Emmett and himself, explaining that the bulk of it would go to Grat and Bill to pay for their lawyers. Bob also intended to pay off some old debts, in particular the money he owed Ririe and Hoots, the men who had posted bond for Bob after the Christmas introducing incident.

It was almost dawn before they calmed down enough to go to sleep, but Bob insisted they keep a guard posted at all times. He made up a schedule on the back of one of the stolen papers, listing himself as the first guard. At the end of each guard's shift, as designated by the stolen pocket watch, that guard would wake up the next guard and give him the list and the watch. As always, Bob warned them of dire consequences if anyone fell asleep during his guard shift, and then finally he let the others bed down.

Even as tired as they were, the boys got little sleep that day. The residual excitement of the robbery, the anxiety about pursuit, and the early summer heat and insects kept them from relaxing enough to fall into a deep slumber. Instead they dozed fitfully, between swatting at flies and fanning themselves with stolen documents.

That evening Eugenia rode out to the cam and regaled them with the stories that were flying in town about the great train holdup. It was already generally accepted that the Daltons were behind it, she warned, and posses were forming all over the territory. Bob gave her a thousand dollars from the haul and instructed her to take it to California for his brothers' defense. When she returned she was to go to Woodward, at the west end of the Cherokee Outlet, and wait until Bob contacted her there. After she left, Bob told the others to saddle up. Officers would soon be scouring the local area, so they had to move out under cover of darkness.

Riding east that night, the gang crossed the border between Oklahoma and Indian Territory and disappeared into the Sac and Fox lands. Few people lived in this area of steep hills covered with scrub oak, but their presence there did not go unnoticed for long. Within a week the Sac and Fox Indian Police had tracked them down, and the gang galloped away just ahead of their pursuers.

Spring rains had swollen the normal trickle of the Canadian River until it overflowed its banks and flooded the lowlands, creating wide tracts of swampy land that most folks considered impassable. With encouragement and a few dollars, however, a local Indian was talked into leading the boys across one of these bogs via an underwater ridge of solid ground. The Indian police, unfavorably regarded as tools of the white man's government by most of the Indian population, were unable to secure such assistance and were forced to abandon the chase.

Bob led them farther east, into the Creek Nation, and let their presence there be known by asking friendly ranchers and store owners to report that the notorious Dalton gang had visited them. Then, as the focus of the posses and detectives shifted to the east, Bob and the others turned back west, traveling across Oklahoma Territory at night and hiding during the day, until they had crossed into the Cheyenne and Arapahoe lands. By the end of May they were safely camped on Jim Riley's ranch on the South Canadian River, about forty miles southeast of Woodward. It was wide open prairie, barely able to support cattle, and there were few residents and even fewer travelers passing through.

Two days after the Wharton robbery, the Santa Fe Railroad and Wells Fargo posted rewards for the capture of the Daltons. Combined with the California rewards and those outstanding for the horse-theft near Claremore, Bob and Emmett were now worth $11,000, and this princely sum brought out the bounty hunters in droves. While the searchers combed the eastern and central territories, Bob and his gang rested quietly on Riley's ranch, protected by a network of friends who kept the Daltons posted on new developments and diverted anyone who passed through looking for them. It was safe and secure there, but after only a few days Bob became restless.

"I been thinking," Bob announced to Emmett as they sat together on the edge of a gully watching the cattle graze below them. With its steep crumbling sides, the gully was the product of a weather cycle centuries old. Long dry spells would be interrupted by sudden cloudbursts and torrents of rain that carved out narrow water courses on its way to the river, but in days the water would again disappear, leaving dry washes that resembled the Grand Canyon in miniature. What little moisture remained was absorbed by the soil at the bottom of the gullies, though, and this sustained the lush green grasses that carpeted the narrow floor and attached hungry cattle.

Emmett waited for Bob to continue, knowing that no response was yet required of him. Bob broke off a piece of sunbaked earth and tossed the clod lazily toward one of the steers below him, smiling with satisfaction as the missile exploded in a puff of dust at the animal's feet. The steer raised its head in dumb confusion, but then placidly returned to munching the succulent grass.

"This ain't much of a life," Bob finally continued.

"What do you mean?"

"You know, running from the law, hiding out all the time. Here we are, famous bandits, with a ton of money in our pockets, and what good does it do us? We can't enjoy it. We can't have normal lives. I don't know."

"I kind of thought we were having fun," Emmett suggested cautiously.

"Well, yeah, but now what? Where do we go from here? Do we just keep robbing trains or whatever until they catch us? I don't want to end up in jail like the Youngers. Maybe we ought to do something else."

"Like what?"

"Maybe we ought to go to South America."

Emmett jerked his head around to stare at Bob, baffled by the unexpected suggestion. Bob paused a moment to let the idea soak in.

"South America?" Emmett asked in disbelief.

"Sure. We've got enough money now, we could live real comfortable down there. They can't extradite us from there, and we could start our own ranch or something."

"I don't know," Emmett said dubiously. "All our family's here, our friends. And they don't speak English down there."

"We can learn Spanish. And I'm gonna ask Eugenia to marry me and go with us. Once we get set up down there, maybe we can send for Mom and the others."

"You think so?" Emmett's wistful tone reflected the glimmer of hope that he felt.

"I don't know why not. What I figured is, we'll ride up into the States, maybe to Missouri, where they aren't looking for us so hard, and take a train to Tampa, Florida. I'll have Eugenia meet us there so we can get married, and then we'll take a ship to South America."

"Have we got enough money for that?"

"We got over $7000, that should be plenty. Stuff is real cheap down in South America."

"What about Charley and Bitter Creek?"

Bob shrugged. "They can come, too, if they want, but I don't think they will. Nobody knows for sure that it was them that helped us rob that train, so they can stay here without any problems."

"Okay," Emmett said, already looking forward to this new adventure. Although he refused to admit it, even to himself, the train robberies terrified him. This proposed journey to foreign lands promised excitement without the deadly danger. The next day they set out.

Monday, June 1, 1891

Bob reined in his horse. "You stay here and stand guard." Emmett nodded. As Bob dismounted, Emmett began to swivel his head methodically back and forth, his hand resting lightly on the handle of his pistol. His eyes, shaded from the bright sunlight by his hat brim, warily scanned the short dusty alley. Kiowa was a tiny town in southwest Kansas, just across the border from the Cherokee Strip, about sixty miles northeast of Woodward. It was the first populated area Bob and Emmett had seen in three days. They had ridden into town very cautiously, and Bob had led them down this alley to a position directly behind a general store.

Bob opened the back door to the store and stepped quickly inside, pausing with the door open to let his eyes adjust to the dimness of the windowless stock room. The room was a jumble of boxes, crates, and barrels, but ahead of him was the curtained doorway that led into the main part of the store. Clutching his Winchester firmly in his right hand, Bob quietly crossed to the curtain and peeked around it. The store was quiet, and there was only one occupant. Behind the sales counter stood a thin man wearing a dark blue apron. Unaware of Bob's presence, he was writing on a tablet. Bob pushed the curtain aside and stepped into the room.

Attracted by the movement, the clerk glanced up at Bob and a series of emotions flashed across his face. Surprise at Bob's entrance was quickly replaced by annoyance that someone would come in the back way, but any planned reprimand was quickly suppressed when he notice the pistol on Bob's hip and the rifle in his hand. Immediately the clerk forced a fake smile, but his eyes wavered with caution and fear.

"Uh, good morning, sir," the man said with false cheer, straightening his back and laying down his pencil. "Can I help you?"

"Need some supplies," Bob said. He took long strides across the room, stopping to search warily out the front window.

"Surely. What would you like?" The clerk nervously wiped his palms on the apron.

"Beans. A couple rashers of bacon. Some flour and salt. Maybe some canned goods." While the man gathered the items and piled them on the counter, Bob kept glancing out the windows to ensure no one would walk in without warning. The store clerk, anxious to please the armed intruder, made several suggestions about items he had on special, and Bob cordially agreed to most of them.

When the pile had grown to a size that Bob considered was the most their pack horse could carry, he asked the clerk how much the charge would be.

"I'm not sure, sir," he said, picking up his pencil. "It will just take me a moment to tote that up." He started jotting down numbers on a tablet, placing his free hand on each item as he noted its price. Bob laid a twenty-dollar gold piece on the tablet.

"Think that will cover it?" he asked with a smile. The clerk stated at the coin a minute, glanced at the pile of groceries, and bobbed his head energetically.

"Certainly, sir, that will be more than enough. Give me a minute to figure out your total, and I'll give you your change."

"Don't need change," Bob told him. "I just need you to carry this stuff out back and load it on our horses."

Relieved that he was not being robbed, and in fact was making a huge profit on the transaction, the clerk was very accommodating. While Bob continued to guard the store's entrance, the other man bustled back and forth carrying the goods out the back door, where he loaded them on the pack horse under Emmett's watchful gaze. When the load had been secured, Bob thanked the man for his help, went back out to the alley, and mounted his horse. Sauntering their horses to avoid drawing attention to themselves, Bob and Emmett headed out of town toward the southwest. Once they were out of sight of any buildings, however, they turned east.

It was a long way to Missouri, and Bob intended to take it slow and easy, zig-zagging across the border between Kansas and the territories to mislead anyone in pursuit. With the supplies they had purchased, and by travelling mostly by night, he hoped to avoid any further contact with strangers. In the days ahead they would have to travel stealthily over three hundred miles, through country where hundreds of men were looking for them. It was a formidable task, but for Bob it had become an exciting challenge.

Monday, June 15, 1891

"The State of California versus William Dalton, charged with the attempted robbery of the Southern Pacific train at Alila on or about the sixth day of February, last." The bailiff's booming voice brought the crowded courtroom to silence. Grat looked over at his brother. Bill had a stricken, yet determined set to his face. Beads of sweat dotted his forehead, although some of them might have been due to the stuffy heat of the courtroom, packed to capacity with newspaper reporters, witnesses, prospective jurymen, and curious spectators. Grat, experienced in this sort of thing, was relatively serene.

The prosecution team, District Attorney Maurice Power and Alfred Daggett, introduced themselves, and then the lawyer next to Bill rose. "You honor, I am J. W. Ahern of Bakersfield. I am not the attorney in this case, but I was asked by J. W. Breckenridge to appear here today. Mr. Breckenridge is at present engaged in a murder trial at Merced and could not be present. He has asked me to be here to request that this case be put over until Thursday, June 18, when the leading counsel could be present."

Power jumped up from the prosecution's table. "We are ready for trial, your honor, and would resist any proposition for a continuance."

Judge Wheaton A. Gray, a big man with white hair and a matching beard, was stern. "This case has already been postponed once," he said. "The date of the trial was fixed by the attorney for the defense, as I recall. Now, there are a lot of witnesses and jurymen who have appeared here today in the expectation that the trial would begin, and some of them have traveled a good distance to be here. Unless you can give me a good cause, I am not in favor of granting a continuance."

Ahern then requested that he be given until the next day to prepare affidavits for a continuance, but the judge refused, sustaining the objections of the district attorney. He did, however, adjourn the court until after lunch to give Ahern a little time to get organized.

When the court reconvened, Ahern presented an affidavit from Breckenridge explaining his absence, and one from himself explaining he was not conversant with the facts in William Dalton's case, and could thus not in justice provide a good defense. Grat and

Bill also made affidavits that they were not ready for trial, due to the fact that several material witnesses that had been subpoenaed by the court had failed to appear.

As the lawyers argued and county clerks were called to establish who were the attorneys of record, Grat morosely stared at Judge W. A. Gray, whose bias was becoming increasingly evident. Not that it was unexpected. During the last political campaign Gray had been chairman of the Republican Central Committee, and thus instrumental in the election of Governor Markham, whose campaign financing was generally believed to have been supplied primarily by the Southern Pacific Railroad. During Grat's grand jury hearing in March, even before the indictments were handed down, Governor Markham had appointed Gray, by telegram, as an additional superior judge for the county. Judge Cross, who had been adequately handling all the cases in the county up to this point, was now relegated to taking only civil cases, and he was ordered to hand over all criminal cases to Gray. It did not take a genius to detect the subtle influence of the railroad in this move.

Although Gray made an attempt to appear impartial, to Grat it was obvious that the judge favored the prosecution. While polite and receptive to all of Power's and Daggett's utterances, he was curt and contemptuous to Ahern, leaving Grat with a cold hard knot in his stomach. He glanced back at where his mother, his brother Cole, and his sister Eva sat, and he tried to give them a brave smile. The worried look on his mother's face did not change.

With a start Grat realized that his name had been mentioned, and he instantly refocused on what was being said. Daggett proposed granting the continuance on Bill's trial, and suggested instead that they could begin Grat's trial. By simply substituting Grat's name for Bill's on the relevant documents, the trial could continue without interruption. Ahern was caught completely off guard by this move, and before he could mount an effective objection, Judge Gray approved the motion. He ordered Ahern, dumb-founded and muttering to himself, to proceed with the trial on the charges against Gratton Dalton, and had the bailiff call the names of the first prospective jurors. As Ahern shuffled papers in confusion, Grat saw that Bill had relaxed a bit, apparently relieved that he was, temporarily at least, out of the fire. That's okay for him, Grat thought, but now I'm the one under the gun, and judge can't wait to pull the trigger. Depression shrouded Grat like a dank fog, and he slumped farther down in his chair, wishing he could just have a drink.

Friday, June 19, 1891

"Your honor, the state moves that the court reporter be required to provide the attorneys for both the prosecution and the defense with a complete transcript of the testimony each day."

Beside Grat, Breckenridge rose ponderously to concur with Daggett. "The defense agrees with the district attorney. It would be an economy to the people to have the testimony so furnished, as it would permit the case to be more closely tried and ensure a proper verdict." Breckenridge had arrived on Wednesday night, and had spent Thursday challenging the manner in which the jurors had so far been selected. It had been to no avail, so the lawyer had then grudgingly participated in the selection of the final jurors.

Breckenridge was an eloquent speaker, and Grat allowed himself a small ray of hope that this man could overcome the court's bias and get him a fair trial. This morning the indictments had been read, and now the matter of the court reporter seemed a foregone conclusion, since both the state and the defense desired the transcripts. The judge, however, was not so disposed.

"Motion denied," Gray pronounced. "I know of no authority for ordering the bills of the reporters paid for such work. You gentlemen will just have to depend on your memory and your own notes."

"If it pleases the court," Breckenridge then said, still standing, "the defense requests that the witnesses in this case be put under the rule and excluded from the courtroom. We would not wish for the witnesses to have their testimony tainted by what they may have heard from other witnesses."

"Objection," Daggett said, rising from his chair.

"Sustained," Gray immediately replied. He bent his head toward the prosecution's table. "Proceed with your opening statement." Breckenridge sat down heavily, a worried frown briefly fleeting across his face. Grat noticed it, and his concern deepened.

Across the aisle Daggett had resumed his seat, and Power had risen and swaggered out in front of the table. He wore a light gray suit, under which could be seen wide red suspenders. His sandy hair was neatly combed, and his face cleanly shaven. In his hand was a sheaf of paper covered with notes; he rarely consulted them.

"May it please the court and the gentlemen of the jury," he began, affecting an oratory style. "It devolves upon me, for the purpose of expediting this matter, to state to you in a general way the line that we will adopt in the presentation of our evidence in this case.

"In the first place, we propose to show you, by legal, competent evidence, by direct evidence—evidence direct and positive—that on the sixth day of February, 1891, at about fifty minutes past seven o'clock in the evening of that day, at the town of Alila, in this county and state, two men boarded a railroad train on the Southern Pacific Railroad, getting upon the engine, and, by drawing weapons upon the fireman and engineer, forced them to run the train out southward from the town of Alila and to get off and dismount from the train and go back as far as the express car of Wells, Fargo, & Co., and there make a demand upon the agent of Wells, Fargo's express for certain treasure, there being eleven sacks of treasure amounting to a little over nine thousand dollars, and that these robbers, those persons who had boarded the train, fired several shots into the car. That in the melee which resulted from the firing, one man was killed, and that the robbers fled without having obtained the coin that was in the car. That in the month of January 1891, there was in the county of San Luis Obispo, about seven miles south of the town of San Miguel, four brothers by the name of Dalton, consisting, in the order of their ages, of the following named persons: First—the defendant who is on trial in this case, Gratton Dalton; Second—William M. Dalton, who is also in custody; Third—Robert Dalton; and Fourth, and the youngest of them all, Emmett Dalton, neither of the latter of whom are in custody, but all of whom were jointly indicted for making an assault to commit robbery upon C. C. Haswell, who was the express messenger of Wells, Fargo & Co., and in charge of said treasure."

Power paused to take a breath and glance briefly at his papers before continuing. "That on the morning or about the morning of the 29th day of January, 1891, three of these boys, Gratton, Emmett, and Robert, left the house of William M. Dalton and proceeded in the direction of Tulare Valley, by easy stages. That they passed in the direction and through Huron, and thence in the direction of Fresno, and thence down along the line of the railroad to the town of Delano, and thence back to the scene of this robbery. We propose also—after they fled from the train—to show that they traveled westward in the direction of the place from whence they came. We propose to show you by circumstantial evidence that there was a conspiracy between these four persons in this case, for the purpose of robbery of Wells, Fargo & Co. and C. C. Haswell, of the treasure in that car, and that in pursuance of this conspiracy this assault and attack was made.

"There will be certain minor circumstances adduced at the trial and valuable time would be consumed in detailing them. It will not be necessary for me to go over them now. I have outlined in a general way the evidence in this case."

Power looked at the jury for a minute, as if trying to gauge their reaction to his speech, then again glanced down at his notes. Addressing the judge, he said, "The state calls as its first witness, C. C. Haswell."

As Haswell came forward and was sworn in, Grat considered what Power had outlined as his case. Except for Grat and Bill having been aware beforehand of the robbery attempt, most of what he said was true. Still, while they could prove Grat was with Bob and Emmett prior to the robbery, Grat could just as easily prove he was in Fresno at the time of the robbery. The question that nagged Grat, however, was whether the judge would allow them to introduce such proof.

After countless nights of tedious riding, Bob and Emmett had finally made it safely to Missouri. There had been occasions when Emmett thought they were caught for sure, but each time they had narrowly escaped detection and continued on their journey. Although Emmett had lived in Missouri for several years as a child, he had not been back since, and his spirits lifted as they traveled through the state. It seemed lusher and greener than Kansas or Indian Territory, with taller trees and more picturesque hills. In Missouri, for some reason, the danger seemed to fade away behind them.

Springfield was a big city, compared to what Emmett was used to. Bustling with activity, it had tall buildings and horse-drawn streetcars, and Emmett discovered it was easy for him and Bob to blend in with the crowd. Bob found a livery stable near the downtown area and convinced the owner to buy their horses and saddles by accepting cut-rate prices. The man also agreed to buy their Winchester rifles, but when Emmett started to protest the ridiculously low amount the man offered, Bob shushed him and quickly closed the deal.

"We've got plenty of money," Bob told him as they walked away, "and we don't want to make a fuss."

Next they went to a clothing store catering to the local farmers and bought new, less conspicuous outfits. Bob found a cheap blue business suit of the type a farmer would buy for Sunday-go-to-meeting or to dress up when going to the bank to ask for a loan. The high-water pants barely covered the tops of his boots, and the jacket was baggy at the shoulders, but it gave Bob the unsophisticated appearance he wanted.

At Bob's insistence, Emmett bought an oversized pair of overalls and a cheap lightweight brown jacket. He replaced his high-heeled boots and spurs with brown lace-up shoes that hurt his feet, and on his head he now wore a straw hat with a wide brim, completing his makeover into a Missouri farmer on his first trip to the city. They had carried their Colt .45 pistols in a satchel while they did their shopping, but in the hotel room that evening, as they tried on their new disguises, Bob had Emmett strap on both their gunbelts under his overalls. The looseness of the denim overalls and the overhang of the jacket effectively hid the bulk of the guns, and Emmett practiced reaching in and drawing them until he had the operation down pat. For his own peace of mind, Bob had a small .38 caliber pocket pistol that he kept in his jacket, ready for immediate use.

The next day they took the train to Memphis, arriving without incident. Bob sent Emmett to the ticket window to buy tickets for Atlanta, the next stop on their journey to Tampa, while he tried to look bored as he carefully scanned the faces of the many people in the station for any hint of recognition. Emmett weaved his way through the crowd, dodging people with arms full of luggage as he made his way to the ticket window. His new shoes gave him an awkward gait, causing three men in business suits to state at him as he hobbled by. Emmett paused to let a woman with two children pass in front of him, and this accidentally allowed him to overhear one of the men comment to the others.

"That young fellow don't look like a real farmer. He walks like a cowboy." Another of the men noticed Emmett's nearness and alarmed expression, and he elbowed the speaker. Casually all three moved a short distance away.

As he stood in line at the ticket window, Emmett kept glancing back at the three men, but they never gave any indication they were still interested in him. Telling himself he was just nervous, he put the incident out of his mind. When his turn came, he gave the ticket seller sixteen dollars and seventy-five cents, put the tickets in his jacket pocket, and rejoined his brother, never mentioning to Bob the remark made by the stranger.

Together they boarded the train and took seats in the smoking car. Bob, sitting next to the window on the platform side of the car, lit up a thin cigar, while Emmett opened a newspaper he had purchased at the depot newsstand. Outside their window people rushed back and forth, climbing onto the train or waving at departing relatives. It was the common commotion associated with a departing train, and Emmett paid little attention to it until Bob suddenly nudged him with his elbow.

Lowering the newspaper a few inches, Emmett glanced around him, following Bob's gaze out the window. Two uniformed policemen were strolling along the platform, scrutinizing the faces of the people on the train as well as those still hurrying to board. Bob put his cigar to his lips and puffed until a thick cloud of smoke shrouded his face. Emmett raised the newspaper again and buried his nose in it. With his elbows he pressed against the two pistols hidden under his clothes, reassuring himself that they were still there, available for instant use. Around the edge of the newspaper he saw the policemen saunter past them toward the rear of the train. They had shown no noticeable reaction to the two Daltons. Emmett relaxed slightly, but he was still unable to concentrate on the printed words in front of him.

A few minutes later the two policemen returned, still striding casually along with the their hands clasped behind them, but they were staring even more intently at the open windows of the train cars. When they had moved on to the next car, a young man in the seat ahead of Bob and Emmett glanced back at them. He, too, had noticed the patrolling officers, and had apparently detected Emmett's reaction. The young man turned sideways in his seat, facing the aisle, and spoke in a conversational tone directed at no one in particular.

"Some people had better be getting wise to themselves," he remarked, looking at the roof of the car.

Emmett felt Bob's elbow press against his arm again. "Go into the next car back," Bob whispered to him urgently. "I'll follow you."

With forced calm Emmett folded the newspaper and rose from his seat. Politely excusing himself, he edged past the other passengers who were making their way to their seats or stowing their suitcases in the overhead racks. After crossing the open platform into the next car, he stopped and gazed around as if looking for a suitable place to sit. Bob brushed past him with a curt nod and strode quickly to the far end of the car. Emmett followed, sneaking quick glances out the windows toward the platform to see if the policemen were in pursuit. No uniforms were visible. When he joined Bob on the open space between the cars, Bob motioned for him to follow, and both jumped down to the roadbed on the far side of the train, away from the platform. Quickly they picked their way across the parallel rows of steel rails and hid behind a motionless freight train. They stayed there, their backs against a freight car, until the passenger train to Atlanta had left the station.

"That was getting too hot for us," Bob said. He leaned sideways to take another look at the empty passenger platform. "We better figure some other way to get out of here."

Staying hidden in the rail yards until nightfall, the two young Daltons finally approached the station again with extreme caution. Lit by flickering gas lamps, the platform was nearly deserted, and they could see no one who looked like an officer of the law. Again Emmett went to the ticket window. There was a train leaving in thirty minutes for New Orleans, Bob had determined after studying the posted schedule, so Emmett purchased tickets for it and hurried back to where Bob waited in the shadows. Emmett still had the tickets for Atlanta, and had considered trying to get his money back, but wisely he decided that it was too big a risk to take.

When the train chugged to a stop at the station, Bob and Emmett joined the few passengers boarding it without further incident. This time they sat in separate seats, pretending to be strangers, but within easy view of each other. Bob had told Emmett that the police were looking for two men together, so as individuals they would attract less attention. Emmett understood the logic of the move, but felt lonely on the long ride south. The train drove through the night, its steel wheels rhythmically thumping over the rail joints, until Emmett's head nodded forward and he fell into an uneasy sleep.

Wednesday, July 1,1891

"The defense calls Mrs. Adeline Dalton." Grat watched with a touch of shame and overwhelming compassion as his mother went to the front of the courtroom and was sworn in. He had told Breckenridge to leave her out of it, but the lawyer had insisted that having her testify was essential to his defense. After a long discussion, and the intervention of Bill on the lawyer's behalf, Grat reluctantly relented.

As Grat had feared, the trial was not going well. The prosecution had presented dozens of witnesses, each of whom was able to confirm one part or another of the state's case against Grat. Even the two witnesses from Delano, who had failed to identify Grat when he was first arrested, now stated they were confident that Grat was the man they had seen with Bob. No one but Grat seemed to notice that it took repeated prompting from the district attorney to make them say so.

There was also a lot of testimony from men who had seen Grat after his first arrest, and Grat was surprised how much emphasis the prosecution placed on the fact that he had shaved his mustache the following morning. While it had seemed of no consequence to Grat at the time, the district attorney harped on it, implying that Grat had done so primarily to confuse witnesses and avoid identification, as if the removal of that thin mustache had dramatically changed his appearance. Grat just scowled at the series of witnesses who pointed him out in court as the man they had seen. From his own experience as a deputy marshal, Grat knew how unreliable eye-witnesses were, and also how readily they were believed by juries.

Yesterday the prosecution had rested its case, after two weeks of testimony, and this morning Breckenridge had begun questioning witnesses in Grat's defense. The series of men from Fresno who swore that Grat had been in that city on the night of the robbery should have made his innocence obvious, but Power and Daggett, on cross-examination, brought out each man's unsavory background. It was an unfortunate fact that Grat had always associated with low-lifes, drunks, and gamblers, all with no permanent address and a history of scrapes with the law. The district attorney easily tripped them up on minor points as their alcohol-addled memories failed them, and continuously made reference to their "occupations" in disparaging terms.

During the prosecution's case, another item of evidence that had received an inordinate amount of emphasis was Grat's overcoat. It was this wild card that Breckenridge now hoped to eliminate by calling Adeline Dalton.

"Mrs. Dalton," Breckenridge intoned with exaggerated politeness, "what is your relationship to the defendant?" He was standing by the witness stand, gripping his lapels and smiling at the jury.

"He is my son," she answered tightly, looking Grat right in the eyes as she spoke. No emotion showed on her face.

"And where do you reside?"

"Kingfisher, Oklahoma Territory."

"Did you not, about three years ago, have a son by the name of Frank Dalton?"

Adeline opened her mouth to speak, but before she could get a word out Daggett was on his feet shouting an objection. "We object to the question on the grounds that the same is irrelevant to any of the issues in this case, and the fact that the witness did or did not have a son by the name of Frank will cut no figure in the trial of this defendant."

Judge Gray looked over at Breckenridge with disinterest and asked, "What do you propose to show by this line of testimony?" Breckenridge drew himself up and spoke to the entire courtroom.

"We propose to show, your honor, that about three years ago this witness had a son by the name of Frank Dalton, that he was a deputy United States Marshal in Oklahoma Territory, and that in the discharge of his duties as such marshal he was killed. That the overcoat which it is claimed by the prosecution was worn by the defendant, and which has bullet holes in it, was worn by Frank

Dalton at the time he was killed, and the bullet which killed him made the holes in this coat.

"Messenger Haswell testified that at the time the train was stopped and the shooting in progress, he hit one of the men who attacked the train, and the bullet holes in this coat may be used by the prosecution to corroborate that portion of Mr. Haswell's testimony. We also wish to show by this witness that the contents of the box which has just been offered in evidence are the underclothes and vest worn by Frank Dalton at the time he was killed." The two previous witnesses had testified about a box that had been shipped from Denver to Mr. Breckenridge.

"Mr. Daggett?" the judge said, looking over at the attorney.

"We still object, your honor, but if it will ease Mr. Breckenridge's mind, we will not use the bullet holes in the coat in connection with Mr. Haswell's testimony. In fact, sir, we will not refer to them at all in our closing argument. Personally, I don't care a thing about the bullet holes in the coat, and they will not figure in this case."

"Is that satisfactory, Mr. Breckenridge?" Judge Gray asked.

"Yes, it is. Thank you, your honor. I withdraw this witness."

"You may step down, madam," Gray told Adeline, and Grat was glad to see her leave the witness stand and return to the gallery. Breckenridge had made his point, and Grat was thankful that his mother had not been forced to recount Frank's death, which would have been extremely trying for her. Meanwhile Breckenridge resumed calling witnesses who could place Grat in Fresno on the night in question.

On Thursday, having finished with the witnesses from Fresno, Breckenridge called Bill Dalton to the stand. Under the lawyer's careful interrogation Bill explained how Bob and Emmett had come to his home the previous October, and how Grat had arrived in January to warn them of their pursuit by lawmen from Oklahoma. He told how he sent Grat and the other two to C. S. Davis's to find work and avoid capture, and how he had next seen Bob and Emmett on the eighth of February. After questioning them at the time about their possible involvement in the Alila robbery, and having heard Bob swear they had nothing to do with it, Bill had helped to keep them hidden until he escorted them south to Daggett in early March. It was only then, he testified, that Bob had admitted the truth.

Daggett's cross-examination was short, and only concerned Bill's conversation with William Smith on February 23, in which Bill had told the railroad detective that Bob and Emmett had gone to Seattle. Bill now admitted that this statement was not true.

Breckenridge then tried to call Jennie, Bill's wife, to confirm that Bob had admitted the crime to Bill, and that they had stated that Bill and Grat knew nothing about it, but Daggett objected on the grounds that such testimony was only hearsay. The objection was sustained. Attempts to call other members of the Dalton family for similar testimony were just as summarily dismissed. Finally Breckenridge called Grat to the stand.

Grat gave short, concise answers to his lawyer's questions, saying no more than was necessary. He described his background and how he had come to California, and told of the trip he had made with Bob and Emmett to Fresno, Traver, and Tulare. Explaining how he left his brothers at Tulare and returned to Fresno, he recounted his later arrest, and admitted he had lied to his interrogators in order to protect his brothers.

At one point Breckenridge asked him, "Can you describe your brother Emmett for the court, Mr. Dalton?"

Grat considered the question for a moment. "Well, my brother is twenty-one years old, and everywhere I go I find we are frequently mistaken for each other. I don't notice the resemblance myself, but people say that of all my mother's children, we look the most alike." Actually, Emmett had just turned twenty that May, but Grat wasn't good with birthdays.

After further questions about events in Tulare before the robbery, the lawyer asked about what happened in the aftermath of the crime.

"Can you tell the court, please, what you thought when you read in the newspapers about the attempted robbery and the description of the men suspected of committing it?

"I was of course uneasy," Grat said, sitting up straight and trying to make eye contact with the members of the jury as he had been instructed., "as it was stated that we had been seen together. More particularly, I was uneasy because the description was of the three of us."

"What do you mean, uneasy?"

"By being uneasy, I mean I was anxious to know the truth, as I was being spoken of and it was not true."

"Were you anxious about anything else?"

"I was anxious to know about the boys."

Breckenridge then led Grat through a description of his several arrests and interrogations, allowed him to explain why he shaved his mustache, and had him admit that he had signed William Smith's statement in order to mislead the detective. Then the lawyer had Grat make an admission that shocked the courtroom and caused an uproar. It took several minutes for the judge to quiet the room down.

While relating how he had never resisted arrest or tried to evade the officers, Grat stated that he had recently had in his possession a key to the Tulare County jail, which he had voluntarily surrendered to his jailer. The key had been given to him by two other prisoners, Maje Walton and a man named Schultz, just before those two had been shipped off to the penitentiary. Breckenridge ended his examination on this note, allowing the jurors to ask themselves whether a guilty man would voluntarily return the key to his own cell.

During the cross-examination, Daggett homed in on Grat's frequent false statements to authorities after the crime, and Grat grudgingly admitted that he had indeed told many untruths. He countered by claiming that he had done so only to protect his brothers, and not for any personal gain. Grat then clarified some other points, and finally he was excused. His testimony had taken most of the afternoon, and court was adjourned until morning.

When court reconvened, Breckenridge announced that the defense was resting its case. Daggett then called witnesses in rebuttal, particularly members of the sheriff's office to explain about the jail key Grat had given them. The sheriff and the jailers insisted that the key would not open any of the doors in the jail, and even if it had, there were other doors with different locks that would prevent someone from escaping.

Just before noon the testimony was concluded, and Mr. Power began the prosecution's closing argument. Pointing out that Bill and Grat Dalton had admitted to many of the accusations brought out by the prosecution, he reminded the jurors of the eye-witnesses who had placed Grat at or near the scene of the crime. As for Grat's alibi, he said, the character of the witnesses from Fresno spoke for itself, and the jury could judge for themselves what credence they could give that testimony. Power kept his summation relatively short, and by three o'clock he was done.

J. W. Ahern, who had remained with Breckenridge throughout the trial, since he had been there at the beginning, made the first argument for the defense. He began by demeaning the character of the testimony by the prosecution's witnesses, implying that it was rehearsed, and pointed out the unreliability of eye-witness testimony. He took apart the evidence point by point, until the judge finally stopped him and adjourned the court at five o'clock. Because it was Friday, and it had been a long trial, Gray set the next session for Monday at 10:00 a.m.

On Monday morning Ahern resumed his summation, arguing cogently that only two men could have ridden from Delano to Alila, since the third saddle had already been shipped. Grat was taken aback when Ahern then began to attack the testimony of Clark Bliven, who had said little that directly implicated Grat or Bill. Ahern claimed that since Bill and Bliven were partners in the Cotton Ranch, Bliven would profit by Bill's being sent to prison. From there Ahern went on to sympathize with Grat's misstatements to authorities, which he said were no worse than the deceptions and entrapments that had been perpetrated by the law enforcement officials in the case. Finally, he reminded the jurors that the railroad had failed to pay their taxes in this county, and thus the ordinary citizens would have to bear the cost of this expensive trial all by themselves.

After lunch Breckenridge weighed in with further defense arguments, and his eloquence was memorable. He played to the jury and the crowd like a Shakespearean actor, making them laugh and cry right on cue. He made fun of the prosecution's key witness, and asked why no photograph of Emmett had been offered in evidence, as had a picture of Bob. Likening the Southern Pacific railroad to the Chinese, who could punish a relative if they could not capture a criminal, he said that the corporation merely wanted a victim, regardless of the victim's guilt or innocence. Winding up with a stirring, albeit largely irrelevant, reference to Pickett's Charge at Gettysburg, Breckenridge brought his speech to a close, and court was adjourned until Tuesday.

On Tuesday morning Daggett made the final arguments for the prosecution, and at noon the case was submitted to the jury. By Wednesday morning the jury had reached a verdict. Guilty as charged.

Although he had known that the odds were against him, Grat was still stunned by the decision, since the evidence of his innocence had seemed so indisputable. His mind was swirling as the judge set his sentencing for July 29, and Grat paid scant attention when the lawyers agreed to postpone Bill's trial until October 5, while simultaneously reducing Bill's bail to $5000. Meekly, his head hung in disgust, Grat let himself be led back to the jail.

Author's Notes

Chapter 9

Bob and Emmett's return from California is covered briefly in *Beyond the Law*, and the search for them was mentioned in several brief newspaper clippings of the era. Emmett's description of the fight with the farmer's posse has sometimes been connected to a similar incident near Ingalls in which a man named William Stormer was killed. The Stormer murder, however, occurred a year later, on May 3, 1892, and the U. S. Marshal at Guthrie told a reporter that his deputies had pursued the culprits into the Creek Nation. During this same interview Marshal Grimes stated that the Daltons were at that time hiding out near Woodward, which matches Emmett's story.

The train robbery at Wharton (now Perry, Oklahoma) was reported extensively in the newspapers, including the *Muskogee Phoenix* of May 14, 1891; the *Fort Smith Elevator* of May 15, 1891; the *Coffeyville Journal* of May 15, 1891; and the *Kingfisher Free Press* in a recap article on August 27, 1891. Emmett also gave a stirring account of the robbery in *Beyond the Law.* Items about the subsequent pursuit of the Daltons by law officials were found in the *Vinita Indian Chieftain* of May 21, June 4, and August 27, 1891, as well as in the *Coffeyville Journal* of May 22, 1891, and the *Kingfisher Free Press* of August 27, 1891, which also reported the stop at Kiowa, Kansas, to purchase supplies.

As mentioned earlier, Grat's trial in Visalia, California, was extensively reported in the *Visalia Weekly Delta* and the *Tulare County Times*, and most of the dialogue in this section is verbatim from their transcript of the trial.

Bob and Emmett's trip to New Orleans is based solely on Emmett's account in *Beyond the Law*, with minor adjustments made for Emmett's often faulty memory.

CHAPTER 10

"They shoulda caught them Daltons by now," the old man insisted, noisily flapping his newspaper as he folded it. He was a thin little man in shirt sleeves and tan suit pants that were held up with unusually wide suspenders, and he had repeatedly reminded them he was a clerk at the New Orleans police court. Every evening he would regale all the residents of the boarding house with blood-chilling tales of crime in the city, all the while explaining how that very crime could be reduced if they would just listen to him. Emmett suppressed a smile as he leaned back in the wicker chair, lazily fanning himself with a paddle-shaped piece of cardboard carrying a printed advertisement for a funeral home.

The air was like warm molasses in the evening twilight, so thick and suffocating that Emmett felt like all the energy had been drained from his body. It was getting too dark to read any more, so the old braggart began waving the folded newspaper in front of his face, trying, like the others, to get some relief from the heat and humidity.

"I had an encounter with the Daltons once," the old man started up again, nodding his head with authority.

"Is that right?" the woman next to him remarked with no real interest. Emmett glanced over at the man again, but he was sure he had never seen him before coming to New Orleans two weeks ago.

"Yes, sir, it was back in 1861, it was. They brought this Emmett Dalton in on a charge of armed robbery." Emmett had to cough to cover his laughter. Not only had he never been to New Orleans before, in 1861 he had not yet even been born.

"He was a mean one," the police court clerk asserted, "with no forehead and beady little eyes. They brought him in and stood him in front of the judge—I believe it was Judge Breaux, but it could have been Judge Anderson. No, I think it must have been Judge Breaux, because Judge Anderson was still in Lake Charles at the time. Anyway, as I was saying, Emmett Dalton was standing in front of the judge when he decides to make a break for it. He slammed his fist into the face of the arresting officer, whose name I do not recall at the moment, but I'm sure I have it written down somewhere, and sent the poor man flying across the room. Now, the judge was behind the bench, so there was nothing he could do, and I saw that it was up to me to prevent this villain from escaping. Quick as a flash, I leapt onto his back and wrestled him down to the floor, pummeling him with my fists until he was nearly unconscious. Other officers heard the ruckus and came in to put manacles on him, once I had him subdued. It was a close call, but I had saved the day."

"My, my," the woman next to him drawled indifferently, "isn't that interesting."

Emmett was about to ask the old blow-hard how this infamous criminal had escaped to continue his crime spree, since the clerk had single-handedly restrained him back in 1861, but at that moment Bob came out onto the porch. He wandered restlessly over to Emmett's chair and stood there fidgeting impatiently.

"I'm bored," Bob told Emmett in a low voice, tapping his foot. "Let's go get our tickets for South America."

"Right now?" Emmett asked.

"Of course not. They're not open now. But first thing in the morning."

"Okay. If you say so."

Changing to a more conversational tone, Bob asked, "So what have you all been talking about?"

Emmett smirked and shook his head. "I'll tell you later."

The cavernous steamship office echoed with the clamor of shouted conversations and squealing luggage wagons. Bob and Emmett, standing at the barred window of the ticket office, had just finished making arrangements for their passage when Emmett remembered he had left the money belt back at their room in the boarding house. Telling the clerk they would be back, the two of them hurried out and walked quickly back to the house through the busy streets of New Orleans. It was a long walk, especially since Bob kept saying things like, "I can't believe you left our money behind."

Emmett rarely replied to these complaints, for there was little he could say other than that he was sorry. It occurred to Emmett that since it was Bob's money, too, he should have been equally concerned about where it was before they left the house, but he saw no point in mentioning it to Bob, who was in a bad enough mood already.

Just outside the boarding house they encountered a Negro boy hawking newspapers, and Emmett took one, flipping a nickel through the air to the boy. Bob had meanwhile barged on ahead, climbing the stairs of the house two at a time as he rushed back to their room. When Emmett followed Bob into the small bedroom, he found Bob already opening the drawer in the dresser where Emmett had hidden the money belt under some clothes. Bob gave an exaggerated sigh as he lifted the belt from the drawer.

"You have got to be more careful, Emmett," he scolded, shaking the belt in Emmett's face.

Emmett, feeling ashamed and a little irritated, took the belt and tossed the paper at his brother. "Look and see where we are today," Emmett told him. It had become sort of a game for them since they had arrived in New Orleans, to read about themselves in the newspapers. The papers had the Daltons committing crimes and escaping capture all over the country, so Bob and Emmett would make bets about where they would erroneously be seen next. Bob sat down on the edge of the bed and scanned the paper's small print, while Emmett undid his shirt and slipped the money belt around his waist inside of it.

"Whoa!" Bob blurted out, jumping to his feet. "Look at that!" He shoved the paper in front of Emmett, pointing to a small paragraph on the front page. Emmett craned forward to read the headline in bold print: **Bandit Grat Dalton Convicted**.

Emmett felt a tightness in his chest and his shoulders sagged. The newspapers had intermittently reported on the extended trial in California, so Emmett was aware that it had not been going well, but he was still shaken by the actuality of Grat's conviction. With the idealism of youth, he had been sure that a jury would see through the railroad's machinations and declare his brother innocent. Now it was clear that such was not the case. Emmett, his shirt still unbuttoned, threw himself down on the bed and fought back tears of anger and self-recrimination. Bob, equally disturbed by the news, paced the room, muttering curses and occasionally slamming his fist down on the top of the dresser. There was no mention of returning to the steamship office.

That evening Bob and Emmett joined the other boarders on the front porch as usual, but they pretended to read the newspaper to avoid taking part in the desultory conversations. They were in no mood to gossip about trivialities. Still, they could not help but overhear what the others were saying. At one point the rambling discussion veered onto the subject of the United States Mint located in New Orleans and how much money it produced. The know-it-all police court clerk authoritatively announced that the mint put out at least a million dollars a day, except for weekends and holidays, and no one bothered to challenge that assertion. When the topic of conversation changed to local politics, Emmett lost interest.

Later that night, as they prepared for bed, Bob stopped in the middle of draping his pants over the back of a chair and turned to Emmett. He had been quietly pensive all evening, but now he said, "Don't you know, we might be able to rob that mint and get away with it."

"Are you kidding?" Emmett dropped the boot he had just removed and stared at Bob with disbelief. "Rob the mint? Why?"

"Well, for one thing, there's a lot of money there."

"Yeah, but there's probably a lot of guards there, too, I'll bet."

Bob shrugged. "Maybe. But it's worth checking out. If we could do it, we'd get enough money to last us the rest of our lives."

"Or go to prison for the rest of our lives," Emmett muttered darkly.

Acting on Bob's idea, the next morning they took a streetcar to the mint, a huge granite structure with few windows. At the impressively tall entrance they were met by a kindly old man in a dark blue uniform who generously offered to give them a guided tour. After signing the guest register with false names, the two brothers followed the guard through the building as he showed them the vaults and the cacophonous stamping rooms, where dimes were being produced by the hundred thousands. At the end of the tour Bob presented the helpful guard with a cigar, and with a friendly farewell he and Emmett went back out into the summer sun.

On the streetcar ride back to the rooming house, Bob said, "I guess we won't do the mint after all. I mean, what a picnic it would be, with just that nice old man guarding it, but there wasn't a damn piece of paper money in sight. I can just see us trying to buy a ranch in South America with ten thousand dollars in dimes."

"We'd have to rent a wagon just to haul our loot around in," Emmett joked. With a chuckle they dismissed forever the idea of robbing the mint.

Eugenia had still not joined them in New Orleans, and Bob evaded Emmett's questions about her. Bob had exchanged correspondence with her since their arrival in New Orleans, so Emmett assumed that there was just a scheduling problem. The day after their visit to the mint, in fact, Bob received a telegram from her. The cable message provided details of Grat's conviction, and informed them as well of the postponement of Bill's trial and the reduction of his bail. Bob read the telegram twice, his frown deepening, and then brusquely handed it to Emmett to read while he paced the floor of their small bedroom.

"Well, I guess we'll have to go back," Bob finally said angrily, stopping to face Emmett with his fists on his hips. "No South America for us."

"Well, maybe it would be too hot down there for us anyhow," Emmett offered in consolation.

"I tell you what," Bob vowed, "it's going to be hot as hell for some people right here in these United States. Pack up, we're going back tonight. I guess they just don't want us to reform."

Bob reined in his horse while he strained to see through the surrounding darkness. Emmett had done the same behind him, but no words were spoken. The day's oppressive summer heat had moderated little since sundown, and the heavy humid air was thick around them. The silence was broken only by the breathing of the horses and the chirps and buzz of insects, although once Bob heard the faint call of a distant coyote. Bob peered at the open countryside, bathed only in the faint blue light of a rising quarter moon, alert for any tell-tale movement or unusual shadows that might signal the presence of someone waiting in ambush. The farm north of Kingfisher seemed quiet and peaceful on this steaming July evening.

A few hundred yards ahead of them was the angular bulk of their mother's cabin. The front door was open to let in the occasional breath of wind, and yellow lamp light spread out across the small porch, only to be swallowed up by the darkness of the yard. A shadow would sometimes flicker across the doorway as someone moved around inside, and Bob caught the muffled clank and thump of pans and dishes being washed. It had been months since he had seen his mother, and Bob was uncertain of the reception she would now give them, after the debacle of Grat's trial in California. He took a deep breath of resolution, then lightly kicked his heels into his horse's flanks to start him walking toward the cabin.

Three days after touring the New Orleans mint, Bob and Emmett had boarded a train going north. Many hours later they finally crossed into Indian Territory and ended the rail portion of their journey at Wagoner, a small town about fifteen miles north of Muskogee. Eugenia had met them there with horses, saddles, and new Winchester rifles.

After all too brief a time with the lovely young woman, Bob tore himself away, and he and Emmett struck out to the west across the heart of the territory. Traveling mostly at night to avoid detection, they maintained a cautious, measured pace. The ride to Kingfisher had taken a week, but now that they were finally here, Bob belatedly questioned the advisability of the visit. What if Mom had become fed up with their antics? What if, God forbid, she had agreed to turn them in to the law? More realistically, what if she just did not want to have anything to do with them anymore? These questions assailed Bob as they approached the cabin.

Emmett apparently suffered from no such doubts, so Bob let his young brother enter the cabin first. Over Emmett's shoulder he saw his mother look up from the kitchen counter when she heard the jingle of Emmett's spurs. Her eyes widened in pleasurable surprise, and she rushed forward with outstretched arms, crying "My boys!" as she took Emmett into her arms. The she released him and hugged Bob just as warmly, and Bob again marveled at the strength he detected in this apparently frail woman.

She stepped back to look at them both, the usual worry lines that creased her face temporarily erased by a joyful smile. "Oh, Robert, Emmett, I've been so worried about you! Have you boys come home to stay?" It was a frivolous question, and all three knew it, so Bob let it go unanswered. Instead he asked questions of his own.

"Have the marshals been here looking for us?"

"A few times."

"When?"

"The last time was about a week ago, I think, right after I got home from California."

With a twinge of guilt, Bob asked, "How's Grat doing?"

"Did you know he was convicted?"

"We read about it in the papers," Emmet said gloomily.

"It was terrible. That railroad is a bunch of crooks. And that judge was in it with them. And now Grat will be going to prison for something he didn't do." She shook her head angrily. Bob was grateful that she did not link Grat's problems to Bob's illegal activities.

"Is there any chance for an appeal?" Bob asked hopefully.

"That takes money, and we've still got Bill's trial coming up. Besides, all the courts in California are controlled by the railroad and the Republicans. But we asked the lawyer to look into it, anyway."

"Well, we can get however much money they need," Bob assured her. She gave him an enigmatic look, then changed the subject.

"You boys must be hungry. Let me fix you something to eat." She went into the kitchen area and began opening cans and putting pans on the stove. While their mother was busy with her preparations, Bob and Emmett sat down at the kitchen table and quietly discussed their future plans. Bob told Emmett they should go back to Riley's ranch and find Newcomb and Bryant, then pull a few "tricks" to raise money for Grat's appeal. If it appeared that the appeal would not be successful, then they would think about going out there again to break Grat out of jail. As always, Emmett agreed, but apparently he had some reservations.

After they ate the hastily prepared supper, Bob and Emmett rose to leave. It was too dangerous, both for them and their mother, to stay long at her home. As she walked them to the door, Bob saw the tears forming in her eyes, and his own eyes began to sting in sympathetic response. Their mother had never been one to show a lot of affection, even to her own children, but now she grabbed the two boys in turn, squeezing them and kissing them on the cheek.

As she hugged Emmett, she whispered, "I wish you boys could stay home and be good." She stepped back and looked at them imploringly. "Could you?"

Bob sniffed, but found himself unable to speak. Emmett, however, smiled at her and said, "Well, Mom, we'll all be good pretty soon."

Mother Dalton followed them out onto the porch and tearfully watched as the mounted their horses. A summer storm had swept in from the west, and the roiling clouds were rent with lightning and bone-jarring claps of thunder. As the first big drops of rain began to pelt them, Bob and Emmett rode away, turning in their saddles one last time to wave at their mother, framed in the light from the doorway. Bob had a bleak premonition that he would never see her again, but he suppressed it as the rain began to come down in earnest. There were more important things to think about right now.

When they arrived at the dugout cabin on Riley's ranch two days later, they found that their gang had expanded in their absence. Black-face Charley Bryant and Bitter Creek Newcomb had been joined by three other men: Bill Doolin, Charlie Pierce, and Bill Power. Doolin was a tall rangy man from Arkansas, with wild hair and a scraggly dark beard. Emmett had met him once when they had both worked as cowboys near Guthrie a few years before. Although poorly educated, Doolin was intelligent and cool, and the Daltons' success had convinced him that they would be good friends to have.

Pierce, a medium-sized man with no distinguishing characteristics, was an old friend of Newcomb's that Bitter Creek had run into on one of this many forays into nearby towns in pursuit of pleasure. Lacking any better prospects, Pierce had gratefully accepted Newcomb's invitation to join the famous Dalton gang.

Power was a handsome young man with wavy dark hair and a broad mustache, and he had come to the hideout with Doolin. He said he was from Illinois and had run away from home at age thirteen. Drifting down to Oklahoma for the land rush, he had staked out some land near Guthrie, but, like Newcomb, he had found he had little patience for farming.

Bob welcomed the new arrivals, for the added personnel would permit the commission of more elaborate crimes, and at the same time they increased his own sense of importance. The Daltons were now so famous and respected that other outlaws were rushing to join them. It was a heady realization, and Bob smiled in anticipation of the headlines that would soon glorify them.

Saturday, August 22, 1891

Charley Bryant had detected the first symptoms just after he left the hideout at Riley's ranch. After telling Bob and the gang that he would return in a week, he had started out early that morning, planning to arrive at his brother's house near Mulhall late that evening. Then the fever had struck. At first he passed it off as too much sun or maybe something spoiled for breakfast, but by noon he was wracked by the familiar chills and sweats of the chronic disease that had never been accurately diagnosed. He had splashed himself with cool water when he crossed the Cimarron River, but it had given him only temporary relief, and he finally conceded that he could go no farther.

Slumped over his saddle horn, groaning from the painful cramps in his stomach, he rode into Hennessey, a small town on the Santa Fe line about twenty miles north of Kingfisher. Weak and disoriented, he rode into a livery stable and slid down from the saddle, grasping a post to keep from collapsing in the straw-covered dirt. The stable hand, understandably reluctant to get near such a sick man, stretched his arm out to take the money Charley offered for the care of his horse.

"Hotel?" Charley croaked. The young man mutely pointed up the street, then led the horse away after Charley drew his Winchester from the saddle scabbard. Charley stumbled out onto the street, emerging into the blazing sun, and squinted at the row of buildings that lined the short main street. The lettering on the signs danced in his blurring vision. Desperately he staggered across the street and down the board sidewalk to the only hotel in town.

With $1800 still remaining from his share of the Wharton loot, he was not concerned about money. He threw down some bills on the clerk's desk and scribbled his real name on the register. He was too sick to care about the suspicious look the clerk gave him as he carried his Winchester up the stairs and into his room. His head was swimming and his bowels were churning as he gingerly removed his clothing and climbed into bed in his undergarments. When he had made himself as comfortable as possible and pulled the sheet halfway up over his body, he laid his pistol and rifle on top of the sheet on either side of him, and then he allowed himself to sink into a restless sleep.

It was a fitful slumber, and he seemed to awaken every five minutes or so, sweating and panting. When he did manage to doze off, his mind swirled with strange dreams of running and falling, jolting him awake just before some unknown horrible fate would strike. When he saw the man standing beside his bed, a pistol in his hand, he initially thought it was yet another of these feverish illusions.

"Bryant," the man ordered, "don't move!"

Charley tried to clear his head, but it was like trying to fight his way out of a briar patch. He fumbled with his hands, searching for the weapons he had left beside him on the bed, but the tall man barked menacingly at him.

"Don't try it. I've got a bead on you. You move and you're a goner." Charley let his arms go limp, which required no effort in his weakened condition, and stared helplessly at his captor. The man was rangy and thin, with a long, unkempt handlebar mustache and a hawk nose. He reached across Charley to grab the pistol from the bed, handing it to a young man behind him whom Charley had not previously noticed. Next the man picked up Charley's rifle and introduced himself.

"I'm Deputy Marshal Ed Short," he announced, "and I'm placing you under arrest."

"What for?" Charley whispered hoarsely, struggling to prop himself up on his elbows.

"Train robbery. Word is that you been riding with the Daltons."

Charley fell back against the pillow, already exhausted by the effort it took to raise part of the way up. "Hell," he muttered, "I don't even care. Do whatever you want, but I ain't gettin' out of this here bed, least not until I'm feelin' better."

Short looked down at Charley for a moment as he considered this statement before he said, "Okay." He handed Charley's rifle to his assistant and pulled a pair of handcuffs from his coat pocket. He latched one bracelet tight around Charley's right wrist, and pulled his arm up as he snapped the other bracelet around the metal bedstead. "They ain't got a jail here, anyway," he remarked.

Resigned to his fate and overcome with apathy, Charley fell back into a troubled sleep, trying to sweat out the illness that had paid him infrequent visits over the last few years. He woke up a few times, blearily noting that darkness had fallen outside, and each time he saw a figure with a gun sitting in a chair a few feet away. Sometimes it was Short, and sometimes it was the young man who Charley assumed was Short's posseman, but there was always someone keeping guard. Escape was impossible in his current condition anyway, but Charley took grim satisfaction in knowing that these lawmen were not getting much rest either.

In the morning Charley felt marginally better, but he decided to keep that to himself. He begged Short to get a doctor for him, and promised to behave if Short would remove his handcuffs. When Short refused both requests, Charley turned to threats.

"You know, the Daltons will be coming to get me," he told Short. "They won't cotton to one of their gang being arrested. They'll kill you and your posse without thinking twice about it, less'n you let me go." It was a bluff, for Charley knew it would be days before Bob and the others even heard about his arrest, but he was pleased that Short took the threat seriously. Short sent his posseman to the train station to buy tickets for Wichita.

"Want me to wire Marshal Grimes?" The young man asked as Short counted out some money. Charley remembered with a jolt the large sum of cash he had been carrying, and ruefully suspected it was now being used to pay for their train fare.

"No," Short told his helper. "It's Sunday, so he won't be in the office. Besides, we need to get this man out of the territory quick, and into a good strong jail. Just get the tickets to Wichita and come right back."

It was just past noon when they boarded the train. Charley, his wrists manacled, was pushed and prodded into the smoking car by Short, who still carried Charley's rifle. Short had ordered his posseman to stay in Hennessey and man the deputy's office, assuring him that he could easily control a sick man like Charley by himself.

Lawman and prisoner took their seats in the car, and the train chugged out of the station on its way north. Charley began to suffer a return of the fever, but it was nowhere near as severe as it had been the day before. Nonetheless, he decided to take advantage of the sweat breaking out all over his body and the quivering of his limbs, and he pretended to throw a fit. While other passengers looked on in horror and revulsion, Charley squirmed and moaned like he was in his death throes, his eyes bugging out wildly as spittle dripped from his mouth.

Embarrassed by the reproachful looks he was getting from the other travelers, Short laid the rifle down in an empty seat and pulled his writhing prisoner to his feet. Alternately stiffening his muscles and letting them go limp, Charley passively resisted as Short pushed and dragged him out the front door of the car, across the open platform, and into the baggage car.

"You can't come in here," the baggageman told them, summoning up all the authority of his menial position. He was a young man in shirt sleeves, with garters on his upper arms to keep the cuffs from falling down over his hands. Whimpering pitifully, Charley artfully staggered over to collapse on a pile of canvas mailbags.

"I'm a United States Marshal," Short explained officiously, "and this man is my prisoner. He is very ill, and there may be an attempt by the Daltons to rescue him. May I have your permission to secure him here?"

Impressed by this pronouncement, the young man nodded and said, "Sure."

Short looked over at Charley, who was watching him with half-closed eyes. Charley trembled and sprawled awkwardly on the bags, giving the appearance that he was virtually unconscious, and was pleased by the resulting look of sympathetic pity on the marshal's face.

"I've got to go back in the smoking car for a minute," Short told the baggageman. He drew his pistol and handed it to the young man, who took the gun reluctantly. "You keep an eye on him, and shoot him if he makes a move." Holding the gun like it was a live rattlesnake, the youth fearfully gaped at Charley, who closed his eyes and pretended to sleep. Charley heard the door slam when Short left the baggage car.

Charley cracked his eyelids just enough to watch the baggageman, who stood nervously by his desk with the pistol held loosely in his hand. The young man shot a look toward the door to the next car, and then stared at Charley a minute. Charley forced himself to remain still. Biting his lip, the baggage handler jammed the pistol into one of the pigeonholes of his desk and disappeared beyond a partition that divided the car in half. No sooner had the young man left the compartment than Charley leaped to his feet, made two quick steps to the desk, and retrieved the pistol. With his hands till cuffed together in front of him, Charley moved rapidly toward the door at the end of the car.

Just as Charley took a position beside the door, the young baggageman returned, his face registering shock as he immediately took in the changed situation. Charley waved the pistol at him and motioned for him to sit on a steamer trunk while he turned his attention back to the door. Carefully he turned the knob with his left hand and opened the door a few inches, pointing the pistol out through the gap. Edging forward, he peeked around the door frame just in time to see Ed Short open the door of the next car, rifle in hand.

Charley slammed the door shut, but then realized there was nowhere else to go. Twisting the knob angrily, he flung the door open wide and began firing. Short, the Winchester now cocked and held at waist level, fired back. Although they were only a few feet apart, they each fired repeatedly, with Charley getting off five rounds and Short managing three. Charley saw one of his bullets put a hole in Short's jacket near his heart, and started to congratulate himself on his skill. Then, with a shock, he realized he had been hit as well.

Charley felt his body go numb, starting at his feet and working its way up, and he grabbed for the platform railing as he fell forward. Short had collapsed next to him, and the dying lawman reached forward with a trembling hand to clamp his fingers around Charley's ankle, as if he feared Charley was still trying to escape. "Help me!" Short called hoarsely, blood flecking his lips.

Crumpled in a heap, Charley was unable to move, and a formless dread was closing in around his mind. With dimming vision he saw the baggageman stoop down beside Short.

As if from a long distance, Charley head Short say, "I got my man, but he got me, too." Short coughed wetly, then cried, "I want to see my mother!"

Lying on the rumbling train car platform, Charley watched Short's eyes glaze and turn sightless in death. He found the process very interesting, and curiously wondered if his looked the same, until death overtook him as well.

Thursday, September 3, 1891

Southern Pacific train #19 had just finished filling its water tank at Ceres, a small station four miles south of Modesto, and gradually it began to pull away and resume its night-time journey south to Los Angeles. Before the train could pick up any speed, however, two men jumped on board the engine and pointed cocked pistols at the two crewmen. Although it was dark and the outlaws wore masks, the engineer could easily discern that one of the gunmen was tall and thin, and the other short and stocky. Harshly the tall one ordered the engineer to stop the train.

Once the locomotive had been brought to a halt, the gunmen escorted the crewmen back to the express car, where the short one demanded that the express messenger open the door. The messenger, a man named Reed, refused. The short robber then produced some dynamite from a sack he was carrying and wedged it against the train car's door. He lit the fuse, and the gunmen and crewmen scuttled aside just before the charge blew a large hole in the door. Giving the fireman a lighted lamp, the robbers forced him to crawl through the smoking hole into the darkened express car. He was no more than halfway inside when Reed cocked his pistol and warned him to get out; the fireman rapidly complied. The short robber then lit another stick of dynamite and tossed it inside the express car, but it failed to explode.

The commotion had drawn the attention of the passengers by this point, and two railroad detectives on board jumped down and made their way forward to the scene of the robbery. When they say what was going on, they opened fire on the bandits, who crawled under the train and returned the fire, wounding one of the detectives. Realizing their cause was now hopeless, the two criminals escaped to their horses and rode off into the night.

Sunday, September 6, 1891

Grat lay on his back and stared at the ceiling, his fingers laced behind his head for a pillow. The glaring light bulb cast ominous striped shadows across the cell's walls and ceiling, and the thin mattress provided little comfort. His mood, never ebullient, was now the foulest he could remember, as anger and depression washed over him in turn, like stormy waves on a lonely beach. The residual heat in the walls from the late summer sun kept him slowly baking, for no breeze could force its way through the narrow barred windows of the Tulare County jail. Downstairs in the basement there was a steady murmur of conversation and occasional laughter; the trusties and minor criminals down there still had the run of the place. Up here on the first floor, though, Grat and John Beck, the cage's only two occupants at the moment, were already locked and barred into their cells. The cage was reserved for the most dangerous types, and for those already convicted and awaiting transportation to the state penitentiary at San Quentin.

Grat's sentencing was less than a week away, but he knew what the outcome would be. Judge Gray would give him the maximum allowed by law, and he would spend at least ten years behind bars. Grat's stomach churned at the prospect. There was no way he could stand being cooped up for that long. The few months he had been here at Visalia had worn him down to a hollow shell, and they had treated him fairly well here, compared to what he could expect across the bay at San Quentin. Breckenridge had promised that he would get Grat a new trial, but Grat had lost all faith in the lawyer, who apparently shared Grat's fondness for hard liquor. Only the continued support and encouragement of his brother Bill had kept Grat from doing something desperate.

There was an increase in noise from downstairs, but Grat paid it little heed until he heard the scraping squeal of metal on metal. The twin rows of cells in the upper cage had two locks on each door. In addition to the key-operated lock at waist level, there was also a sliding bar at the top that was operated by a series of levers controlled from inside the jailer's office. The bars on the empty cells across from Grat's were being moved into the open position; that could only mean that someone was to be placed in these cells.

When Grat heard the clump of footsteps on the stairs up to the cage, he swung his legs over the side of the metal cot and stood up, casually ambling over to the front of the cell. Grasping the cold iron bars in his hands, he leaned forward to peer through the door that led down the stairs from the cage. Williams, the jailer, appeared first, and as he rattled the keys to unlock the grated door of the cage, he gave Grat a warning look.

"You got company, Grat," he called. Williams had been somewhat sympathetic to Grat's plight, and this remark was not a taunt; in fact, Grat thought he detected a tone of regret in the jailer's voice. Williams swung the door open and stepped inside; three men followed him into the wide corridor between the two blocks of cells. Grat's chest went tight as he recognized his brother Bill, his hands cuffed behind him and his usually neat blonde hair in disarray. Behind Bill was a frightened young man Grat had never seen before, and bringing up the rear was Deputy Witty.

"What happened, Bill?" Grat asked anxiously, his grip tightening on the bars.

"Hi, Grat," Bill replied with forced cheerfulness. He smiled and shrugged as he was stopped in front of the cell diagonally across from Grat's and his cuffs were removed. Responding submissively to Williams' gesture, Bill trudged into the cell. The stranger was placed in the cell directly opposite Grat, and both doors were slammed shut with a clang.

"What's going' on?" asked Beck from the cell next to Grat.

"None of your damn business, Beck." Witty said, giving him a scowl. Witty did not like any of the prisoners, but in deference to Williams he refrained from abusing Grat. Beck, however, was fair game for his tormenting.

Williams locked the cell doors with his key and motioned for Witty to go on out of the cage. Witty descended the stairs to catcalls from the prisoners below, while Williams stopped at the cage door to lock it behind him. Turning the key, he looked at Grat and Bill, shook his head slowly, and muttered, "It's a damn shame, that's what it is." Then he, too, was gone.

"Now what?" Grat demanded of his brother, whose smile was now fading.

"Yeah," Beck added, "what the hell's goin' on?" Grat gave Beck a threatening frown, and the young farmhand sat down on his bunk and pouted.

"Did you hear about that attempted train robbery up at Ceres on Thursday?" Bill asked.

"I heard something, but didn't pay any attention to it. Why?"

"They think I did it."

"You?" Grat let that sink in, and then asked worriedly, "You didn't did you?"

"Of course not! I'm already under indictment for one train robbery I didn't do, so why would I try to rob another one, for real this time? Jeez, Grat, you know me better than that."

"Well, I had to be sure. Why do they think you did it?

Bill gave a disgusted look. "Because I'm a Dalton. What other evidence do they need? Everybody knows that all the Daltons are train robbers." His sarcasm was cutting and vicious. "That damned railroad has to find somebody to blame, and I'm an easy target."

"What happened? I mean, how did they arrest you?"

"I was over at Traver, staying at Maggie Rucker's boarding house like I've been doing for weeks now, when Kay and Witty ride up and call me out. I came out with my hands up, and the next thing I know I'm in handcuffs and they're searching the house for 'evidence', which, of course, they can't find. Instead they find this poor man. . ." Bill nodded at the young man in the cell next to him. "I'm sorry, sir, what did you say your name was?"

"Dean," he said with an introductory nod to Grat and Beck, "Wiley Dean."

Bill continued his story. "They said he was my partner in the robbery, and brought us both in. We told Kay we were both in Traver on Thursday and can prove it, but he wouldn't listen. Said he knew we did it, and he would get the third man tomorrow."

"What third man?"

"Who knows? Apparently he thinks three men held up that train. Of course, on Friday he was announcing that Bob and Emmett did the robbery, even though everybody knows they're back in Oklahoma."

"Are you sure they're still there?" Grat had sort of hoped that Bob and Emmett would come back and break him out of jail.

"Am I sure? Yes. I just got a letter from Mom, and she saw them just a few days ago. They're fine, but God only knows what they'll get into next. Tell you the truth, if I didn't know they were back east, I would have suspected them of this robbery myself."

"Well," Grat said with a shrug. He felt the same way.

"How are you doing?" Bill asked solicitously, changing the subject.

"Okay, I guess."

"You don't sound okay."

"This jail's getting to me. I just can't go to San Quentin, Bill, I won't make it."

"Yeah, you will, Grat. You're tough. Besides, we'll get you a new trial somewhere else and you'll be acquitted. I promise."

"Yeah, sure."

"Hey, you don't see me moping around about being in jail, do you?"

"No, and why not?"

"Because I'm innocent, and I can prove it."

"That's what *I* thought a couple months ago." Grat's words were so full of despair that Bill raised his eyebrows.

"Don't give up on me, Grat. Something will turn up, you'll see."

"I shouldn't have given them that key back at the trial," Grat grumbled. At the time he thought the act of honesty would sway the jury in his favor, but that had been a forlorn hope.

Beck, who had sat listening to the entire conversation, could no longer contain himself. "Maybe you'll get another key," he said mysteriously. Grat stared at the horse thief for a minute. Beck returned his gaze, the corner of his mouth curling up slightly. Grat scratched his ear and turned back toward Bill.

"How is Mom?" he asked. Bill began recounting her last letter, but Grat was only half listening while he mulled over what Beck had said. A germ of an idea was forming, and later, long after the light was turned off, Grat lay awake considering all the angles and making plans. There was no way he would go peacefully to prison.

Author's Notes

Chapter 10

Bob's and Emmett's adventure in New Orleans and their return to visit their mother were taken from Emmett's book, *Beyond the Law*. Although there is no corroborating documentation of these events, Emmett's description rings true for the most part. Again, his memory played him false sometimes, as he claimed they heard of Grat's escape from jail while they were still in New Orleans, when in fact it did not occur until almost two weeks after they robbed the train at Lillietta, described in the next chapter.

Charley Bryant's capture and shoot-out with Ed Short was described in detail in the *Kingfisher Free Press* on August 27, 1891. Emmett also recounted this incident, with embellishment, in his book, but his version, by necessity, must have been drawn from this same newspaper account.

Bill Dalton's arrest and incarceration for the Ceres train robbery was headline news in both the *Sacramento Union* and the *San Francisco Call* on September 7, 1891. Grat's despondency was described in a later article in the *Visalia Weekly Delta* on September 24, 1891.

A year after the Ceres robbery a man named George Sontag confessed that he, his brother John, and a man named Chris Evans had robbed Southern Pacific trains at Pixley, Goshen, Ceres, and Collis. In September 1892 railroad detective William Smith and Deputy Sheriff George Witty tracked John Sontag and Evans into the mountains. Evans and Sontag ambushed the posse and wounded Witty twice before escaping. A different posse cornered the pair the following summer, and severely wounded both men. Sontag died two weeks later, and Evans went to Folsom prison, but escaped a few months after arriving there. He returned to Visalia, his house was surrounded, and he peaceably surrendered to Sheriff Kay. This time he remained in Folsom until his parole in 1911.

CHAPTER 11

September 13, 1891

"The State of California versus William M. Dalton and Wiley Dean," the bailiff proclaimed in a monotone to the small hearing room packed with reporters and curiosity seekers. Bill and his lawyer, J. W. Breckenridge, were already standing in front of the bench; Dean, his eyes wide and his face pale, trembled next to Bill, while his own lawyer, a man named Maddux from Modesto, hung back from the others. Bill winked at Dean, and the gangly youth managed a weak smile. Dean's red hair had resisted all attempts to comb it down, and his tie was comically askew, but his eyes were filled with dread. Bill gazed at him and tried to somehow silently reassure his young friend that everything would turn out all right.

Bill had felt great compassion and sorrow for Wiley, whose only crime was taking a room at the same boarding house as Bill. It had been six days since they were arrested, and the forced proximity had cultivated a spirit of companionship. They had whiled away the long hours in their cells by talking and joking, and even Grat had shaken off his depression and joined in. Bill had challenged Dean's intellect with revelations about the political machinations of the railroads and the insidious corruption of the Republican Party and their minions, while Grat had thrilled him with lurid tales of his career as a deputy marshal. Comrades in adversity, the three men had become fast friends. Lying on their bunks in the dark last night, talking about the future, they had agreed that if ever one of them got free, he would do everything in his power to help the others. Bill had known at the time that it was a hollow promise, but was glad that Dean had found comfort in it.

As the hubbub in the courtroom subsided, Bill was relieved to see the friendly face of Justice Towns looking down at him rather than the hostile glare of Judge Gray. Gray, whom Bill considered a

Republican pawn of the Southern Pacific Railroad, was clearly prejudiced against the Dalton family, whereas Towns was a local Democrat with no personal or political ax to grind. But then, this was only the arraignment.

Towns silently perused the papers in front of him. He glanced up at the men assembled before him, but before he could speak, Breckenridge began addressing the court in his usual theatrical style.

"If it pleases the court, we would like to make a preliminary statement regarding this unconscionable act of barbarity that brings us here today."

"Barbarity?" Towns asked dryly, raising one eyebrow at the portly lawyer.

"Indeed, your honor. Mr. Dalton has been arrested and charged with this crime with absolutely no evidence against him other than his very name. The officers and detectives have ignored incontrovertible proof that Mr. Dalton was in Traver on the day in question, and could not possibly have had anything to do with the attempted robbery in Ceres. The Southern Pacific Railroad, embarrassed by its inability to solve or prevent the attacks upon its trains, have viciously laid the blame on an innocent victim whose only crime is having the name Dalton."

"It's a little early to be pleading your case, Mr. Breckenridge," the judge said. "Could we at least hear the charges first?" He shifted his gaze to the district attorney, who had been nervously biting his lip. "Mr. Fulkerth?"

"Uh, your honor," Fulkerth began haltingly, "I have investigated this case thoroughly, and I must beg the court's indulgence. The detectives who first brought this case to our office have gone back on everything they said, and my own investigations lead me to believe that neither Mr. Dalton nor Mr. Dean was anywhere near the scene of the attempted robbery. Therefore, I move that they be discharged immediately."

Bill clenched his fists in restrained joy. Finally something had gone right. His raised eyebrows indicated that Towns was as surprised by the unexpected turn of events as Bill was. With a barely suppressed smile the judge nodded at Bill and his lawyer.

"Mr. Breckenridge, do you have any objections?"

"Certainly not, your honor."

"Mr. Maddux?"

Dean's lawyer took a step forward and shook his head. "No, your honor."

"Then the motion is granted. You gentlemen are free to go."

Bill was surrounded by reporters and well-wishers as he left the courtroom, all wanting to shake his hand and ask him questions. As he tried to accommodate them, Bill nodded and smiled to Wiley Dean, who was politely pushing through the crowded hallway. Dean's face had regained its color, and his expression was a mixture of happiness and confusion. He gave Bill a thumb's up as he passed.

"Who do you blame for your arrest, Bill?" one of the reporters asked, jostling for position with a pencil and notebook in his hands.

"The Southern Pacific," Bill answered. "They have hounded me for months, trying to get some kind of mud to stick to me. They are bound and determined to lock me up in order to shut me up, and they will do anything to keep me from telling the truth about them." Bill paused to let the young man write this down, and noticed Deputy Sheriff McGinnes shouldering his way through the crowd. In his hand was a folded document, and his solemn eyes were fixed on Bill.

"William Dalton," McGinnes announced officially as he firmly grasped Bill's left arm, "I have a warrant for your arrest."

Breckenridge, who had been waxing eloquent to a group of admirers nearby, broke away and swiftly took the warrant from the officer's hand.

"On what charge?" he demanded.

"The Alila case," McGinnes explained. His distaste for Breckenridge was obvious. "One of Dalton's bondsmen here in Visalia has withdrawn."

Bill's former elation now collapsed into despair. McGinnes tugged on his arm, but Bill resisted a moment in order to make one last statement to the reporter who still stood poised with his pencil.

"They have succeeded," Bill told him angrily.

Bob was down at the river target shooting when Emmett ran up and told him that Eugenia had just ridden in. Gathering up his box of cartridges, Bob hustle back to the ranch house to greet her. Bob and the gang had arrived there at Younger's Bend only two days earlier, and he had been anxiously awaiting the opportunity to actually touch Eugenia and talk to her again. After Bob's return from New Orleans she had stayed at Wagoner, on the eastern side of the Twin Territories, while he had hidden at Riley's camp 250 miles to the west. The separation had been a source of restiveness for Bob, whose affection for Eugenia was intensifying. When he had learned of Charley Bryant's capture, Bob used it as an excuse to lead the gang back east.

Although the survival of the gang depended on mutual trust, Bob reminded the others that Charley had been very ill, and he might have talked out of his head about where he had been. There was also the possibility that the lawmen could backtrack from where Charley was captured to the camp at Riley's. It only made sense, he said, to seek a new hideout. Besides, funds were getting low, and Eugenia had written him that there were reports of large cash shipments on the Katy line through Wagoner. This last reason especially appealed to Doolin, Pierce, and Power, since they had joined the gang after the Wharton robbery, and thus they had not shared in its proceeds.

The ride east had been a cautious and round-about trip. On September 22 there was scheduled to be another land run, this time for the tribal lands of the Iowa, Pottawatomie, Shawnee, and Sac and Fox tribes. These small tracts of mostly uninhabited hill country were right in the middle of the Twin Territories, dividing the newly formed Oklahoma Territory in the west from the shrinking Indian Territory in the east. The prospect of another land run had drawn hordes of land-hungry settlers into the area, and the number of peace officers had been increased accordingly. Bob and the gang took advantage of the resulting social turbulence to slip past into the Creek Nation, where they took shelter at a secluded ranch on the Canadian River south of Muskogee.

The ranch had originally been owned by a man named Jim Reed, a horse thief who was one of Belle Starr's several husbands. When Reed was killed by lawmen, Belle took charge of the ranch and named it Younger's Bend, in honor of Cole Younger. According to Belle, Cole had secretly married her in Texas and fathered her daughter Pearl. In 1889 Belle was killed by a shotgun blast to the back while riding along the Canadian River. Purportedly the murderer was a jealous lover; this was entirely possible, for despite her remarkably homely countenance, Belle Starr had had many affairs. Pearl Younger, an independent young lady who was far more attractive than her mother, now ran the ranch, which had gained a widespread reputation as a brothel.

Since her father was the Dalton's first cousin, Pearl had welcomed them and their friends. Although Pearl spent most of her time in Fort Smith, running a brothel there, she frequently returned to Younger's Bend so she could retain title to the land under Creek Nation law. She had also introduced Bob to Dick Broadwell, a young drifter from Kansas who desperately wanted to join the Dalton gang. Swayed by Broadwell's open admiration of his exploits, Bob accepted him into the group, although he had misgivings about Broadwell's exuberance and wild nature.

While the other men in the gang welcomed the entertainment Pearl and her girls offered them, Bob remained faithful to Eugenia. Emmett, suffering from painful shyness, pretended he was not interested. The temptation was one of the reasons Bob was so glad to see Eugenia arrive, but he was also anxious to learn how his brothers were doing in California. More importantly, it was not safe to stay long at Pearl's; word of their presence would spread like wildfire through the neighboring communities.

When Eugenia showed Bob the newspaper clippings about Bill's arrest for the Ceres robbery, he became enraged, cursing the railroad and all it stood for. He reassured Emmett that Bill was undoubtedly innocent, but secretly he wondered if his own actions had encouraged Bill to try train robbery himself. It seemed unlikely, for Bill had never shown the sort of courage and aggressiveness such an undertaking demanded, but he was a Dalton, after all. True or not, the accusations against Bill renewed Bob's resolve to strike back at the railroads and express companies, which he now viewed as the root of all evil in America.

Seated together on a brocade divan in Pearl's luxuriously furnished parlor, Eugenia gave Bob some current train schedules and told him what she had heard about shipments of cash. On the coming Tuesday, she said, the night train from Kansas City would be carrying the payroll for the Lehigh coal companies. Since the companies were in Indian Territory, the money would probably be shipped in the smaller way safe, rather than the stronger through safe that supposedly could only be opened at Gainesville, Texas. She suggested that they assault the train at Lillietta, a cattle station and water point about four miles north of Wagoner; she had reconnoitered the area and felt it was ideal for their operation.

When Eugenia prepared to leave the next morning on the long ride back to Wagoner, she made it clear to Bob that she did not approve of Pearl Younger, nor of Bob's staying at Pearl's ranch any longer than was absolutely necessary. Bob promised her they would depart as soon as they had made their plans and equipped themselves for the job ahead, then watched longingly as she galloped away.

Tuesday, September 15, 1891

"Wait till I give the signal," Bob warned the others. They were crouched down beside a cattle chute only about fifty yards from the tiny one-room train station, and the southbound train had just pulled in to take on water. The weak glow from the station's windows and the flickering beam of the locomotive's headlamp did little to relieve the surrounding blackness. Bill Doolin, chewing tobacco as he patiently waited, leaned to one side and quietly spit on the ground. Doolin's calm reassured Bob that he had made the right choice regarding who would accompany him to the engine. Behind them Newcomb, Pierce, Power, and Broadwell shuffled their feet and jostled each other, whispering and joking until Broadwell let out a loud horselaugh.

"Keep it quiet!" Bob ordered them in a strangled voice. Reluctantly they complied, but even in the dim moonlight Bob detected a momentary scowl on Pierce's face, resentful at being chastised. As long as he does what he's supposed to, Bob thought, not seriously worried about threats to his leadership. Still, he wondered if maybe he should have left Pierce to hold the horses instead of Emmett. There was a clank as the water spigot was raised from the engine, and Bob put such concerns out of his mind. Now was the time to act.

Clutching his rifle, Bob said, "Let's go!" Immediately they all swung into action, fanning out to take their allotted positions around the train as it prepared to leave. The harsh shadows across the uneven ground made running treacherous. Bob bounded to the cab of the locomotive, grabbing a hand rail to swing himself up to face the engineer.

"Hold up," he ordered, just as Doolin appeared on the other side of the cab.

"It's the Daltons!" the engineer blurted out, jerking his hands up like he had just touched a hot stove. Bob was momentarily flustered by the instant recognition, since the man surely did not know Bob by sight. Then he realized that the engineer simply assumed that anyone robbing a train must be a Dalton. Bob had decided after the last robbery to stop wearing a mask, and this incident merely confirmed the wisdom of his decision.

"Get down," Bob ordered the two crewmen, who jostled each other in their haste to comply. With Doolin prodding the train men from behind with his rifle, all four walked back along the train to the express car. Power and Newcomb were already there, banging on the door and shouting threats to the express messenger inside.

"Everybody get back!" Power warned ominously, giving Bob a big wink. "I'm gonna light the fuse on this dynamite." He held nothing in his hand but his pistol, but the messenger cowering inside had no way of knowing that.

"Wait!" came a shrill voice from inside the car. "I'm opening the door." There were some clicks as bolts were thrown, and the wide door rumbled open, the terrified clerk holding up his hands as soon as he finished sliding it aside. Doolin clambered into the car, rudely shoving the messenger to one side, and Newcomb climbed in after him. Bob and Power kept their guns trained on the engineer and fireman as they heard Doolin gruffly command the young clerk to open the safe.

Farther back along the train a couple people climbed down from the passenger cars, but they were quickly corralled by Broadwell and kept from raising a fuss. If he was following Bob's orders, Pierce was performing the same function on the other side of the train. Nervously Bob licked his lips and glanced from one side to the other. He waited impatiently as the seconds seemed to drag by.

"Lookee here!" Doolin said with a guffaw, suddenly reappearing in the doorway of the express car. He held the top of a large canvas sack that was dragging the floor beside him. With obvious effort he lifted the bag and swung it out to drop on the ground in front of Bob.

"Is that all money?" Power asked, awestruck.

"No, it's horse manure," Newcomb said sarcastically as he pulled the messenger to the edge of the doorway. With a shove he sent the young man sprawling in the dirt and gravel beside the train. The he and Doolin jumped down to join Bob and Power. Bill Power had bent over to grasp the neck of the money sack, and he was now struggling to lift it off the ground.

"Here," Doolin told him, taking the sack. "You better let me do that." Doolin was long and lanky, but his thin arms and broad shoulders were solid muscle, and he swung the bulky bag over his shoulder with impressive ease. "You ready?" he asked Bob.

Bob nodded and let out a piercing whistle, signaling to Pierce and Broadwell that it was time to leave. Swiftly the men ran down and across the tracks to the wooden pen where Emmett was guarding the horses. It took them a few moments of confusion to find their own mounts in the dark, but as soon as they were all up in the saddle they took off across the open fields to the west of the station, galloping for the hills barely visible on the horizon.

Once they had put some distance between themselves and the train, they slowed down to a more prudent pace and began laughing and whooping over their success. Bob was especially pleased that the robbery had gone so well; not one shot had been fired, no one was injured, and they had made off with what appeared to be more money than they would ever need. All in all, a good night's work.

Monday, September21, 1891

The gentle morning sunlight that slanted into the Visalia courtroom did little to brighten Grat Dalton's mood. Slumped in the hard wooden chair, his legs stretched out straight under the table and his hands loosely clasped in this lap, Grat stared gloomily at the dust motes dancing in the sunbeam and wondered how things could possibly get any worse. Next to him sat his two lawyers, Breckenridge and Ahern, but Grat had already lost all confidence in them. Ahern was scribbling notes on a legal pad while consulting a thick leather-bound text; Breckenridge just sat erect staring at the door to the judge's chambers, attempting to look infallible.

There was a constant chattering from the room full of spectators behind him, but Grat kept his unfocused gaze on the top of the table in front of him. Without really being aware of the action, he brought his right hand up to his mouth and began to pick and scrape his teeth with his fingernail. The previous week's events had emphasized the fact that just when he thought things couldn't get any worse, they did. First Bill had been released on the Ceres charge, only to be re-arrested because of the bond dispute. This time he had been placed in a basement cell, which was too remote for him to console and encourage Grat with his lighthearted conversation. Then, on Tuesday, the great J. W. Breckenridge had gotten into a street fight with a journalist over a disparaging remark in an editorial, a circumstance unlikely to improve the lawyer's standing before the court. Finally, on Thursday, Williams, the jailer, had told Grat about the train robbery at Lillietta in Indian Territory, one that all the papers insisted was the work of the notorious Dalton gang. That, too, Grat thought, would hardly make the court consider his request for a new trial more favorably.

Eventually Judge Gray was announced, and Grat rose lethargically to his feet as the stocky bearded jurist swept into the room, his robes flowing behind him, and took his seat behind the bench. This was to be Grat's sentencing hearing, and when he sat back down he searched Gray's impassive face for a clue about his intentions. The judge's expression was unreadable, however, and Grat slumped back again as the case was called and Ahern rose to speak.

"Your honor, inasmuch as the court reporter has not yet finished his transcript of the trial, the defense moves that sentencing be postponed until such a date as the court deems expedient."

"Is the court reporter present?" Gray demanded.

"I am, your honor." A. H. Murray Jr., the official reporter for department number one, identified himself for the record after he was called to the stand. He stated that the work of transcribing the notes was about half finished, and would be completed by October first.

After Murray stepped down, Breckenridge stood and addressed the judge, his hands gripping his lapels as he spoke in a deep rumbling voice developed through years of practice. "Your honor, if I may, I would like to suggest that this case be taken up again on Tuesday, October sixth. This would allow me and my associate counsel sufficient time in which to examine the transcript and then prepare a bill of exceptions to be used in a motion for a new trial."

District Attorney Daggett had no objection, so Gray had his clerk note the change. He adjourned the case for the time being and returned to his chambers. The temporary reprieve raised Grat's spirits a little, and he even managed a weak smile to his brother Cole when a deputy led him out of the courtroom and back to jail. Still, it was only temporary, and it only served to harden his resolve to regain control of his life. When he returned to his cell and the guards had left the cage, he would begin serious discussions with his fellow inmates, Beck and Smith.

Sunday, September 26, 1891

"What time is it?" Grat asked.

"Five-fifteen," Smith answered. William Barton Smith, a short, heavy-set fireplug of a man, was standing at the front of the cage staring down through the bars at the jailer's office, outside of which was mounted a large wall clock. Smith had been a railroad brakeman, but detectives had caught him breaking into a freight car to steal a few cigars. Although it was a minor theft, the railroad had insisted in fully prosecuting the case, and Smith had just been found guilty of second degree burglary. Like Grat, he was awaiting sentencing, and he would almost certainly be sent to San Quentin. Also like Grat, he was determined to avoid that fate.

"He's late," Grat noted with a touch of concern.

"He'll be here," Beck assured him, rising from his bunk to stand at the open door of his cell. John Beck was still awaiting trial on a horse theft charge. Taller and thinner than either Grat or Smith, Beck was a sandy-haired farm boy whose innocent looks belied a cunning criminal mind. Although uneducated and illiterate, Beck was sly and adept at manipulating others, and he had been instrumental in setting up this evening's plan. "Ever'thing else has worked, ain't it?"

Grat nodded in grudging agreement. They were waiting on Diss, the little Dutch boy who brought Grat's dinner every evening from the hotel. He usually came around 4:30, and the delay, on this of all nights, was especially worrisome, due to what he was bringing along with the food.

Grat heard the sound of a door opening and the clink of keys. Smith turned away from the bars and said, "Here he comes." Complying with jail rules, all three men withdrew to their cells and pulled the doors closed. In a moment Diss appeared outside the cage door. In one hand he had a big ring of keys and a black coffee pot, and in the other was a wicker basket with a plaid towel over it. The jailer Williams, who had remained at the foot of the stairs, called for

Diss to hurry up. Diss set the coffee pot on the floor while he unlocked the cage door, then picked it back up and entered the cage. He walked over and set the pot and basket down on the overturned wooden box that the prisoners used as a table, gave Grat an exaggerated wink, and then turned and strolled casually back out.

Grat waited until Diss had relocked the cage door and descended the stairs before he swung open the cell door and rushed over to the basket. In it were sandwiches, pickles, and a wormy apple; at the bottom, wrapped in a white kitchen towel, was a Colt .45 caliber pistol. Smith and Beck came out of their cells and joined Grat in admiring the gleaming weapon, grim smiles on their faces. Beck glanced over his shoulder to make sure they were not being watched, then reverently picked up the pistol and fondled it, holding it close to his chest. Grat, ravenously hungry all of a sudden, took a huge bite of one of the sandwiches as he moved the basket and pot into his cell.

While Grat sat in his cell and ate, Beck and Smith furtively examined the gun and whispered to each other what they might do with it. All three men jerked when they were startled by the shout from below.

"All right, you guys, it's bed time!" Williams yelled. "Everybody back in their cells." Smith, who had been aiming the pistol at imaginary targets, nervously stuffed it under his shirt and then assumed a false nonchalance while he walked to his cell. Grat stood up and pulled his cell door closed as Beck and Smith did the same. With a metallic squeal and clunk, the sliding rods at the top of Smith's cell moved into place, but the rods on Grat's and Beck's adjacent cells scraped only a couple inches and jammed. Downstairs Williams worked the levers back and forth, trying to get the rods to seat, but this only resulted in a frantic clashing of iron against iron. Grat and Smith exchanged worried glances.

"Hey, Grat," Williams called up, stepping just outside his office door. "Shut your door again. Somethin's not lined up right."

"Okay," Grat yelled back cooperatively. He opened and slammed his door noisily, while at the same time he stretched up to manipulate the nut on the locking rod bolt that they had earlier loosened. Down in his office Williams swung the lever again, and this time it locked into place properly.

"Thanks," Williams told him a couple minutes later when the jailer came up to lock the individual cell doors with his keys. When Williams returned to his office without noticing the loose rods or the odd behavior of the inmates, Grat heaved a sigh of relief. This operation was getting far too nerve-wracking. Grat sat back down on his bunk and picked up the remaining sandwich, but he found his hunger had vanished. He replaced it in the basket and poured some more coffee into his cup. For the next half hour he sat there sipping it, wishing the flutter in his stomach would go away.

Grat estimated that it was just after six o'clock when he heard the door to the jailer's office open again. He listened to the sound of a single pair of boots climbing the metal stairs to the cage, and the rattle of keys as the cage door was opened. It was Billy Brewer, the young trusty everyone called "Dutchy," bringing them some matches, just as they had counted on. Although the cage had an electric light, the power was shut down every night at 1:00 a.m., so the prisoners were provided with candles in case they needed light during the night. For safety and security reasons, they were given only a few matches at a time.

Billy was trembling but game as he came to each cell with the ring of keys. Grat was the first, and wrapped his blanket around the locking mechanism while Billy cautiously inserted the key and twisted it in the lock, striving to minimize any sound of metal on metal. The same was done for Smith and then Beck.

"Thanks, Dutchy," Beck whispered to him as he handed the boy a slip of paper torn from an accounts ledger. Beck had shown it to Grat earlier; it was a promissory note for $100 payable by Beck's lawyer, a note Beck had asked someone in the basement cells to write for him. Billy shoved the note into his pants pocket and anxiously left the cage, fumbling as he relocked the cage door. Grat's stomach began to feel better, for now the main hurdles had been overcome. It was all downhill from here.

At 6:30, as previously arranged, the plucking of Bill Dalton's guitar was heard from below, and in moments all of the men down there were singing lustily. Just like the last three nights, they were led in song by a former English sailor who seemed to know every tune ever written. Many accompanied their raucous singing by pounding on the bars or stomping their feet, anything to raise the level of noise. With the ruckus downstairs masking their actions, Grat and his partners used their fingers to undo the nuts and bolts on the sliding rods of their cells. These had been loosened earlier with a wrench that a trusty had smuggled in, and in only a few seconds the rods were pushed aside and the cell doors swung wide.

When Grat stepped out of his cell, he looked back to see how it appeared from outside. Using the basket, pot, and spare blankets and pillows, he had created a lumpy form on his bunk that might pass for a sleeping person, as long as the lighting stayed dim and no one looked very carefully. Quietly he closed the door and slid the locking rod back into place, finger-tightening the metal nuts as best he could. Beck and Smith had done the same, and Beck had already overturned the wooden box that sat between the cells. Under it were the tools that trusties had brought them on the sly: a file, a knife with its blade serrated by the file into a saw blade, a whetstone, the wrench, and a section of broom handle blackened to resemble an iron bar. Grat grabbed the file and went to crouch by the back wall of the cage.

For three evenings they had been filing away at one of the bars while the men downstairs sang and yelled to cover the racket. By lights out the previous night they had made deep cuts through the bar at both ends, leaving only a thin stand of iron to hold the bar in place. Grat wiped away the mixture of soap and dirt with which he had disguised the cuts and began furiously sawing away the sliver of metal that remained. Behind him Beck used the wrench to retighten the bolts on the locking rods, while Smith hovered near the front of the cage watching the door to the jailer's office, his hand clutching the pistol in his belt.

"How's it going?" Beck asked, leaning over Grat with the wrench hanging loosely by his side. He had finished his job and was anxious to get going.

"Just. . .a little. . .more. . ." Grat panted as he frantically dragged the file back and forth. Then the cut at the bottom was through. Grat grabbed the bar in both hands and pulled; at first the bar bent outward only an inch, but suddenly the top of the bar broke with a snap, sending Grat sprawling backwards.

"All right!" Beck said gleefully. "Let's get out of here." Dropping to his knees he twisted his body and began worming his way through the narrow opening. Meanwhile Grat placed the iron bar under the box and arranged it just like it had been. When Beck had pulled himself through and gained his feet on the outside of the bars, Grat handed the tools to him, and then contorted his own body to squirm out of the cage. Once Grat was clear, Smith left his post to follow them. He refused Grat's offer to take the gun, maintaining his grip on it as he clumsily pushed his way through the bars. Because of his thick trunk and broad shoulders, Smith momentarily became stuck. Grat and Beck had to pull on his arms and clothes to squeeze him through, but finally he was able to scramble to his feet beside them. Beck handed the broom handle to Grat, who knelt down and forced it into the gap where the iron bar had been.. When he stood up again, he nodded at the others, and Beck led them around the cage to the stairs.

As the basement resounded to the second verse of "Midshipmate," the three men edged down the stairway to the lower level. Grat kept his gaze locked on the door to the jailer's office. It was rare for any of the deputies to enter the jail after lockup, but there was always a chance. Behind him was Smith, the pistol cocked and ready, and it belatedly occurred to Grat that Smith should have been first to go down the stairs instead of the last.

When he reached the bottom step, Grat turned to face the inmates in the lower cells. Bill was sitting on his bunk strumming his guitar, and Grat gave him a grin and a wave. Then, as the singing crescendoed and some of the men began clapping in time, Grat bowed to them like a stage musician. With a final sweep of his arm he followed Beck across the corridor to the kitchen door. Fumbling with the tools he was carrying, Beck drew a key from his pants pocket and handed it to Grat. After Grat cautiously unlocked and opened the door, they entered the darkened room beyond. Grat relocked the door behind them and carefully made his way across the room after Beck and Smith, who had arrowed their way to the wood storage room at the northwest corner of the building. This room had a grated window high on the far wall, through which fire wood was delivered.

The room was lit only by the meager glow of the streetlamps outside, and Beck's face was a latticework of light and shadow as he worked at the window. Beck cursed under his breath as he fumbled with the padlock that secured the grate. He was trying to break it with the wrench, but the tool kept slipping out of the hasp, making a dangerous clank.

"Here," Smith ordered, handing the pistol to Grat, "let me do that." He took the wrench from Beck, carefully judged the angles, and on his second try he snapped the hasp from the lock. The metal grating, hinged at the bottom, creaked as he lowered it, but freedom was too near for the men to care now. Beck shoved past Smith, scrambled up the grate, and crawled out the window. Grat handed the pistol up to him, then accepted Smith's boost to reach the high opening and squirm out onto the dry grass of the courthouse lawn. While Beck stood guard with the gun, Grat stayed on his hands and knees and reached back through the window to help Smith. They gripped each other's wrists, and with great effort Grat dragged the bulky man through the narrow opening. Grat stood and dusted himself off, waiting while Smith pulled the grating back up and jammed it into place with a stick. Once Smith was ready, the three men cautiously moved away from the jail.

It was Sunday evening, and the courthouse plaza was silent and empty. The lights were on over at the Methodist church for their evening services, but the rest of the buildings were dark and deserted. Across the plaza, near the church, a buggy with a two-horse team was parked. Grat smiled at their good fortune.

At Grat's suggestion, the three escapees strolled across the plaza as if they were in no particular hurry, climbed into the buggy, and casually drove off down the street. Their absence from jail would not be noticed until twelve hours later.

Grat drove the buggy six miles west to Goshen, where he let Beck and Smith off so they could catch a train going south. The three men shook hands and insincerely agreed to look each other up later; finally Grat flicked the reins and drove away, this time heading north.

It was a pleasant late summer evening, with clear skies and a cool breeze, and Grat's spirit soared with the joy of freedom. He had been foolish to turn himself in, he thought, but he would never make that mistake again. If they insisted that Grat Dalton was a criminal, then so be it. He would never let himself be jailed again.

When he arrived at Maggie Rucker's boarding house near Traver, Wiley Dean was waiting for him in the yard. Dean seemed to have been pacing nervously for hours, and his welcome for Grat was exuberantly relieved.

"Any problems?" Dean asked after Grat climbed down from the buggy.

"Nope. Went just like we planned."

"You didn't need the gun?" Dean's voice had a worried tone.

"No, but I'm still glad you sent it. Just in case."

"That's great. So no one got hurt or anything?"

"I might have pulled a muscle in my arm," Grat joked, rubbing his left shoulder. "Cutting those bars is hard work."

"What about Bill?"

"He's fine. He played a real mean guitar tonight. We could have gotten him out, too, if he had wanted."

"I know," Dean said. "I think he shoulda escaped with you, but you know Bill. He's convinced they'll acquit him."

"Yeah, like they did me," Grat said bitterly. "Well, what's done is done. You got the horses ready?"

"Back in the barn."

"Go get 'em. I want to take this buggy somewhere and leave it, so you follow with the horses. Okay?"

"Sure, Grat. Whatever you say."

It was after midnight when they reached Tulare City, ten miles south of Visalia. Grat drove the buggy into a cornfield and unhitched the horses to let them graze. Then he mounted the saddle horse Dean had been leading and the two men trotted off. To the east were the Sierra Nevada Mountains, where they could hide in the pine forests and craggy canyons.

Around ten the next morning the guards came for Bill. The jail had been a beehive of activity in the three hours since the escape had been discovered, and Bill had chuckled as he heard the accusations and recriminations from the various deputies and jailers. They were still trying to reconstruct how the escape had been managed, and all the while they fended off the questions of persistent reporters with vague explanations and promises of early recapture. The damage to the cage itself had been quickly repaired, and now Under Sheriff Hall was standing outside Bill's cell waiting while Bill gathered up his coat and his guitar.

"You know Grat's gone?" asked the trusty who was with Hall.

"Yes," Bill replied with satisfaction. "I always said that Gratton would never cross the bay."

"It's your turn next," Hall warned him, pointing him toward the stairs.

"Oh, I'm all right," Bill answered jauntily. "There may be a few flies on the guards, but there are none on the Dalton boys." Carrying his coat and guitar he climbed the stairs to the cage, smiling and nodding regally to the rest of the basement inmates, who all shouted encouragement to Bill and insults to the guards.

They placed him in Beck's old cell, double checking the lock and the sliding bar to make sure it was secure. When Hall left the cage and locked its door behind him, Bill dropped the coat on his bunk and moved his guitar into playing position. He strummed it a few times to check the tuning, then broke into song, one he had written especially for this occasion. It was called, "You Will Never Miss My Brother Till He's Gone."

When they could keep from laughing the men downstairs began to join in on the chorus. The jailers fumed and scowled in embarrassment, ineffectually demanding silence. It was a rare moment of triumph for Bill Dalton.

Author's Notes

Chapter 11

On September 14, 1891, the *Sacramento Union* carried an article about the hearing for Bill Dalton and Wiley Dean, describing how the charges were dropped and Bill's subsequent arrest due to the withdrawal of his bond.

The Dalton gang's visit to Pearl Younger's ranch is based solely on rumor, but a rumor that seems very plausible. Pearl and her mother had a history of associating with criminals, and the purported kinship between the Daltons and Pearl via Cole Younger would certainly have encouraged Bob to seek refuge there. Emmett, on the other hand, claimed that they were still at Riley's camp when Eugenia rode out to tell them about the payroll shipments, but this is difficult to believe. For an attractive young woman to make such an arduous and dangerous trip of 250 miles each way, alone on horseback, would have been folly in those days, as well as pointless. She could much more easily have taken a train to Woodward and then rented a horse to ride out to the camp, if that is truly where they were at the time.

Because of time constraints, the death of Charley Bryant, and other factors, it is more logical to assume that the gang had already moved to the east, and Younger's Bend would have been a convenient destination, both because of its reputation and its location near Lillietta. Emmett's failure to mention Pearl Younger may be attributed to his standard reluctance to name those who had aided and abetted the Daltons, as well as perhaps embarrassment about staying at a widely known house of ill repute.

The Lillietta robbery was reported by the *Vinita Indian Chieftain* on September 17, 1891, and by the *Fort Smith Elevator* on September 18, 1891. Emmett's description of this robbery in *Beyond the Law* is remarkably dissimilar to the newspaper accounts. Since Emmett's book was written almost 25 years later, it is probable that he confused this robbery with another, since all of their train robberies were done under similar circumstances. It may also be that since Emmett was apparently left guarding the horses, his recollection would necessarily be based mainly on what the others had told him later, complete with typical exaggerations and embellishments.

The *Visalia Weekly Delta* published an article about Grat's initial sentencing hearing on September 24, 1891, which included an observation on Grat's obvious mental and physical deterioration. This same newspaper also had articles about Breckenridge's street fight with an editor, and William Barton Smith's conviction on the burglary charge.

On September 29, 1891, the *San Francisco Call* ran a long report on Grat's escape from jail, including wood-cut drawings of Grat and W. B. Smith. On October 1 the *Visalia Weekly Delta* published a remarkably thorough and even-handed investigative report on the escape after conducting numerous interviews. Much of the information came from a written statement by an anonymous source within the jail. This "educated and intelligent" inmate provided insider knowledge of how the escape was planned and carried out. Judging from the tone and content of this statement, it is entirely possible that it was written by Bill Dalton himself, especially in light of Bill's demonstrated penchant for using the press to influence public opinion.

Wiley Dean's part in the escape was not revealed until later, when he was captured after hiding in the mountains with Grat. This was reported in the December 31, 1891, issue of the *Weekly Delta*.

Bill Dalton's actions and remarks on the morning following the escape are exactly as reported by the October 1 issue of the *Delta*.

CHAPTER 12

Bob's nerves were beginning to fray like an old rope. In the weeks following the Lillietta robbery the search for the Daltons had intensified, and the gang had constantly been on the move to elude their pursuers. Breaking camp every evening, they traveled through the night to a new location, tracking back and forth across the Creek Nation to stay one jump ahead of the law. No longer did they seek assistance from friendly farmers and ranchers. The rewards for their capture were increasing almost daily, reaching a level that Bob feared would tempt even the most loyal of friends.

Whenever they needed supplies, Bob would send Emmett into the nearest town. Emmett was not as well known as Bob, and he had an innocent appearance to carry him through safely. As an added insurance, Emmett normally paid at least twice what the goods were worth, buying gratitude and silence from the store owners, who often sympathized with the Dalton's war on the railroads.

While primarily worried about external pressures on the gang, Bob was also becoming concerned about the growing internal friction. Having such a large gang made the robberies easier and less risky, but it also reduced each member's share of the proceeds. It also afforded more opportunities for disagreements and personality conflicts. This had been brought home to Bob a few hours after the Lillietta robbery, when the gang had stopped to count and divide the loot.

Riding west across the prairie in the moonlight, they had paused at the banks of the Verdigris River to dismount and examine their plunder. Bob had been disappointed to discover that the remarkable weight of the mail sack was due to its containing a large quantity of silver coins, mostly dollars and halves. When he asked Bill Doolin why he had bothered with the small change, Doolin had taken the question as criticism. Reacting angrily, Doolin told him money was money, and said it was not his fault that the train had not carried the big payroll that Bob had promised. It took Bob several minutes to smooth the ruffled feathers and return to the job at hand, counting the money, but the seeds of dissension had been sown.

Although the total came to over $20,000, it had to be split seven ways. Thus each man received only about $3000, much of it in coin. While the newer members of the gang were quite pleased with earning this much for a single night's work, Bob suspected it would quickly be frittered away on high living. For him and Emmett, the proceeds were a letdown; their combined funds were still insufficient to disappear and start a new life elsewhere, Bob's continuing goal. To make matters worse, Doolin, backed up by Newcomb and Pierce, protested the way the split was made. Doolin implied that since Bob had done the counting and dividing, perhaps it had not been totally equitable. Possessing virtually no education, Doolin was always suspicious of those who were comfortable with reading, writing, and arithmetic, and he was convinced that Bob had somehow shortchanged him using mathematical legerdemain.

Patiently Bob recounted the money and explained the division, and with some grudging assistance from Bitter Creek he finally persuaded Doolin that each man had received the same amount. Unable to let it go completely, however, Doolin then suggested that since Emmett had done nothing more than hold the horses, his share should be reduced or eliminated. The other men, realizing that they could easily be in Emmett's position during a future holdup, quickly voted this idea down and encouraged Doolin to shut the hell up. Reluctantly accepting defeat, Doolin sullenly took his money and stuffed it inside his saddlebags.

As they mounted up to resume their ride, Bob told them that it would be best if they split into two groups. Seven armed men traveling together would draw attention wherever they went, he explained, and by dividing they would also impede the tracking and pursuit by lawmen. He suggested that Doolin, Newcomb, and Pierce take off in one direction, and while he, Emmett, Power, and Broadwell would go another. Both groups would eventually reassemble back at Riley's camp out in the Cheyenne and Arapahoe lands.

Unspoken was Bob's desire to separate himself from Doolin, who seemed to be challenging his leadership. Bob was also concerned about the fondness shown by Doolin, Newcomb, and Pierce for saloons and loose women, fearing that their lack of caution could lead to the gang's downfall. Doolin was shrewd and capable, and Bob was unsure of his own ability to fully control this wild man from Arkansas.

Doolin, for reasons of his own, welcomed the suggestion to split up, and soon he and his two companions rode away and were swallowed up by the darkness. Bob and the other three, leading two pack horses, moved out to the northwest, in the general direction of Tulsa. At sunrise they found a small patch of woods on a hilltop. There they made a hidden camp among the trees and rested in the shade, waiting for nightfall when they could again travel undetected. It was a pattern that would repeat itself in the coming days and weeks.

It was a bright autumn day, but there was a cool wind from the north. Bob lay on his back in the high grass on the south side of the hill, his hat pulled down over his eyes, and tried to sleep. He could feel the sun's rays heating his clothing, generating a pleasant boundary of warmth that would be swept away by the occasional breath of cold air as the wind shifted and eddied around the hill. The smell of earth and dried grass filled his nostrils, and for a while he was completely relaxed and content. Then he heard a muttered "Uh-oh" from Dick Broadwell. Instantly he scrambled up into a crouching position, pushing his hat back with one hand while the other reached for the butt of his pistol.

"What?" he asked urgently, his eyes darting to scan the immediate vicinity.

"Over there," Broadwell said, pointing to the south. He was standing by a small tree, a recent stain on its trunk revealing what his purpose had been.

Bob's eyes searched the rolling plain below them for whatever had caught Broadwell's attention. They were surrounded by open land, an essentially flat terrain that was carpeted with wild grass and dotted with clumps of bushes and scrub oak trees. This hill was the highest point in the area, and Bob had wisely chosen its vantage point for their camp. Now, as the afternoon sun began to sink toward the horizon, there was movement in the distance. Squinting his eyes, Bob made out the silhouettes of four mounted men riding slowly towards them. Emmett and Power, who had been sleeping amidst the unloaded supplies, rushed over and crouched beside Bob.

"What's up?" Power asked, rubbing his eyes.

"Four riders coming our way," Bob answered curtly. "Get the horses out of sight."

All four men scrambled to work, hastily throwing their saddles over the horses without cinching them and grabbing their guns and blankets up into their arms. They led the horses around the hill to the north side, avoiding the crest where their figures would stand out against the bright blue sky. Once they were out of sight from the approaching strangers, they cinched their saddles and packed their belongings, getting ready to mount up and ride at a moment's notice. Some of their food supplies had been left on the ground at their original camp, but Bob told them to leave it alone; they could always get more food.

After he finished buckling up his saddlebags, Bob reached inside one of them and drew out the field glasses he had bought several months ago. They were the finest pair he had ever seen: black enameled brass and pebbled leather, equipped with the finest German lenses, and stored neatly in a tooled leather case with velvet interior. With the binoculars in one hand and his Winchester in the other, Bob ran diagonally toward the top of the hill and dropped into an eroded gully that provided him a protected view of the land to the south. Carefully laying his rifle on the grass in front of him, Bob stretched out just below the edge of the ravine and brought the glasses to his eyes, propping his elbows in the dirt. He heard the others take positions to either side of him, but his concentration was on the distant figures swimming into focus in front of him.

It took only a few seconds to adjust the glasses properly, to get only one sharp image, before he could begin to identify the distant riders. In the lead, studying the ground intently, was an Indian. The man, his long black hair in braids, looked up and swept his gaze across the hill where Bob lay hidden. Bob's stomach tightened as he recognized the weather-beaten face. It was Tiger Jack, a Yuchi Indian with the reputation for being one of the best trackers in the country. If he found their trail, there would be hell to pay.

Bob shifted his gaze to the three white men who rode behind Jack, and cursed under his breath. The man on the right behind Tiger Jack was Burrill Cox, the hated deputy marshal from Claremore who had arrested Grat and taken him to the Fort Smith jail the year before.

"Who are they?" Emmett whispered.

"Shh!" Bob commanded, his eyes pressed against the opticals. Next to Cox rode an older man, paunchy, with a long gray handlebar mustache. It was their old friend Heck Thomas, now doggedly on their trail, and Bob sensed the irony of the reversal in their relationship. Once Heck had helped bring Frank Dalton's killer to justice, and he had often worked with Bob and Grat when they, too, had been deputy marshals. Back then they had depended on each other for support and assistance. Now he was their enemy, continuing to enforce the laws that the Daltons now violated. Still, Bob felt no antipathy toward the man; he was simply doing his job, and doing it well, and Bob respected and admired the loyalty and perseverance of the man.

The last man in the group was someone Bob had never seen before, yet he somehow seemed familiar. Dressed all in black, the stranger had a prominent nose under which sprouted a thick dark mustache. His angular features and rigid posture implied a no-nonsense attitude, and suddenly Bob realized who it was. From the description Bill and Grat had given him back in California, Bob was sure that this must be their nemesis, railroad detective William Smith. He had heard that Smith was still searching for them, and sure enough, determined as ever, there he was.

Quietly, without looking up from the binoculars, Bob told the others who they were facing. Forbidding any discussion, he continued his surveillance of the small party as it came ever closer. Bob was about to order a retreat when he saw the men pull up and dismount. In a few minutes it became obvious that they were making camp for the night, and Bob watched with relief as the bedrolls were laid out and a campfire started. Watching their lips and expressions, Bob guessed at what they were saying, and he related this to Emmett and the others in short muttered phrases.

Tiger Jack, after tying his horse to a sapling, began to wander around the campsite in ever-widening circles, stopping every few steps to bend down and examine the ground. Suddenly he turned and walked swiftly back to the camp, where he spoke animatedly with Heck Thomas.

"I think Jack's found our tracks," Bob told his companions. "But I don't think he wants to find us."

The Indian went over and mounted his horse, obviously intending to leave. Smith ran over and grabbed the reins of Jack's horse, arguing angrily with him. Jack kept shaking his head and repeating a short phrase.

"What's he saying, Bob?" Emmett asked.

Bob had no idea, but to keep Emmett happy he said, "Jack's saying, 'Squaw heap sick.' He doesn't want to meet up with us, so he's telling Smith he has to go home." It was as good an explanation as any, and perhaps even correct. With angry gestures and disgusted expressions the three lawmen gave up and repacked their horses. With Tiger Jack far in the lead, the party rode back the way they had come. Bob took the glasses from his eyes and let out a long noisy sigh as the previously unnoticed tension ebbed away from his body.

"That was close," Bill Power remarked unnecessarily.

"Think they'll be back?" Broadwell asked, sitting up and brushing dirt from his shirt.

"We're not going to wait and find out," Bob told them. "They might be going to get more men." He picked up his rifle and stood up on the sloping side of the ravine. "Let's mount up and ride west. If we push it all night, we can be out of Heck's territory by morning. By the time he gets permission to keep chasing us, we'll be long gone."

"Where we goin'?" Power asked as they climbed up the opposite bank of the ravine.

"Back to Riley's camp."

"How much have we got all together?" Bob asked out of the blue. Emmett had been listening to Power's story about a man he knew who had fallen down a well, and was caught off guard by Bob's abrupt question. They were all huddled in the dugout cabin at Riley's ranch, vainly striving to keep warm and dry. Outside a fine cold rain was falling, blown almost horizontal by the sharp north wind that whistled unimpeded across the high plains, and inside the dark musty hut dug into the side of a ravine, Emmett, Bob, Power, and Broadwell sat shivering. Each had moved a box or cot to sit on so that it was clear of the many small leaks dripping through the canvas roof. While the other three had entertained each other with stories and jokes they had all heard before, Bob had been off in a corner brooding, wordless until his unexpected query to Emmett.

Emmett lifted his shirt and laboriously removed the money belt from around his waist. As the others waited silently, he licked his thumb and whispered to himself as he methodically slid the bills from his left hand onto his lap.

"A little over seven thousand," he said. He straightened the stack of money before returning it to the belt.

"Then we're through," Bob announced quietly with a grim finality.

"Through?" Bill Power blurted out in consternation. "What the hell is the matter with you? Why, I haven't even started yet." Emmett was equally bewildered by Bob's statement, but he allowed the others to risk Bob's wrath by questioning it.

"I don't care if you're started," Bob told Power with a touch of annoyance. "You can't keep this up and always get away with it. They're on to us, they know who we are. Heck Thomas almost caught us the other day, and he won't quit looking. We're bound to slip up sometime."

"Aw, hell!" Broadwell scoffed. "Nothin' like it. That bunch didn't have enough nerve to fight a sick cat." Emmett admired Broadwell's bravado, but the young man did not know Heck Thomas like Bob and Emmett did; the Daltons were certain that Thomas would be a persistent hound dog on their trail, and he would give them no quarter when he found them.

In the gloomy shadows Bob shrugged. “Well, it don’t make any difference to me what you boys think. I’m saying that I’m through.” Bob turned to look at Emmett, and his expression seemed to soften for a moment. “I don’t give a whoop in hell for all the deputies they send after me,” Bob assured them, deflecting any possible accusations of cowardice. “They’ll never get me alive, to stick behind any prison bars, and I’m not gonna let Emmett get put behind any either, not while I’m alive. So you just take that as it lies. We’re through. You guys have your wad, and I helped you get it. I don’t care what you do with it. You can gamble with it, or blow it any way you want, but from now on we’re through. Here is where I call it quits.”

Emmett viewed his older brother with renewed respect and affection. Bob resisted repeated attempts by Power and Broadwell to change his mind, much to Emmett’s satisfaction. For some time Emmett had felt a growing trepidation about their future, a gnawing concern that despite their careful planning and Bob’s skillful leadership, they would someday be caught or even killed. In fact, he sometimes wondered which fate would be worse. Being caught and locked up would bring them down to the same level as the common criminals he and Bob had put in jail when they were deputies. More significantly, at least to Emmett, their incarceration would also bring shame and disgrace to their family. He often worried that there seemed to be no other alternatives facing them, but Bob’s announcement had given him new hope that Bob had devised a plan to save them.

After the rain drifted away and the clouds broke up, the men moved outside to soak up the afternoon sun. With a suddenness typical of the area, the wintry cold of the October morning was replaced with an Indian Summer afternoon. Power and Broadwell continued to pester Bob, using challenges, pleas, and any other tactic they could devise to change his mind, all to no avail. For Emmett, their insistence emphasized how vital Bob’s leadership was to the gang. Power and Broadwell could not even conceive of committing their crimes without Bob, and they depended totally on him for guidance. Leaning erect against the side of the dugout, one boot casually crossed over the other, Bob calmly fended off all their blandishments. Tall and slim, clean and well-dressed, Bob was the image of a hero, and Emmett had never felt closer to him.

Toward nightfall Bop saddled his horse and announced he was going to Woodward. The others quickly followed suit, and the four started off through the gathering darkness. Power and Broadwell, still appealing Bob's decision, tried to pry out of him his intentions for the immediate future. Emmett was also extremely curious about this subject, but he let the other two do all the questioning for him. Bob, in response, simply repeated that he was quitting, and refused comment about his future plans. Emmett rode along in silence, confident that Bob would fill him in when the time was right.

Eventually the conversation died away, and the four men rode quietly under the stars, each absorbed in his own thoughts and dreams. Emmett's mood had improved, knowing that the anxiety he normally experienced prior to one of their crimes was to be a thing of the past. There was still danger ahead, of course, but there was also a promise of better things. This seemed to be a turning point in their lives, one that would eventually lead them away from a vortex of self-destruction.

The sky had begun to lighten with the approach of dawn when they came to a ranch they had visited on previous occasions. The owner was sympathetic to the Daltons, and Bob suggested they could get some breakfast there. The two-room cabin showed a light in the window, implying that the rancher was up early preparing for his daily chores. Bob signaled for Emmett to let Power and Broadwell go through the gate ahead of them. Not noticing in the dark that the Daltons had lagged behind, the other two rode up to the house, dismounted, and tied their horses to the hitching rail.

Bob leaned down and closed the gate from the outside, then shouted to Power and Broadwell, "So long boys. You'll hear from me later on. Good luck!"

Spinning his horse around, he called out, "Come on, Emmett," and rode away. In the misty twilight Emmett could barely discern the looks of surprise on their friends before he, too, turned his horse around and galloped off.

Once they were out of sight, Bob and Emmett slowed their pace and continued on toward Woodward in the half-light of approaching dawn. Emmett was bursting with questions for his enigmatic brother, but he knew it would do no good to pressure Bob for answers. He held his tongue and waited as patiently as he could. Finally, without preamble, Bob spoke up.

"We are really through," he said conclusively, keeping his eyes focused on the road ahead. "We just can't beat this game forever. I don't know, but I guess we've taken enough out of the express company for what they did. I mean, Grat's been convicted, so there's not much we can do about that, but he'll probably get out all right sooner or later, and I don't figure we're doing Bill's case any good."

Bob paused, and Emmett gave a grunt to show that he was listening. After shifting his position in the saddle a little, Bob continued, a touch of regret in his voice.

"There ought to be some justice in this old world. Maybe we should have stuck it out in California and fought it out ourselves, instead of leaving it for Bill and Grat, but we didn't, and here we are. So now I think we better beat it down south, get down to the Gulf, and then it'll be us for South America. We'll go into the cattle business down there. We got us a good stake, and we'll be safe there. They can't bring us back from there for what we've done, and they can't punish us down there for what we didn't do. Far as I can see, that's the only way we can go, so what do you say? Are you through?"

Emmett had heard this all before, in one form or another. While he agreed with the concept, he had serious doubts about their ability—and about Bob's commitment—to carry it out. He pondered how to express his concerns without offending his brother, who was very sensitive to any criticism.

"Well, you see, Bob . . . " Emmett began hesitantly, but Bob interrupted before he could continue.

"See nothing!" Bob replied sharply. "I said we're through, and that's all there is to it. Come on!" With that Bob spurred his horse into a trot, and Emmett had to do likewise to keep up. Emmett sighed and dropped the topic. He just hoped Bob really meant it this time. Emmett had long ago realized the futility of continuing their career in crime, but he also suspected that their funds were insufficient to accomplish Bob's grandiose plans. Unless land and cattle in South America were a whole lot cheaper than here in the United States, they would probably just end up working as cowboys for someone else. Still, Emmett admitted to himself, that was certainly better than being hounded across the country by the law. The hard reality was that they had very few options open to them.

It was full daylight by the time Woodward was visible in the distance, so they found a clump of low trees and high brush in which to conceal themselves. With a clear view of the surrounding prairie, the tangle provided a secure and secluded place to rest and wait until nightfall. While alternately standing guard, the two boys spent the cool autumn day sleeping and engaging in sporadic conversation. Whenever Bob brought up the subject of South America and what they would do there, Emmett forced himself to show as much enthusiasm as he could muster.

Shortly after sundown they mounted up and rode on into Woodward. With money supplied by Bob, Eugenia had rented a small cabin on the outskirts of the frontier town, and cautiously they approached the back of this cabin, which showed a lantern shining in a tiny window at the side. Leaving Emmett to stand watch with the horses, Bob dismounted and disappeared around the corner. Emmett heard a soft knock on the front door, and then the sound of the door opening and closing swiftly. For the next half hour he just paced back and forth, alert for any movement in the darkness and straining to hear any unusual noise. Lights shown from the scattered buildings of the town, and infrequently someone would carry a lantern to the outhouse. Otherwise all was peaceful.

Emmett nearly yelped out loud when he suddenly felt a hand on his arm. He was so startled by Bob's silent approach that at first he could not really comprehend what Bob was excitedly whispering to him.

"Give me the money belt."

"Why?" Confused, his heart pumping wildly from the fright, Emmett fumbled with the lower buttons of his vest and shirt.

"He escaped, Emmett! Isn't that great?"

"What?" Emmett tried to gather his scattered wits. "Who escaped?"

"Grat! He escaped from jail. Him and two other guys. They cut their way through the bars and just walked out. Bill had guns and a horse waiting for him, and now he's hiding out in the mountains."

"Grat's escaped? That's wonderful! But what about Bill? I thought he was in jail, too."

"That's the best part. Bill was acquitted, so he's off scot free."

"When did all this happen?"

"A few weeks ago. Eugenia says it was in all the papers, and Mom got a letter from Bill."

Emmett finally managed to free the money belt and snaked it out from under his shirt. "What do you need this for?"

Bob snatched the belt from him. "Bill spent all his money on that damn lawyer, and Grat needs money to make it through the winter. I'm gonna give some of our money to Eugenia to take to Grat and Bill. Wait here, I'll be back in a little while." As suddenly as he had appeared, Bob was gone again, back in the cabin with Eugenia.

Hours later Emmett was still waiting, noting with concern that the stars on the eastern horizon were beginning to fade. Sunrise was only an hour or so away. He was just working up the nerve to go knock on the cabin's door when Bob returned, the smile on his face obvious even in the dark.

"Let's go," Bob ordered, and they both climbed on their horses and rode away from the town, back toward Riley's camp. Later, as the morning sun warmed their faces, Bob informed Emmett that the trip to South America was postponed again. Instead they would wait to see how Grat fared; they would also need more money, since much of their stake was on its way to California. Emmett dejectedly wondered if they would ever leave the Twin Territories, or if there would ever come a time when they were not being pursued. He was beginning to doubt it.

Thursday, December 25, 1891

"Hell of a way to spend Christmas," Grat said glumly, and spit a stream of tobacco juice down the slope in front of them. Wiley Dean, sitting huddled under a blanket with his arms around his knees, just nodded. Between them lay the greyhound that had wandered into the camp and attached himself to Grat; the dog was curled on a flat rock, his long thin legs stretched out and crossed alongside. Sitting in front of their camp in the mountains east of Fresno, Grat and Dean were trying to warm themselves in the morning sunshine that glittered off the patches of frozen snow dotting the rugged landscape.

Wandering around in the mountains in the days following Grat's jail break, they had eventually come to this remote location. High on a peak near the head of a steep canyon, they had found an outcropping of rock that provided some protection from the elements. Stretching a sheet of canvas out from the shallow cave using tree limbs and rope, they had made themselves an open-sided shelter. Inside were blankets and food, and near the entrance was a circle of rocks in which a fire was usually kept burning. From this aerie they could see miles in all directions, and the only practical approach was up the steep incline directly in front. It was a safe hideout, but it was rugged and austere, and Grat sometimes had to remind himself that it was better than being in jail.

"We need some fresh meat for our Christmas dinner," Grat proposed, to break the monotony. "Let's go deer hunting."

"Okay," Dean agreed. He shrugged off the blanket and struggled to his feet on the uneven ground. There was little enthusiasm in his voice or movements. The thrill and adventure of helping a famous outlaw escape had apparently faded with the long weeks of hiding in the mountains. The dog, however, jumped up and wagged his tail at Grat, excited by the prospect of any activity. Grat figured the dog would stay around longer than Dean.

Both men strapped on their pistols and grabbed their Winchester rifles, and Grat reached into his saddle bags to retrieve the small folding telescope that Bill had sent him. Slipping it into his jacket pocket, he joined Dean in stumbling and jumping down the rocky mountain side below their camp until they reached the edge of the forest. The line of trees marked the beginning of a more gradual incline, and Grat paused to check on the horses they had left there to graze. That done, the two men followed the bounding dog on down into the canyon, winding through the tall pines until they reached the stream that coursed through the bottom of the canyon. The frigid clear water tumbled over and between the rocks and boulders of the creek bed, making a pleasant gurgling sound.

Following the stream as closely as the terrain allowed, Grat and Dean crept down the canyon, always vigilant for a deer that might have come to get a drink from the creek, or a lawman that might be waiting in ambush.

By noon Grat estimated they had gone about two miles, and they had seen no sign of any deer. The canyon had widened considerably, and near the stream a rocky knoll rose above the pines and aspens. Clambering to the top of this pile of smooth granite boulders, they stopped to rest, taking in great lungfuls of the crisp mountain air. While the dog darted around sniffing and lifting his leg, Grat found a convenient rock formation to sit on and took out his telescope to look around. Sweeping it slowly in a circle, he at first saw nothing but rocks and trees. On down the canyon the land leveled out, and in the distance he could make out the Elwood farm. The ground was too rocky and the winters too harsh to make for good farming, but Elwood and his wife struggled along anyhow. Bearded and eccentric, Elwood was an independent old cuss who despised "city folk," but he and his wife had welcomed Grat and Dean as neighbors. Through the haze Grat could now distinguish Elwood himself, plowing behind a gray mare. No other movement, animal or human, could be seen. Grat took the telescope from his eye and collapsed it.

“Let me look,” Dean requested, holding out his hand. Grat passed the tube over to his companion and dug out a chaw of tobacco from his coat. Biting off a chunk of the pressed tobacco leaf, he stood up and walked around a rock to urinate, leaving Dean to search the terrain with the telescope.

When Grat returned, Dean was standing with his rifle on his shoulder looking bored. “Now what?” the sullen youth asked with a raised eyebrow.

“Head back to the camp, I guess,” Grat answered around the wad in his mouth. “Maybe we’ll see something on the way back. Come on, boy,” he said to the dog, who immediately rushed to Grat’s side, his tongue lolling expectantly. As soon as he understood what direction they were now going, he trotted off ahead of them.

There was no conversation as they climbed the dusty path back up the canyon, watching their step to avoid twisting an ankle on the uneven ground. Then, as they neared the trees where their horses were pastured, Grat patted his coat pocket.

“You got my looking glass?” he asked Dean worriedly.

Dean stopped and looked back at Grat. “No. I gave it back to you.”

“When?” Grat was still checking all his pockets.

“Up on the rocks. I put it right where you were sitting.”

“Shit!” Grat clenched his jaw to keep from blowing up at the younger man. Dean had frequently demonstrated such stupidity, and Grat was getting tired of it. When he had regained control of his anger, Grat gruffly ordered Dean to go on to the camp while he and the dog went back down the canyon to find the telescope. Dean shrugged and did as he was told.

Muttering to himself the entire way, Grat stomped down the path and kicked rocks as he returned to the knoll. He climbed back up on the outcropping and found the instrument just where Dean had said he left it. Grat pocketed it, shook his head in disgust, and for a second time began the trek back up the canyon.

About a mile from the camp the path veered away from the creek and passed through a thick stand of tall evergreens. Grat was still thinking dark thoughts about Dean when his dog, who was about fifty feet ahead of him, suddenly halted and barked. Grat froze and brought up his rifle. The dog was pointing at a tree on the left side of the path, and from behind the tree stepped a man with a revolver in his hand.

"Drop the gun, Dalton!" the man shouted.

Grat squeezed the trigger of his rifle, firing wildly from the hip, and when the man ducked for cover behind the tree, Grat ran to his right toward the creek, which at that point flowed through a steep-sided gully. With a shower of stones he slid down the bank and began splashing down the jumbled stream bed. Behind him he heard the shouts of his pursuers, a full-sized posse by the sound of it. It was probably that damn Wiley Dean, Grat thought as he jumped, stumbled, and ran down the rock-strewn creek. Since Dean wasn't wanted for anything, it was always he who had gone into town for supplies or to meet with Bill to get money and messages. Dean must have led the lawmen there somehow. Whether Dean had betrayed him intentionally, or just through his own stupidity, was of no immediate importance. Right now Grat had to outrun this posse; he could worry about Dean later.

From the various shouts and noises, Grat surmised that some of the lawmen were chasing him on foot, but others had gone for their horses. While the mountainous terrain gave Grat a slight advantage, mounted riders would eventually run him down. He had to find a horse for himself quickly.

Another advantage Grat had over the lawmen was an intimate knowledge of the canyon and its trails. At the first opportunity he left the creek and scampered down one of the many game trails he was familiar with; soon he was outdistancing the posse, and their bellows became less distinct.

Panting from the unaccustomed exertion, Grat broke out of the trees onto a mountain pasture. Just as he had hoped, Elwood was still plowing his fields. He stopped and looked up when he heard Grat's shouted "Hey!" and waited with a puzzled smile. Grat ran up to Elwood and halted, bending over to take deep breaths while he glanced warily back at the tree line. The dog had gotten there ahead of him, and was now wiggling happily as Elwood scratched behind his ears.

"I need your horse," Grat gasped. He kept his rifle pointed at the round, hoping he would not have to threaten the old man.

"Sure thing, Grat," Elwood said without asking for an explanation. Hurriedly they unbuckled the plow harness and dropped the shanks to the ground. Elwood laced his fingers together and held his linked hands out low in front of him. Grat put one boot in Elwood's hands and was boosted up onto the horse. Once Grat was settled on the horse's bare back, Elwood handed up the long plow reins, which Grat hastily coiled up to a more manageable length.

"Thanks," Grat said. "I'll get it back to you."

"Who's that?" Elwood warned, looking past Grat. Grat twisted around and saw a buggy with two men in it, bouncing up the rocky road in a mad dash to Elwood's farmhouse. Grat brought the plow horse around and raised the rifle to his shoulder. He fired off two rounds in rapid succession at the buggy, causing his horse to rear up in panic. Grat and Elwood quickly calmed the animal, a task made more difficult by the greyhound's frantic barking.

Grat raised the rifle again, but the buggy's driver had hastily guided it behind some rocks. Swearing at the dog to shut up, Grat kicked his mount's bare flanks and galloped away, heading up a canyon that angled away from the one where his camp had been. It had been a close thing, but he was still free.

With no supplies, little money, and his face on wanted posters all over the state, Grat needed outside help, and it had to be soon. To make matters worse, he felt physically drained, and he believed he was coming down with pneumonia. He had evaded the posse in the mountains; now he rode down into the open expanses of the central valley and headed northwest toward Merced. Bill had told him that there was a prominent man living outside Merced who would aid

Grat if it became necessary, and Grat decided that now was just such an emergency.

Judge W. W. Gray welcomed Grat at his ranch and put him in a secluded room to recover from his illness. A Chinese cook was assigned to care for Grat, and he took his job very seriously, becoming quite attached to the gruff outlaw. Judge Gray, no relation to the W. A. Gray who had presided over Grat's trial in Visalia, was a well-known Democrat. He had served on the Merced County Board of Supervisors, and he had once been the Chief of Police in Oakland, California. His wife and Mrs. Breckenridge, the wife of Grat's attorney, were sisters. From what his brother-in-law had told him about Grat's trial, and based on his inside political knowledge of the railroad's corruptness, Gray had no doubt that Grat was innocent. He also had no reservations about aiding and abetting this particular felon.

After two weeks of needed rest and proper diet, Grat again felt able to travel. Judge Gray had sent word to Bill Dalton about Grat's presence at the ranch, and Bill had quietly dispatched their brother Cole to look after him. Cole brought Grat up to date on the posses still searching for him, and described how their friends and family were being harassed by reporters and amateur detectives. The resulting guilt made Grat decide that he had imposed on the judge's good will enough. At breakfast one morning he announced he was returning to Oklahoma. Politely hiding his relief, Gray provided Grat with a horse and saddle and wished him all the best. The dog was left behind with the Chinese cook, who promised, in broken English, to care for the faithful animal.

Although Grat had planned to ride alone, he was eventually persuaded to take Cole along. Cole's presence would provide insurance in case of accident, as well as assisting with security. Unlike Grat, whose distinctive description had been posted all across the Southwest, Cole could ride into towns along the way and purchase supplies. In their pockets was the money that Bob had sent out with Eugenia.

On a cool January morning they began the long arduous journey back east. Their route would take them south around Bakersfield, bypass Los Angeles, and then cut straight east across

Arizona, New Mexico, and the Texas panhandle. By the time they reached the territories, the epic ride would take one hundred and four days—three and a half months of desert, mountains, and prairie. Grat was not even sure what awaited him in Oklahoma, but it had to be better than what he had left behind in California. At least, that's what he kept telling himself.

On April 19, 1892, the Cheyenne and Arapahoe lands were opened for settlement. These lands, in the far western part of the territory bordering the Texas panhandle, were considered much less desirable than the tribal properties farther east. Consisting mainly of flat, almost treeless prairie, the area was too dry for most farming, and even cattle were an iffy proposition. The official opening was more of a land stroll than a land run.

Jim Riley, though, had been ranching there for years. Technically speaking, he was there illegally, which may have been one of the reasons he allowed the Dalton gang to use his ranch as a hideout for so long. Regardless, his cattle operation had prospered, and when the lands were opened, he wanted to ensure that no one took the land he had settled years before. Grateful for Riley's assistance, and bored from weeks of inactivity, Bob, Emmett, Broadwell, and Power rode out from their camp in various directions and staked out claims for Riley. While they could never file the claims themselves, since they were famous fugitives, the boys could, and did, mark the claims and drive off any interlopers.

Bob had tried to get Doolin and his partners involved, but the rangy Arkansan was uninterested in such good deeds. He, Newcomb, and Pierce had become close friends who always stuck together, and none helped with staking the claims. The three men shared an aversion to work and a desire to play hard with the money they had stolen, and they derided the others as do-gooders. This time, as so often before, they rode off together, going to such lawless towns as Ingalls, where bandits were welcome and illicit money was readily accepted in the bars and brothels. The gang had somehow split into two factions, and Bob, naturally enough, was beginning to favor his group over Doolin's.

To Emmett it seemed that Grat's arrival at Riley's camp at the end of April caused a noticeable improvement in Bob's attitude. All winter long the gang had languished on the barren plains of western Oklahoma, with no definite plans and a steadily diminishing supply of money. Doolin, Newcomb, and Pierce were often absent for weeks, off carousing in bars and perhaps committing a few crimes on their own, while even the loyal Broadwell and Power began to complain about the inactivity and lack of direction.

As he rested from his long ride, Grat told the others of his many adventures in California, and of the perfidy of the railroads, express companies, and the politicians. He, in turn, listened as Bob and the others recounted their own thrilling escapades, bringing out newspaper clippings to verify their notoriety.

Grat's ire over the injustices done to him had seethed and festered during his trek back to Oklahoma, and he grinned in appreciation at Bob's tales of vengeance on the railway express cars. Grat was easily convinced that he should join his brothers in their war against the railroads, and this decision reinvigorated Bob, turning up the flame in him that had for a while been flickering near to extinction. As soon as Grat was recuperated, Bob told them, the Dalton gang would strike again.

While Bob gathered intelligence and made his plans, Emmett showed Grat around the area, introducing him to Jim Riley and showing him their planned escape routes if a posse were to ever dare attack them. The latter seemed unlikely, for among the clippings Bob had shown Grat were articles deploring the timidity of citizens who declined to join posses in search of the Daltons. Many such search parties were abandoned due to lack of interest, despite the huge rewards now being offered for the Daltons' capture. One editorial realistically observed that the rewards would only be paid if the Daltons were brought in alive. Since the gang members had supposedly sworn to fight to the death, the prospects for collecting the rewards seemed insufficient for citizens, or lawmen for that matter, to risk their lives in the attempt. According to the newspapers, the marshals were reasonably certain where the Daltons were located, but they were unable, or unwilling, to mount an operation to capture them.

A few days after he had joined his brothers at Riley's camp, Grat went out scouting around with Emmett and Dick Broadwell. It was late spring, and already the thick carpet of prairie grasses was beginning to yellow in the baking sun. Only occasional clumps of bushes and stunted trees disturbed the panorama of slender stalks waving in the constant wind. While riding leisurely across this vast countryside, the three outlaws spotted a lone rider near the distant horizon. At first the stranger had been traveling slowly at a diagonal to their own line of travel, but when he noticed them, he turned his horse and approached at a gallop. Grat halted his horse and had Emmett and Broadwell do likewise, waiting patiently as the figure drew near.

It was a soldier, his blue uniform covered with dust, and he nodded curtly as he reined in his horse in front of them. "Good morning, gentleman," he said. There was a slight slurring of his words, and Grat noticed a bottle-shaped bulge in the man's military jacket.

"Morning," Grat answered politely. Emmett and Broadwell touched their hats in salutation.

"I'm putting out sooners," the soldier informed them pompously. "May I ask what you are doing in this area?"

"We're United States Deputy Marshals," Grat answered blandly. The soldier's eyes flickered as he evaluated this unexpected statement and tried to judge its veracity. There was a pause before he spoke again.

"Could I see your commission, please?"

"We don't carry those with us," Grat explained innocently. "We left them back at the marshal's office in Guthrie. You could go there and check with the marshal."

The soldier locked his lips as he looked searchingly at the three men. This situation was clearly not covered in his general orders. "I believe you need to talk to my corporal. If you will follow me, I'll take you to our camp."

Grat, tired of the charade, shook his head slowly. "Not interested."

Drawing up in his saddle, the soldier frowned and said, "I'm afraid you'll have to."

"Oh, go to hell!" Grat barked at him. For emphasis he placed his left hand on his hip, right next to his holstered forty-five. The soldier's eyes darted to his movement, and then shifted quickly to Emmett and Broadwell, who had made similar gestures. Without a further word the soldier twirled his horse around and galloped off, presumably in the direction of the corporal's camp.

Emmett and Broadwell laughed at the soldier's sudden departure, but Grat was not so amused. The three continued their journey to visit a Cheyenne Indian camp over on the North Canadian River. Broadwell, who had made friends with many of the tribe and spoke a little of the Cheyenne language, introduced Grat to them. He also told the Indians of their encounter with the soldier, and they laughed in appreciation. The Indian Wars were not long past, and many Cheyenne still harbored deep resentment of the way soldiers had treated them.

Grat passed around a bottle of whiskey he had brought, and the Cheyennes offered the white men some jerky to gnaw on. Carrying on conversations that consisted mainly of grunts and gestures, with occasional translation by Broadwell, outlaws and Indians enjoyed each other's company, sharing the camaraderie of the outcast. Barely an hour had passed since their arrival at the camp when Grat noticed the approach of more soldiers.

There were six of them, and their arrival caused the Indians to immediately go for their outmoded rolling-block rifles and buffalo guns.

"Tell 'em not to shoot," Grat told Broadwell, fearing some sort of massacre. Broadwell began shouting in Cheyenne and making gestures to calm the Indians, whose anger had been fueled by the liquor. Somehow Broadwell managed to shepherd most of them into their teepees.

The soldiers had halted their mounts about three hundred yards away when they saw the Indians pick up their guns, and now a single man detached himself from the group and rode cautiously toward Grat and the other two white men. Grat walked over to his own horse and drew his Winchester from its scabbard. Gripping the stock in this left hand, his fingers through the cocking lever, he tilted the gun back onto his shoulder and strolled out to meet the lone soldier, who had reined in his mount a few feet away.

"Vhat are you doing here?" the man asked in a thick German accent. He was a solidly-built man, but with a noticeable paunch. His head looked like it had been carved from a block of wood, and a long, straw-colored handlebar mustache drooped over his mouth. Small blue eyes peered out from under prominent eyebrows. On the sleeves of his dark blue tunic were the double chevrons of a corporal. Grat felt an instant dislike for the man.

"None of your damn business," Grat told him.

"It is much so my business! It is forbidden for you to be here. You are in fiolation of federal regulations vhich prohibit the presence of any personnel who are not Indians in this territory until this territory is opened to settlement at a future time. My orders are to apprehend and escort any such fiolators out of the area and turn them over to civilian aut'ority. I must demand that you gentlemen lay down your veapons and accompany me to our headquarters."

Behind Grat, Emmett and Broadwell were snickering at the corporal's accented and bureaucratic pronouncement. Grat brought the rifle forward off his shoulder and cradled the barrel in his right hand, pointing it just over the corporal's head. "Not today," Grat told him. "Now, let's see how fast you can get back to your comrades." Conspicuously he cocked the rifle, the metallic ratcheting adding emphasis to his action.

The corporal narrowed his eyes, and then pulled the reins to turn his horse around. "In twenty-four hours," he threatened over his shoulder, "the whole United States Army vill be here. Then ve vill see!" Spurring his horse to a gallop, he started off back to where the other soldiers were waiting.

"Yeah! Get out of here!" Broadwell yelled, then raised his rifle and fired two shots into the air to encourage the corporal's departure. Grat swung around and tried to stop Broadwell's reckless action, but he was too late. Thinking the shots were a signal, the Cheyennes came pouring out of their teepees, formed a ragged line abreast of the Daltons, and brought their guns up to fire at the retreating soldiers. Broadwell wave his arms and shouted at them to stop, but not in time to keep most of them from shooting. Fortunately, in their haste, the Indians had not taken careful aim. The soldiers all fled with no apparent injury, other than to their pride.

Broadwell explained to the Cheyennes what the corporal had said; concerned that the corporal might make good on his threat to bring more troops, the Indians began to break camp. Thinking that perhaps they had caused enough trouble for one day, Grat told Emmett and Broadwell to mount up. It was time to return to Riley's camp.

Author's Notes

Chapter 12

Emmett's description in *Beyond the Law* of their encounter with Heck Thomas is confirmed by an article from the *Muskogee Phoenix* that was reprinted in the *Coffeyville Journal* on October 23, 1891. The account of Bob's decision to quit again and the visit to Eugenia in Woodward is from Emmett's book.

Grat's narrow escape in the mountains of California was covered extensively in the *Visalia Weekly Delta* on December 13, 1891. This article mentioned that Grat's mother had sent a check to a woman in Hanford to be cashed and forwarded to Grat, and implied that this was how they had tracked him down. The newspaper had interviewed Dean, who they referred to as Riley Dean, as well as the various lawmen involved. Dean was jailed and charged with grand larceny and aiding and abetting a felony, belying Grat's belief that Dean had betrayed him.

Emmett's depiction of Grat's activities that winter is essentially the same, although he says that the man who had been hiding with Grat was someone named Middleton. As with others, Emmett probably changed the name to avoid implicating someone who had aided the gang. The aid that Grat received from Judge Gray was confirmed in interviews done many years later with Littleton Dalton, who also said that Cole accompanied Grat on his ride back to Oklahoma.

For obvious reasons, Emmett is the only source for the boy's staking of claims during the Cheyenne and Arapahoe land run, as well as for the encounter with soldiers. According to the curator of the Fort Sill Museum, no Army records of this incident have been located, and these records are currently not available for research.

CHAPTER 13

Emmett's eyes swept the empty spaces between the randomly dispersed buildings of Woodward; reassured that he was unobserved, he stepped up onto the wooden porch of Eugenia's cabin and knocked gently at the door. The sun was just peeking over the horizon, making him blink whenever his gaze shifted to the east, but as yet there was no one on the streets. The eastern walls of the houses and shops were bathed in the orange glow of sunrise, but the western sides were still deep in shadows that stretched away from them. The air was cool and fresh, pushed along by a whispering south wind. Afraid that he might have knocked too gently the first time, Emmett rapped on the wooden door a little harder, a knot of concern—not fear, he told himself—forming in the pit of his stomach. Farm people start work early, and soon the town would be bustling; he felt exposed on the sun-drenched porch.

He had just raised his fist to pound on the door a third time when it suddenly swung open. Clutching a dressing gown closed at her neck, her tousled brown hair falling in cascades around her shoulders, Eugenia frowned at Emmett through puffy half-awake eyes. Emmett felt a catch in his throat, for he thought she was incredibly beautiful; he envied his brother's ease with women in general, and in particular Bob's good fortune in finding such a wonderful and understanding woman as Eugenia.

"Good morning," Emmett managed to mumble to her, trying not to stare.

Squinting against the light, Eugenia looked up and down at Emmett, then craned her neck to look past him. "Where's Bob?" she asked, her voice raspy from interrupted sleep.

"On the trail," Emmet answered, remembering belatedly to remove his hat in the presence of a lady. "I have a message for you."

"Get in here before someone sees you," she ordered, pulling on his arm. Emmett allowed himself to be tugged into what passed for a parlor and waited, hat in hand, while she scanned the neighborhood before closing the front door. There were a couple wooden chairs in the room, but when Eugenia remained standing to face him, Emmett politely did the same. Emmett assumed her annoyed expression was because she would have preferred to see Bob.

"Why didn't Bob come?" she asked, combing her hair back with her fingers.

"Him and the rest of the gang are on their way east. We heard there's going to be a big shipment of the Sac and Fox annuity money on the Santa Fe."

"Why aren't you going?"

"I am. I'm taking the train from here. Bob's worked out a really terrific plan. See, I'll be on the train, and . . ."

Eugenia cut him off with a shake of her head. "Don't tell me. I'll read about it later." Emmett was impressed that she was so concerned about maintaining secrecy. His admiration for her went up another notch. "So, what's the message?" She turned away and shuffled into the adjoining kitchen; with practiced ease she began building a fire in the small iron stove, using correspondingly small logs from a pile in the corner. Emmett watched her bend over, then averted his eyes and silently chastised himself for what he was about to imagine.

"Bob wants you to go back to New Mexico and wait for him there."

Eugenia struck a match and lit the fire, waiting to make sure it was going to catch. When the flames began to crackle and spread, she closed the door and put a blackened tin coffee pot on top of the stove.

"Why?" she asked as she continued to fuss with the stove. Emmett was disconcerted by the unexpected question. When Bob had given him the message, Emmett had never considered the possibility that she would question the decision.

"Well, I think he wants you to go someplace safe. After this next trick they'll be looking for us all over the place, so he won't be able to come see you. Once we get enough money, then we'll all go to South America."

Eugenia turned and looked at Emmett. "South America. That's what he said last year." Emmett could not read her expression.

"This time is different," he assured her earnestly. "Since Grat's got out of jail and Bill's been acquitted, all we need now is the money. We don't have enough right now, but after this next job we'll have plenty. We'll meet you in New Mexico, back at that same hotel, and then we'll all go somewhere and catch a boat for South America. Bob's got it all figured out."

"I'm sure he does," Eugenia agreed. Emmett figured that her lack of enthusiasm was due to her not having had her coffee yet.

"I've got some money for you," Emmett said, digging into his inside coat pocket. He withdrew a wad of crumpled bills and stepped forward to hand them to her. "Bob said this should be enough to pay for your train ticket and your hotel bill out there."

She absently leafed through and straightened the stack of bills, then laid them on the rough wooden kitchen table. "When does he plan on meeting me there?"

"I don't know for sure. I guess it depends on how long it takes for us to avoid the posses and ride out there. Three or four weeks, I reckon."

"Okay," she sighed. "You want some coffee?"

"No, thank you, ma'am. I have to put my horse up at the livery stable and get my train ticket."

"Just like that? Aren't you worried about getting caught?"

Emmett shrugged. "They don't have any pictures of me, and Bob says I look so innocent no one would ever think I was a Dalton."

Eugenia gazed at him appraisingly for a few seconds. "Well, that is a nice suit you're wearing, but there aren't that many innocent young men who wear a pistol on their hip."

"Oops," Emmett said guiltily, "I forgot." Hastily he unbuckled the bullet-laden gunbelt and rolled the leather strap around the holstered Colt. Glancing around the house searchingly, he asked, "You got something I could wrap this in?"

Eugenia found some brown wrapping paper and string and quickly turned the gunbelt into an innocuous parcel. He thanked her profusely, said his farewells, and cautiously slipped outside. After mounting his horse, he happened to ride by the side of the cabin on his way to the livery stable and glance in the small kitchen window. Eugenia was sitting at the kitchen table, a cup of coffee in her hand, staring blankly at the pile of money. He waved, but she never looked up.

Wednesday, June 1, 1892

All day long the blazing sun had seared the prairie of the Cherokee Strip, and nightfall had brought little relief. The blast-furnace wind that had roared during the day had lost little strength, but the air blustering around them at least helped evaporate the sweat and kept the torment of the mosquitoes to a minimum. A figure appeared out of the darkness, and Dick Broadwell walked casually up to where the others were waiting.

"The operator's asleep," he snorted derisively. "Stretched out on a bench, snorin' away." Bob had sent Broadwell over to check out the lonely depot, and was pleased with this report. Things were going just as planned.

Red Rock was nothing more than a one-man depot and telegraph office stuck out in the middle of nowhere. Twelve miles north of Wharton, where the gang had robbed a train a year earlier, the station was located in the largely unoccupied Otoe and Missouri tribal reserve at the eastern end of the Cherokee Strip. Surrounded by miles of flat prairie, it was one of the loneliest places Bob could imagine, perfect for robbing a train. The only problem had been figuring out a way to make sure the train stopped there, since the night train usually blew right on by. Then the idea to use Emmett had occurred to him. Emmett would board the Santa Fe at Arkansas City, Kansas, just across the state line, and ask the conductor to let him off at Red Rock. When the train stopped to let him disembark, the gang would strike. It was an extremely clever plan, as Bob kept reminding himself and anyone else who would listen.

Bob leaned on the fence rail and peered through the dark toward the little depot, the only source of light other than the stars. Broadwell stood beside him, checking his pistol for what seemed like the hundredth time, and Grat sat on the ground near Bob's feet, his knees up and his back supported by a fence post. A few feet away Doolin and the others quietly talked and smoked, the glow from their cigarettes briefly illuminating their faces whenever they took a drag. They were all waiting at the cattle pens a few hundred yards south of the depot, their horses tied nearby, trying to hide their nervousness from each other.

Bob tilted his head various ways, attempting to detect any unnatural sounds over the rush of wind across his ears. The prairie grass rustled in the breeze, and insects made various clicking and buzzing noises; the only other sounds came from the men waiting with him. It had rained the last few days, and the air was suffused with the smell of rich soil and wildflowers, although these pleasant odors were occasionally overpowered by the acrid tobacco smoke from his friends.

Bob drew his pocket watch out of his vest and clicked the cover open, but it was too dark to make out the hands. He borrowed a match from Broadwell and after turning his back to the depot, struck the match and held the flaring head cupped in his palm over the watch dial. Eleven-forty-five. With rapid economical movements he blew out the match and tossed it while he clicked the watch shut and dropped it back in his pocket. Now he was getting worried.

"What time is it?" Broadwell asked, keeping his voice quiet.

Bob told him. They all knew the train was due at eleven-twenty, so it was way overdue. It was probably just running late, as night trains often did, but Bob could not help imagining all the possible calamities that might have befallen. What if someone had recognized Emmett? What if the rains had washed out a bridge? Worse, what if someone else had robbed the train earlier? Bob was already contemplating a withdrawal when Broadwell yelped in his ear.

"There it is!" Far on the northern horizon a speck of light flickered and began to expand. It was the headlight of the Chicago-Galveston Express #403, running half an hour late. The south wind carried the sound of the distant train away from them, but they all knew it was time to spring into action. Following Bob's carefully laid-out strategy, Doolin and Broadwell loped off toward the station, where they would wait in the shadows for the train to stop. Bob and the others grabbed their Winchesters and jacked the first round into the chamber. Grat stood up slowly, brushed off the seat of his pants, and waited silently behind Bob.

"Put your masks on," Bob reminded them as he pulled his own up over his nose. On one of his shopping trips to town Emmett had bought a bolt of black cotton cloth from which identical bandannas had been made for all the members of the gang. Bob like the neat, professional, and menacing look the matching masks gave them.

The train had been slowing as it neared the tiny wood-frame depot, and it halted with a spout of steam when the passenger cars drew abreast of the platform. Someone carrying a package stepped down from the train and walked quickly across the platform into the darkness behind the depot. Bob could tell from the man's rolling gait that it was Emmett. Once Emmett had disappeared, Broadwell and Doolin ran to the locomotive and sprang into the cab. The conductor had already signaled the crew to pull out, and he had climbed back into the passenger car without concern. The depot operator was apparently still asleep inside the station, so no one other than the engine crew noticed the boarding.

Sluggishly the train gathered steam again, approaching the waiting men at a walking pace. According to plan, Bill Power walked across the tracks and took up a position that would prevent anyone from surprising them on the far side of the train, while Bob, Grat, Charley Pierce, and Bitter Creek Newcomb walked over closer to the rails and waited, their rifles held at the ready. With a screech of the metal brakes and a hiss of steam, the engine crept to a stop beside them. There was some scuffling in the cab, and then the fireman and the engineer jumped to the ground, followed by Doolin and Broadwell. The fireman carried a pickax in his hand.

"Let's go," Doolin said, his voice somewhat muffled by the mask. Together the group marched back along the train, Doolin and Broadwell poking the crewman in the back with their pistols. In the reflected light from the cars Bob got a good look at the engineer, and there was a flash of recognition. Instantly he remembered where he had seen the man before: it was Carl Mack, the same man who had been engineer on the train they had robbed at Wharton last year. Under his mask Bob smiled at the irony, but he said nothing. There was no point in providing the railroads any more clues to their identity than they already had.

At the tail end of the train a man with a lantern climbed down and started toward them. It was the brakeman, wondering what the problem was. Newcomb sprinted down the tracks and took him in custody. Meanwhile Bob and the rest of the group had reached the first car behind the engine's tender, which was the postal car. Doolin rapped on the door with the butt of his pistol. With a click the door opened, and the yellow glow of the lantern inside made a halo around the young postal clerk who stood in the doorway with one hand on the handle. Behind him another young man craned his neck, trying to see what was happening.

"Come out of there!" Doolin ordered gruffly. Gaping with terror and excitement, the two young clerks raised their arms and rapidly complied. They joined the engine crew in the center of the growing group of men who now proceeded on back to the express car. Engineer Mack stumbled when he tripped on a railroad tie in the dark, and Broadwell grabbed him roughly by the arm.

"Watch out, you son of a bitch!" Broadwell cursed at him. Bob gave Broadwell a dirty look, but it was lost in the darkness. The crowd of men stopped beside the broad sliding door of the express car. Newcomb, meeting them there, shoved the brakeman forward to join the other train crew members. Pierce broke away and strolled on down the train to the passenger cars. When the conductor appeared and stepped down, apparently intending to find out what the delay way, he met the barrel of Pierce's Winchester. Meekly he returned to the car.

Realizing what was happening, the express messenger and guard had already locked the express car's door and blown out the lights, and they refused Bob's shouted command to open up.

"Open up or we'll start shooting," Bob warned them.

"We can't do that," was the shaky reply. "It's against company policy."

"If that's the way you want it," Bob said. Aiming high on the car, he fired a shot that splintered the wooden wall above the door. Like a rolling thunder other guns joined in as the gang poured round after round into the car at locations that were judged least likely to injure the occupants. Bob had insisted on this in their planning, knowing that their reputation among the common people would be seriously blackened by any unnecessary deaths. It was the tacit support of those ordinary citizens that had kept them uncaptured for so long, and Bob did not want to risk losing that support. After a minute Bob called a cease-fire.

"Are you coming out?" he yelled at the men inside. Their answer was a pistol shot that left a ragged hole in the door. The gang resumed firing; Broadwell even climbed under the car and fired his pistol through the floor. When they stopped again, the guard inside fired two more rounds at the door, splintering the wood and emphasizing their unwillingness to submit.

"You!" Bob called to the fireman, who was huddled in terror with the other crewmen under Doolin's watchful eye. "Use the pick to chop a hole in the door."

"They'll shoot me!" the man protested, his voice rising in fear.

"No, they won't," Bob told him. "Now do it."

The man tentatively edged over to the express car, lifted the pick in both hands, and swung it at the door, burying the blade in the wooden panel. Immediately there was a shot from inside the car, and the fireman jumped away, leaving the pick jammed in the door. Broadwell and Newcomb fired a couple rounds each into the car to discourage the occupants, then Bob ordered the fireman to try again.

"It's me, Fireman Rogers," he called out. "Don't shoot anymore." There was no sound from inside. After a moment's hesitation, he grabbed the pick handle and pried it out, ripping pieces of pine from the door in the process. Gaining confidence when there were no more gunshots, he swung the heavy tool again, smashing through the soft wood, and jerked out another jagged section of door. In a few minutes he had made an irregular hole about two feet across. Sweating from the exertion in the humid night air, he rested the pick and looked to Bob for further instructions.

"Go in and unlock the door," Bob told him. Even in the dark Bob could see the man's eyes open wider in fright. Bob lowered his rifle until it pointed directly at Rogers' stomach. Rogers dropped the pick and gingerly grasped the sides of the hole. There was another loud bang from inside, and a bullet crashed into the door just above the shaking engineer.

"Don't come in here!" the guard hollered, his voice cracking.

"It's me, Rogers. Don't shoot. They're making me come in."

"Whittlesy!" the engineer yelled at the messenger. "It's me, Carl Mack. Quit shootin'. You're gonna hurt one of us. There's too many of them out here for you to mess with."

There was no answer, but at Bob's insistence Rogers tried again to go through the hole. Begging the messenger and guard not to kill him, he wiggled through the battered opening until he was sitting on the floor inside. Grat had moved up as Rogers pulled his feet into the car, and he trained his rifle through the aperture directly at the frightened man.

"Unlock the door," he ordered, speaking for the first time that night. Scrambling to his feet, Rogers threw the catch and slid the door back. From the dark recesses of the car another shot rang out, causing Rogers to drop to the floor and cover his head with his arms. Bob and Grat both saw the flash of the gun from the front left side of the car, and they shouted this information to the others. While Bob, Grat, and Newcomb peppered the front end of the car with rifle fire to keep the guards' heads down, Doolin and Broadwell leaped into the express car with their pistols ready.

Seeing it was now hopeless, the express company men gave up their valiant defense and surrendered. While Broadwell took their guns and pushed them into a corner, Doolin had the fireman relight the lanterns. Bob stayed on the ground to supervise as Doolin forced the fireman to take a sledgehammer from its rack. At gunpoint Rogers began pounding on the top of the larger through safe. Each swing produced only minor damage, the massive hammer clanging as it bounced off the steel safe. This was going to be a time-consuming operation. Bob stepped away from the pool of light pouring out the open door and looked down the length of the train. Several passengers had climbed down and were gathered in small groups smoking and observing the robbery, ever mindful of Pierce and the rifle he kept vigilantly pointed in their general direction.

Grat was standing guard over the four remaining train crew, who were starting to talk now that the shooting had stopped. Bob ambled over to them.

Addressing Carl Mack, the engineer, he said, "I'm sorry about that rude remark my friend made." He sympathized with working men, especially someone who had now been held up twice.

"What do you mean?" Mack asked, puzzled by the statement.

"When he called you a son of a bitch. He was just excited. It won't happen again."

"Okay. Thank you." Mack stared into Bob's eyes for a moment, as if trying to figure something out, so Bob quickly turned away and strolled down the roadbed toward Pierce.

"Everything okay?" Bob asked when he reached where Charley was standing.

"No problems here," Pierce assured him. "Everyone's behavin'." Bob nodded in satisfaction. Squatting down, Bob peered under the train cars and recognized Bill Power's boots on the other side. Everything was under control over there as well. Bob straightened back up and walked over to a farmer who was smoking a cigarette as he watched the evening's activities.

"Evening," Bob said with a tilt of his head.

"Howdy," the man answered politely.

"Could I trouble you for some tobacco," Bob asked. "I'm fresh out, myself."

"Sure," the man said with a smile. He opened his jacket and reached around under it toward his hip pocket.

Bob simultaneously raised both his rifle and his left hand in an unmistakable gesture to stop. "If it's in your hip pocket," he said with a negative shake of his head, "then you better not go for it. Don't want to take any chances, do we?"

"I guess not," the man agreed, slowly bringing his empty hand back out.

"Thanks, anyway," Bob said. Casually he walked back toward the express car. He could hear the clang of the sledgehammer on the safe, evidence that they were not yet ready to leave. This was taking too long, Bob told himself, even though there was no chance of any interference at this remote location. When he rejoined Newcomb, who was standing at the open door of the express car watching the fireman attempt to bash open the safe, Bob checked his watch again. Twenty minutes after midnight, and they were still here. Somehow they had to speed things up.

"There!" Doolin yelled happily as a final crash of the sledge hammer stove in the top of the through safe. He reached through the narrow opening and began pulling out the safe's contents, stuffing them into an empty mail sack Newcomb had brought over from the postal car.

"Now the other one," Doolin told the fireman, who had paused to catch his breath. Doolin motioned with his head toward the smaller way safe as he continued to fish around in the through safe for its bounty. Broadwell, who still had the messenger and guard covered at the end of the car, back away from the flying hammer. It took only a few blows to shatter the way safe, and Doolin swiftly cleaned it out as well.

"Ain't much here," Doolin told Bob with disgust. "Where's the rest of it?" he demanded, scowling at the messenger who cowered in the corner.

"That's all there is," Whittlesy insisted.

"Shit," Doolin said disbelievingly. Angrily he pulled out drawers and opened cabinets, dumping the contents on the floor. Then he began ripping open parcels and had Rogers use the sledge hammer to smash open some wooden crates. No more money was found. "I ought to shoot you sons of bitches," Doolin barked at the express men as he tore through the compartment.

"Don't kill anybody," Bob reminded him. "Just hurry up. We're wasting time."

Up at the front of the car Broadwell ordered the express company men to empty their pockets. The guard came up with fifty dollars and a gold watch, but Whittlesy had nothing. He had probably hidden it somewhere, but they didn't have time to look for it now.

"Come on, that's enough. Let's go." Bob waved Doolin and Broadwell out, and hurriedly they picked their way over the mess Doolin had strewn in the car to jump to the ground.

"Mount up!" Bob shouted for all his men to hear. With one last warning to their captives, the men all ran to their horses, where Emmett was waiting. The robbery had taken almost an hour, and no one was still excited enough to yell or joke as they rode away. They were all just relieved that it was over.

"Damn, it's hot!" Newcomb said, fanning himself with his hat.

"Oh, yeah,?" Broadwell replied sarcastically. "I hadn't noticed."

Bob gave them both a sour look, but did not have the energy to say anything. They were all lounging around the cramped dug-out cabin at Riley's camp, and tempers were starting to flare. The Red Rock robbery had stirred up a hornet's nest of pursuing posses, and they had been forced to remain in hiding at the camp southeast of Woodward. The barren plains of western Oklahoma were shimmering in the relentless heat, and all eight of the gang members had squeezed into the only shade around, their shabby sod and canvas hut. When eight rowdy young men were cooped up together in such a small space, however, it was too much to ask that they remain congenial.

The robbery had netted far less than they had hoped. The way some of the gang threw money around for liquor and loose women, along with the generous payments Bob usually made for supplies, meant that the proceeds were unlikely to last more than a couple of months. As for the three Daltons, their take was far too meager to finance Bob's long-delayed plans for South America. Exacerbating the situation, Doolin continued to insinuate that the Daltons were taking more than their share, especially since Grat had joined them. At the same time, he kept goading Bob to lead another raid as soon as possible. It was a powder keg with a short fuse; all of them felt confined at the remote camp, and there were too many opportunities to grate on each other's nerves.

"I'm gonna go drain my lizard," Power announced, rising to his feet. The others ignored him. Emmett, who was watching Grat and Pierce play cribbage, scooted aside to let Power by. Bob swatted at a pesky fly that kept bouncing off his face and ears, and he wondered what Eugenia was doing at that moment. Time dragged by.

The open doorway, the only source of light in the one-room cabin, was darkened as Power returned and stopped at the entrance.

"Hey, Bill," he said to Doolin. "Yours and my horses done wandered away. You want to come help me look for 'em?"

"Oh, hell," Doolin sighed. "Yeah, I'm comin'. Let me get my rifle." While Doolin found his rifle and put on his hat, Power snagged his own rifle from the corner; both men walked out into the bright burning daylight. Bob stared after them for a moment, and then went back to day-dreaming.

When the two men returned a couple hours later, they were both hooting and laughing, anxious to tell their friends about what had just happened. Everyone, including Bob, perked up as Doolin and Power crowded into the cabin and took turns telling their tale.

"You won't believe it," Power exclaimed.

"We was walkin' down that creek over north of here, a mile or so," Doolin said, "when we come around this bend and ran smack dab into four men on horses."

"It was a posse," Power said dramatically, "and two of 'em was deputies."

"Said their names were Swayne and Cook," Doolin added, looking to Bob for confirmation.

Bob nodded. "Yeah, I know them."

"Well, sir, we got the drop on 'em" Power continued. "Covered 'em with our rifles, made 'em put up their hands. I told this Swayne fellow that he was riding my horse, and told him to get the hell off it. And he did. Right smartly, too."

Doolin took up the story. "I told them to give me all their cartridges, and then threw 'em in the creek. Coulda killed 'em right then and there, but I figured they was just doin' their job. So we told 'em to get out of the country and don't come back."

"They took off like a pack of scalded hounds," Power boasted. "From the way they looked, I don't think they'll be botherin' us again any time soon."

"That's a fact," Doolin agreed. He leaned his rifle against the sod wall and sat down on the floor. He and Power both had pleased expressions on their faces, but Bob did not share their good feelings.

"They'll tell others," Bob warned ominously. "We could have a whole army of lawmen down on us. Since you were on foot, they'll know we're around here someplace close."

"You really think so, Bob?" Emmett asked worriedly.

"They didn't know who we were," Power argued.

"You don't know that for sure," Bob pointed out. "And even if they didn't, they'll probably figure it out pretty quick. I think it's time for us to move out. They're getting too close for comfort."

"That's what I been sayin'," Doolin remarked smugly. "We need to get out of here and rob us another train."

"Start getting your stuff ready," Bob said, speaking to everyone in the room. "We'll ride tonight. Let's go over to Indian Territory, see what we can find there."

Thursday, July 14, 1892

The lingering summer twilight had just faded into darkness when they approached the northern edge of Adair. It was a typical railroad town in the Cherokee Nation, just fifteen miles south of Vinita. A stop on the Missouri, Kansas, and Texas line—MK&T, or Katy for short—Adair was about twenty miles north of Lillietta, where the gang had robbed a train in September of the previous year. The depot was on the west side of the tracks, and the town had grown out from the depot, with Main Street perpendicular to the tracks.

The eight outlaws had originally ridden up from the south, circling the town to the east and north until they reached the railroad tracks leading south into town, scouting their escape routes. This was flat open country, with scattered clumps of woods and meandering creeks lined with willow trees and bushes. To the southwest, however, the land began to rise and fold into rugged forested hills, and it was there they had been hiding, and there they would return.

When they encountered the first occupied buildings on the northeast outskirts of Adair, Bob had them all dismount. Leaving Charley Pierce in charge of the horses, Bob led the rest of the gang in on foot. Cloaked in darkness, they quietly followed the tracks south until they were a few hundred feet from the depot. Bob held up his hand to halt them, then gestured Grat, Power, and Newcomb into position across the tracks.

It had been a hastily conceived plan, and Bob was not entirely happy with it. They had received word yesterday via a friendly rancher that tonight's train from Denison, Texas, would be carrying a large shipment of cash. The short notice had prevented Bob from carefully scouting the area and selecting an ideal location, as he had always done in the past. Instead, he had relied on his memory of the area, which he had last visited two years ago, and hoped for the best. The abundance of glowing windows in the town demonstrated to Bob that Adair had grown considerably since he was last there. Always optimistic, he decided the town's larger size might prove to be an advantage, since the railroad would not be expecting a robbery attempt there.

When Grat, Power, and Newcomb had become only transient shadows in the gloom of the railyard, Bob strode forward to the well-lit depot; Emmett, Broadwell, and Doolin followed in his wake. The wide plank platform was empty, since the 10:10 express from Denison was not scheduled to stop at Adair. The four men went up the short steps and marched across the wooden platform, their boots producing a rhythmic marching cadence, counterpointed by their jingling spurs. All of them carried Winchesters in their hands, and each had a Colt .45 on his hip. Dressed in business suits and dark slouch hats, they wore no masks. This time Bob wanted them to know that it was the Daltons.

Bob burst into the station operator's office, and Doolin crowded in behind him. Holding his rifle aimed casually above the startled operator's head, Bob assumed as stern a look as he could manage, narrowing his eyes at the young man dressed in shirtsleeves and vest.

"The express?" Bob said, raising one eyebrow. The young man bobbed his head to show he knew what Bob meant. "Flag it down," Bob ordered.

"I'll have to go down the track and set the signal," the operator stammered.

"I know. Go to it." Bob jerked his head toward the door, and the young man jumped to his feet and edged past Doolin out onto the platform. Bob caught Emmett's eye and told him, "Keep an eye on him. Make sure he does it right."

With his lips pressed tightly together beneath his thin mustache, Emmett acknowledged the command with a single nod. Waving his rifle, he herded the operator off into the night. Leaving Broadwell to wait there in the office for Emmett to return with the operator, Bob and Doolin left the station's halo of light and went back up the tracks to hide behind the water tower, where the train's engine should come to a halt. Everything was ready. Bob allowed himself to relax a notch; so far it had gone exactly to plan, despite the minimal preparation.

It seem like hours, but it was actually only minutes later that the train appeared, its headlamp flickering over the gleaming rails as it squealed and shuddered into the station. No words were necessary. The gang now worked together like a well-oiled machine. Bob and Doolin broke into a run and leaped onto the footboards of the engine cab just as it rolled to a stop, shouting at the engineer and fireman to throw up their hands. The trainmen immediately complied, but Bob noticed the knowing look that flashed between the two men. He briefly wondered what it meant, but he had no time to dwell on it.

"Get down," he ordered. Wordlessly the crewmen climbed down to the ground, stumbling as they strove to keep their hands in the air. Bob and Doolin jumped down behind them. Doolin had grabbed the fireman's pick before he left the cab, and he shoved it roughly at the man. The fireman accepted it without question.

The express car was by the north end of the depot platform, and Bob kept his eyes in motion as they neared the car's door, searching for any unusual movement. Newcomb was poised at the south end of the platform, his rifle held ready to dissuade any interference from the passengers. Broadwell came out of the station office stuffing money in his pants pockets. Through the window Bob could see Emmett standing guard on the operator. The cash drawer was overturned on the counter. All was as it should be. Bob tried to shake off a feeling of impending doom.

Lifting his rifle and pounding on the express car door with the butt of his gun, Bob yelled, "Open up!"

He waited for a few seconds, but there was no response. Bob had a hunch that tonight, especially, they could not afford to waste time. "Chop it open," he commanded the fireman, standing back to give the man room to swing the pickax.

Uncertainly the fireman took the pick in both hands, his eyes darting and his knees trembling. "Williams!" he called out at the express car. "Don't shoot! It's me." After a few seconds hesitation, he swung the pick and smashed the first small hole in the door. When there was no gunshot from inside, he seemed to gain confidence, and he went to work with increasing strength and intensity. In a couple minutes he had a hole big enough to crawl through, so he stepped back, resting the pick on the platform as he glanced toward the rear of the train.

At Bob's insistence, the fireman dropped the pick and squeezed through the opening to unlatch the door. When it rumbled open, the fireman was standing expectantly in the middle of the doorway. Bob had just motioned the man to step back off the car and rejoin the engineer when a single gunshot rang out from the far end of the train. Bob twirled into a crouch and brought his rifle up ready to fire, fleetingly hoping that the shot had been an accidental discharge. It was not, and an explosive crackle of gunfire erupted.

Two men had jumped down from the smoking car at the end of the train and were shooting wildly at the robbers, while other men fired pistols from the windows of the car. Newcomb ducked behind a bench to return fire with his rifle, while Bob, Broadwell, and Doolin crouched behind the train crew and opened up as well. Immediately wounded by the gang's accurate fusillade, the two lawmen on the ground hastily ducked back into the smoking car. When the glass around them began to shatter, the men at the windows of the car also retreated. Shots from the far side of the train indicated that Grat and Bill Power had engaged armed men as they tried to exit over there. After the previous uncertainty, the battle brought Bob a measure of relief, for now he knew what they were up against. The situation was desperate, but not impossible.

"Jack!" Bob yelled to catch Broadwell's attention. They had agreed to only use aliases during the robbery, and Broadwell liked to be known as "Texas Jack" Moore. Motioning for him to follow, Bob leaped into the express car, ready for a fight, but found Williams, the express messenger, quaking beside his desk with his hands already raised. Broadwell came in low behind Bob, prepared to provide covering fire, but he straightened and relaxed as he took in the situation.

"Open the safes, NOW!" Bob yelled in his most menacing tone. There was not time to be polite tonight. Williams' eyes grew wide in reaction to Bob's threatening glare, and he dropped to his knee and began spinning the dial on the large through safe like a man possessed. It was open in seconds, and Williams needed no prompting to immediately move over and work on the smaller way safe. Outside the gunfire had died down, which Bob sincerely hoped was a good sign.

While Bob stood over Williams at the way safe, Broadwell laid his rifle on top of the large safe and started groping around inside, pulling out bundles and slipping them into a gunny sack he had been carrying draped over his pistol belt. Williams swung open the small safe's door and scrambled backwards until he sat against the wall, his hands again high in the air. Bob glanced over to see how Broadwell was doing, and suddenly all the nerves in his body jangled.

Next to the through safe was a large crate stored halfway under a long counter, and just visible next to it were the tips of two boots. Bob touched Broadwell on the shoulder and held his finger to his lips. Following Bob's silent gestures, Broadwell stood up and moved back, picking up his rifle and keeping his eye on the cowering messenger. As soon as his partner was out of the way, Bob crept forward, his rifle poking at the shadows under the counter.

Kicking the soles of the protruding feet, Bob roared "Come on, get out of there!"

"Okay, don't shoot," a muffled voice answered. There were scrabbling sounds as a huge man unfolded himself from under the counter. Even taller than Bob, and muscular in build, the man deliberately kept his hand away from his holstered pistol.

"What the devil are you doing in here?" Bob asked as he took the man's pistol with his left hand.

"Why, uh, I just came as a guest of Mr. Williams. I'm just taking a ride." Bob grunted with disbelief as he threw the pistol out the open door. While Broadwell finished cleaning out the safes, Bob kept the messenger and his "guest" covered. He tossed William's pistol and Winchester out the door as well, and the weapons clattered on the wooden platform. Broadwell stuffed the last of the money in the sack and stood up. Bob tilted his head toward the door, and Broadwell scooted past him and out onto the platform.

"Well," Bob said congenially to the two victims with a friendly wave, "so long." He jumped down to the platform and nodded to Doolin, who was still holding the engineer and fireman hostage. Doolin shoved the crewmen back toward the engine, while cordially greeting Pierce, who had brought the horses down to the north end of the platform. There were still sporadic gunshots as Newcomb, Grat, and Power reminded the men in the smoking car, presumably a posse or special train guard, to keep their heads down and their weapons silent. Emmett was standing at the door to the station office, nervously keeping an eye on the operator as he waited for Bob's signal to leave. Bob gave him a wink, and was pleased with the hesitant smile it provoked.

In a few minutes Doolin had accomplished his assignment; the train crew fired up and the train began pulling away from the station. When the smoking car, now riddled with bullet holes, rolled past the depot, Bob and the others fired a few more warning shots into the upper part of the wagon. There was no response. After the last car had rattled away from the station into the dark, the gang members all ran for their horses. As they mounted up, Bob took a quick head count. All were present and accounted for, and none seemed to have been hit in the gun battle. With a joyful yelp Bob spurred his horse into motion, painstakingly guiding his mount over the treacherous railroad ties toward the pitch-black countryside to the east.

Bob was congratulating himself on a successful job that had overcome unexpected obstacles when he heard shots and shouts behind him. Twisting around in his saddle, he saw that not everyone had followed him across the tracks. Doolin, Newcomb, and Pierce were instead riding the opposite direction down the main street of Adair, whooping and firing their guns in reckless abandon. With a flash of anger at this violation of his orders, Bob scowled at Doolin's disobedience. It further confirmed his conviction that Doolin's group was too wild for the Daltons, even as he recognized that the deviation from his plan was not terribly important. Besides, the group with Bob had the money.

Author's Notes

Chapter 13

Emmett's visit to Eugenia in Woodward and the encounter Doolin and Power had with deputies are drawn from *Beyond the Law.*

The Red Rock robbery was widely reported in the newspapers of the Twin Territories, to include the *Fort Smith Elevator* on June 10, 1892, the *Kingfisher Free Press* on June 16, 1892, the Guthrie *Oklahoma State Capital* on June 11, 1892, the *Edmond Sun* on June 10, 1892, and the El Reno *Oklahoma Democrat* on June 11, 1892. Surprisingly, Emmett devoted only a brief paragraph to this robbery in his book. It may be that he did not want to reveal the integral part he played in the crime.

Despite its more sensational shoot-out, the Adair robbery received less newspaper coverage than Red Rock. There was a long article in the Vinita *Indian Chieftain* on July 21, 1892, and a shorter article in the *Kingfisher Free Press* on the same day. Perhaps because this crime occurred in rival Indian Territory, most of the Oklahoma Territory papers never even gave it a mention. Emmett described this robbery in detail, although it is obvious that his account was somewhat colored by the newspaper reports he undoubtedly read later.

CHAPTER 14

In the aftermath of the Adair robbery, lawmen and posses scoured the Indian Territory for the Daltons, investigating every sighting and rumor in the hopes of bringing in the elusive bandits. The pursuit was hindered, however, by the continuing popularity of the gang. Their attacks on the despised railroads, their gentlemanly manners and appearance, and their determination to avoid killing anyone had earned the respect of the territorial residents, many of whom had a dubious past themselves. With the active aid of farmers and ranchers who fed and sheltered the gang, along with the passive support of other citizens who declined to report them to the law, the Daltons had little difficulty making the long journey back to Riley's camp.

By virtue of crossing the line dividing the Twin Territories, the bandits escaped the jurisdiction of their pursuers in Indian Territory, who had few leads anyway. Meanwhile, in Oklahoma Territory, the furor created by the Red Rock robbery had already subsided, and one by one the search parties had returned to their normal daily activities. By taking advantage of the political rivalries of the divided territory, Bob played both ends against the middle and came out ahead. Although the gang reached their camp near the South Canadian without incident, other factors were putting a strain on their personal relations.

When Doolin and his friends had ridden wildly through Adair and out the west end of town, Bob had resolutely led the rest east to deceive any observers. A mile or so outside of town they turned south for a couple miles before finally heading back west to the rendezvous. Doolin's group was waiting for them there, and they shrugged off Bob's remonstrations in their rush to divide up the money. The take was far less than they had expected, and Newcomb wondered aloud why it had taken the others so long to reach the campsite. Bob ignored the implication that the Daltons had siphoned off part of the money before they had rejoined Doolin's group, but Emmett could tell that it disturbed him.

By the time they wearily climbed down from the horses at the cabin on Riley's ranch, relations between the two factions had almost returned to normal, but there was still an underlying current of dissatisfaction. Along the way they had picked up newspapers carrying accounts of the Adair affair, and the reports implied that the railroads had been expecting the robbery, hence the special guard on board. Bob told the others that this probably explained the small amount of cash in the express car, and said he suspected that the prediction of large sums that had been given them before the event was part of a railroad plot to entrap them. This interpretation quieted some of Doolin's complaints, but still left the men with little to show for their efforts.

Emmett suspected that Bob was less troubled by the cash shortfall than by the death of an innocent bystander. During the robbery, with all its attendant gun play, a doctor sitting in the drugstore across from the depot had been killed by a stray bullet that had pierced the thin wooden walls. The doctor's companion had been seriously wounded by a second round. Most of the gang were of the opinion that the death was almost certainly a result of the wild shooting done by the special guard, since the gang's gunfire had been primarily aimed in the opposite direction from the drugstore. Privately, though, Bob told Emmett he feared that the man had been killed by Doolin and his group as they had ridden through town firing blindly at the buildings.

The special guard in the smoking car, a posse led by Indian Police Chief Charley LeFlore, Katy railroad detective J. J. Kinney, and Deputy Marshal Sid Johnson, had acquitted itself poorly, according to the newspapers. Since LeFlore and Kinney were both wounded in the shoot-out, Emmett felt that these two, at least, should have been given some credit.

While most of the men took justifiable pride in thwarting the railroad's best attempt to capture them, Bob fretted over the close call. He became withdrawn, rarely participating in the card games or joshing of the rest of the gang during the long hot summer hours at the dugout cabin. Emmett watched sympathetically as his brother would count and recount their cash, shaking his head sorrowfully as the amount was never sufficient to take the three of them to South America. Doolin, whenever he and his friends were not off visiting some friendly bar or brothel, kept pressuring Bob to plan another robbery to replace the funds that were steadily being depleted. Bob just kept saying that he was working on it.

In September, after weeks of lethargy, an incident occurred that galvanized Bob into action. Shortly before noon Bob and Emmett were sitting together on the creek bank beneath the shade of a twisted oak tree, daydreaming out loud about what they would do when they got to South America. They were in the middle of a discussion about what breed of cattle would be best to raise there when Bob abruptly stopped and stared off into the distance. Following his gaze, Emmett saw the dust of a single rider, and in silence they observed his approach. Automatically they retrieved their rifles, which they had left leaning against the tree, and laid them across their laps. When the figure drew nearer, Emmett easily recognized him, but Bob informed him anyway.

"It's Jim Riley," Bob announced. He climbed to his feet and stretched. "I'll go see what he wants." Emmett had intended to go meet their friend as well, but he settled back down at Bob's implicit command. Bob strode out into the burning sun and waved a friendly greeting. Riley reined in his horse next to Bob, nodding to Emmett. Emmett could not hear their short conversation, but he saw Riley hand an envelope to Bob, wheel his horse around, and ride off back toward his ranch house. Bob unsealed the envelope and unfolded the enclosed letter. He began reading it as he leisurely walked back toward Emmett. Abruptly he stopped, a stricken look on his face, and he appeared to read the letter again. Emmett jumped to his feet and hurried over.

"What is it?" Emmett asked. He feared that it was bad news about their mother.

Bob opened his mouth a couple times, but no words came out. His eyes were glistening with moisture, and the tendons in his neck stood out.

“Is it about Mom?” Emmett inquired anxiously. Bob shook his head.

“Look here,” Bob finally managed, his voice rough with emotion. He held the letter out, but then snatched it back when Emmett reached for it. Instead Bob methodically folded the letter and slipped it back into the envelope. Emmett dropped his outstretched hand and waited for Bob to explain.

“It’s Eugenia,” Bob said, visibly struggling to contain his feelings. “She’s . . . dead.”

“Dead? How?”

Bob swung his head from side to side, his lips pursed. When no answer was forthcoming, Emmett tried another tack.

“Who sent the letter?”

Bob cradled his Winchester in the crook of his elbow and gripped the letter in both hands, staring hard at the face of the envelope. “Ben Canty,” he eventually muttered. The man they had met in New Mexico.

Then, with short sharp movements, Bob ripped the letter into tiny pieces and lete them scatter in the ever-present wind. Emmett was at a loss for words, unsure how to comfort his brother.

With a faraway look Bob walked back to the tree where they had been sitting and leaned his rifle against it. Emmett followed, but remained standing, the butt of his rifle dragging in the dirt. Bob dropped to the ground, forcefully leaned back against the trunk of the tree, and quietly cursed.

“Damn, damn, damn, damn, damn her!”

Emmett felt helpless. He was confused by Bob’s apparent anger, distressed by the awful news, and uncertain how to help.

Bob reached inside his jacket and withdrew his black leather wallet. Opening it, he slid out the photograph of Eugenia that he always kept there. He gently balanced it on his knee while he put the wallet back in his pocket. He picked up the picture with both hands and started at it blankly for several minutes; Emmett chewed on his lower lip and waited. Finally, his eyes narrowed, Bob shredded the picture, flinging the bits of paper into the air. Blindly he watched the fragments flutter away until they had all scattered in the grass and dirt. After more time had passed in silence, he looked up at Emmett with grim determination, his hands gripping his knees like talons. In a harsh prophetic voice he swore, "Now I will make them understand that 'Hell on earth' is a reality."

For the rest of that day and through the following morning Bob never said a word. He took long walks by himself, or sat alone with his thoughts. Bob's depression was so palpable that even Grat noticed it. Emmett told Grat about the letter and Bob's reaction to it, and admitted he was puzzled by the fact that Bob seemed more irate than grieved by the news of Eugenia's passing. Although he said nothing to Emmett about it, Grat concluded that the letter's contents were not quite as Bob had described. From Bob's behavior, Grat surmised that the letter had in fact been from Eugenia, telling Bob that she wished to end their relationship.

Grat had never really been in love, much to his regret, but he could still imagine what Bob was going through. In the end it did not matter whether Eugenia had actually died or had simply broken off their engagement; either way, Bob had suffered a loss, and there was little his brothers could do about it. Grat advised Emmett to let Bob work it out on his own. Their brother was a strong man with tremendous resilience and drive; left to himself he would soon overcome this setback, just as he had survived other disappointments in the past.

Grat leaned the rickety wooden chair back until his head rested against the sod wall of the cabin. He had brought the chair out to the shaded east side in the hope of catching a cool breeze. Broadwell and Power were just inside the door playing cards, and no one had seen Doolin, Newcomb, or Pierce for almost a week. Emmett had dragged a wooden crate over beside Grat, and together they sat and watched Bob pace aimlessly out in the sun, kicking up little clouds of reddish dust with each jingling step. In the last hour Bob's demeanor had grown more lively and animated, and Grat hoped that signaled a recovery from his despondency, because he needed Bob's usual vitality to counteract his own tendency toward lassitude and cynicism.

Bob suddenly came to a standstill. He paused for a minute, tilted his head back to look at the sky, then decisively turned and marched over to his brothers. He faced them with his hands on his slim hips, towering over them. There was no smile, but Grat was impressed by the fierce intensity of Bob's gaze.

"We're going to Coffeyville," he announced. His eyes flickered between them, waiting for a reaction.

"Why?" Emmett finally asked.

"To do one last trick."

"They all know us in Coffeyville, and they're watching the trains too close now anyway."

"Who said anything about trains? It's banks this time."

"What bank?" Grat asked suspiciously. He could justify robbing trains because of the way he had been railroaded out in California, but a bank was a different matter.

"Not one bank," Bob replied earnestly, holding up two fingers in their faces, "but two." The corners of his mouth curled up in the beginning of a smile.

"Now, look here," Bob continued quickly in order to stifle their protests. "It's getting too risky to go after another train right now. They're just waitin' for us. And no one's been hurt so far, but that won't keep up forever. Now, we all want to get out of the country, but we'll be here forever unless we do something. So I say let's go to Coffeyville. We can take the Condon and the First National at the same time, and that ought to give us enough to get out all right."

As with most new ideas, Grat's initial reaction was negative. "How are we going to do that without getting killed?"

"It's no more dangerous than robbing a train," Bob explained patiently. "We'll ride in, get the banks, and ride out. That's all there is to it. Easy, huh?"

"I don't know," Emmett said doubtfully. "Someone could get hurt. And the people in Coffeyville never did anything to us."

"No one is going to get hurt," Bob insisted. His face had clouded and his voice turned petulant at the unexpected opposition to his idea. "Anyway, what's a better idea? You got any suggestions?"

Emmett shrugged and looked at Bob's feet to avoid his challenging stare. Grat leaned forward until his chair rested on all four legs and crossed his arms across his chest. He could foresee a lot of problems with Bob's plan. He was about to enumerate them when he took another look at Bob's face and realized the futility of it. When Bob got an idea in his head, there was no changing it. It was usually best to just agree with him and allow him to eventually talk himself out of it. Grat certainly hoped that would be the case this time. To Grat's way of thinking, robbing two banks at the same time in their home town was a recipe for disaster.

Over the next few days Bob expounded on his plan in detail, using all his powers of persuasion. Broadwell and Power were much more responsive to the idea than Grat and Emmett had been, and with their support Bob badgered his brothers into at least tacit approval. Broadwell and Power were not exactly intellectual giants, and Grat certainly knew better than to trust their judgment, but sometimes he felt that he had reached a stage where nothing really mattered anymore. Besides, Bob had almost always been right before; why should this time be any different?

A week passed, and Doolin, Newcomb, and Pierce had still not returned. Anxious to set his plan in motion, Bob left a note for them with Jim Riley and then started out with the rest of the gang on the long ride east. The second day out they camped on the Cimarron River just north of Kingfisher. Emmett was sent into town for supplies with strict orders to avoid their mother's house, which was almost certainly under surveillance. When Emmett brought someone back with him from town, Grat was at first alarmed, but he was pleased when he saw who it was. Riding into camp with a big grin was their brother Bill, who had come to Kingfisher a few months earlier to try and rebuild his life.

"So, how are Jennie and the kids?" Grat asked him after they had all shaken hands and Bill had been introduced to Power and Broadwell. They were in a small grove of trees near the river, leaning against the tree trunks as yellowed leaves occasionally floated down among them.

"Fine," Bill answered, although his tone suggested otherwise. "They're still in California, staying with her family."

"When are they coming out?" Bob asked.

Bill shrugged. "As soon as I get settled and start making some money, I guess."

"How's Mom?" Emmett inquired.

"She's doing okay. Ben's helping her out. It isn't easy for her, what with you boys in the papers all the time."

"I know," Emmett admitted miserably.

"Well, that'll just happen one more time," Bob assured him.

"What do you mean?"

"We're gonna do one more trick, and then we're heading for South America. Mom won't have to worry about us then."

"Haven't you done enough?" Bill's scorn was obvious, but Bob seemed oblivious to it.

"Not yet. We still need some more money. Say, Bill, you want to come with us?"

"Are you serious?" Bill was dumbfounded. Grat suppressed a smile, knowing that Bill was the one member of the family whom Bob could not manipulate. "Why would I want to go with you?"

"You said you needed money. We're going to get a whole lot of it, and we could use another man."

"Yeah," Broadwell chipped in enthusiastically. "Six would make it go easier."

"What would go easier?" Bill asked warily.

“We’re going to take a couple banks,” Bob explained succinctly, spreading his hands in front of him. He deliberately left out any mention of Coffeyville.

“At the same time!” Broadwell added proudly.

Bill’s mouth hung open as he looked around the group for confirmation. Grat raised his eyebrows and nodded.

“Are you crazy?” Bill demanded, shaking his head slowly in consternation.

“Bob’s got a plan,” Grat offered wryly. Bill searched Grat’s face.

“And you’re going along with it?”

Grat shrugged.

“Come on, Bill,” Emmett begged. “We need you.”

Bill shook his head again, firmly this time. “No,” he said with finality. “No, I do not want to go rob banks with you. I don’t even want to talk about it. That’s just . . .” He raised his hands palms outward, and tried to push the idea away. Grat, out of sympathy for his brother, steered the conversation away to less controversial topics. He asked about their sisters, and politics, and anything other than the impending robberies. Bob walked away, clearly frustrated and disappointed by his inability to enlist Bob in his scheme.

After an hour or so Bill announced that he had to go back to Kingfisher and made his good-byes. While Bill mounted his horse, Bob made one last attempt to sway him.

“If you change your mind,” Bob told him, “we’ll be at Zue Mitchell’s the first week of October. You remember how to get there?” Bill had gone to live in California ten years earlier, just after the family had moved to Coffeyville, and Bob wanted to ensure he knew how to find their cousin’s farm near Lenapah.

“Yeah, I remember,” Bill told him, but it was clear he had no intention of showing up there. With a final wave he rode away.

After Bill had gone a somber mood settled over the gang. Bill’s adamant refusal had caused all of them to reconsider their plan, and that in turn had raised a lot of questions. One of the most important of these was how, exactly, were they going to get to South America afterwards without getting caught. There was a long rambling discussion, with Bob uncharacteristically encouraging and accepting suggestions from the others. Finally they developed a strategy that was simple and workable.

During the next two nights they continued their journey east, detouring north around Guthrie, the territorial capital. Twelve miles east of Guthrie they stopped at the farm of Amos Burton, a black cowboy originally from Texas. The Dalton boys had all known him for several years, and they trusted him completely. He had homesteaded the small property with his widowed sister and her children, but the unproductive farm barely kept them all fed. They told Burton that they needed his help, and that they were willing to pay for it. By pooling most of their remaining funds, the five men were able to offer Burton more than enough to persuade the destitute farmer to assist them.

He was to use some of the money to buy a covered wagon with team and stock it with provisions and ammunition. They agreed on a familiar location in the Cherokee Strip where Burton would go with the wagon and wait for them. After the robbery the gang would meet him there, load up the wagon, and send Burton home. Most of the gang would then hide in the back under the canvas; the drivers would dress like farmers and pose as horse traders, thus explaining the five horses being led behind the wagon. In this guise they would drift westward until the furor died down, and then find a place to hole up until spring. By that time they should be able to safely travel by train to Seattle, where they would split up and catch separate ships for South America. It was an excellent plan, and it might have worked.

Friday, September 30, 1892

"Who is it?" Emmett asked quietly. Bob had his spyglass up to his eye, watching the two men in the distance as they walked from the barn to the ranch house. He and Emmett were astride their horses, hidden in the trees that bordered Bill Halsell's ranch; they had left Grat, Power, and Broadwell at the Mitchell ranch a few miles to the west, camped a mile up California Creek from the house.

"The one on the left is Bob Thornton," Bob said, concentrating on the moving figures. Thornton was Halsell's ranch foreman, the man they had come to see about supplying some fresh mounts. "Oh, hell!" Bob said, jerking the telescope down and forcefully collapsing it with a loud click. "The other one's Chapman."

"Deputy Marshal Chapman?" Emmett asked, hoping he was wrong. They knew him from their days as lawmen, but he had never been a particularly close friend.

"Yep," Bob confirmed. The two men disappeared into the house, and Bob spurred his horse forward. Emmett trotted after him across the pastures and through the open door of the Halsell barn. Thornton, who had heard their arrival, came out of the house and walked into the barn, his face showing no surprise at the identity of his visitors.

"Howdy," he greeted them.

"Who's here besides Chapman?" Bob asked, foregoing any small talk.

"Just him."

"Tell him to come out and chat with us."

While Thornton returned to the house, Bob and Emmett dismounted and took up positions on either side of the barn door. They gripped their Winchesters and waited. It took a while for Thornton to convince Chapman it was safe, but finally the deputy trudged into the barn with his Winchester held loosely beside him. When he spied the two Daltons he stopped, but he judiciously kept the rifle pointed at the ground.

"Howdy, boys," Chapman said with a forced smile. "Glad to see you."

"Chapman," Bob acknowledged, nodding. "Been a while."

"Yes, it has. Guess I don't need to ask what you boys have been up to."

"Guess not," Bob agreed good-naturedly. "How about you?"

"Oh, you know. This and that. Got me a place down at Tulsa. Just up here visitin'."

"You still a deputy?"

"Well, you could say so. But say, I'm gettin' damn tired of this marshal game. Ain't a cent in it for a fellow, and he's got a good chance of being kicked off any time."

"Yep," Bob agreed. Emmett suspected that Chapman, aware of Bob's history with the marshals service, had said this just to ingratiate himself.

"In fact," Chapman said, as if it had just occurred to him, "why don't I join up with you?" Emmett saw a frown start to form on Bob's face. Chapman saw it, too. "Oh, I don't mean to ride with you. But I could act as a scout. I'll stick right on the job as a deputy, and then if I get in with any posse that's after you, I can steer them away. What do you say?"

"And have you double-cross us, too?" Bob said, shaking his head. "Not by a long shot."

Emmett thought it was a poor idea to antagonize Chapman, regardless of his reprehensible willingness to violate his marshal's oath, and he rushed to smooth things over. "We don't really need anyone right now," Emmett explained in a conciliatory tone. "We're leaving the country, and won't be pulling any more jobs. We appreciate your offer, though."

"Well . . ." Chapman shrugged.

"But we are going to need some fresh horses," Emmett continued. "Mine's been hobbling a little, not serious or anything, but, you know, we can't take any chances."

Bob was still scowling, and Chapman seemed anxious to appease him. "Why, you boys can take my horse, there." He nodded at a strong-looking brown horse in a nearby stall. "It's as good a colt as you'll find anywhere in Indian Territory. You're welcome to it."

Emmett walked over and inspected the horse. Chapman's pride in the animal was justified. "I'll give you my horse and a hundred dollars for it," Emmett offered.

"Sure!" Chapman readily agreed, holding out his hand as Emmett dragged a wad of bills from his pocket and counted out the required amount.

"We better draw up a bill of sale," Emmett told him when he gave him the cash. "Don't want people to think you stole my horse." He was smiling, but he was serious. Somewhat reluctantly Chapman found some paper and wrote out two copies of a statement describing the transaction. Both men signed each copy; Emmett stuffed his copy in his saddle bag.

Reassured by the lack of gunfire, Bob Thornton strolled back into the barn. He appeared pleased to see that Chapman and the Daltons were getting along. While Chapman and Emmett chatted, Thornton showed Bob some other horses in the barn, and Bob made a deal to buy four of them. Everyone would need fresh mounts for the Coffeyville job.

Saturday, October 1, 1892

Emmett sat at the kitchen table, chewing the end of a pencil. In the next room he could hear his cousin Zue Mitchell getting her children ready for the trip into town. Her husband, John, was already out at the barn hooking up the wagon team. The calico curtains had been tied back so that the morning sunshine flooded the kitchen with warmth and brightness. Emmett's mood, on the other hand, was far less cheerful. He picked up the lined tablet paper and reread the letter he had written

________________, Ind. Ter., October 1, 1892

Dear Mother:

Get somebody to see Bob at once. He has planned to rob two banks in ____________ on the 5th. Am with him now, but he will not listen to me. If he pulls off this job, I will have to go with him. Grat is in it too, and I won't let them think I am a quitter, so will go with them unless somebody talks them out of it. It's going to be close to where we used to live. If Will is in Kingfisher, send him. He knows where we are.

Yours, E.

He could not think of anything to add. With a small sigh he folded the letter and slipped it into the envelope Zue had given him. He sealed the envelope, smacking his lips to get rid of the foul taste of the glue. Carefully he printed his mother's address on the outside. Pushing his chair back from the table, he stood up and went to look for Zue. He found her in the parlor, tying her bonnet in front of a mirror.

"Do you need money for postage?" he asked, handing her the letter. She smiled and shook her head.

"You boys have already given me a couple hundred dollars to buy the clothes and stuff. That should more than cover a couple cents worth of stamps."

"When do you think Mom will get it?"

Zue looked pensive for a moment. "Well, today's Saturday, so I imagine it will get there Monday, if the train don't get robbed." She gave him a wry grin and a wink.

"I don't think it will," Emmett responded, trying to join in the joke, but his heart just wasn't in it. Zue patted his hand reassuringly and put the letter in her knit handbag.

"Anything else I can do for you in town?"

Emmett shook his head.

"Well, I've got the list Bob made out, and I'll see what I can do. I hope I can find everything."

“We sure appreciate it. I just hope you don’t get into any trouble on account of us.”

“Don’t you worry about it. After all, we’re family.” Emmett nodded. Zue gave Emmett another encouraging smile and went to the front door.

“There’s some muffins on the stove you can take out to the other boys. We’ll see you this evening.”

Emmett stood in the door and watched as she and the children climbed into the wagon John had brought around. In a minute they were rumbling off down the rutted farm road. Reluctantly Emmett gathered up the muffins and went out the back door to being the long walk back to their camp on a wooded hilltop. They were all accustomed to staying up all night, so Bob and the other three were probably still asleep.

Tuesday, October 4, 1892

When Bill Dalton first sighted the Mitchell’s farmhouse, he noted the many changes that had occurred since his last visit ten years ago. There was a new addition on the side of the house, and the barn had been recently painted. Flowers and shrubs had been planted around the porch, and the place had a generally prosperous look. A boy had been playing in the yard, but he had run inside the house the moment he spotted the stranger approaching. By the time Bill reached the front gate, John Mitchell was standing on the porch eyeing him suspiciously, his hands tucked inside the bib of his overalls.

“Afternoon, John,” Bill called out, waving his empty hand. John squinted at him, and then his face broke into a smile.

“Bill? Is that you? Well, I’ll be damned!” He gestured for Bill to come up to the house and climb down from his horse, before twisting around at the waist to yell through the open front door. “It’s Bill Dalton! Come on out and say hello.”

Bill was relieved to see his brothers, Bob, Grat, and Emmett, file out of the house. Emmett was still pushing his pistol back into its holster. Behind them came Dick Broadwell, followed by Bill Power, who incongruously had a table cloth tied around his neck. Last out was Zue Mitchell, who held a comb and scissors in her hand, explaining Power's strange garb. There was a long and raucous exchange of greetings, with hugs, handshakes, and backslapping. Bob and Emmett seemed especially glad to see him, although Bill imagined each had a different reason.

Bill was peppered with questions, and he gamely tried to answer all of them, despite the rapidity with which they were asked. Mom was doing fine, and so were their sisters and brothers. Ben had been helping out on the property. Jennie and the kids were still back in California, and no, he didn't know when they would be coming out yet. He had taken the train to Lenapah Station and rented a horse there. He had only gotten lost once trying to find the Mitchell's ranch. No, he hadn't seen any marshals or detectives.

Finally Zue broke up the interrogation and told them to get in the house so Bill could relax. Bill politely declined her offer of food, saying he had eaten dinner in Lenapah. Gradually the four Dalton brothers drifted back into the parlor. Zue took Power back to the kitchen to finish his haircut, and Broadwell went with John and the boy to put Bill's horse in the stable and do some other evening chores.

Bob and Emmett sat together on the couch, looking at Bill expectantly. Grat settled on the piano bench; the music sheets and open keyboard cover implied that he had been playing earlier. Bill hung his hat on the hat rack by the front door and took a seat in a wing-back chair. Bob leaned forward.

"So you decided to go with us after all?"

Bill's shoulders sagged. "No, I didn't. I don't even know where you're going." He doubted that Emmett had told Bob about his letter to their mother, so he did not reveal the true purpose of his visit.

"It'll be spectacular," Bob enthused. "It'll be better than anything the Youngers ever did, even better than the Northfield raid.

This will be something that no one has ever done before. And it will be the Daltons who did it, and everyone will know it was us. How can you pass up something like that?"

"Easy. So where are you going to commit this spectacular crime?"

Bob lowered his voice and glanced around. Zue was still in the kitchen with Power, and they could hear her constant stream of chatter. "Coffeyville," Bob declared. "We're going to take the Condon and the First National."

Bill stared at Bob for a long minute. Bob's eyes sparkled as he awaited Bill's reaction. His face fell when Bill finally responded. "That is the stupidest thing I've ever heard. I can't believe you're my brother."

"It is not stupid!" Bob flared, sitting back with a jerk. "I've got it all worked out. We ride into town tomorrow morning when the banks first open, so they'll still have plenty of money. We'll wear disguises, and we'll just waltz in and hold them up. By the time anyone figures out what's going on, we'll be out of there and on our way back into the territory. No one gets hurt, and we end up with enough money to go to South America."

"You're going to do this in broad daylight?" Bill asked.

"Of course. Banks aren't open at night, you know."

"What if you run into some lawmen?"

"The only law in Coffeyville is the town marshal, an old man named Connelly who's getting ready to retire and become a school teacher. Hell, most times he don't even carry a gun."

"There might be some deputies in town from the territory," Bill suggested.

"Yeah, and there might be a blizzard, too. We'll be in and out of there so quick it won't matter who's in town, anyhow."

"But two banks?" Bob kept hammering away, but he was starting to think it was a losing battle. Bob was totally convinced, it seemed.

"Twice as much money," Bob pointed out, now thoroughly warmed to the subject. "The Condon and the First National are right across the street from each other, so we can give each other cover if we have to. You ought to come with us, Bill. We could use a sixth man, to make it three at each bank, and then it would really be a Dalton job."

"Why would I want to?"

"After the way they treated you out in California? I'd think you'd want to get even."

"That was the railroad's doing," Bill explained patiently. "That's got nothing to do with the banks."

"Yeah, but . . . " Bob struggled to find the words, clenching his fist on his knee. "You told us the railroads and the banks were in it together, all a bunch of damn Republicans trying to squeeze money out of the working man. That's what you said."

Bill looked at the ceiling in supplication. "Bob, that doesn't give you the right to go robbing them. And not all banks are run by Republicans."

"Well, these banks are. Back in '88 when they tried to send me and Grat to jail for shooting Charley Montgomery, when we were just doing our job, that bastard Kerr said the First National would give Charley money to escape, 'cause Kerr was a Free Mason just like them."

Bill briefly considered trying to explain the difference between Republicans and Free Masons, but dismissed the idea as futile. He stared into Bob's intense eyes and tried to fathom what was going on behind them. "But, Bob," he persisted, "why do you have to rob banks at all? Why can't you just quit? Don't you know what you're doing to Mom?"

"Quit? And do what? Go to prison?" Bob reached back and scratched the back of his neck. Tiny clippings of hair clung to his neck and collar from his recent haircut. "We just don't have a choice, Bill. We don't have enough money to leave the country, and if we stay we'll get caught some day and go to prison. They ain't gonna just let us walk in and say, 'We're the Daltons, and we're real sorry, can we go home now?' They mean to get us, and if we don't have any money, they will. We got to have money to survive, and the only way we can get it now is to steal it."

"But you could get killed."

Bob nodded solemnly. "That's true. Might get sick and die, too, or get struck by lightning. Those are just the chances you take. But if it works, we'll have plenty of money, and can go to South America and live like kings. Hell, we can even bring Mom and the little kids down to live with us. It'd be great."

Sensing defeat, Bill turned to Grat for support. "And you're going with him?" Bill asked accusingly.

"Guess so," Grat admitted.

"Why?"

"Like Bob said, we don't have a lot of choice. We're wanted in California and both territories. I've already seen what kind of justice we'd get if we're caught." Grat shrugged, a mournful expression on his face. "What else are we gonna do?"

Emmett was hunched over on the couch, his lower lip pushed out and his eyes downcast. He did not look up when Bill addressed him.

"Emmett, what about you?"

Emmett took a deep breath and let it out slowly. In a hesitant, barely audible voice, he said, "I'm with Bob." Bob gave Emmett a brotherly pat on the knee.

Bill rubbed his eyes with both hands, trying to think of a new tack he could take, some suggestion he could offer as an alternative. Nothing came to mind.

"Your turn, Grat," Power said as he walked into the room, brushing the hair from his shoulders with his fingers. Bill slumped in his chair, feeling like a failure, but not yet willing to give up. The robbery would not occur until tomorrow; he still had time to try and change Bob's mind. Mom would never forgive him if he failed.

Author's Notes

Chapter 14

Most of this chapter is drawn from *Beyond the Law*, since Emmett was the only surviving witness, but several aspects were either confirmed or altered in light of other documentation. The meeting with Deputy Marshal Chapman became a major news item after the robbery, when Chapman swore that Emmett had stolen the horse, and Bill Dalton had to take legal steps to reclaim it. This affair was covered in a series of articles in the *Coffeyville Journal* in December, 1892.

When he was interrogated two days after the robbery, Emmett told newsmen that the day before the robbery the gang had been camped on a timbered hill by Hickory Creek, twelve miles from Coffeyville, as reported in the *Kansas City Star and Kansan* on October 7, 1892. In his book, however, Emmett stated that they were on California Creek, twenty miles from Coffeyville. Topographic maps do not show a Hickory Creek in that area; California Creek, on the other hand, does exist, but it is twelve miles from Coffeyville, not twenty. It would seem, therefore, that they were probably on California Creek, twelve miles from Coffeyville, which also happened to be the location of the ranch belonging to John and Zue Mitchell. In the 1890 preliminary hearings in Lenapah against Grat on the horse-stealing charge, the Mitchells had testified that they lived on California Creek, and that Zue was related to the Daltons. This testimony is on file at the National Archives in Fort Worth.

Thus it is only logical to assume that the Daltons stayed with their relatives. This would help account for the fact that the photographs taken of their bodies after the raid clearly show that they had all had recent haircuts. They were reported to have come into town wearing new clothes and theatrical disguises, and they had brought fresh-baked biscuits and hard-boiled eggs for their breakfast that morning, according to the editor of the *Coffeyville Journal* in his book, *Last Raid of the Daltons*. All of these things point to their having been in fairly civilized surroundings, not camped out as Emmett claimed.

The letter Emmett wrote to his mother on October 1 was not revealed to the public until 1908, after it had been used in an ultimately successful ploy to have Emmett pardoned by the governor. According to the *Oklahoma City Times* of April 17, 1908, which reprinted the letter, Mrs. Dalton did send Bill to try and dissuade Bob. After he left, she also went to William Grimes, then the U. S. Marshal in Guthrie, and told him of the letter. He dispatched couriers to where he thought the boys might be, but they failed to find them in time. These facts were confirmed by Grimes in 1908.

A significant line in the letter is the last, which said that Bill Dalton knew where they were. This implies that they must have spoken with him as they rode by Kingfisher on the way to Coffeyville, as I have depicted. More importantly, it supports that they must have been at the Mitchells, since Bill, who was unfamiliar with the area, would only have been able to find a place he had previously visited, such as the home of a relative.

That Bill found them is indicated by the existence of the "sixth man" on the road to Coffeyville. The *Coffeyville Journal* reported that four witnesses had seen the Daltons west of town early that morning, and all four reported seeing six men. Since two of these witnesses, Mr. and Mrs. R. L. Hollingsworth, were my great-great-grandparents, I am predisposed to accept the veracity of their account. By the time the gang reached the city limits, though, there were only five. The identity, or even existence, of the sixth man was hotly debated in the days following the robbery, and remains controversial to this day, but the evidence clearly points to Bill. The *Topeka Daily Capitol* of October 8, 1892, reported that Bill Dalton had arrived in Guthrie from the direction of Indian Territory the day after the robbery. He reportedly was in need of a shave, and his actions were termed suspicious.

Emmett always contended that Bill Dalton never committed any criminal acts, and his failure to mention Bill's presence at Coffeyville was probably an effort to keep that image untarnished.

Likewise, his omission of mention of the Mitchells was for their own protection.

In a letter to the city of Coffeyville a few days after the raid, Bill Doolin claimed he had meant to be in on it, but had gotten the date wrong. According to Emmett, though, Bob left Doolin and his friends out intentionally, and he may have done so by telling Doolin the wrong date, giving him some plausible deniability if the raid had been successful and Doolin asked why they had been excluded.

CHAPTER 15

Wednesday, October 5, 1892

The wind had shifted to the north as the cold front moved through, and the precipitous drop in temperature had chilled Bob and the boys to the bone. Down along the creek bed, sheltered by the high banks and the trees, the wind was reduced to a fluttering breeze, but the night air was still too cool for comfort. They had all dressed in their new summer-weight suits, and now, caught off guard by the cold snap, they were suffering for their stylishness.

Bob paced back and forth near the edge of the triangular clearing, rubbing his hands together for warmth. Most of the other men were doing the same, striving to keep warm while they waited for the dawn. Only Bill Dalton was asleep, huddled in a pile of horse blankets under a tall bush.

They had left the Mitchell's ranch at ten that evening. On the ride north Bill had continued to harangue Bob; pleading and pestering, cajoling and castigating, he employed every trick he knew to dissuade Bob from his rash plan. Bill had been eloquent and persuasive, but Bob's mind was set, and nothing could deter him.

Bob, in turn, had countered with his own arguments in favor of Bill joining them in the robberies, and a few times he thought there was a waver in Bill's determination to remain law-abiding. Bob acknowledged that those apparent chinks in Bill's armor might merely have been due to his brother's extreme fatigue. While the gang members had long ago adjusted to a night owl schedule of sleeping during the day, Bill was accustomed to a more normal schedule. By the time they had arrived at Onion Creek, three miles west of Coffeyville, Bill had been awake and active for almost twenty-four hours straight.

After cutting through a barbed wire fence on P. L. Davis's farm, the gang had made its way across a plowed field to make camp in a stand of timber along the creek. Bob had then sent Emmett and Power over to a nearby cornfield to gather forage for their horses, and while they were gone he had helped Bill bed down. Bill protested weakly at first, but gave in when Bob assured him that they would all go to sleep as soon as the horses were fed. Bill was unconscious as soon as he laid his head down, and Bob smiled affectionately at his older brother. He appreciated what Bill was trying to do, but it was too late for that. The plan had been set in motion, and like a runaway train on a downhill track, it could not be stopped.

Emmett came out of the shadows and began pacing alongside Bob, his hands jammed into his pants pockets for warmth. "What time is it?" he whispered.

"Don't know," Bob answered. "Around four-thirty or five, I think."

"Wish the sun would come up."

"You anxious to go rob some banks?"

"I'm anxious to get warm."

"Well, go put on your duster," Bob suggested.

"You're not wearing yours."

"I'm not that cold."

"Hmm," Emmett grunted, but made no move toward his horse. Bob thought about getting his own coat, just so Emmett would not be embarrassed about wearing one, but decided against it. As leader of the gang, he had to set the example.

After several minutes of silence, Emmett drifted away again. A minute later Bob heard Emmett's voice joined with Broadwell's in a murmuring conversation. That was fine. Bob did not want to talk to anyone right then. He needed to concentrate, to go through his plan step by step again, to make sure he had covered every contingency. They had never done a robbery in daylight before, nor ever robbed a bank, and there were many unknowns involved. Bob hoped he had anticipated all the potential problems, but worried that he had not.

Yesterday evening the gang had all gathered around Zue Mitchell's kitchen table as Bob drew a crude map of downtown Coffeyville and plotted out their movements. Like most towns in Kansas, Coffeyville had been laid out in a rectangular grid that was aligned with the compass. The east-west streets were numbered, and the north-south streets were mostly named for trees. Near the center of town, however, the railroad angled through from the northeast, creating a trapezoid-shaped plaza that had become the center of the business section.

The north side of the plaza was Eighth Street, and bordering it on the south was Ninth. Perpendicular to these numbered streets was Walnut, which formed the western side of the plaza. The fourth side was Union Street, which ran northeast to southwest at an oblique angle, parallel to the railroad tracks that were one block over.

Jutting into the plaza at the wider north end, between Walnut and Union, was a building with a floor plan that matched the plaza in shape, so that the north end of the building was much wider than the south. This odd-shaped edifice belonged to C. M. Condon & Co. The narrow end of the building held the Condon Bank, and the wider end, fronting on Eighth Street, was an opera house. Facing the plaza on Union was a row of storefronts, all of which had wide porch awnings over the brick sidewalk. The backs of these buildings all faced the railroad tracks. Near the middle of this block, directly across from the Condon, was the First National Bank.

On the west side of the plaza were more businesses, mostly general stores and dry goods shops. Between Slosson's Drug Store and McKenna's Dry Goods the block was split by an alley that ran west to Maple Street, behind the Long-Bell Lumber Yard. Since it had no part in his plan, Bob gave the alley little mention. He would later regret this omission.

With arrows and X's Bob had explained the course of events to the men, going over each man's responsibility. They would ride into town from the west on Eighth Street until it crossed Maple. After dismounting and tying their horses to the hitching rail on Eighth in front of Long-Bell, they would walk together down the block to Walnut. Grat was to take Broadwell and Power down Walnut to the southwest entrance of Condon's, while Bob and Emmett would continue on Eighth and turn right down Union to hit the First National. After the robberies they would all retrace their steps to the horses, intentionally left out of sight of the plaza, and ride back the way they came in. It seemed foolproof. With any luck they should be on their way out of town before any alarm was raised. Broadwell had openly praised the plan, and the others had agreed that it was very well conceived. Now, though, as he waited for the sun to rise on the fateful day, Bob was beset by doubts.

Bill's pleas and arguments continued to haunt him. At one level he knew Bill was right, that he was just digging himself in deeper and deeper, but at another level he rationalized that it was the best way out of a bad situation. What was most disturbing was the awareness that deep down he felt a growing desire to end it all any way he could. While the Daltons had gained loot and notoriety, they had also found that their options were progressively diminished by that fame, along with the profits from their crimes. Now that Eugenia was gone, Bob found himself with nothing to look forward to. South America was a dream, one that was too unreal to foster genuine hope.

So far his life had been an exciting adventure, filled with gun battles, chases, and flattering newspaper articles, but now what? More robberies, more gun battles, and more headlines? These had all lost their appeal, but what else was there? He was ready to move on, but with no firm destination in mind. The one thing he knew for sure was that his raid on Coffeyville would settle things one way or another. Either they would ride away with enough money to do whatever they wanted while simultaneously staking a claim on the boldest crime of the century, or they would die in the attempt. Whichever it was, Bob would have his glory, and his future would be decided for him. He took morbid comfort in the thought.

The first rays of the sun brightened their spirits as well as their surroundings. The onset of autumn had transformed the grove into a riot of color, the reds, yellows, and browns contrasting with the remaining greens like a beautiful landscape painting. The sun also brought warmth, and the men began their preparations with a growing good humor. Bill continued to sleep, despite the boisterous conversations around him, and Bob saw no reason to wake him. Zue had boiled some eggs and baked some biscuits for them, and Bob unwrapped them and passed them around. Greedily the young men gulped down this welcome breakfast, leaving the shells and crumbs on the ground to be carried away by the ants.

At Bob's insistence, all the men shaved that morning. Grat protested that it was too cold to shave, since Bob had not permitted a fire for hot water, but Bob just glared at him until he complied. Bob explained that not only did they need to look presentable on this glorious occasion, they needed to be clean-shaven in order for their disguises to remain secure. Zue had procured some false beards and mustaches intended for a theatrical production, and the three Dalton brothers would wear these to avoid recognition as they entered the familiar town. Since Power and Broadwell were unknown in Coffeyville, they would need no disguises initially, although both had bandannas around their necks to wear over their faces once they entered the bank.

Bill woke up while Emmett was applying spirit gum to Bob's false goatee, in preparation for affixing it to his brother's chin. Complaining that they should not have let him sleep so late, Bill was only slightly appeased when Bob gave him some eggs and biscuits that he had held back for him. Rumpled and unshaven, with bits of leaves and grass in his hair, Bill gobbled down the food with a grouchy expression on his face while he watched his brothers don their fake facial hair.

When Emmett had finished with him, Bob admired his image in a small shaving mirror. A handlebar mustache and goatee gave him the look of a southern gentleman, he thought.

Grat put on a bushy mustache connected to mutton chop side whiskers, and the combination made his already wide face look puffy and somewhat ludicrous. With effort Bob refrained from teasing him about it.

Emmett sported a full beard, the most artificial-looking of the three disguises. Not only did it not match his dark brown hair color, it looked out of place on his young face. Bob dismissed any concerns, rationalizing that they would keep their distance from the citizens of Coffeyville as long as possible; by the time someone noticed the false beards, it would be too late. Bob put the mirror away in his saddle bags. Next to him Bill was washing down his breakfast with a drink from Grat's canteen.

"You comin' to town with us?" Bob asked casually. Bill screwed the lid back on the canteen and replaced it on Grat's saddle. He looked at Bob searchingly.

"You're still going to do it," he said, making it more of a statement than a question.

"I told you we were. I'd sure like to have you along."

"This is insane!" Bill muttered. Shaking his head, he walked away to get his hat, then went over to check the saddle cinch on his rented horse. Bob grinned. Maybe he would talk Bill into yet.

Bob checked his pocket watch and saw that it was after eight-thirty. The banks would be open in a few minutes; time to get a move on.

"Let's go, time's a-wastin'," he told the others, and they all climbed into their saddles. With Bob in the lead, they filed out through the trees onto the open field. Bill brought up the rear, mumbling something about stupidity. They left through the hole in the fence they had cut the night before and turned north again, following an old wagon trail that wound between the fields and over the creek.

Thirty minutes later they skirted Allin's Hill and came to the dusty road that led east into Coffeyville. With almost military precision they wheeled onto the road and formed two lines of three abreast, pulling down their hat brims in front to shade their eyes from the morning sun.

Bill found himself in the second row, along with Emmett and Bill Power. Emmett's eyes were wide with apprehension as he gave Bill demanding looks and motioned toward Bob with his head. Bill shrugged helplessly at his younger brother, out of ideas on how to discourage Bob. At this point Bill wondered if he really wanted to try. Maybe Bob was right. Maybe this was the only way. Then he looked again at Emmett, whose fright was evident, even behind the ridiculous whiskers, and he remembered his mother's pleas that had sent him here. Taking a deep breath, he tried one last time.

"Bob," he called. Bob, riding in the middle of the front row, half turned his head. "Bob, how about you all go to Alaska. I hear there's lots of opportunity up there, and no one would look for you there.

"Too cold," Bob answered succinctly.

"Well, then, maybe we could talk to the Marshal in Guthrie. I hear Mr. Grimes is a reasonable man. Maybe we could work a deal for a pardon or something."

"I don't think so, Bill. He couldn't do that even if he wanted to. He has to answer to Washington, and . . . " Bob broke off and squinted at the road ahead of them. "Somebody's coming. Everyone act natural."

Bill wondered what acting natural meant in this sort of situation. Six men, five of them heavily armed, and three of them with fake beards, were probably not a natural occurrence around here. Shifting to see around Grat, Bill spied the plume of dust behind an approaching buggy. As it grew near the men edged their horses off the road and waited for the buggy to pass.

When it came abreast of them Bill could see that the occupants were an older couple, well dressed and in no hurry. Bill tilted his head down so that his hat brim shielded his face from view. Bob gave them a friendly greeting and a wave, and they returned it. In a moment they were gone, the dust of their passing drifting in the breeze as it settled back to earth.

"Do you think they recognized us?" Emmett asked anxiously as they resumed their ride toward town.

"Do you know them?" Bill asked Emmett quickly, alarmed at the idea.

In a calm voice Bob replied, "I've seen them before around town. They didn't seem to be worried when they saw us. You guys just take it easy."

For Bill that was not a reasonable request. Here he was riding with a gang of wanted outlaws on their way to commit a spectacular robbery of two banks. The reality of that was starting to finally hit home, and he was about to tell Bob he was leaving when Bob guided them off the road again. Another buggy was headed their way. Keeping his head down, Bill moved to the back of the group, allowing himself only a peek as the buggy passed with cheerful greetings exchanged. Two farmers, who looked to be brothers, were driving the buggy. Bill didn't even bother to ask if Bob knew them as well.

As soon as the buggy was past, Bill spoke up. "I'm leaving, Bob. I think you all ought to turn around and forget this Coffeyville idea. Why don't you come back with me to Oklahoma? We'll figure out something."

"Go ahead, Bill," Bob said. "You do what you want. But we're going into town and rob us some banks."

Bill looked at Grat, but Grat was starting off to the east, ignoring the conversation. Bill turned his gaze to Emmett.

"Emmett? How about you?"

Emmett glanced at Bob, then studied the reins he held in his hands. "I'm stickin' with Bob," he said.

Bob had a grim smile on his face. "You tried, Bill," he said sympathetically. "Tell Mom you tried. That's all you can do." Clicking his tongue he wheeled his horse and trotted it on down the road. One by one the others followed him, leaving Bill alone in the settling dust. Bill stared after them, watching them assume a new formation, with the three Dalton brothers in front, Power and Broadwell behind. Bill was certain that he would never see them again. When the gang crested a rise and sank from view, Bill turned his horse and headed back to Lenapah. He had to catch a train. Mrs. Dalton was going to need his support.

Grat glanced to his left. Bouncing gently in his saddle, Bob was as cool as a cucumber, showing no more emotion than a man on his way to town to buy supplies. Emmett, on the other side of Bob, was not nearly so calm. Emmett's eyes blinked rapidly against the dust their horses' hooves were churning up, and the muscles in his jaw were visibly taut. Behind the three Daltons Power and Broadwell, enveloped in a cloud of yellow dust, were making nervous jokes to each other. Grat examined his own feelings and found a queasiness that he attributed more to nervous anticipation than fear. Still, at the back of his mind lurked a premonition of disaster, but he consciously forced it away and closed a mental door on it. There was no longer time to think about things; there was only the time to act.

They had entered the outskirts of the city, and Grat scanned the houses as they rode past. Several people looked up from their yards or porches at the five strangers on horseback, but no one showed any signs of alarm. All five men had their suit coats buttoned to cover their pistol belts, and their Winchesters were put away in their saddle scabbards. Bob had told them that people would think they were marshals riding in from the territory. Bob's prediction was accurate, and that realization gave Grat a more positive outlook on the coming activities.

Once they were within the Coffeyville city limits, the road they were on had become Eighth Street, and soon they approached the Episcopal Church, at the intersection with Maple Street.

"Oh, hell!" Bob grumbled, stretching up in his saddle to see better. Grat's hand jerked to his hip; he fumbled with his coat tail, trying to reach his pistol. Then he, too, saw what had upset Bob, and he settled himself down. All of Eighth Street between Maple and Walnut was an obstacle course, with gaping holes and piles of rock and dirt. Several Negro laborers were working in the street, digging with shovels and carrying stones in wheelbarrows. The hitching rails on both sides of the street were gone, and the street itself was impassable. Only the covered sidewalks were clear.

Grat wondered what they would do now, for they were already entering the intersection with Maple, and had to either turn or stop. Reacting decisively, Bob said, "Take a right."

Without hesitation, and without breaking formation, the five men wheeled their horses south on Maple. The Long-Bell lumber yard on their left occupied the entire northwest corner of the block, from Eighth halfway to Ninth. When they reached the south end of the lumber yard, Bob simply said, "The alley," and all five turned left. The alleyway provided access to the rear of the businesses on Eighth and Ninth Streets; its eastern end opened onto the plaza.

Across from the back of the lumber yard was an empty lot with a split-rail fence around it. Following Bob's lead, Grat and the others halted, dismounted, and tied their horses to the fence. Each took his rifle from its scabbard and checked its operation. Bob pulled a couple two-bushel grain sacks out of his saddle bags and handed one to Grat. Grat held the rolled-up burlap sack in his right hand, and his Winchester hung from his left. He was ready. Bob gave each man a quick visual inspection, and nodded in mute approval. When Bob jerked his head to the side, they all began walking down the alley.

Each man knew where he was supposed to be, so they shuffled around like a square dance team until Grat, Broadwell, and Power were walking abreast in front, with Bob and Emmett directly behind them. Grat kept his eyes scanning from left to right for signs of danger. The unpaved alley was quiet and almost deserted. The buildings which fronted on Eighth and Ninth Streets were not uniform in size or depth, so the width of the alley varied from ten to thirty feet. Behind some of the stores were sheds, barns, and stables, and in the middle of the alley, on the south side, was the small city jail, a tiny stone building that appeared to be empty. On the ground in front of the jail was a large pile of paving stones, and picking through them was one of the black laborers. He briefly glanced at the passing Dalton gang without interest.

Just past the jail, parked in the center of the alley, was an oil tanker, its two-horse team still hitched to it. The five men veered around it, arriving at the alley's exit onto the plaza, a narrow passage between two tall brick buildings. On the left was McKenna's Dry Goods store, whose front faced the Condon Bank. On the right was Slosson's Drug Store, which had an outside wooden staircase leading up from the alley to the second floor. Like many of the buildings on the plaza, both stores were two stories tall, solidly constructed of the dark red bricks that were manufactured just north of town.

Bill Power and Dick Broadwell moved closer to Grat, keeping formation in the confining passageway. Ahead, out on the plaza, Grat could now see the Condon Bank on the left. Directly across the plaza was Isham's Hardware, with its huge plate glass windows flanked by tall, narrow doors with full-length glass in them. Through the reflections on the glass Grat could dimly make out the shapes of stoves and farm implements on display. One door up from Isham's was the modest First National Bank. All of the buildings on the plaza had wide elevated brick sidewalks, and over these sidewalks were equally wide wooden awnings supported by metal poles.

Exiting the alley, Grat noted with concern that the plaza was very busy for a Wednesday morning. The sidewalks were teeming with people, and several wagons were parked in front of Boswell's General Store, two doors down from Slosson's. Glancing back to his left, Grat recognized Aleck McKenna standing on the sidewalk in front of his store. McKenna gave the group a cursory look, and then did a curious double-take, staring hard at Grat. Grat turned his face away and increased his pace. Directly ahead was the Condon.

The C. M. Condon & Co. building had been erected in 1890, forming a prominent focal point in the center of the plaza. The southern end of the building was the bank proper, and its floor plan resembled the lower half of an octagon. Facing the plaza were two huge plate-glass windows; on either side of these windows were the doors, which faced southeast and southwest respectively. The brick building was decorated with pseudo-classical stone facings, and it was topped with a gingerbread overhanging façade. Despite its small size, the bank building made a strong impression.

Stepping up onto the sidewalk at the corner of the bank, Grat paused to take one last look around. McKenna continued to watch them with a puzzled frown, but no one else seemed to have taken any special interest in them. Power and Broadwell joined him under the awning, while Bob and Emmett continued on across the plaza to the First National. The clock was now ticking.

A bell tinkled as Grat pushed open the southwest door and stepped inside, and he was pleased to see that there were no customers in the bank. A wedge-shaped counter, made to match the floor plan, dominated the lobby. Grat could see only one man working behind the metal screen that rose up from the counter, and he did not look up when they entered. Grat pointed his rifle at the man while Power and Broadwell, pulling their bandannas up over their noses, spread out behind him and shut the door. Power stayed at the southwest entrance, his back against the door frame, while Broadwell took a similar position at the opposite door.

Finally reacting to the clump of their boot heels, the man in the cage raised his head and assumed a pleasant expression, expecting to be greeting customers. His face fell and his jaw dropped open when he saw the rifles pointed at him.

"We've got you, God damn you!" Grat roared, intending to cow him into submission. "Hold up your hands!" Quickly the man obeyed, his eyes wide with terror. From his fine suit and tie, Grat figured the man was the bank manager.

The left end of the counter abutted a tiny office with two entrances, one from the lobby and the other providing access to the cage area behind the counter. There was a rustle of paper, and then a dapper young man with a receding hairline rushed out of the office into the cage. He stopped short when he saw Grat.

"You, too," Grat ordered, motioning with his rifle at the new arrival. The cashier raised his hands as well, but his demeanor remained calm and assured. Grat ran through the cashier's office, dodging a heavy wooden desk, and confronted the two bankers in the cage.

“Hold this open,” he commanded the cashier, shoving the grain sack into the man’s hands. The cashier fumbled a few seconds as he unrolled the sack and found its opening.

“Fill it,” Grat told the manager. Moving cautiously, his eyes transfixed by Grat’s rifle, the trembling man opened the cash drawer and began emptying it into the sack. When he was done he raised his hands again, which were now quivering like leaves in a high wind.

“Where’s your gold?” Grat scowled at both men. The manager, with his hands raised, just shook his head.

The cashier, still holding the sack, blithely said, “We don’t have any.”

“Horse shit,” Grat grumbled. “Get in the vault.” At the back of the cage was a metal door leading into the brick vault room. Pushing the two bankers ahead of him, Grat went through the narrow metal door frame into a cramped room furnished only with a bookcase, a tall double-door safe, and a smaller combination safe. As they crowded into the room, Grat spied a young man vainly trying to hide behind the bookcase.

“Come out of there, you bastard!” Grat yelled at the man, kicking at his exposed buttocks. “You stupid son of a bitch! Are you trying to get killed?” Meekly the bookkeeper straightened up and shuffled over to join the cashier and his manager.

The doors for the large safe stood open, and inside were three large canvas money bags. Pointing his rifle at the manager, he said, “Empty those bags into the sack.” The cashier held open the gunny sack as the manager did as he was told.

“What is that you’re putting in there?” Grat asked, curious about how much they were getting.

“Silver dollars,” the cashier answered. By the time the last bag had been dumped into the sack, the cashier had to bend over and rest the bottom of the sack on the floor, so heavy had it become with all that silver.

Grat leaned down to make sure the big safe had been thoroughly cleaned out of anything valuable, then straightened and gestured toward the small chest. "Open up the door," he said.

"It's not time for that to open," the cashier responded blandly. Grat was aware that some bank safes had time locks, but he had never seen one before.

"What time does it open?" he demanded.

"Half past nine o'clock."

"What time is it now?"

The cashier pulled his pocket watch from his vest and looked at it. "Twenty minutes after nine."

This was an unexpected problem. Grat pondered his options. So far the take had been nothing to brag about, probably no more than a couple thousand from the cash drawer and a thousand from the silver in the safe, at most. Visible through the narrow vault door was Power, nervously waiting by the outside door. There were still no customers in the bank, and no alarm had been raised. Grat made an impetuous—and fateful—decision.

"We can wait ten minutes," he told the bankers.

The First National Bank of Coffeyville was a single-story brick building, with double doors flanked by plate-glass windows. When Bob and Emmett entered there were three customers standing in the lobby area. As Emmett closed the door behind him, another customer tried to follow him in, pushing the doorknob against Emmett's hand. The man was halfway through the door before he saw Emmett's rifle and stopped in mid-stride. Emmett motioned him on in with the rifle, then closed and latched the door. Bob aimed his rifle at the cashier in the counter window, a man named Tom Ayres that Emmett had known for years.

"Everyone throw up your hands!" Bob shouted. "Stay right where you are and don't move." Arms shot into the air around the room. It was like the gunshot that starts a horse race. Emmett realized that there was no going back. A thrill coursed through his body, and suddenly he had boundless energy.

"You heard him, you bastards!" Emmett screamed with a rising pitch, cocking his rifle and waving it around menacingly. "I'll kill anybody that moves!"

Emmett was surprised at his own ferocity, but gratified by the frightened responses it caused. He moved over closer to the counter, so that he could cover both the cashier and the customers. This allowed him to see a teller sitting at a desk near the vault, his hands high above his head.

"Watch 'em," Bob told Emmett, and ran down the short hallway to the right of the counter. In a moment he was back, pushing ahead of him another young man. It was Tom Ayres' son Bert, the bookkeeper. Bob shoved Bert into the area behind the counter and thrust the grain sack at him. "Fill it up," he barked. Bert took the sack and walked over to the counter. Mechanically he lifted the money from the counter and the cash drawer and lowered it into the burlap sack.

"Hurry up, God damn it!" Emmett screeched at him. "I'd just as soon shoot you as look at you!" Bert began to tremble, but his movements remained slow as he finished his task. He turned to Bob and held out the sack.

"Now get the money in the safe," Bob told him gently.

"I don't know the combination," Bert said plaintively.

Bob turned to the cashier. "Tom, you go and get it." Tom Ayres, startled by the use of his name, searched Bob's disguised face for a moment, and then opened his eyes wide in recognition. The corners of his mouth tilted up in a barely perceptible smile, and he nodded and went into the vault. He came back out with his hands full of money and dropped the bundles into the sack that his son held open for him.

"Is that all of it?" Bob asked calmly.

"There's some gold in the vault," Tom answered. "Do you want that, too?"

“Yes,” Bob said impatiently, “every damn cent of it.” Tom returned to the vault, and came back out with a heavy bag of coins that he dropped into the gunny sack.

“Is that for sure all of it now?” Bob asked for the second time.

“That’s it,” Tom assured him. Tom’s eyes were darting around, and he licked his lips to moisten them.

“I’ll check,” Bob said, walking into the vault himself. He came back out holding two stacks of bills. “What’s this?” he said accusingly, shaking his head in disgust. He tossed them into the sack, and went back into the vault. Emmett heard him rummaging around in the safe. He brought a locked metal box to the vault door and asked what was in it. Tom Ayres told him it was important papers, so Bob put it back. He came out of the vault and took the bulging sack from Bert Ayres shaky grasp.

“Tie this up,” he told Emmett, tossing it over the counter. Emmett was fumbling with the string, pleased that the robbery had gone without a hitch, when he heard the first gunshots.

In the Condon vault Grat fidgeted as he waited for the time lock to open. The manager was sweating, and he kept shooting worried glances at the cashier. The cashier, on the other hand, was calmly watching Grat, with perhaps a hint of a smile. In a flash it dawned on Grat that he had been fooled by one of the oldest tricks in the book.

“God damn you!” he swore at the cashier. “You’re lying through your teeth! I’ve half a mind to put a bullet through you. Now open that chest.” This last command was directed at the manager, and Grat emphasized it by roughly poking the man in the stomach with the barrel of his rifle.

On wobbly legs the manager tottered over to the chest and crouched down beside it. He grasped the locking handle and pushed it down, but the door remained close. “See?” the manager squeaked, pleading with his eyes.

“Where’s your gold?” Grat demanded again, his ire rising to the boiling point.

“We haven’t any,” the cashier smugly replied. Grat nudged the grain sack sitting at the cashier’s feet with his rifle. “How much is in this sack?”

“Four thousand dollars.”

“How much cash did your books show last night?”

“Four thousand dollars,” the cashier answered. His tone became more cooperative, as if he were explaining accounting procedures to a customer who was overdrawn on his checkbook. “One thousand dollars in currency, and three thousand dollars in silver, all of which you have in your sack. There’s nothing in the burglarproof chest except some nickels and pennies. We ordered some currency, but it hasn’t been delivered yet; it’s over in the express office.”

Suddenly there were voices and the sound of a scuffle out front. Grat stepped backward and leaned through the vault door to take a look. Two customers had come in through the southwest door, and Bill Power had swiftly corralled them, backing them against the counter with their hands raised. Reassured that Power had the situation under control, Grat had just turned back to the bank employees when the tomb-like silence of the bank was shattered by the crack of gunfire and breaking glass. Grat ducked automatically, and scuttled out of the vault to the counter, surveying the situation with a hasty scan through the big windows that were already pockmarked with bullet holes.

Someone out on the plaza—several someones, in fact—were firing at the bank from hidden positions. Broadwell and Power were trying to make themselves thinner behind the narrow doorposts, occasionally returning fire by poking their rifles through the jagged holes that had suddenly appeared in the glass panes of the doors. The newly arrived customers had dropped to the floor and covered their heads with their hands.

There was movement behind the wagons parked at Boswell’s store, and puffs of smoke from across the plaza at Isham’s Hardware. With evil pops new holes appeared in the windows, the glass spidering around them. A bullet thunked into the wooden counter not far from Grat’s head.

Grat poked his rifle through the teller's window grill and fired at the wagon, but the figure had already taken cover. Power and Broadwell also were shooting, blasting away in different directions at a number of targets. The roar of the gunfire was deafening, and the smell of gunpowder and fear permeated the small room.

Keeping low, Grat scuttled back into the vault, where he found the bank employees huddled together in the corner, out of the line of fire.

"Is there a back door?" Grat yelled over the noise.

"No," the cashier answered.

Grat leaned against the inside door jam, his mind churning as he searched for a solution. They could not stay where they were; for their attackers it was like shooting fish in a barrel. The longer they waited to escape, the harder it would be.

"Take the sack!" Grat ordered the manager. The man's eyes bugged out in fright, and he was shaking like an epileptic. He grabbed the neck of the sack and pulled, but his knees buckled under the weight, and despite frantic struggling he was unable to lift it from the floor. Desperately he began dragging the bag across the wooden floor in short, stumbling jerks. With a look somewhere between pity and disdain, the clean-cut cashier grabbed the bottom of the sack and began helping the manager.

"Out front," Grat directed them, following close behind them. The bookkeeper, thankful he was not needed, stayed cowering in the corner.

The three men were bent over as they bolted from the vault, turned right, and crab-walked into the cashier's office. Grat bullied them around the desk and into the short hallway beside the counter, but there they were met with a hail of bullets. Cracking through the air and slamming into the woodwork, the deadly slugs scared the bankers far more than Grat had. Panic-stricken, they dropped the money sack and pushed Grat back into the office, where all three squatted, taking shelter behind the door and desk. Grat again rack his brain for some practical solution, but his thoughts were a jumble. Then he heard a yelp from out front.

"I'm shot!" Bill Power cried with surprise. "I can't use my arm!"

Grat peered around the door frame and saw Power clutching his left arm. His right hand still held his Winchester, and blood smeared the wooden stock and the fingers that gripped it. Grat turned and glared at the cashier. "Go get the sack!" he snarled.

Flinching at the continued gunfire, the cashier crawled forward on his hands and knees to the office doorway, stretched out his hand, and hastily dragged the bag into the office as he shuffled backward.

"Dump it out," Grat told him. The man pulled a small pocket knife from his pants and cut the string tying the mouth of the sack. Grasping the bottom seam, he lifted until all the coins and currency spilled on the floor; some silver dollars rolled away unnoticed beneath the desk. Ignoring the coins, Grat grabbed the stacks of currency and stuffed them inside his vest. He paused to prepare himself. He took a deep breath, held his rifle in both hands, and sprang into a run for the front doors.

"Let's get out of here!" he yelled at Power and Broadwell as he jerked the door open on a dead run. Bullets snapped all around him as he sprinted across the sidewalk and onto the street. He did not look around to see if his partners had followed; instead, he pumped lead from his rifle at any suspicious location. Ahead of him was the narrow opening of the alley. If he could make it to there, he thought, he would be safe; the brick buildings would shield him from his assailants while he ran to the horses. He could hear Power and Broadwell right behind him, shouting and shooting. Miraculously Grat made it to the sanctuary of the alley, and it was like ducking into a barn in a hailstorm. With a wave of relief he spied the horses still waiting at the far end of the alley, and he lengthened his stride. That was the moment when he felt the hammer-blow of a bullet striking him in the back.

At the first sound of gunshots, Emmett's stomach lurched like it had been clutched with an iron fist. Through the First National's front glass he could see the windows on the Condon bank being shattered, and he briefly exulted when a Winchester's barrel poke out and barked an angry reply. At least they aren't shooting at us, he said to himself, wincing with guilt when he remembered that it was his brother and friends who were drawing all the fire.

Bob, unfazed, herded the three bank employees out from behind the counter into the front lobby.

"All right," Bob yelled above the din, "everybody out the front door. Now!" He waved his rifle at the customers and bankers, who obediently crowded toward the door but hesitated about actually going through it. Finally someone turned the knob and the door swung open; like water from a broken dam, the customers stumbled out on the sidewalk and turned left, holding their hands up and pleading at the top of their lungs not to be shot. Emmett and Bob were close behind the three bank employees, who paused as they reached the doorway to observe the fate of the customers. Over their shoulders Emmett got a better view of the plaza.

"Look out there to the left," he warned Bob. He had seen someone raise his head up from behind a wagon parked across the plaza in front of Boswell's. Bert Ayres and the teller each had Bob's and Emmett's rifles pressed into their backs, so they eased slowly out onto the sidewalk as the Daltons used them as shields. Tom Ayres, in the lead, broke away and ran down the sidewalk to the left, ducking into the doorway of Isham's Hardware. At the same time there were two blasts from a rifle somewhere nearby, and Emmett felt the bullets zip past his face. Bob and Emmett both jumped back into the bank, and the two young bankers tumbled in after them.

Emmett belatedly realized he had not finished tying the money sack as Bob had requested, and suddenly that little detail was of utmost importance. Draping the rifle over his forearm and pressing the stock against his side with his upper arm, he concentrated on the unusually difficult task of tying a square knot. At the door, Bob leaned forward to take a quick look, then raised his Winchester to his shoulder and snapped off a quick shot to the left. He turned to the two bank employees and said simply, "The back door." With the bankers leading the way, all four rushed down the hall to the back of the bank. They halted in a bunch around the blank-faced door that led into the back alley.

"Open it," Bob ordered the teller. The young man released the bolt and pushed the door wide, stepping down onto a small platform to hold the door open for the robbers. Bert Ayres flattened against the wall of the hallway to let the Daltons past. Bob and Emmett plunged out into the alley, their eyes flicking back and forth searching for potential danger. It was not long in appearing.

The bank building did not extend as far back as its neighbors, whose walls stretched on either side about twenty feet farther toward the railroad tracks. Emmett was right behind Bob as they moved away from the rear of the bank, when suddenly a young man came running around the back corner of Isham's Hardware on the right. Sporting his first mustache and wearing a suit with a bow tie, he carried a pistol down at his side. There was a look of anticipation on his face, and he smiled when he spied the three men at the back door of the bank.

"Stop!" Bob and Emmett shouted simultaneously, raising their rifles in warning. There was a flicker of confusion in the young man's eyes, and he slowed, but he kept coming toward them. Silently Emmett willed the man to halt, but to no avail.

"I'll have to get that man," Bob muttered with obvious reluctance. Grimly he fired his rifle from the hip, and with a stunned look of incomprehension the young man stumbled backward and fell to the ground.

"Come on!" Bob barked at Emmett, sprinting toward the north end of the alley. After a moment's hesitation while he stared at the pool of blood forming around the fallen man, Emmett took off behind him.

They met no one else in the alley, nor was there anyone in sight when they reached Eighth Street. Making a sharp left, they trotted up to the front corner of Mahan's and Custer's, the northernmost store on the block. The rattle of gunfire was still intense on the plaza as Bob sneaked a glance around the front of the building, giving him a clear view of the plaza down Union Street. He looked back and gave Emmett a wink, saying, "You hold the bag, and I'll do the fighting. Go on down Eighth Street to Maple. I'll be right behind you. Now take off."

Clutching the bag to his chest with his left arm, the Winchester dangling from his right, Emmett broke into a run across Union and leaped up onto the brick sidewalk that fronted the opera house at the north end of the Condon bank building. There were rifle shots behind him, and once he was protected by the corner of the building, he turned and looked back. Bob still stood at the end of the sidewalk on the other side of Union, firing the last of four rapid shots at an armed man in front of Rammel's drug store, one door up from the First National. When the man dropped his rifle and collapsed on the bricks, Emmett recognized him as George Cubine, a well-known bootmaker. Things were quickly going to hell in a handbasket.

Bob began side-stepping across the street toward Emmett, keeping his rifle ready and scanning for other guns. Emmett watched helplessly when old Charles Brown, a shoemaker from Cubine's shop, darted out and picked up the rifle Cubine had dropped. Bob saw it, too, and before Brown could raise the gun to his shoulder Bob cranked off four more rounds. The old man crumpled next to Cubine and lay still. Bob caught up to Emmett and frowned at him impatiently.

"Go!" Bob said, and Emmett did, hurrying down the sidewalk toward Walnut Street. Behind him Bob took a last shot down Union, and then ran to catch up with his brother. Together they dashed across Walnut, safely attaining the shelter of Mitchell & Ulm's restaurant on the corner, and kept on running down Eighth Street. The normally busy shopping street was empty; at the sound of gunfire people had fled indoors. Emmett hoped the alley would be the same.

By the time they reached Maple Street, Bob had taken the lead, and Emmett noticed that somewhere Bob had discarded his false beard and mustache. With his hands holding the money and his rifle, Emmett was unable to remove his own disguise. They rounded the corner of the Long-Bell lumber yard office, ran south past the open sheds stacked with boards, and cut back into the alley where the horses were tied. While Emmett secured the money sack to the pommel of his horse's saddle, Bob scanned back and forth down the alley while he methodically and efficiently pulled rifle cartridges from his belt and slammed them into the Winchester.

At the far end of the alley, around the oil tanker and through the narrow opening between McKenna's and Slosson's, Emmett could see only the front windows and doors of Isham's Hardware, but there seemed to be furtive movements behind the appliances. The steady rattle of gunfire popped and echoed from the plaza, and Emmett could not control his flinching with each shot.

"What's the matter with the boys?" Bob muttered anxiously, sliding the final round into his gun. "What's taking them so long?" He glanced over at Emmett, who had just finished tying the sack on his horse. "I guess they're having a hot time of it," Bob told him grimly. "Guess we'd better get back there and get them out."

Emmett nodded, but when Bob strode away purposefully toward the other end of the alley, Emmett followed him with great trepidation. Trotting cautiously down the alley, they stayed close to the back walls of the buildings on the north side, unseen by the riflemen on the plaza. With both hands tightly gripping his rifle, Emmett trailed right behind Bob, praying that no one would see them and that Grat and the others would suddenly appear in the alley so they could go back to the horses and ride away. Irrationally he blamed Grat for the danger they were in. Grat's unexplained delay was risking all their lives, just at what should have been their moment of triumph. Emmett's thoughts were interrupted when Bob stopped short, causing Emmett to stumble to avoid running into him.

A teenage boy had jumped out in front of them, emerging from the back door of one of the stores that faced Eighth Street. In his hand was a small pistol, a .22 caliber revolver. He had apparently intended to go down the alley toward the plaza, but when he saw Bob and Emmett he stopped, staring at them in wide-eyed confusion.

"What are you fellas doin' here?" he asked, showing no trace of fear.

Bob tapped the boy on the head with the barrel of his rifle. "Run home, boy, or you'll get hurt," he said with a short laugh. Comprehension dawned on the boy's face. He turned to run back into the store, and Bob paddled his bottom with the stock of his rifle to hurry him along. When the door closed behind him, the Daltons resumed stalking down the alley. The boy's sudden appearance had put Emmett's heart in his throat, and he forced himself to be calm as he scampered after Bob.

At the back of McKenna's Dry Goods was a passageway that led north between the buildings to Eighth Street. Bob took a quick glance down the narrow opening to ensure it was clear, and edged forward to the alleyway leading to the plaza. Just as Bob reach the back corner of McKenna's, the level of gunfire out on the plaza rose to a crescendo, and Emmett knew that Grat, Power, and Broadwell must be making a break for it. For some reason Bob looked up and rapidly raised his rifle to his shoulder. Emmett followed Bob's aim and saw a man climbing out a back window on the second floor of Slosson's with a rifle in his hand. Bob snapped off a quick shot, and the window frame splintered, driving the man back inside.

Pressed against the side of a small shed near the pass-through to Eighth, Emmett had only a partial view of the brick-walled passage between Slosson's and McKenna's. There were shouts and footsteps barely audible over the roar of the guns, and the next instant Broadwell appeared, his legs pumping as he sprinted through the gap and around the parked oil tanker. Right behind him came Grat and Power, but both men were pausing every few steps to fire back at targets in the plaza behind them. Bob jumped out into the middle of the alley to join them, his head back as he scanned the rooftops for snipers.

Thinking they were now making their getaway, Emmett ran a few steps back up the alley in pursuit of Broadwell, but then he slowed to see if the others were following. Just as he looked back Bob staggered backwards and sat down hard on a pile of paving stones on the south side of the alley. Power was scrambling for refuge in an alley entrance to McKenna's store, but the threshold was too shallow to offer any real protection, and the door refused to open. With a wet spot spreading across his back, Power pounded at the door while bullets thudded into the wooden door frame or ricocheted off the brickwork beside him. Shrinking back against the stone wall of a store, Emmett watched in horror as Power pushed away from the door and ran haltingly up the alley, desperately trying to escape the rain of bullets.

Grat had momentarily taken cover behind the oil tanker, but immediately scuttled across the alley to the front of a barn on the south side, about halfway to the horses. The wooden stairway on the side of Slosson's shielded Grat from the withering fire that Emmett now realized was coming from Isham's Hardware, but as Grat edged along the barn, he left a red smear on the weathered wood.

Emmett backed down the alley, transfixed by the terrible scene unfolding before him. He glanced toward the horses and saw Power sprawled lifelessly on the ground a few yards short of his goal. He could not see Broadwell anywhere. Emmett felt like he was trapped in a barrel of molasses, his every movement labored and slow. Back to his left Bob was still firing from a sitting position, but red splotches discolored the yellow stones on which he reclined. The staccato blasts of the guns had merged into a continuous roar, and there were puffs of dust and flying splinters as the bullets crisscrossed the narrow alley in a deadly fusillade.

Bob staggered to his feet, and Emmett felt a surge of hope. Grat was also moving now, and both began stumbling toward the horses. Emmett turned and ran in the same direction, keeping to the north side of the alley, out of the line of fire. At last, Emmett thought feverishly, they were going to make it. He sprinted down the alley and jumped behind a pile of boards at the lumber yard, and he was surprised to find Broadwell there already. Broadwell, lying in the dirt with his rifle beside him, looked up at Emmett hopefully. His hands were bloody, and his sleeve was wet with crimson stains.

Emmett popped his head up to look back down the alley, and his stomach clenched. There was no longer any visible movement. Bob and Grat were both sprawled on the ground, only feet from where Emmett had seen them last. Between them, on his back and moaning as he clutched his stomach, was town marshal Connelly. Emmett had no idea where he had come from.

It took Emmett a moment to realize that the shooting had stopped. Broadwell was faster to realize the significance of this fact, and without a word he scrambled up and ran to his horse, leaving his rifle behind. With only a second's hesitation, Emmett followed him, abandoning his own rifle as well. They were met with a hail of renewed gunfire. Even before he reached the horses, which were only ten feet away, a bullet slammed into Emmett's hip. He stumbled but kept upright; a numbness began rapidly spreading throughout his body as he pushed between the horses to the hitching rail and struggled to untie his horse. Temporarily shielded by Bob's and Power's horses, he finally worked the knot loose and threw himself up into the saddle. Mortally wounded by the rain of lead hurled down the alley, Power's horse collapsed on its side, and next to Emmett Bob's horse sank to its knees with a pitiful scream.

Broadwell had managed to mount up faster than Emmett, and he was already galloping out the alley onto Maple before Emmett was ready to ride. Emmett saw Broadwell's back convulse as another bullet struck home, and then he was out of sight, leaving Emmett all alone with bullets buzzing around him like hornets. He pulled on the right rein to point his own horse west when another slug struck his right arm, shattering the bone. He vainly squinted down the alley for the source of the bullet, and saw to his amazement that Bob was still alive. He had crawled back to the pile of rocks and taken cover behind it, leaning on one of the stones for support.

Emmett's mind raced as he weighed the alternatives. He could turn and ride away, carrying all the money, but where would that get him? He had always depended on Bob, and now, for the first time, Bob was depending on him. The decision was made in an instant. Swinging his horse on around, he spurred it into a gallop down the alley. The pain from his wounds was growing, gnawing away at his strength, but he had only one thought in mind. He was totally focused on rescuing Bob, and he was almost oblivious to the stream of bullets zipping past him.

When he reach Bob he wheeled his horse around, presenting his back to the alley's plaza exit, and with his left arm he reached down toward his brother. Weakly Bob raised a bloody hand a few inches and smiled sadly at Emmett.

"It's no use," he croaked, and his hand dropped limply to the ground. Unwilling to concede defeat, Emmett leaned over farther, off balance because his shattered right arm was useless. His fingers were stretched toward Bob's collar when the popping of rifles was drowned out by a tremendous boom close behind him, and instantly his back felt like it was on fire. Emmett felt himself falling forward, sliding headlong from the saddle to crumple face down on the ground next to Bob.

He had to save his brother. That thought kept recurring to Emmett, but for some reason he felt sleepy. He should have gotten more sleep the night before, he decided, and cursed his own stupidity. Beside him Bob gurgled. Emmett turned his head, dragging his nose through the dust, and saw Bob's pale face only inches away. With his mouth open and his eyelids drooping, Bob expired, a last whistle of air escaping from his lungs.

The guns had stopped, and Emmett's ears rang in the ensuing silence. As from a great distance he heard someone shout, "They're all down."

Emmett gradually became aware that men had gathered around him, but their voices merged into a garbled hubbub. He could also hear women weeping, children shrieking, and wounded horses whinnying in terror.

"Hold up your hands!" someone yelled at him. With his right cheek pressed into the dirt, Emmett could only see shoes and boots, but then a rifle barrel was waved in his face. Summoning all his strength, he raised his left hand in a feeble show of surrender.

"No, please," he moaned pitifully.

"Let's hang the son of a bitch!" a vicious voice suggested, and another responded, "Yeah, get a rope!"

Other, calmer voices, opposed this move, much to Emmett's relief. Roughly someone grabbed his shoulder and rolled him over on his back, as other hands pulled his pistols out of their holsters and tore away his false beard.

"Who are you?" a man demanded.

"Charley McLaughlin," Emmett lied.

"This one's Bob Dalton," a man announced authoritatively, nudging Bob's body with the toe of his boot.

"This is Grat Dalton over here," Someone called from a few feet away.

"I'll bet you this one is Emmett," one of the men said, looking down at Emmett, who was squinting against the sun. Emmett wiggled his head back and forth in denial.

"Don't matter. Let's get him to a doctor."

"Why? Let's just let him die, the bastard."

"We can't do that."

"Yeah, we'll have a trial, and then we'll hang him."

"I've got some questions I'd like to ask him."

"Come on, someone grab his feet."

Emmett felt himself being lifted, and the pain was so excruciating that his tenuous hold on consciousness slipped away completely.

Author's Notes

Chapter 16

Naturally enough, the *Coffeyville Journal* devoted almost its entire next issue, on October 7, 1892, to the Dalton raid, complete with a map and detailed descriptions of all the events. David Stewart Elliott, the newspaper's editor, also published a small book only weeks later called *The Last Raid of the Daltons*, which gave an even more vivid description. In 1903 the *History of Montgomery County, Kansas* was published which included a section on the raid, which was still fresh in the minds of Coffeyville residents. This account drew heavily from Stewart's book, as was acknowledged in the text. All of these sources are virtually identical in their recounting of events; Emmett's book, *Beyond the Law*, diverges somewhat, but not significantly. Emmett, of course, had a different perspective, and he wrote his account sixteen years later, so variations are to be expected.

What Emmett and the other members of the gang did not know at the time was that Aleck McKenna had recognized Grat's walk and the peculiar shape of his head, and he immediately alerted the other citizens of the town. Isham and Boswell handed out new Winchesters and cartridges, and the citizens, thinking that only the Condon was being robbed, took up positions on the south side of the plaza. In the subsequent gun battle, four of the armed Coffeyville defenders died, and several were wounded, but no innocent bystanders were hit at all. Ironically, if the gang had been able to tie their horses on Eighth Street as Bob had originally intended, they would probably not have been recognized, and could have easily made their getaway.

Death Alley, as it is now known, is partially preserved as it was. Visitors to Coffeyville can walk the plaza, view the restored Condon Bank building, shop at Isham's Hardware, and walk down the alley where the gang was slaughtered. Bullet holes are still visible in the brick walls, and outlines of the fallen outlaws are painted on the pavement that passes in front of the original jail.

Nearby, not far from where Bob shot young Lucius Baldwin behind the First National, is the Dalton Defenders Museum.

CHAPTER 16

Wednesday Evening, October 5, 1892

Dr. Wells made one last check of the bandages and the splint on Emmett's right arm before pulling the blanket up to his chin. "Thanks," Emmett whispered with heart-felt gratitude. The doctor had been unexpectedly gentle while treating Emmett's wounds; from the way the townspeople had talked as they carried him to Dr. Wells' office, Emmett had feared the doctor would share their fury and handle him brutally. Not that he would really have blamed the doctor, for the people of Coffeyville had reason to be upset.

During the several hours it had taken to remove the buckshot from Emmett's back and dress all his wounds, visitors to the doctor's office had curtly informed him that four Coffeyville citizens had died in the gun battle, and two others had been wounded. The young man Bob had shot behind the First National was a store clerk named Lucius Baldwin, and he had died three hours after the battle. As a result of Bob's accurate fire down Union, George Cubine had been dead when he hit the sidewalk in front of Rammel's drug store, and old Charles Brown, who had picked up Cubine's rifle, had died in agony only three hours later. Emmett was told that Grat had shot Marshal Connelly in the alley just before he himself was killed, and the marshal had outlived his murderer by only minutes. Bob had promised that no one would get hurt in the raid, but instead it had taken a terrible toll. It was natural that the citizens would hold Emmett responsible for the appalling loss of life.

Tom Callahan, the Montgomery County sheriff, had arrived from Independence to take charge of things. He stood mutely at the end of Emmett's bed, waiting for the doctor to finish. Apparently he held no personal animosity toward Emmett, since he had occasionally smiled encouragingly at him as the doctor had applied the bandages. Dr. Wells nodded at Callahan and began gathering up his tools and left-over gauze.

"You feel up to answering some questions, boy?" Callahan asked. The sheriff was a tall man with a small mustache. He wore his badge on the vest of his brown suit, and he had a wide tie knotted thickly at the neck of a white shirt. Emmett wanted to say he was too weak, but he also wanted to get it over with. Besides, if he refused to cooperate, they might go ahead and carry out the threatened lynching. He nodded to the sheriff, swallowing hard.

Callahan went to the door of the small operating room and opened it about a foot. The hall outside was jammed with men, all of whom seemed to be talking at once. Callahan pointed at three men. "You two and the reporter can come in," Callahan told them, raising his voice to be heard over the din. "The rest of you hold it down out here. We're going to be doing some questioning, and I want to be able to hear myself think." The voices subsided to a low murmur. The three designated witnesses shoved their way forward and squeezed through the half-open door to gather in a semi-circle near Emmett's bed and stared at him in undisguised curiosity. Emmett felt like an exhibit at a freak show. Embarrassed, he turned his head to look at the wall.

"Bring in the first one," Callahan called out through the door that he was still holding partially open. There was a scuffling in the hallway, accompanied by impatient suggestions for everyone to get out of the way. Emmett rolled his head back to see what was going on. Two men were struggling to bring a corpse into the room, one man backing in holding the body's arms, and the other with his hands under its knees. When they reached the foot of the bed they unceremoniously dropped the cadaver on the floor, out of Emmett's sight. Bending down to get a different grip, they raised the lifeless form to a standing position, grasping its arms to hold the limp body erect. Emmett gulped and struggled to catch his breath. It was his brother Bob.

Bob's hands were tied in front of him, and his shirt was torn and bloody. Large patches of cloth had been ripped from the cuffs of his pants, presumably by souvenir hunters, and his belt, hat, and boots were all missing. His eyes were closed and his mouth was slightly open, as if he were about to speak. Emmett's eyes burned from trying to hold back the tears, and his throat ached with stifled moans.

"Can you identify this man?" Callahan asked.

His voice quavering, Emmett answered, "I identify that as my brother, Bob Dalton." He squeezed his eyes shut and turned his head to the wall again as Bob's body was lowered back to the floor.

"How old was he?" Callahan asked gently.

Emmett sniffed and turned back to face the room. The reporter was scratching away at a notebook with a pencil, while the other two strangers stared at Bob's body in morbid fascination. "Twenty-three," Emmett said, gradually regaining his composure. "Turned twenty-three last May thirteenth."

"And he did all those train robberies in the territories?"

Emmett coughed to gain time while he thought about what he would say. He concluded there was no reason to implicate himself any more than was unavoidable. "I guess so," he finally said. "I haven't been with my brothers for a year and a half, at least not until the first of October. That's when I met up with them down south of Tulsa in the territory. Bob told me then that he was in the Adair robbery. I believe he said he was in the California robbery in January of 1890, too."

"Who was with him in the Adair robbery?"

"That would have been Grat, Tom Evans, and Jake Moore."

As Emmett talked, Bob's body was carried back out and another brought in. When they stood the second corpse up, its head flopped unnaturally. One of the men grabbed the dead man's hair and pulled his head up so Emmett could see his face. It was Grat. A hole in his Adam's apple showed that a bullet had broken his neck. Like Bob, his hands were tied, and his boots, hat, and belt were missing. Emmett sobbed and turned his face away, trying to bury it in the pillow. Gathering his strength, he finally looked back around, and was relieved to see that Grat's body had been laid down again where he could not see it.

"That's Gratton Dalton, my brother," he admitted.

"Was he in the California robbery, too?"

"That's what Bob told me."

"How old was he?"

"Thirty-one."

Next they brought in Bill Power. In case Power had some family somewhere that were good people, Emmett identified him as Tom Evans. When Broadwell was carried in, Emmett said his name was Jake Moore. He told the sheriff that he had just met both men on October first.

"Is this Jake Moore the same man as Texas Jack?" Callahan asked.

"Don't know anything about any Texas Jack," Emmett lied.

After Broadwell's body was carried out, Sheriff Callahan closed the door, again warning the men in the hall to keep quiet. He walked over and put one shoe up on the footboard of Emmett's bed. "How'd this bank robbery come about?" he asked. Emmett paused to consider his reply before he began making his statement.

"On the first of October I met the boys twenty miles south of Tulsa. They asked me how much money I had, and I told them about twenty dollars. I asked them what amount they had, and they replied about nine hundred." Emmett wanted to get those amounts on the record, or otherwise someone might claim it was part of the bank money.

"I asked them what they were going to do. They said this here town of Coffeyville had been talking about them, and some of the people at Coffeyville had been trying to have them captured. I told them that was a lie, that they used to have lots of friends there. Then Bob said he was going to discount the James boys' record, and go up and rob both banks in one day. I told him that I didn't want any of it in mine. But they said I had better go along and help so I could get some of the money and leave the country. They said that if I stayed around here by myself, I would be sure and get caught or killed."

The reporter was scribbling way at his notebook, and Emmett paused to let him catch up. Callahan was watching Emmett closely as he spoke, and Emmett suspected the sheriff was catching every one of his lies. One of the other witnesses, apparently at Callahan's instruction, had also begun taking notes. Emmett took a drink from a glass of water that had been left beside his bed, carefully replaced the tumbler on the bedside table, and plowed on with his story.

"On the morning of the third we were north of Tulsa, in Osage Nation, and we rode twenty miles toward Coffeyville. We talked the bank robbery over as we came along that day. I tried to persuade them not to come, 'cause the people here had never done us any harm, so they said all right, if I didn't want to go along, then the four of them would go and that would give them a round up. So I told them if that was the case, I might as well go along, and I went for the love of my brothers. Besides, I knew the people would chase me just as hard if I wasn't along, and I had no money to get out of the country on."

"We camped yesterday, the fourth, on a timbered hill on Hickory Creek, about twelve miles from Coffeyville. During the night we saddled up and rode to Onion Creek, and camped on Mr. Davis's farm. This morning we fed the horses some corn, and I asked them if they were still in the notion of coming up here, and they said they were. I told them they had better not go, that it wouldn't be treating the men right who had always defended us. I asked them how they were going to do it.

"Bob said we'd ride in here about 9:30 a.m. I asked him what his idea was for that, and he said there wouldn't be so many people to hold up in the morning, and we wouldn't have to hurt nobody. He told me he would like to have me go with him because I was quick on foot, and he and I would go to the First National Bank, and let the other three go to the other bank. So he said we would ride and hitch our horses north of the lumber yard. We would hitch there, as people wouldn't see us until we were right in the bank. When we got out to the lumber yard, though, we saw there were no hitch racks, so we came around near the cooler."

Emmett stopped to take another drink of water. The reporter stopped writing and held his pencil up like a pointer. "Excuse me, Mr. Dalton," the reporter broke in. "Is it true that you are related to the Youngers?"

"I am a full cousin of the Younger boys. My mother is a sister to Cole Younger's father."

"How about the James boys?" the reporter persisted.

"They and the James boys are no relation." Emmett had been asked this question many times over the years. For some reason people believed the Youngers and the James boys were related, just because they had ridden together.

Callahan was now scowling fiercely at the reporter, but the young man took no heed. He said, "There have been reports that there was a sixth man in your group. Is that correct?"

"Five were all there were of us," Emmett answered, shaking his head. He wanted to keep Bill's name out of this at all costs.

"What about Allie Ogee?"

Emmett had earlier overheard some men suggesting that Ogee had been the sixth man, so the question came as no surprise. "I have not seen Allie Ogee for two years," Emmett said truthfully.

"Let's get back to the robbery," Callahan said dryly, shooting a warning look at the reporter. Emmett nodded.

"Bob and I started to come out the front way of the First National Bank. Bob stepped out on the street and shot his Winchester south once. We then went back and went out of the back door to the alley." Emmett bleakly relived that awful moment, and his voice cracked. "Met a man with a six-shooter. Bob killed him. Then we went west and went in back of Wells Brothers to our horses.

"Did you all do any shooting on the plaza?" Callahan's tone was kindly but insistent.

"Bob shot several times going up the street," Emmett admitted.

"Did you see George Cubine get shot?"

"I didn't see Cubine."

"Do you know who he is?"

"I know him," Emmett said quietly, looking down at his chest in shame.

"What about in the alley?"

"I could have got away," Emmett said in his own defense, "but I saw Bob fall, and rode back to him." He sniffed again, tears forming as he remembered that terrible scene. "He held up his hand, and I was endeavoring to get him on my horse, when I was disabled." Emmett pushed his head back and stared blindly at the ceiling while the reality of what had happened rushed in on him. "Oh, God!" he croaked, "Bob and Grat are dead!" Great choking sobs overwhelmed him, and tears flowed unchecked down his cheeks and into his ears.

"That's enough for now," Emmett heard Sheriff Callahan announce. "Let's go and let this boy get some rest."

On Friday morning Sheriff Callahan came to Emmett's room and told him to get ready to leave. They were taking him to jail in Independence, where he would formally be charged with bank robbery and two counts of murder. The evening of the robbery Emmett had been carried from Dr. Wells' office to a room at the Farmer's Hotel, where he had been kept under constant guard. Weak from the loss of blood, crippled by the bullet wound through his hips, and emotionally drained by all that had occurred, Emmett dreaded the idea of going anywhere, much less taking a train ride to the Independence jail. When the trip was canceled at the last minute, his delight was somewhat tempered by the explanation that the Coffeyville citizens had threatened to take him away from Sheriff Callahan and lynch him if the sheriff tried to move him from the hotel.

Just before noon on Friday his guard announced that Emmett's family had arrived in town, and after some minor disputes they were allowed to visit him. With conflicting feelings of joy and shame Emmett watched them file into the hotel room and gather around his bed. First in was his mother, gaunt and haggard, continually dabbing at her red and swollen eyes with a lace handkerchief. With her was Emmett's oldest brother, Ben, his sister Eva, Bill, and his youngest brother, Simon. Their greetings were brief and strained. With guards present, there was little they could say about what was most on their minds, and for this Emmett was truly grateful. He was in no condition to explain to his mother what had gone wrong, or why two of her sons were now dead while a third was accused of murder.

Emmett lamely assured her that he would be all right, and told her not to believe all the stories in the papers, even though he knew that for once the newsmen had been fairly accurate and truthful. Ben kept his arm around Mrs. Dalton, providing both physical and emotional support for her through this heart-rending ordeal. Eva, typically, kept shooting Emmett disapproving looks; clearly she blamed him for all the suffering their mother—and by extension, herself—was suffering. Simon, thirteen years old and full of mischief, simply gazed at Emmett in adoring wonder, proud to be related to someone so famous and daring. It was Bill, however, who took charge of things, informing Emmett that he would be paying for Bob's and Grat's burials, hiring a lawyer for Emmett, and generally ensuring that Emmett was treated fairly.

Finally, feigning exhaustion, Emmett closed his eyes and lay back on his pillow. The emotional demands placed on him by his family were draining his weakened resources. Characteristically perceptive and understanding, Bill recognized Emmett's needs and hustled his mother and siblings out of the room. When they were gone and the room was once again silent, a genuine fatigue overcame him, and Emmett fell into a feverish sleep.

Over the weekend his family members came back to visit him, albeit only in two's and three's, and they kept him abreast of the latest news. Bob and Grat had been buried on Thursday in unmarked graves not far from that of their brother Frank in the Elmwood cemetery. Upon reconsideration, Emmett had provided the real names of Power and Broadwell on Thursday morning, and Power had been buried with Bob and Grat. Dick Broadwell's body was claimed by his brother George from Hutchinson, Kansas, who shipped it home for burial.

Bill told Emmett how all the bodies had been stripped for souvenirs, as had their horses, and how the bodies had been photographed in front of the jail like hunting trophies. Bill was incensed by this outrage against common decency, and he vowed to set things right.

On Sunday Eva left to go back to Kingfisher, and on Monday their mother, Ben, and Simon departed as well, leaving only Bill to keep Emmett company. On Tuesday deputies brought a cot to the hotel room, and with Bill's assistance Emmett was lifted onto it and furtively carried to the railroad station. Accompanied by a heavily armed guard and his brother Bill, Emmett was put on a train to Independence, where he was transported to the county jail and locked in a cell. He was to remain there for the next four months.

Saturday, October 15, 1892

Bill Dalton was reaching for the door to the Montgomery County jail when it was thrown open from inside and a young woman brushed past him in a huff, without offering even a semblance of an apology. She briskly pranced away sniffing haughtily, her skirts swaying across the sidewalk. Bill shook his head and went on into the jail. The deputy at the front desk was leaning back in his chair with a knowing grin.

"You'd think he was an actor or something," the man remarked to Bill.

"Who?" Bill asked, stopping in front of the desk.

"Your brother. Them women keep comin' here wantin' to see him, leave him love letters and all. I ain't never seen the like."

"Emmett?" Bill was amazed. Although he was not bad looking, Emmett had never been a ladies man. He was usually so shy with women that Bill doubted that Emmett had ever been kissed.

The deputy rose from his chair, chuckling, and motioned for Bill to follow him. "Come on back. He's been expecting you."

Emmett had been placed in a cell separate from the other prisoners, and a straight-backed chair had been left by the door to his cell for his frequent visitors. Bill thanked the guard, who then left them alone. It was not until Bill took a seat and looked in at Emmett lying on his cot that he noticed the flowers. There were several bouquets scattered around the cell, on the floor by the cot and on the small table next to it.

"Morning, Emmett," Bill said slowly, gazing at the blooms with bewilderment. "Where'd all the flowers come from?"

Emmett, propped up on pillows into a semi-reclining position, smiled sheepishly at his brother. "Some girls sent 'em to me," he explained with just a touch of pride.

"Okay," Bill said doubtfully. "Do you know these girls?"

"Not yet," Emmett admitted with a mischievous grin. Bill just shook his head in bemused wonder. He was glad to see Emmett recovering his spirits, although his physical healing was certainly going to take a lot longer. The bullet through his hip had done serious damage internally, and his right arm had been shattered; the shotgun blast to his back had fortunately resulted in only superficial wounds. Despite his injuries, however, Emmett was looking healthier every day. He was fed well there in the jail, and two local physicians, Dr. McCullough and Dr. Masterman, made daily visits to dress his wounds and monitor his recovery.

"Well, it's a good thing Mom has already gone home," Bill chided him. "I don't think she would approve of all these girls chasing after you."

"We don't have to tell her, do we?" Emmett seemed genuinely concerned.

"No, I guess not," Bill reassured him. "Frankly, I'm kind of glad Mom and the others left. They were driving me crazy with the complaining and crying. I don't think it was helping you any, either."

“No,” Emmett conceded. “I was getting tired of explaining everything that happened over and over, talking about Bob and Grat all the time. How many times do I have to tell her I’m sorry?” Bill nodded with understanding.

“Good news,” Bill said, changing the subject. “They’ve finally admitted that they recovered $900 more than was stolen from the banks, so that’ll be your money. They’ve also recovered some of the other property that was robbed of you and the others in the alley. They’re appointing a probate judge, and I’m going to administer on the estate, as soon as I can hunt it all down. There’s already some creditors claiming Bob and Grat owed them money from a long time ago. So far, with the $900 and the saddles and guns and so forth, the estate’s worth about $1300, and I have to get a bond of twice that amount in order for me to administer on it, so I’ve got to come up with about $2600 somewhere.”

“How are you going to do that?”

“Don’t know for sure,” Bill said ruefully. “People aren’t real anxious to loan money to a Dalton right now. You know anybody that might help?”

Emmett chewed on his lower lip in concentration. “You might try Bud Heady,” Emmett suggested.

“Bud Heady? Who’s he?”

“A good friend of Bob’s. Remember when Frank was killed, and Bob escorted the body back to Coffeyville? The guy who came with him was Bud Heady. He was a deputy marshal for a while, but then he got into some kind of business and did real well.”

“Where would I find him?”

“Last I heard he was in Wharton. Probably still there. I’m pretty sure he’d be willing to help.”

“Okay.” Bill took a pencil and a small notebook from inside his coat and wrote down the name and city. “Oh,” he said, “I just remembered. Tuesday some man named Chapman claimed the horse you were riding. Said you stole it from him, had witnesses to back him up.”

"That lying son of a bitch!" Emmett exploded, wincing as he tried to raise up more. "I bought that horse from him fair and square. Gave him my horse and a hundred dollars. Hell, I've even got a bill of sale."

"A bill of sale? Where is it? If we've got a bill of sale, then I'll get the damn horse back or know why not. Jeez! These people are just trying to steal you blind."

"It's in my billfold," Emmett told him. "The sheriff's got it in his safe."

"I'll get that and then I'll just straighten this fellow Chapman right out," Bill promised vehemently. "Which reminds me. Elliott, the newspaper editor, has your pistols. He says you gave them to him. Is that right?"

"Not exactly," Emmett said, still angry about his horse. "He took them off me in the alley while I was giving up. He was trying to keep them from hanging me, so I told him he could hold on to them for me. I didn't mean he could keep them forever."

"Then I'll straighten him out, too."

"Now, Bill, don't go off half-cocked here. Mr. Elliott was real nice to me when he didn't have to be. There's no need to go making him mad. I'm sure if I explain the situation to him, he'll give back the guns."

"I don't know, Emmett. He didn't strike me as an honest gentleman." Emmett gave Bill a long pleading look. After a moment Bill heaved a big sigh in resigned defeat and nodded. Then he reached into his coat pocket and brought out some ragged newspaper clippings.

"Mom wrote a thank you note to the people of Coffeyville," Bill said with mixed feelings. He admired her graciousness and civility, but he opposed any conciliatory gestures towards the people who had killed his brothers. "You want to hear it?" Emmett nodded. Bill unfolded the scrap of paper, cleared his throat, and began to read.

"'We desire to return our sincere thanks to the citizens of Coffeyville for their uniform kindness to us during our stay in their midst. We have no enmity against any one what ever on account of the late terrible tragedy. We desire to return our thanks, also, to Dr. Wells for his kind attention to Emmett.'" Bill refolded the clipping without comment.

"That was nice of her," Emmett remarked.

"Uh-huh," Bill agreed without conviction. He unfolded a different clipping. "You know that letter to John Kloehr they were all talking about?"

"That one from Doolin?" Emmett said.

"Yeah. One of the papers printed it. You want to hear it?"

"Sure."

John Kloehr was the man credited with killing three of the gang members, including Bob and Grat. On Wednesday, a week after the bank robberies, he had received a letter signed by the "Dalton Gang" that threatened revenge on Kloehr and the people of Coffeyville. The letter had created an uproar, and people had called for additional Winchesters to be shipped from Parsons and Kansas City to defend the town. Of course, no such raid of vengeance had actually occurred.

Bill cleared his throat again and began to read out loud.

From Arkansas City, October, 1892

To John Kloehr.

Dear Sir: I take the time to tell you and the city of Coffeyville that all of the gang ain't dead yet by a hell of a sight and don't you forget it. I would have given all I ever made to have been there on the 5th. There are three or four of the gang left and we shall come to see you some day. That day—the 5th of October—we were down in the Chickasaw nation. We did not know it was coming off so soon. We thought it was coming off November 5. We shall have revenge for your killing of Bob and Grat and the rest of them. You people had no cause to take arms against the gang. The bankers will not help the widows of the men that got killed there, and you thought you were playing hellfire when you killed three of us, but your time will soon come when you will soon go into the grave and pass in your checks for the killing of Bob and Joe Evans and Texas Jack. So take warning. We will leave you in the hands of God for this time.

Yours truly,

Dalton Gang

"Sounds like Doolin," Emmett commented. "Newcomb or Pierce must of wrote it for him, though, since he can't hardly write." Suddenly Emmett got a worried look on his face and darted his eyes around the jail area. "Is there anyone close by who can hear me?" he whispered anxiously.

"No," Bill answered wearily. In spite of everything, Emmett wanted to keep protecting the identity of his former gang members, but Bill considered it a waste of time. Doolin and his friends were already well known throughout the area.

"I wonder why he thought it was November 5th?" Emmett mused in a much lower voice. "And did you notice how he didn't mention Grat there at the end? He never did like Grat, you know."

"You think he meant that business about taking revenge?" Bill asked.

"I don't know. He can be pretty mean, but there wouldn't be no point to it."

"Well, I don't know if you heard or not, but Thursday, while everybody was busy trying to defend Coffeyville, four armed men robbed the train south of Caney." Caney was a small town 25 miles straight west of Coffeyville.

Emmett chuckled appreciatively. "I'll bet that was them. Bill may not be educated, but he's real clever. He probably wrote that letter to get everybody's attention on Coffeyville so no one would be around while he robbed the train at Caney. You got to hand it to him. How much did they get?"

"Paper says they only got a hundred dollars."

"Yeah, well, the express company always lies about stuff like that."

“I’ll take you word on that,” Bill commented with a wry smile.

From there the conversation rambled on about other topics as Bill tried to entertain his ailing brother and prepare him for the trial ahead. Bill knew the prospects were bleak, but for Emmett’s sake he remained outwardly confident that things could be worked out. Finally he got up to leave, telling Emmett that he would be gone a few days trying to round up the bond money. He gave Emmett a wink, and was pleased when Emmett responded with a warm smile. Maybe things would turn out all right, he mused.

For Emmett the next few months dragged by, for he had nothing to do but lie in his cell and endure the pain and boredom. His hips were not healing as rapidly as he hoped, and he was still unable to walk or even stand for more than a few seconds. But while he counted the lonely quiet days in jail, Emmett was kept informed about all the activity that was occurring beyond his cell door.

Bill was unable to raise the bond money he needed, so Sheriff Callahan was appointed to administer the estates of Bob and Grat. His inability to borrow the necessary funds irritated Bill, and he became touchy and morose. In late October, frustrated in his attempts to reclaim the property taken from his brothers after the bank raid, he threatened to sue the city of Coffeyville for damages. A reporter claimed that Bill had even made disparaging remarks about his older brother Ben, and that he had suggested he might have to shoot a reporter or two.

Further fanning the flames of outrage were the remarks of a controversial Kansas state congressman named Simpson, who reportedly said, “The Dalton boys were no worse than the national bankers and thousands of others in Kansas who are engaged in pretended lawful pursuits, while really they are robbing the people. They are to be no more condemned for their acts than the bankers they robbed.” While Emmett read this statement with a euphoric sense of vindication, prominent business leaders and Republicans decried the Democrat congressman’s comments as a disgraceful insult to the brave men of Coffeyville.

To make matters worse, Bill took legal action to recover Emmett's pistols from David Stewart Elliott, the editor of the Coffeyville newspaper, and Elliott responded with a series of scathing articles about Bill and his claim. To Emmett's dismay, Elliott's displeasure with Bill began to extend to Emmett, and the formerly amiable newspaperman began publishing contemptuous remarks about Emmett as well. Since bad press could prejudice his upcoming trial, Emmett pleaded with Bill to back off, but Bill was adamant about securing their legal rights.

On November 8, 1892, Emmett was carried to the courtroom of Judge J. D. McCue, who wished to proceed with Emmett's trial as soon as possible. This haste may have been related to the judge's upcoming re-election campaign. Propped up in a chair, still weak and crippled by his wounds, Emmett sullenly insisted he was not yet ready to stand trial. As yet he had no lawyer, nor funds to hire one. For now he was represented by the city attorney, Joe Fritch, but this was supposed to be only on an interim basis. When Fritch called Emmett's two doctors to testify about his physical condition, McCue was forced to relent and to continue the case until mid-December. Emmett, while grateful for the temporary reprieve, was also filled with righteous indignation by the blatantly political attempt to rush him to judgment.

The war of words between Bill Dalton and David Stewart Elliott raged on, and soon other newspapers joined in the fray, sensing that Bill and his obstinance were easy targets for editorial scorn. Although these taunts made Bill furious, Emmett felt that Bill had brought them on himself by his uncompromising attitude. One article, in particular, made Emmett smile at its cleverness, even as he condemned its libelous nature. It appeared in the *Kansas City Star*, and read:

> *The theory of the people of Coffeyville that Mr. William Dalton likes to drink whiskey better than he likes shooting scrapes is doubtless in the main correct, for it is probable that human nature is as strong in the Daltons as it is in other men, and that the desire to become a corpse, however natural the features may look, is easily controlled. While, on the other hand, the desire to accumulate a richly scented jag and paint*

Michelangelo frescoes on the sky is doubtless, in a low-browed citizen as Mr. Dalton is said to be, hard to suppress.

While annoying to some of the local citizens, Bill's efforts finally began to pay off. On the second of December Bill had a constable serve Elliott with a writ of replevin, and Elliott was forced to turn over Emmett's guns. In the report on this outcome that appeared in his own paper, the *Coffeyville Journal*, Elliott contrived to portray himself as a magnanimous man who was being swindled, and he disingenuously implied that the guns were to be delivered directly to Emmett so that he could shoot his way out of jail. Emmett, for his part, just hoped that Elliott would now find some other outlet for his invective and let Emmett's situation fade from the headlines.

A week later Emmett's Winchester, unaccounted for since the battle in what was now called "Death Alley," turned up in the possession of a man in Independence. He relinquished the weapon without argument, stating that there were no unfired cartridges in it when he acquired it. Because Emmett was facing murder charges, this statement did little to help his case, which was largely predicated on his contention that he had never fired a shot that day. As Joe Fritch pointed out to him, however, the rifle's condition was moot, since the man who surrendered it had received it from someone else, a person whom he refused to name, so there was no reasonable chain of evidence to prove the bullets had been fired instead of simply removed in the interim.

In the middle of December Bill's actions again raised a furor, and this time it was taken up in the United States Congress. Chapman, down in Indian Territory, still refused to return Emmett's horse. Bill had taken his evidence to Marshal Yoes at Fort Smith, and after reviewing it Yoes had issued Bill a limited commission to go into Indian Territory and recover the horse himself. The newspapers distorted this incident by claiming that Bill Dalton had been made a deputy U. S. Marshal, an affront to the law-abiding citizens of Coffeyville. Scandalized by this apparent malfeasance, the senator from Kansas, a man named Vest, made an impassioned speech on the floor of Congress condemning this offensive state of affairs and demanding an immediate inquiry into why a member of such a notorious family of outlaws would be appointed as an officer of the law.

Marshals past and present immediately responded in writing that Bill had never been made a deputy marshal, and the tempest in a teapot quickly subsided. Bill shrugged it all off with a now-rare flash of good humor, telling Emmett how he had tracked down Chapman and cowed him into surrendering the horse. To Emmett, Bill's behavior was becoming a little erratic, but he attributed it to the stress of the situation and Bill's separation from his family. Bill had intended to bring his wife and children out from California, but so far he had been too busy and too broke to do so. Bill and his wife exchanged letters regularly, and Bill clearly missed seeing his wife and watching his children grow up. Emmett felt sure that once Bill was reunited with his family, he would calm down and return to his normal pleasant personality.

On December 19, 1892, Emmett once again went to court. Sheriff Callahan had his deputies lash a chair to two poles like an old-fashioned sedan chair, and with Emmett precariously perched on the seat they carried him to the court room like pallbearers with a casket. When they first brought him in and set him down, there were few in the court room beside the jurors and court officers, but as word spread about the unannounced trial, spectators flocked into the small paneled chamber. With his hips in agony and a general fatigue caused by the long weeks of inactivity in his cell, Emmett had no enthusiasm for such proceedings.

McCue called the court to order. Directing his stern gaze at Emmett, he asked, "Mr. Dalton, are you ready for trial at this time?"

"No, your honor," Emmett croaked, exaggerating his infirmity by only a little.

"Are you ready to enter a plea regarding the charge of murder?"

"No, your honor," Emmett repeated, wincing as if he were in more pain than he really felt.

"I see you have no counsel present. Do you not have a lawyer?"

"No, your honor." Emmett motioned with his head toward the man sitting behind him. "I've consulted with City Attorney Fritch some, but it was more in regard to other matters."

"Mr. Fritch," the judge inquired, "could you represent this man?"

Fritch rose. "I'm sorry, your honor, but I have to leave town on the morning train, so I am unable to look after this matter at this time." Judge McCue nodded, and Fritch sat back down.

McCue looked back at Emmett after making some notations on the papers in front of him. "Mr. Dalton, do you possess the funds necessary to hire an attorney?"

Emmett tried to look pitiful. "Well, your honor, I guess I could raise some, maybe."

McCue frowned at him as if he didn't really believe Emmett's act, then consulted his papers again. "Well," he finally announced, "as it happens I am unable to hold court this week anyway. My wife's condition is weak, and I must attend to her. However, Mr. Dalton, you will need to be ready for trial at nine o'clock next Monday morning. I would hope that by then you will have a lawyer, for you will certainly need one. This court is adjourned until next Monday morning." With a rap of the gavel it was over, and Emmett was carried back to his cell.

As it happened, the trial was postponed several more times for various reasons, and Emmett ended up spending the entire winter in the Independence jail. In January Sheriff Callahan held an auction to sell of the recovered property of Bob and Grat Dalton as part of the probate process. The estates were then settled, but by the time the creditors were paid off and legal fees were deducted, virtually nothing remained. Declaring that he had accomplished all that he could, Bill returned to Kingfisher to arrange for his family to join him, and thereafter Emmett rarely heard from him. His mother and his oldest brother Ben made occasional visits to the jail, but Emmett's closest confidants now were his jailers.

Unable to pay for a lawyer, Emmett continued to rely on Joe Fritch for legal advice. In early March 1893 Fritch told him the district attorney was ready to make a deal. The state was willing to drop the specifications of bank robbery and the murder of Lucius Baldwin if Emmett would plead guilty to a reduced charge of second degree murder in the case of George Cubine. Fritch was confident that if Emmett accepted, the court would only sentence him to fifteen or twenty years.

At first Emmett refused. He had not killed anyone, and they had no real proof otherwise. He opposed pleading guilty to a crime he did not commit, and he had almost convinced himself he was truly innocent of any serious crimes. Bob, Grat, and the others had done all the shooting, after all, and Emmett had been only an unwilling accomplice, participating only out of commendable family loyalty. This unwarranted belief that he might convince a jury of his innocence was hard to shake, and Fritch and Emmett's other friends and acquaintances at the jail spent days persuading him that this deal was the best he could expect. They pointed out that if he made this deal, the court would be more receptive to the idea of commuting his sentence at a later time. Swayed by their arguments, Emmett finally conceded and agreed to the deal.

On March 8, 1893, Emmett hobbled into Judge McCue's court room on crutches and took a seat at the defendant's table. When the court was called into session, Fritch and a deputy helped Emmett stand up again and face the judge, his shoulders hunched over the crutches. The judge glanced at a document in front of him and then gazed at Emmett.

"Mr. Dalton, I understand you are now ready to make a plea in your case."

"Yes, your honor."

"Well, then, to the charge of murder in the second degree, how do you plead?"

Emmett took a deep breath. "Guilty, your honor."

The judge wrote something on the paper. "Having pled guilty to the charge, the court now finds it has the duty of sentencing you. In consideration of the circumstances of your crime, and the many good men who died on that day in October, I feel I have no choice but to pronounce the maximum sentence the law allows. You are hereby remanded to the state penitentiary at Lansing, where you will remain for the rest of your natural life. This court is adjourned."

Emmett was stunned. He stared blankly as the judge gathered up his papers and swept out of the court room. It was almost beyond comprehension. He had only agreed to plead guilty because he had been promised a light sentence, but the judge had broken that promise. Too shocked and numb to be angry, Emmett meekly allowed Fritch and Callahan to lead him out of the courthouse and back to the jail.

Within an hour they had hustled him to the train depot and escorted him across the platform to a waiting train. When the shock of his sentence had worn off, Emmett broke down and cried. Tearfully he gave away his possessions as he said good-bye to his brother Ben, the only member of the family present to see him off, and the friends he had made in Independence. He presented his Winchester to Sheriff Callahan and his pistols to Joe Fritch, who then assisted him onto the train that was to take him to prison. Sobbing as tears ran down his cheeks, he waved out the window until the train pulled out and the depot had disappeared from sight. For Emmett this last train ride truly went to the end of the line, for he feared he would never see freedom again.

Author's Notes

Chapter 16

The events in this chapter were derived from a number of articles that appeared in the *Coffeyville Journal* and the *Kansas City Star and Kansan* in the months following the bank robberies, along with Emmett's book, *Beyond the Law*. There was also a letter Bill Dalton wrote to his wife on October 16, 1892, that was published in the *Dallas Morning News* on June 15, 1896, and two articles published in the Visalia, California, *Weekly Delta* on October 13, 1892. The letter sent to John Kloehr threatening the people of Coffeyville was reprinted in the *Oklahoma Herald* of El Reno, Oklahoma Territory, on October 21, 1892.

EPILOGUE

Emmett spent fifteen years in prison at Lansing, and prison authorities described him as a model prisoner. By 1907 he was a trusty who was so well liked by prison officials that he was allowed to go into town unescorted for prison business. His mother came to visit him at least twice a year, and she continually lobbied government officials for clemency. Her efforts finally paid off, and on November 1, 1907, the governor of Kansas granted Emmett a full pardon.

Upon his release Emmett returned to Kingfisher to live with his mother, where he finished the manuscript for his book, *Beyond the Law*, published in 1908. He became active in civic affairs, and in September 1908 he married a woman named Julia Johnson Gilstrap Lewis. In his second book, *When the Daltons Rode*, Emmett claimed that he and Julia had been sweethearts since their first meeting in 1887, and that she had faithfully waited for him to be released from prison. The facts regarding Julia's personal history, thought, make this heart-warming story seem very far-fetched.

In January 1887, the year she and Emmett purportedly met, sixteen-year-old Julia Johnson had married Bob Gilstrap, a half-blood Cherokee. In November of that year she gave birth to their daughter Jennie, and two years later, in December 1889, her husband was killed in a shoot-out at Jake Bartle's store in Bartlesville. Julia, now a widowed mother, apparently remained single until around 1903, when she married a man named Earnest Lewis. Lewis was later arrested for train robbery and bootlegging, and in November 1907, a few days after Emmett was released from prison, Julia's second husband was killed in a gunfight with two deputies.

A year after becoming a widow for the second time, Julia married Emmett, continuing a tradition of marrying reckless men. Julia's granddaughter stated that Julia had never met Emmett prior to his release from prison, and in light of her checkered past, this seem far more probable than Emmett's romantic version of their courtship.

Regardless, Emmett's marriage to Julia was a lasting one. Initially they resided in Bartlesville, but when Emmett became involved in producing a silent film version of his book, they moved to California. Emmett subsequently invested in several other movie deals, and none were very successful. Next he tried real estate and land development, and in this endeavor he enjoyed moderate success.

After a stroke and failing health, Emmett died at home in July 1937, and his ashes were buried at Kingfisher next to his mother's grave. Julia may have married again before she died in 1943.

Bill Dalton's activities in the months following Emmett's conviction are a matter of some debate. The newspapers insisted he had joined up with Bill Doolin, and reportedly they were committing crimes together all across the central plains. Hard evidence linking Bill Dalton with most of these crimes is nonexistent, however. That Bill Doolin and a changing cast of gang members were robbing trains and banks is certain, but Bill Dalton's participation is merely conjecture, based primarily on the then-current assumption that Bill was the leader of a band that newspapers continued to call the Dalton Gang. According to their memoirs, lawmen of that era, on the other hand, generally regarded Bill Doolin as the gang's driving force, and discounted Bill Dalton's active participation in all but a few of the gang's crimes.

Although he might not have taken part in their felonies, there is little doubt that Bill Dalton at least associated with the Doolin gang. There are two incidents in which there is overwhelming evidence that Bill Dalton was involved with Doolin and his gang members. The first, and most notorious, is the great raid on Ingalls. The tiny town of Ingalls, Oklahoma Territory, a few miles southeast of Stillwater, was a haven for outlaws in those years, a wild collection of saloons and brothels. On September 1, 1893, in an attempt to clean up the town and round up some of the more brazen outlaws, Ingalls was invaded by 27 deputies who sneaked in by hiding in covered wagons. There were several reports that during the long ride from Guthrie the lawmen had been sampling illegal liquor to bolster their courage for their assault.

At the time the lawmen were piling out of the wagons and dispersing with guns drawn, Doolin, Dalton, and other members of the gang were drinking in Ransom's saloon. Bitter Creek Newcomb, who had just left the others to go visit his girlfriend, spotted the posse and raised the alarm. A tremendous gun battle erupted as the deputies tried to surround the saloon, but most of the outlaws, including Bill Dalton, made it to the stable next door, where they mounted their horses and escaped in a hail of gunfire. One outlaw who did not escape was Tom Jones, also known as Ray Daugherty and Arkansas Tom, who was upstairs at the hotel with a woman when the fighting broke out. Poking his rifle through a hole in the roof of the hotel, Tom used his elevated position to wreak havoc on the deputies, killing three of them.

When he ran out of ammunition, Arkansas Tom surrendered, and he was later convicted of second degree murder and served seventeen years in Lansing. As for Bill Dalton, there is no reliable evidence that he even fired a shot in the exchange, although everyone agrees that he was there and escaped with the others.

In March 1894 Bitter Creek Newcomb and a man reported to be Bill Dalton entered a general store at Sacred Heart Mission, south of Shawnee, Oklahoma, to purchase supplies. The store owner, a part-time deputy named William Carr, apparently recognized the two men, and when they asked to buy some whiskey, he pulled a gun and began shooting. One, or possibly both, of the outlaws returned fire in self-defense, killing Carr in front of several witnesses.

Significantly, in neither the Ingalls battle nor the death of Carr were warrants ever issued on Bill Dalton, confirming the lack of proof concerning his criminal participation. In fact, the only surviving warrants with the name Bill Dalton on them are two that were issued on the charge of introducing in 1896, two years after Bill Dalton had been killed in Ardmore. Presumably these warrants were for someone else of the same name.

On May 23, 1894, a bank at Longview, Texas, was robbed by four men, and thereby hangs a tale. Longview is in far eastern Texas, very near the Louisiana border. Four men came to rob the First National Bank that day, but lawmen were alerted to the robbery and a gunfight ensued. One robber and two citizens were killed before the other bandits were able to make good their escape with the money. The identity of the robbers remains controversial, but some facts are clear.

The dead robber was identified as Jim Bennett, also known as Jim Wallace, and he wore a hat labeled "L. B. Roberson, Ardmore, I.T. (Indian Territory)". A second robber was identified as Jim Jones, a man who worked at a Longview sawmill and had married a local girl named Prudie Robinson (sometimes written as Roberson). The third robber was first identified as the dead robber's brother, George Bennett, and then later as Jim Jones' brother Will. The fourth man was described as a horse trader named Oscar Speight.

For two weeks posses trailed the robbers, who headed northwest into Indian Territory and the Arbuckle Mountains, where reporters surmised they were going to join up with the infamous Dalton gang.

When the robbery occurred, Bill Dalton, along with his wife and two children, had for several months been staying with a bootlegger named Houston Wallace at a cabin about 25 miles north of Ardmore, a town in the south central part of the Twin Territories. On June 4, 1894, Houston Wallace and an unidentified woman went to Duncan, about 25 miles west of their cabin, to purchase supplies. Reportedly some of the money they used was somehow identified as coming from the Longview robbery. Two days later Wallace went into Ardmore with Mrs. Bill Dalton and Prudie Robinson (Mrs. Jim Jones) to buy more supplies and to pick up some packages at the express office. His suspicions aroused by Wallace's extravagant spending, Deputy Marshal Selden Lindsay stopped the trio and searched the packages from the express office, revealing that they contained illegal liquor. Wallace and the two women were immediately arrested.

That night a posse of nine deputies departed Ardmore for the Wallace cabin. It is likely that questioning of Wallace and the women had elicited the fact that Bill Dalton was there, and they, for some reason, concluded that he must have been involved in the Longview robbery. It should be noted that despite his notoriety, Bill Dalton was not officially a wanted man at this time. During the night the deputies took up positions in the woods around the cabin and waited for Dalton to appear. According to the deputies, the next morning either a child or a woman spotted them and yelled a warning to Dalton, who came out with a pistol in his hand. When he refused to halt, either C. Loss Hart or Selden Lindsay (witnesses disagreed) fired his rifle and killed Bill with a .44 caliber bullet that entered Bill's lower right back and ranged up to lodge in his left breast.

Emmett claimed that Bill was shot as he leaned down to pick up his crippled daughter, and that scenario would in fact account for the odd trajectory of the bullet. The official explanation was that Bill had been falling when the shot was fired, hit by another shot to the chest. Unfortunately the autopsy revealed no such wounds to the chest.

Witnesses from Longview came and identified the body, but their identification is extremely suspect. The main witness was not even at the robbery, but he claimed to have loaned the robbers his fishing boat the day before. After viewing the body, he confirmed that Bill Dalton was "the big one," despite the fact that the autopsy showed Bill was only 5' 9" tall and weighed about 180, hardly an imposing figure. This witness based his positive identification primarily on the boots Bill had been wearing, which had diamond-shaped patches decorating them. A reporter present noted that these patches were barely attached to the boots, casting doubt on how long the patches had actually been there.

On June 10 Sheb Williams, the U. S. Marshal from Paris, Texas, arrived at Ardmore to take charge of the investigation. He immediately dismissed charges against Mrs. Dalton for receiving stolen property, and he ordered the money, guns, and letters that had been confiscated from Bill Dalton be returned to her. This is especially strange in light of the fact that the $275 they had found on Bill was purportedly the proceeds from the Longview robbery.

Three days later Mrs. Dalton, Houston Wallace, and Prudie Robinson (or Roberson) had a preliminary hearing on the introducing charge, and the two women were released on their own recognizance. Mrs. Dalton returned to the Wallace cabin, which the deputies were supposed to have searched thoroughly, and recovered an additional $850. Interestingly, no one made any attempt to seize this money.

On June 14 Mrs. Dalton was presented with a bill for the expenses of the men who had guarded her husband's body from souvenir hunters. Furious at this outrageous demand, but anxious to leave, she reluctantly paid the bill and boarded a train that was also carrying Bill's body. She took him back to California, where he was buried on Bliven family property.

According to various newspaper reports, of the three bank robbers who had left Longview alive, deputies had killed five and captured two (!). The last to be brought to justice was Jim Jones, whose real name was Jim Nite. In February 1897 Nite was charged with the murder of George Buckingham and Charlie Learned, the two civilians killed during the Longview robbery, and eventually he was convicted and sent to prison.

In 1896 the nine deputies who had been present when Bill Dalton was killed were charged with his murder and released on bond. As happened with Bob Dalton in the case of Charley Montgomery, this was not an unusual occurrence when a suspect was killed without a warrant, but it is curious that the charges were filed two full years after the event. Due to courthouse fires and other reasons, the records of the deputies' trial no longer exist, but since all continued to work as lawmen, we can safely assume that they were acquitted.

Whether Bill Dalton actually took part in the Longview robbery may never be known, but he certainly associated with those who did. Houston Wallace, the man with whom Bill was staying, admitted that the robber killed at Longview was his brother Jim. Jim Nite, using the name Jim Jones, and who was later convicted for the murders that took place during the robbery, was married to Prudie Robinson, who was also staying at the Wallace cabin. The identities of the other two men in the robbery were never firmly established. Bill Dalton was not linked to the robbery until after he had been killed, conveniently, perhaps to give the deputies some justification for their precipitous actions. From any point of view, the circumstances surrounding Bill's death remain exceedingly strange.

All of which begs the question, what was Bill Dalton doing between March 1893, when Emmett was convicted, and June 1894, when Bill was killed? Had he indeed joined Bill Doolin's gang and perpetrated various crimes? Since he was clearly a devoted family man, it seems unlikely he would expose his wife and children to such dangers by having them join him in such a desperate situation, but it was during this period that he had brought them out from California. Surviving documents and the descriptions of those who knew him also indicate he was not a reckless, or even unusually brave, man. On the other hand, he had been vilified by the newspapers following the Coffeyville raid, and as a result he may have been unable to secure honest work and discovered that his company was welcomed only by criminals.

Another possibility, admittedly remote and unprovable, is that he was working as an undercover informant for the U. S. Marshals Service. This would account for the flap in Congress over his appointment, and for Marshal Williams' intervention at Ardmore in favor of Mrs. Dalton. It would also explain his association with known criminals, and why he felt safe enough to have his family join him. It may be pertinent to note that Mrs. Bill Dalton never gave any interviews about her deceased husband, and to this day his descendants decline to discuss his career.

It has also been suggested that the man killed at Ardmore was not, in fact, Bill Dalton, and that Bill used this misidentification to disappear into obscurity. This could explain the 1896 warrants for introducing, and the later appearance of the name William Dalton on voter rolls in California. Or not.

Whatever the truth about Bill Dalton, Bill Doolin certainly continued his career of crime for several years, employing a number of associates. In 1895, however, things got very hot for the Doolin gang. Original members Bitter Creek Newcomb and Charley Pierce were killed in July by two ranchers they had mistakenly trusted. In December 1895, hoping to avoid a similar fate, Doolin sent word to Marshal E. D. Nix in Guthrie that he wanted to make a deal. Nix was agreeable, but in Washington the Justice Department vetoed the idea. The following month Doolin was captured without a fight at a bath house in Eureka Springs, Arkansas, and there is speculation that Nix, a political hack with no background in law enforcement, but who had a knack for personal promotion, had made a secret, unauthorized deal with Doolin in order to improve his own image as a tough lawman who was cleaning up the territory.

A few months later Nix lost his job when it was revealed he had diverted almost a million dollars of government funds to his own personal use. With this official leverage gone, Doolin saw his deal crumbling and escaped from jail, possibly with the assistance of Nix and his associates. In August 1896, acting on a tip from an informant, deputies staked out the house of Doolin's mother-in-law in the tiny settlement of Lawson, and when Doolin showed up they gunned him down.

As a final note to illustrate why so much misinformation has been published about the Daltons, there is the story of Deputy Marshal Ransom Payne. Only two months after the raid on Coffeyville, a "flash literature" book was published that portrayed Payne as a heroic lawman who had tracked the Daltons for months, and who had been only minutes behind them when they entered Coffeyville. Obviously written with Payne's assistance, the book first came out under the title *The Life of the Daltons* by "An Eye Witness."

The book was so full of falsehoods that Marshal Grimes immediately fired Payne, and then took the unprecedented step of allowing his letter of dismissal to be published in the *Coffeyville Journal* on February 17, 1893. In his open letter to Payne, Grimes pointed out some of the more egregious lies in the book, and he denied he had ever entrusted the former deputy with any important duties, especially any pursuit of the Daltons. Grimes made it clear that he considered Payne incompetent at best, and implied strongly that Payne was a coward as well as a liar.

The marshal's condemnation seems to have had little effect on sales of the book, though, and many later authors, who presumably were unaware of Grimes' denunciation, have used this book as a primary source of information. Other books that were published in the following years were almost equally flawed, but they have likewise been taken as gospel, resulting in the current abundance of myths and distortions about this criminal gang.

The Daltons are all gone now. Bob and Grat are still in their graves, saying nothing at all to everyone who visits. To most of the world they are known, if at all, as a footnote to history, but in Coffeyville their exploits live on in the people's memory. The raid was the most exciting and important thing that ever happened in Coffeyville, and the town has built a museum to honor the stalwart men who defended the city in 1892. They have restored the Condon Bank building and the old city jail to the way they were more than a hundred years ago, and they have marked where the bodies fell in Death Alley. The fate of the Dalton boys may be a fading memory elsewhere, but the people of Coffeyville will never forget.

Author's Notes

Epilogue

Almost all the information in this section was provided by Nancy B. Samuelson. Much of it came from her book, *The Dalton Gang Story* (1992, Shooting Star Press), and was supplemented by articles she has published in the Quarterly of the National Association for Outlaw and Lawman History, Inc., as well as by personal conversations and correspondence. The 1896 warrants for a Bill Dalton are held in the National Archives.

ACKNOWLEGEMENTS

First and foremost I wish to thank Nancy B. Samuelson, whose research into the Dalton family blazed a trail for me. Her exhaustive search for the truth debunked many of the myths about the Daltons as she tracked down the original documents that established the framework around which this book was created.

Many government and private organizations were of tremendous assistance to me in researching the Dalton story. These include the U.S. National Archives, especially the people in Fort Worth and Kansas City; the Oklahoma and Kansas State Historical Societies; the Oklahoma State Archives; the Western History Collection at the University of Oklahoma; the Chisholm Trail Museum in Kingfisher, Oklahoma; the Dalton Defenders Museum in Coffeyville, Kansas; and the Wells Fargo Historical Museum in San Francisco.

I am extremely grateful to the many individuals who took time to help me with this project. Lorraine M Lineer did a fantastic job of researching the newspaper files in Sacramento so that I could tell the entire story of the Daltons' California adventure. Joel Jacobsen provided information on the New Mexico incident, and Robert R. Ernst gave me insight into the marshals service of the era. My family, in addition to their support and encouragement, also supplied me with research materials and oral histories that fleshed out the story. Among these family members I want to particularly thank my mother for her recollections about Bartlesville, and my uncle Tom Allin and my aunt Doris Whitmore for their help researching the Coffeyville story.

Of course, I could never have written this book without my wife, Jan, who never complained about the time and money I spent to complete this speculative enterprise, and whose love and encouragement made it all worthwhile.

Last, but not least, I wish to thank my friends, who (usually) pretended not to be bored when I rattled on about the progress I was making and the obscure facts I had uncovered. Thanks to David, Roger, David, Stan, and especially David.

Printed in Great Britain
by Amazon

20123266R10267